Advances in
Instructional Psychology

VOLUME 1

Advances in
Instructional Psychology

VOLUME 1

Edited by

ROBERT GLASER

 LAWRENCE ERLBAUM ASSOCIATES, PUBLISHERS

1978   Hillsdale, New Jersey

DISTRIBUTED BY THE HALSTED PRESS DIVISION OF
JOHN WILEY & SONS
New York   Toronto   London   Sydney

Lawrence Erlbaum Associates, Inc., Publishers
62 Maria Drive
Hillsdale, New Jersey 07642

Distributed solely by Halsted Press Division
John Wiley & Sons, Inc., New York

Library of Congress Cataloging in Publication Data

Main entry under title:

Advances in instructional psychology.

Includes indexes.
1. Educational psychology.   I. Glaser, Robert,
1921–
LB1051.A3176   370.15   78-13400
ISBN 0-470-26519-1

Printed in the United States of America

Contents

5. ASSESSMENT OF LEARNING OUTCOMES
Robert M. Gagné and Jacob G. Beard

Preface

The rubric "instructional psychology" was first used to name an area of work in the 1969 *Annual Review of Psychology*. Since then, the field has taken on enough shape that it can be generally characterized as consisting of research on the acquisition of knowledge and cognitive skill and how this competence is developed through the design of conditions for learning. The emergence of this field marks a significant change in the relationship of psychology to education.

In the 1950s and early 1960s, experimental psychologists generally were not hospitable to the investigation of instructional problems. The border between basic psychological research and research on the acquisition of skill and competence in the subject matters of schooling defined a "no-man's land" that relatively few had the training or the inclination to explore. During the intense activity of the years of teaching machines and programmed learning, those who cared about the relationship between behavioral science and educational technology were concerned that the rush toward immediate practicality would pull the field away from its loose ties with the scientific study of behavior. And as recently as 10 years ago, it was difficult to attract outstanding psychologists to consider working on problems that had an educational taint.

Psychology and education have not always been so separated; in the early part of this century, the psychology of learning and educational psychology were intimately connected in the work of many of the great figures of that time. The sporadic engagement of experimental psychology and educational psychology over the years provides an interesting perspective for viewing the field of instructional psychology, and a synoptic history is presented in the introduction to this volume.

At the present time, the scene has substantially changed as a result of the impact of behavioristic psychology's intrusion into the technology of teaching and the emergence of modern cognitive psychology as today's dominant theoretical force in the study of human learning and performance. This change has been accompanied by a change in research tactics. In the old mode of research, findings established in controlled laboratory environments were extrapolated to complex learning with little investigation of the limitations and boundary conditions involved. This has now been replaced by research that, in large part, picks its problems and develops its theory from complex realistic human performance. There is the growing realization that study of the acquisition of human knowledge and competence in relatively formal instructional situations can be a significant test of a theory's adequacy, as well as a useful social contribution. As a result, a psychology of instruction is emerging within the context of a rapidly growing science of cognition and learning.

The purpose of this new series is to foster this trend by publishing outstanding work that appears to be contributing to the knowledge and theories required to systematically address the problems of instruction. This serial publication is intended to provide a forum for psychologists in diverse areas engaged in research on specialized topics relevant to understanding instructional processes. Since the field is in an active and expanding phase, *Instructional Psychology* is broadly conceived and will be shaped by the workers in it. Toward this purpose, the *Advances* will be responsive to the current scene and not become committed to particular viewpoints. The activities of the field will determine the future scope and definition of instructional psychology, so it will be necessary to be eclectic in range of coverage. The major criteria for inviting contributions are that the authors have been actively involved in high-quality work of significant interest to the interaction of psychological science and the problems of instruction, and that they have something informative and provocative to say. In particular, the invited contributors are encouraged to present a detailed view of their current work and thinking, to relate it to other existing work, and to describe it as they see fit in a way they believe to be exciting and significant.

The chapters in this volume are representative of work now underway that is defining instructional psychology. Chapter 1, by James Greeno, is an example of research on the analysis of the structure of knowledge. He presents a model of problem solving in the domain of high-school geometry. The model is developed in the form of a computer simulation using the framework of current information-processing theory and includes a detailed representation of the thinking processes students use when they solve geometry problems.

Chapter 2, by Ann Brown, focuses on the development of certain metacognitive skills that influence learning and problem solving in young children. These skills of thinking facilitate the active control of one's own learning by means of predicting, checking, monitoring, and reality testing, and they are indicative of efficient problem solving in a variety of situations. Brown reviews the empirical research on metacognitive skills, instructional attempts to train these skills in slow-learning children, and the cultural relativity of these abilities.

In Chapter 3, Robbie Case discusses the kinds of questions that must be addressed when applying principles of cognitive development to instruction. He takes Piaget's general principles of intellectual development and organizes them into a set of procedures for optimizing children's acquisition of the skills and concepts normally taught in school. He describes research centering around a neo-Piagetian theory of intellectual development that addresses questions that Piaget's theory leaves unanswered: how to identify the operational structures of relevance to skills taught in school, how to assess a child's current level of operational functioning, and how to bring children from their current level of functioning to the one desired.

Chapter 4, by Patrick Suppes, Elizabeth Macken, and Mario Zanotti, moves away from the cognitive-processing approaches of the previous chapters to more global models appropriate for organizing instruction. The authors present in detail two examples of global models and sketch how these models can be of use in systematic thinking about curriculum and teaching. In the first example, they develop a model for the prediction of student progress in computer-assisted instruction in three curriculum areas—language arts, mathematics, and reading—and use the model to regulate the amount of time spent in these curriculum areas. The second example investigates the use of radio as an instructional technology in developing countries. The concern here is with the use of a quantitative model for optimizing the organization of instruction for group learning.

In Chapter 5, Robert Gagné and Jacob Beard examine current formulations of measurement rationale and technology for the assessment of learning outcomes. The concept of criterion-referenced measurement is reviewed in the context of various categories of learned performance: intellectual skills, verbal information, cognitive strategies, motor skills, and attitudes. The authors consider questions involved in specifying the task domain to be assessed, the quality and quantity dimensions of performance assessment, the process of test construction, determination of the adequacy of assessment measures, and decisions required in test selection and design.

The completion of this volume has been a cooperative effort from its inception during a conversation between the publisher, Lawrence Erlbaum, and myself. Most obvious are the efforts of the authors who took time from their often overcommitted lives to make extensive presentations of research with which they have been concerned for some time. Less apparent, but an indispensable part of the final product, are the efforts of the busy individuals who critically reviewed the early manuscripts: Lloyd Bond, Michelene Chi, Alan Lesgold, Jay Millman, James Pellegrino, and Alexander Siegel.

The details of all the stages involved in working with the authors and publisher were competently handled by my assistant, Joan Jewell. Without her assistance, this volume would never have reached the readers' bookshelves. My thanks also go to Marlene Daurora for typing the final manuscript, to Pat Stanton for typing and editorial assistance, and to Donna Rottman, who prepared all the figures and tables for publication. Throughout, the work on this book was facilitated by the resources of the Learning Research and Development Center of the University of Pittsburgh.

University of Pittsburgh   ROBERT GLASER

Advances in
Instructional Psychology

VOLUME 1

INTRODUCTION:
Toward a Psychology
of Instruction

Robert Glaser
University of Pittsburgh

In increasing numbers, experimental psychologists are turning their enterprise to analyses and investigations useful to the study of the instructional process. This trend is apparent in many different fields of psychology, including the study of learning, cognitive performance, human development, and social processes. There are many reasons for this surge of interest: the increasing prestige that has come from working on socially relevant as well as purely disciplinary problems; the capability of current psychological theory for investigating more complex cognitive behaviors; and the conviction that the interaction between task-oriented and discipline-oriented research can be mutually beneficial for society and for psychological science.

For many psychologists interested in educational phenomena, the boundaries between basic and applied research are becoming increasingly blurred. Examination of recent work on the nature and development of human knowledge and intellectual skills makes it apparent that research directed toward educationally relevant areas, including the psychological processes underlying intelligence and aptitude, can be both highly fundamental in character and, at the same time, directed toward practical understanding. Much exciting work at the moment looks in these two directions — toward basic research and toward realistic educational events. Research of this kind can contribute to both application and basic knowledge by attempting to understand and improve instructional practices and, at the same time, advance scientific theory. This attitude is cogently stated by John Anderson (1976), who writes:

> I am less interested in defending the exact assumptions of the theory and am more interested in evolving some theory that can account for important empirical phenomena. By a theory that accounts for "important empirical

1

phenomena" I mean one that addresses real world issues as well as laboratory phenomena. Such real world issues . . . would include how to improve
people's ability to learn and use language, to learn and remember text,
to reason, and to solve problems. This reflects my belief that the final
arbiter of a cognitive theory is going to be its utility in practical application. Thus, I am proposing a change in our interpretation of what it means
to understand the nature of human intelligence. I once thought it could
mean unique identification of the structures and processes underlying
cognitive behavior. Since that is not possible, I propose that we take
"understanding the nature of human intelligence" to mean possession of a
theory that will enable us to improve human intelligence [pp. 15–16].

The development of theories of this type requires an alternative approach to
psychological research. The goal of most approaches is to describe, after the fact,
phenomena of learning and performance. The alternative to be considered is
theory and experiment that contribute to prescribing optimal ways for acquiring
knowledge and skill. Indeed, there is a growing concern with the normative, prescriptive aspects of our knowledge of learning and cognition (e.g., Atkinson &
Paulston, 1972; Bruner, 1964; Gagné, 1977; Glaser, 1976; Groen & Atkinson,
1966). This prescriptive task is different from the work of purely descriptive
science but still requires, as the basis for optimizing learning and performance,
a detailed description or hypothesis of underlying processes.

I.   THE PRESENT SCENE

Progress is now being made toward the integration required for building a
psychology of instruction based on research and theory in learning and cognition. Some of the particular areas that show this interaction include: psychological task analysis of the subject matter of instruction; early childhood education
and developmental psychology; the interpretation of intelligence and aptitude
in terms of cognitive processes; learning from text and discourse comprehension;
assessment of the outcomes of learning; and behavior modification. A brief
description of the research in these areas provides an introduction to the problems that are shaping the field of instructional psychology.

Task Analysis of the Subject Matter of Instruction.   Psychologists are
expanding their attention to include the study of human behavior considerably
more complex than that usually studied in the laboratory. The concepts of
modern cognitive theory are being applied to understanding the stages of competence in many domains of knowledge and skill relevant to educational
practice, such as text comprehension, reading music, theorem proving in
geometry, and solving problems in physics. Techniques are being developed for
specifying the nature of competent performance in terms that allow access to

theoretical concepts and experimental data but preserve fidelity to real-life situations. Task analysis is playing a central role in this work and instructional tasks are being studied by means of simulation techniques, information network analysis, cognitive process models, and learning hierarchies. Analytic description is required of what has been learned by an expert in a particular subject-matter domain. What is it that distinguishes a skilled reader from an unskilled one, a student skilled at mathematics from a less skilled one, or a chess master from a novice player? Task analysis is being used to describe such differences in terms of the cognitive demands placed on basic psychological processes, including attention, perception, memory, and language, and to identify structural units and sequences of instruction that might serve to facilitate the acquisition of knowledge and skill. Since an individual's capabilities change over time, task analysis must also consider the processes available at different stages of development.

Early Childhood Education and Developmental Psychology. Psychologists are showing increasing involvement in educational intervention and compensatory education programs for young children. This movement into the field of education coincides with increased interest in intellectual development and how it might be enhanced through instruction. Developmental psychologists are involved in research and development efforts that are multifaceted and varied, reflecting differences in psychological theory, the interests of psychologists and educators, and the complex goals of education. Overriding theoretical and practical issues continue to be the plasticity of intellectual development, the nature of cultural influences, critical periods of development, and the timing of educational intervention. Key questions concern the general and specific effectiveness of instruction or any deliberate form of intervention in altering or accelerating the biologically and culturally influenced course of intellectual development.

At present, the proliferation of new programs in early childhood education has diminished, and efforts are now focused on designing methodologies for evaluating their effects and on understanding the instructional processes that are involved. General tests of the trainability of Piagetian tasks are no longer in vogue, but more detailed analytical and experimental work is being conducted on the cognitive transformations that take place between the levels of competence that define developmental change. More precise thought is being given to what it might mean to design an educational environment on the basis of principles of cognitive development.

Intelligence, Aptitude, and Cognitive Processes. Many factors are forcing a breakdown between the traditionally separate areas of the psychometrics of individual differences and experimental psychology. These include questions about the use of and theoretical basis for tests of intelligence, research on the interaction between individual differences and instructional variables, investigations of the process aspects of intellectual development, and cross-cultural studies of cognitive performance. These factors are making it necessary and possible for us to understand intelligence and aptitude in different ways than we have in the past and to change the way in which individual differences might be viewed and assessed for the purposes of education. One approach that seems likely to be fruitful for future progress is conceptualization of individual difference variables in terms of the process constructs of cognitive theories. Research along these lines is accelerating. The nature of the cognitive processes involved in the performance of test tasks used to measure and define intelligence is being investigated. As cognitive strategies and metacognitive processes are identified, attempts are being made to assess how they might be influenced by instruction.

Discourse Comprehension.   There has been a pronounced increase in the number of studies concerned with meaningful prose materials of paragraph length, typical of the kind of material employed in textbooks and everyday written communication. This is in contrast to the more artificial materials of traditional verbal learning experiments or the specifically designed sentences and short paragraphs of early psycholinguistic studies. The organizational structure of text is being studied as it influences learning and retention. Work on text organization and the comprehension of meaning has essentially replaced classical verbal learning studies, and appropriate techniques are being developed for this new research. These studies are beginning to address directly the problem of how people learn from text. Investigators are asking how facts are organized by readers, how inferences and conclusions are drawn from written passages, and how to best instruct individuals in text-processing skills.

Study continues on the processes of beginning reading, such as letter and word decoding, phonemic analysis, and syntactic constraints. Accompanying this work, there is an increasing amount of research on the advanced semantic processes involved in comprehending discourse, including the influence of cognitive schemas and internalized representations of prior knowledge on understanding. Intensive task analysis of the nature of reading comprehension and the increased attention to learning from written materials constitute an exemplary trend in attempts to examine the relationship between knowledge, cognition, and instruction.

Assessment of Learning Outcomes and Educational Processes.   The nature of psychological testing and its underlying discipline of psychometrics is now undergoing examination. With respect to the measurement of achievement, there are attempts to break away from the traditions of aptitude testing to measurement techniques more concerned with identifying the characteristics of levels of competent performance. Measurement models are being developed for the design of tests that can be interpreted in terms of performance criteria rather than in terms of relative norms. The general goal is to more closely articulate assessment with the conduct of instruction so that constantly updated information about a learner's attained capabilities can be used in making educational decisions.

A related active area of investigation is concerned with detailed analyses of the conditions under which learning takes place in school contexts. There is a growing sophistication in the study of classroom processes. Past studies designed to evaluate curriculum innovations (1) attempted to describe school learning by relating the nature of student input to the quality of student output, and (2) only very generally described the processes intervening between the two. Detailed information was rarely obtained about differences between effective and less effective classroom processes in terms of some model of classroom instruction. Models now are being developed that attempt to explain the variance obtained in achievement measures in terms of the initial ability of the student, classroom process variables, and the interaction between the two. Of particular interest is the possibility that research on the dimensions of classroom instructional processes can be related to underlying theories of the acquisition of competence in the subject matters of schooling. Each endeavor should be able to reinforce or challenge the findings of the other.

Behavior Modification.   Behavior modification, representing the application of operant theory and systematic reinforcement contingencies, first appeared in the context of clinical psychology. Educational applications now are burgeoning, and many guidebooks for teachers are available. Behavior modification practices are being implemented widely in elementary schools, and higher education is adopting operant techniques in the form of personalized systems of instruction. The successes and failures of these applications are influencing research. Classroom behavior modification studies are beginning to focus on intellectual performance, extending earlier work primarily focused on decreasing disruptive behavior and increasing attention to task. The cognitive aspects of behavior modification, represented by studies of modeling, of vicarious and self-reinforcing processes, and of self-regulatory performance are of increasing concern.

II.   HISTORICAL PERSPECTIVE

The activity just described roughly characterizes the current scene in the emerging field of instructional psychology. A synopsis of the history of the relationship between experimental psychology and education can be helpful in placing this work in perspective.

At the beginning of this century, many of the great psychological figures who were concerned with the development of a scientific psychology assumed that there would be an active intercourse between psychological science and its applications to educational and social practices. James Cattell, John Dewey, G. Stanley Hall, William James, Edward Thorndike, and John B. Watson all suggested in one way or another that the search for knowledge about learning, cognition, and human development should be related in some fundamental way to establishing a disciplinary base for the design of educational settings. Among the numerous conceptions that might have dominated psychological thought in this early period, association theory and functional psychology had great attraction because of their practical appeal. By their nature, these theories appeared to promise that changes could be brought about in the environment to influence the human condition and would lead to improvements in such areas as child development, mental health, and education (Boring, 1950; Robinson, 1932).

Thorndike, heavily involved in laboratory work on the psychology of learning, applied the theory of S–R bonds to the psychology of instruction in various subject matters and to educational experimentation exemplified by the influential studies with Woodworth on transfer of training and the doctrine of formal discipline. His research proceeded in a very direct fashion. There were certain laws of learning – the laws of S–R bonds, the law of effect, and findings about the specificity of transfer – that could be immediately applied to the design of instruction and materials for teaching. Thorndike came armed with laboratory-tested principles and theory that could be applied directly to the design of learning conditions and teaching practices in the classroom.

Dewey resisted the prominent associationistic trend and was a contrast to Thorndike, not only with respect to his beliefs about the nature of human behavior, but also with respect to his view of the relationship between psychology and its application. Dewey envisioned a special structure, which he called a "linking science," to intervene between scientific theory and practical application. Such a linking science would provide a conceptual framework into which knowledge obtained from both scientific work and educational practice could interact, cumulate, and modify each other. In his own work, Dewey elected to leave the translation of science into practice to the long-term venture he conceived it to be. It was most immediately important to move to implementation in laboratory schools, even though the underlying principles of human behavior were only very generally defined. In Dewey's thinking, the findings of science would eventually work their way into practical application, but the immediate development of schools needed to proceed on the basis of available, more intuitive principles. The question that remained, however, was whether the direct application of laboratory findings and related theoretical abstractions would necessarily lead to the development of a "linking science" of instructional psychology that could be generally available to practitioners and scientists. In order for such a linking structure to develop, what appeared to be required was a coupling of the experimental and theoretical style of Thorndike and the cumulative, conceptual framework of Dewey. Each had only described half of the job.

Despite the early pragmatic inclinations of American psychology, it has displayed an erratic history with respect to translating scientific knowledge into educational practice and, of coordinate importance, translating practice into research problems that test scientific theory. A spirit of close affinity between the science of psychology and the practice of education persisted for a short time after the strong impetus by Thorndike and Dewey and others at Columbia and Chicago. Following this period, however, education and psychology appeared to go their separate ways. The isolation of the two fields was fostered by activities that preoccupied each of them.

It may not be too much of an oversimplification of history to say that each field addressed the immediately demanding problem of building its own discipline — with little apparent need for external relationships with one another. Psychology, on the one hand, aspired to become a natural science and take its place among the "hard" sciences. In order to accomplish this, psychologists went into the laboratory to work out experimental techniques using tasks designed more for theoretical purposes than for relevance to realistic educational subject matters. Education, on the other hand, and particularly educational psychology and the psychometrics of educational testing, found their challenges primarily with practitioners and with the practical problems of teacher training, teaching methods, curriculum development, and testing for the schools. The primary concern of education was to build the educational profession; less effort was devoted to nurturing its scientific and disciplinary roots. As psychology and education set about these urgent and different tasks, psychologists and psychology departments were established in faculties of arts and sciences, and most educational psychologists joined separate departments in faculties of education. The two enterprises, the main body of experimental psychology and educational psychology, took on different characteristics because of the climate in which they worked and their constituencies.

During this period of mutual insularity — lasting roughly from after the immediate influence of Dewey and Thorndike to World War II (with some relaxation during World War I) — educational psychologists abstracted general instructional principles from extant learning theory. These principles were subjected to appropriate classroom experiments and case studies that could be presented to teachers as illustrations of general guiding principles that could influence their practices. For experimental and theoretical psychologists, direct involvement in the development of instructional practices and materials was of little concern. Also of little concern was the study of problems in learning and performance that arose in practical educational contexts — problems that could influence psychological theory and laboratory experimentation. In the "true" psychology departments of the faculties of arts and sciences, educational psychology and concerns with instruction were not prestigious activites.

This lack of a strong link between psychology and education led to certain interesting paradoxes. The field of testing and psychometrics, strongly influenced by the needs of education and training in society, developed a strong technology and theories of mental tests bolstered by factor analysis but unsupported by an underlying psychological theory of learning and performance. Psychometrics was largely an engineering enterprise, and questions that arose in the application of this technology did not generally feed back into the work of experimental psychology and related theory. In contrast, work on learning, memory, problem solving, and thinking was essentially a theoretical and descriptive enterprise that showed little inclination for the development of a framework necessary for application. Theoretical problems and results that could have been generated by application were unavailable to challenge theories and findings from the laboratory.

Following World War II and during the 1950s, there were two major attempts at rapprochement between psychology and instructional technology. The first was a large research effort sponsored by the military concerned with problems of training. Many psychologists, both those recognized at the time and those who were to become well known later, became involved in the effort. In both the United States and Europe, they brought various points of view and method-ologies, including techniques for the analyses of skilled performance, to the investigation of instruction (Glaser, 1964, 1965; Melton, 1957). The second was the movement of Skinner's operant psychology into the educational scene. In the late 1950s and 1960s, teaching machines and programmed instruction had a tremendous surge of interest, which has been well documented.

In regard to these two attempts, it is of interest to note the comments of two of the leading psychologists involved. Melton, who directed the United States Air Force Personnel and Training Research Center that employed a major peace-time concentration of psychologists, had the following to say (1960) when the Center succumbed after 9 years for lack of continued support:

> Lost somewhere along the line was their [psychologists] warning that the technology that could be supported by contemporary psychological science was primitive — only a first approximation — and that substantial support of certain critical areas of fundamental psychological science should pro-ceed concurrently with the initial implementation of the technology, if the technology were to become reliable and effective. . . . Now we are witnes-sing the elaborate employment of a technology . . ., but with the scientific underpinning on starvation rations. . . .
>
> Now, this is not the only case where enthusiasm for a psychotechnology has been coupled with relative apathy for its scientific foundations. I think here again of mental testing, progressive education, guidance, visual education. My concern is that this not be the history of the next ten years [p. 663].

Skinner, in 1965, also felt called upon to express some concern about the ap-plication of operant psychology to education:

A special branch of psychology, the so-called experimental analysis of behaviour has produced if not an art at least a technology of teaching from which one can indeed "deduce programs and schemes and methods of instruction." The public is aware of this technology through two of its products, teaching machines and programmed instruction. Their rise has been meteoric. . . . Unfortunately, much of the technology has lost contact with its basic science. . . .

Teaching machines are widely misunderstood. . . . The programming of instruction has also been widely misunderstood. The first programmes emerging from an experimental analysis of behaviour were copied only in certain superficial aspects [pp. 427–428].

The concern of Melton and Skinner provides a lesson for future work that needs to be considered. New applications that have been too quickly separated from the theory underlying them appear to become superficial and sterile, and the theory also is not improved. Maintaining contact through appropriate linkages can encourage a mutually correcting system in which failures and limitations in both application and theory might be understood and modified.

In the late 1950s, major efforts in curriculum design were launched by leading scientists and mathematicians. The widely publicized book, *The Process of Education*, by Bruner (1960) was the result of a conference that brought together subject-matter experts, professional educators, and psychologists in different fields with different theoretical points of view. Bruner writes, "Strange as it may seem, this was the first time psychologists had been brought together with leading scientists to discuss the problems involved in teaching their various disciplines [p. ix]." The curriculum reforms of the 1960s have been extensively discussed and debated from many points of view. From the viewpoint of an instructional psychology, it is clear that no strong psychology of subject-matter acquisition emerged from these reforms that could assist efforts at curriculum design. One integration of subject-matter instruction and psychological theory of some influence, however, was the concept of learning hierarchies developed by Gagné (Gagné, 1970; Gagné, Mayor, Garstens, & Paradise, 1962), which was applied to the development of the AAAS science curriculum for elementary schools.

The foregoing attempts to integrate education and psychology, with attendant frustrations, were encouraged by the social and scientific Zietgeist. Society urged improvements in the educational system, educators asked for research and development, and many psychologists found relevance, remote or somewhat more immediate, to their liking and a reasonable test of their work. A scene was set, and a new field of instructional psychology appeared to be taking shape. In 1964, Hilgard was the contributing editor of the NSSE Yearbook on *Theories of Learning and Instruction*. This volume included chapters by many prominent psychologists including Bruner who discussed the nature of a theory of instruction and made a distinction between descriptive theories of learning and prescriptive theories of instruction.

In 1966, the respected classic textbook by Hilgard on *Theories of Learning*, first published in 1948, found for its third edition (Hilgard & Bower, 1966) enough activity in the field to include a chapter on "Learning and the Technology of Instruction." In the later 1975 edition (Hilgard & Bower), the chapter was called "Theory of Instruction" and included, among other things, Gagné's hierarchical theory, Bruner's cognitive-developmental theory, Atkinson's decision-theoretical analysis for optimizing learning, Carroll's model of school learning, and Skinner's programmed learning.

The first review, entitled "Instructional Psychology" (Gagné & Rohwer), appeared in the 1969 *Annual Review of Psychology*. This review, reflecting the field of learning at that time, included such topics as attention and set; pretraining and transfer; stimulus characteristics in learning; conditions of responding; prompting and guidance in learning discriminations, concepts, and rules; feedback effects; and studies of the variables influencing retention in verbal learning. Also included were a few studies of reading and language, and training on conservation tasks. A second review of "Instructional Psychology" (Glaser & Resnick), appearing in the 1972 *Annual Review*, identified areas of investigation, such as those described at the beginning of this introduction, that have been defining the field of instructional psychology. Later reviews (McKeachie, 1974; Wittrock & Lumsdaine, 1977) have identified other areas of research. Recent symposia continue to reflect the search for a strong psychology of instruction (e.g., Anderson, Spiro, & Montague, 1977; Klahr, 1976).

III.   ADVANCES IN INSTRUCTIONAL PSYCHOLOGY

Given this trend, it is time to begin a series concerned with advances in instructional psychology. The series begins in the midst of a change. At present, modern cognitive psychology is the dominant theoretical force in psychological science, as opposed to previous years when behavioristic theories of learning were in ascendance. At the same time, the impact of behavioristic psychology is currently widespread and pervades many settings where the learning and relearning of behavior is a significant phenomenon, particularly in therapeutic situations, institutional environments, special education, and "personalized instruction" at all levels of education. Relative to behavioristic psychology, cognitive psychology is a fledgling with respect to the extent of the application of its findings and techniques to practical human endeavors.

This state of affairs is of interest because attention to applied problems was a significant influence in the development of modern cognitive theories. The psychological research on the skills required in complex man-machine systems stimulated by World War II forged a link between the study of cognition and models of human performance in terms of information-processing systems, probability theory, computer simulation, and concepts of artificial intelligence. In this sense, major theoretical concepts of present-day cognitive psychology emerged, to some extent, out of practical concerns with complex human behavior — behavior at a level of complexity much greater than that upon which behavioristic theories were derived and nurtured. At the moment, behavioristic theories are being changed by practical applications, and cognitive theories are striving for theoretical organization in the course of investigating complex areas of human performance such as problem solving, language development, thinking, understanding, memory, imagery, intelligence, and the comprehension of discourse. Perhaps the lesson learned is that not only might basic scientific work and theory be useful for application, but that attempts at application can be a significant influence in shaping psychological knowledge and theory. What seems to be required for mutual progress is the continuous contact between theory and application through some intermediary, bridging activity. It is anticipated that developments in the field of instructional psychology will contribute toward this end.

REFERENCES

Anderson, J. R. *Language, memory, and thought.* Hillsdale, N.J.: Lawrence Erlbaum Associates, 1976.

Anderson, R. C., Spiro, R. J., & Montague, W. E. (Eds.). *Schooling and the acquisition of knowledge.* Hillsdale, N.J.: Lawrence Erlbaum Associates, 1977.

Atkinson, R. C., & Paulston, J. A. An approach to the psychology of instruction. *Psychological Bulletin,* 1972, *78,* 49–61.

Boring, E. G. *A history of experimental psychology* (2nd ed.). New York: Appleton–Century–Crofts, 1950.

Bruner, J. S. *The process of education.* Cambridge, Mass.: Harvard University Press, 1960.

Bruner, J. S. Some theorems on instruction illustrated with reference to mathematics. In E. R. Hilgard (Ed.), *Theories of learning and instruction: The sixty-third yearbook of the National Society for the Study of Education.* Chicago: NSSE, 1964.

Gagné, R. M. *The conditions of learning* (2nd ed.). New York: Holt, Rinehart & Winston, 1970.

Gagné, R. M. *The conditions of learning* (3rd ed.). New York: Holt, Rinehart & Winston, 1977.

Gagné, R. M., Mayor, J. R., Garstens, H. L., & Paradise, N. E. Factors in acquiring knowledge of a mathematics task. *Psychological Monographs,* 1962, *76*(7, Whole No. 526).

Gagné, R. M., & Rohwer, W. D., Jr. Instructional psychology. In P. H. Mussen & M. R. Rosenzweig (Eds.), *Annual review of psychology* (Vol. 20). Palo Alto, Calif.: Annual Reviews, 1969.

Glaser, R. Implications of training research for education. In E. R. Hilgard (Ed.), *Theories of learning and instruction: The sixty-third yearbook of the National Society for the Study of Education.* Chicago: NSSE, 1964.

Glaser, R. (Ed.). *Training research and education.* New York: Wiley, 1965. (Originally published, 1962, University of Pittsburgh Press.)

Glaser, R. Components of a psychology of instruction: Toward a science of design. *Review of Educational Research,* 1976, *46,* 1–24.

Glaser, R., & Resnick, L. B. Instructional psychology. In P. H. Mussen & M. R. Rosenzweig (Eds.), *Annual review of psychology* (Vol. 23). Palo Alto, Calif.: Annual Reviews, 1972.

Groen, G. J., & Atkinson, R. C. Models for optimizing the learning process. *Psychological Bulletin,* 1966, *66,* 309–320.

Hilgard, E. R. *Theories of learning.* New York: Appleton–Century–Crofts, 1948.

Hilgard, E. R. (Ed.). *Theories of learning and instruction: The sixty-third yearbook of the National Society for the Study of Education.* Chicago: NSSE, 1964.

Hilgard, E. R., & Bower, G. H. *Theories of learning* (3rd ed.). New York: Appleton–Century–Crofts, 1966.

Hilgard, E. R., & Bower, G. H. *Theories of learning* (4th ed.). Englewood Cliffs, N.J.: Prentice-Hall, 1975.

Klahr, D. (Ed.). *Cognition and instruction.* Hillsdale, N.J.: Lawrence Erlbaum Associates, 1976.

McKeachie, W. J. Instructional psychology. In M. R. Rosenzweig & L. W. Porter (Eds.), *Annual review of psychology* (Vol. 25). Palo Alto, Calif.: Annual Reviews, 1974.

Melton, A. W. Military psychology in the United States of America. *American Psychologist,* 1957, *12,* 740–746.

Melton, A. W. Some comments on "The Impact of Advancing Technology on Methods in Education" by S. Ramo. In A. A. Lumsdaine & R. Glaser (Eds.), *Teaching machines and programmed learning: A source book.* Washington, D.C.: National Education Association, 1960.

Robinson, E. G. *Association theory today.* New York: Century, 1932.

Skinner, B. F. Review lecture: The technology of teaching. *Proceedings of the Royal Society,* 1965, *162,* 427–443.

Wittrock, M. C., & Lumsdaine, A. A. Instructional psychology. In M. R. Rosenzweig & L. W. Porter (Eds.), *Annual review of psychology* (Vol. 28). Palo Alto, Calif.: Annual Reviews, 1977.

1
A Study of Problem Solving

James G. Greeno
University of Pittsburgh

I. INTRODUCTION

A major objective of instruction, especially in mathematics and science, is to strengthen students' skills in solving problems. In mathematics, most of the activities that students perform in order to learn the material involve problem solving, and problems are used to test the amount that each students has learned. At a minimum, the instructional objectives of a course must be that students acquire the specialized knowledge they need to solve problems in the domain of the course. There may be more ambitious objectives as well; it may be hoped that students will strengthen general skills in problem solving and reasoning. But if students fail to acquire the more specific knowledge required for solving the problems given as exercises and in tests, they will fail the course.

What must a student know in order to solve problems in a domain? One answer is that the necessary knowledge is represented in the texts and other instructional materials used in the curriculum. This information is certainly needed, but it is not sufficient. In addition to knowing the concepts and propositions given in a text, students must also have knowledge of how to apply those concepts and propositions to find the solutions of problems. This "how to" kind of knowledge is in the general category of "skills," and until recently, very little was known about the skills needed for solving problems.

The main content of this chapter is a review of results obtained in a program of research concerned with problem solving in high school geometry. This research has been done using the framework of current theories of information processing, and the results include a relatively detailed representation of the processes that students use when they solve geometry problems. The representation has been developed in the form of a computer program called *Perdix* that solves geometry problems. The procedures represented in Perdix are hypothetically the same as those that students typically use in solving the same kinds of problems. Therefore, Perdix is a candidate for a model of the knowledge that students acquire in order to solve problems in geometry. The work is not finished; I do not offer Perdix as a complete model of the knowledge that a successful geometry student acquires during the course. However, the model does apply to a substantial part of the content of the course, and as far as it goes, I consider its principles to be plausible hypotheses about the nature of knowledge that students are expected to acquire when they study geometry in high school.

The use of computer simulation as a theoretical method imposes an important discipline, partly because it ensures that the components of knowledge that are assumed in the model are sufficient for the tasks that the model is able to perform. This is particularly important for instructional applications. If it is found that a certain component of knowledge is needed in order for a program to solve a problem it is reasonable to suppose that human problem solvers also need that kind of knowledge. The kind of information that we gain from computer simulation is similar to that obtained in task analyses of the kind that educational psychologists have been conducting for some time (e.g., Landa, 1974; Resnick, 1976). As with traditional task analyses, a computer simulation includes analyzing performance on a task into its significant components. By requiring that these components function together in a running computer program, we impose the additional requirement that the component processes are sufficient for the task, and that they are mutually compatible so that they can be integrated in a single functioning system.

An important goal of this research is that the model of problem solving should be a realistic representation of students' thinking processes. To achieve this, the model's development has been guided by a set of thinking-aloud protocols given by six ninth-grade students who were taking a geometry course. I interviewed each student approximately once each week over a period of 8 months. In each session, each student solved a few problems; sessions typically lasted 15 to 20 minutes. The problems were not part of the students' course work, but they were selected to be appropriate for the stage of the course that the students had reached at the time. In addition to these protocols, which form the basic data for these studies, data have been obtained in further experiments using tasks designed to highlight specific aspects of problem-solving processes.

The representation to be given here is much more detailed than is usually the case in discussions of school learning and curriculum. However, a detailed representation is needed in order to obtain a clear understanding of the nature of the knowledge that students acquire and the way it is used in solving problems. It is generally true in sciences that provide basic knowledge relevant to applications that analyses in basic science include details that are not used directly in applications. Examples that come to mind include the theory of electricity in relation to electrical engineering and scientific physiology in relation to the practice of medicine. Scientific analyses of cognitive processes are in an early stage of development, and as work continues, we may find ways of expressing basic principles without the accompanying detail that seems necessary at present. However, at the present time, relatively detailed descriptions of theoretical systems are required if the content of the theories are to be communicated.

Section II of this chapter presents a brief sketch of relevant background literature in the psychology of problem solving. This is by no means a complete review (for a somewhat more complete discussion, see Greeno, 1977a); however, the section mentions some recent developments that seem to me to be particularly salient and relevant to the material that is presented later. Section III presents a general overview of the model Perdix, including a sketch of Perdix' performance on a sample problem, to provide a general idea of the way the model represents the process of solving a problem. Sections IV, V, and VI present the main findings of the research. These are descriptions of the representations in Perdix of the main kinds of knowledge needed for solving geometry problems. Section IV describes knowledge for perceptual pattern recognition. Section V describes the representation of propositional knowledge used in making inferences. Section VI describes strategic knowledge: representations of problem goals and subgoals and knowledge used in planning during problem solving. Section VII presents some implications of the findings concerning issues in instructional practice. Section VIII presents some implications of the findings concerning issues in the general theory of problem solving.

II. GENERAL BACKGROUND

In recent years, cognitive psychologists have developed detailed analyses and descriptions of psychological processes involved in many cognitive tasks. A few years ago, the common style of psychological analysis was to specify variables that influenced the effectiveness of perception, memory, learning, problem solving, or whatever process an investigator was studying. Now, with increasing frequency, investigators go beyond identifying variables that have effects on processes and specify relatively detailed models of how they believe the processes occur, including the nature of component subprocesses and the way in which subprocesses are organized into a complete procedure for doing the task.

This trend toward greater specification of processes has occurred in the psychological study of problem solving no less than in other areas of cognitive psychology. Following Newell and Simon's (1972) fundamental contributions, psychological analyses of problem solving now attend to the nature and organization of component processes that interpret information, set goals, and select among available actions in the process of solving the problem. This contrasts sharply with work that was done during the dominance of behaviorist and associationist concepts in experimental psychology. Work on problem solving done in these frameworks included identifying experimental conditions that facilitated solution of anagram problems or concept identification. Another line of work provided conceptual analyses of functional fixedness in terms of behaviorist hypotheses of reinforcement and extinction. In general, the analyses provided were much more abstract than the detailed analyses now being developed. [Bourne, Ekstrand, and Dominowski's (1971) discussion is representative.]

Efforts to analyze processes of problem solving in detail were carried out earlier by Gestalt psychologists, such as Duncker (1945), Köhler (1927), and Wertheimer (1959). These investigators considered problems as situations in which a desired goal could not be achieved because the individual did not understand important relations among components of the situation. There was special interest in cases where a problem was solved suddenly, with an apparent experience of insight. Duncker's concept of functional fixedness called attention to cases in which understanding could not be reached because some limited conceptualization of a component of the situation was incompatible with finding a way to fit that component into a needed relation with the rest of the problem.

Most current work on the psychology of problem solving considers a solution as successful achievement of a search. In many problem situations there is a specified initial stiuation and a goal. The problem solver has a set of operators that can be used to make changes in the situation. To solve the problem, a sequence of operations must be found that changes the initial stiuation into the goal. Because there are several different operators available, there are many different sequences that might be tried. Most of these sequences are incorrect; that is, they do not lead to the solution. Because only a few of the possible sequences (or perhaps only one) will lead to the goal, the task of finding a successful solution path can be quite difficult.

A number of important concepts have been developed in analyzing problem solving as a search that occurs in a large space of possible sequences of operations. One idea is means-end analysis, which is a general heuristic used in organizing work on a problem. In means-end analysis, the problem solver compares the current situation with the goal situation to identify the differences between them. These differences become the focus of work on the problem, and the problem solver sets subgoals of trying to reduce the various differences that are found. Problem solving is further organized by a priority system that provides a basis for deciding which subgoal to work on first. In means-end analysis, the number of possible actions to be considered is reduced by knowledge of which operators are relevant for each of the various different subgoals that occur in the problem situation. The concept of means-end analysis and the related concepts of ordering differences and relating operators to differences have been developed in relation to the problem-solving system called the *General Problem Solver* (Ernst & Newell, 1969; Newell & Simon, 1972).

Another important set of concepts involves general methods for planning solutions. An idea developed in relation to the General Problem Solver is that a general sketch of a solution can be found by considering certain essential features of the situation and the goal and forming a plan to remove the differences involving those features. The solution of the problem must also remove differences in the features ignored in the planning phase, but the finding of the solution can be greatly facilitated by having an appropriate plan (see Newell & Simon, 1972). Planning often requires substantial knowledge about the problem domain, including knowledge of the main subproblems that must be solved (Sacerdoti, 1975), knowledge of the kinds of partial solutions that can be developed and used intact (Fahlman, 1974), and knowledge of procedural deficiencies, sometimes called "bugs," that enables the problem solver to anticipate and avoid actions that produce new problems rather than progress toward the solution (Sussman, 1973).

A third important set of concepts developed in recent work on the theory of problem solving involves the kind of information that must be stored in memory as the problem solver proceeds with work on the problem. In most problem-solving systems, work is organized according to a series of subgoals, and a record is kept of the subgoals that have been tried. This record is essential for keeping one's place in the problem. When a subgoal has been established for a subsidiary purpose, then after working on that subgoal, the problem solver must return to the higher goal for which the subgoal was intended. A record of subgoals also provides information that permits the problem solver to avoid trying the same thing over and over, once it is found that it does not succeed. In some experiments, analyses have begun to relate the requirements of information storage to general models of memory processes and capacity limitations (Atwood & Polson, 1976).

The part of the theory of problem solving that has been developed most strongly might be called the *mechanics of problem solving*. There is now a strong body of concepts concerned with the procedures that are followed in successful problem solving in a wide variety of situations. Less attention has been given to what might be called the *semantics of problem solving*, involving issues of how problems are represented and how meaningful relationships in the problem are used in finding and understanding problem situations. However, some important beginnings have been achieved. In analyses of the process of understanding a text that describes a problem, important relationships between the structure of the description and the individual's representation of the task have begun to emerge (Hayes & Simon, 1974; Simon & Hayes, 1976). In experimental analyses of some elementary mathematics problems, the importance of a process of detecting troublesome conditions in the problem has been demonstrated (Resnick & Glaser, 1976). In addition, important theoretical analyses have shown that strong procedures for analysing patterns in the problem situation can reduce the requirements for memory storage by large amounts (Reitman & Wilcox, 1976;

Simon, 1975). These analyses show that there is a great advantage to having sophisticated concepts to use in representing the problem situation, permitting large economies in the processing demands of problem solving.

III.   OVERVIEW OF PERDIX

The formal structure used in writing Perdix is a production system. This means that each element of knowledge is represented as a production containing a condition and an action. When the program is running, the process involves a series of cycles. On each cycle, the conditions specified in various productions are tested. Eventually, the condition of one of the productions is found to be true. Then the action of that production is performed. Performance of an action completes a cycle. On the next cycle, the conditions of the various productions are tested again until one of them is found true. Then the action of that production is performed, and so on. The formalism of a production system is a useful one for constructing psychological theory, because the components of the process are easily identified in the elementary productions, and there must be a relatively explicit specification of the way in which different parts of the process interact. General discussions of production systems as models of psychological processes have been given by Anderson (1976), Hunt and Poltrock (1974), Klahr and Wallace (1976), Newell (1972, 1973), Newel and Simon (1972), and Simon (1975).

A simple example of a production system is given in Table 1.1. These productions would be used in a situation where one wished to enter one's house. In each production, the condition is stated, and an arrow separates the condition from the action of that production. Suppose that initially the door is closed and locked. Then tests of the conditions of P1, P2, P3, and P4 will all fail, and P5, which is a default condition, will always be true. Thus, the action on the first cycle is to find and grasp the key. On the second cycle, the conditions of P1, P2, and P3 are false, but the condition of P4 is true. This leads to the action of inserting the key into the lock. On the third cycle, the conditions of P1 and P2 are false, but P3's condition is true, so the action of turning the key is per-

TABLE 1.1
A Simple Production System

Production	Condition	Action
P1.	Door open ⟶	Walk through doorway, close door.
P2.	Door unlocked ⟶	Turn knob, open door.
P3.	Key in lock ⟶	Turn key.
P4.	Key in hand ⟶	Insert key in lock.
P5.	Else ⟶	Find key, grasp key in hand.

formed. On the fifth cycle, with the door open, P1's condition is found true, so the action of walking through the door is performed.

Notice that the production system takes appropriate account of some circumstances. For example, each cycle begins with a test of whether the door is already open. Thus, if the door is open initially, the system will not go through the unnecessary steps of finding the key and unlocking the door. On the other hand, this example is deliberately sketchy and incomplete. A serious psychological theory of the knowledge used in unlocking and opening doors would involve detailed representations of routines for finding keys, tests whether turning the key had successfully unlocked the door, and other components.

The productions that represent knowledge of geometry in Perdix involve conditions that test for patterns of information in problems and actions that produce new information and relationships. Perdix is intended to represent problem solving that is based on processes of pattern matching and pattern completion. (The model's namesake is a character in Greek mythology, apprentice to Daedalus, whose invention of the saw was inspired by a fish skeleton, and whose invention of the compass was inspired by a crab claw.) The idea of a pattern used here is very general. Some patterns are combinations of visual features of diagrams. Some patterns are general concepts, such as the idea of congruent triangles. Some patterns are abstract general structures, such as the pattern of relationships between propositions in a proof.

The general programming framework used in writing Perdix is a system called *ACT*, developed by Anderson (1976). Production systems written in the ACT framework use representations in the form of labeled networks. At any time, the problem situation is represented as a network. The nodes denote elements of the situation, and patterns are represented by the ways in which the nodes are interconnected in the network. In geometry problems, some elements are parts of diagrams, such as points, segments, angles, and triangles. Other nodes in the network include general concepts, such as the names of relations like congruence or vertical angles. The elements are linked together in ways that correspond to problem situations. For example, the node representing an angle is connected to the nodes that represent the vertex and the sides of the angle. If two angles have been found to have the relation of vertical angles, the node representing the relation of vertical angles is linked to the nodes representing those two angles.

When Perdix works on a problem, there is a network that represents the situation at the beginning of the problem. This includes the information given in a diagram as well as other given information, such as relations of parallel lines or angles that are bisected. The goal of the problem is to have the problem solver produce a relation that is not present in the network. The conditions of productions specify patterns that allow the inference of new relationships. On each cycle of the process, a series of tests is carried out involving patterns that are relevant to the problem goal. When a relevant pattern is found in the network, the action of the production generally involves adding new connections in the network corresponding to relationships that can be inferred. Thus, problem solving involves modifying the situation by adding new relational material to the network. Solution of the problem corresponds to adding the particular relational pattern that is called for in the problem goal.

A. An Example Problem

I illustrate these ideas by presenting a sketch of Perdix' solution of a problem involving parallel lines. The problem is shown in Panel (a) of Fig. 1.1. Solution of this problem illustrates the general idea of solving problems by pattern matching/pattern completion. In addition, it illustrates the three main kinds of knowledge for solving problems that I discuss in detail in Sections IV, V, and VI, and which I describe only briefly now. In the following discussion, I refer to various angles in the diagram of the problem using designations show in Panel (b) of Fig. 1.1.

One general kind of knowledge required for solving problems like this is that a student must be able to identify angles that have particular geometric relations. For example, if angle A1 and angle A6 are considered, the student will recognize that they are vertical angles. This part of the process involves *visual pattern recognition*.

A second general requirement is knowledge of propositions that enable inferences to be made. An example is that A1 and A6 are congruent because they are vertical angles. This inference is based on the proposition, "vertical angles are congruent," and students of geometry know many propositions of this kind. This part of the process of solving problems can be referred to as knowledge of *propositions for inference.*

A third requirement is knowledge that enables setting goals and subgoals and forming plans for achieving goals. These processes provide organization of the problem-solving process and guide the pattern recognition and inferential processes. For example, a student must know that in order to find the measure of an angle, one needs to find a quantitative relationship between that angle and some other angle whose measure is already known, such as congruence or being supplementary. The part of the problem-solving process involving setting goals and forming plans can be called *strategic knowledge.* Table 1.2 shows the specific strategic procedures that are involved in solving the problem in Fig. 1.1.

At the beginning of work on the problem in Fig. 1.1, the situation is represented by a rather large network of elements and connections. There are nodes representing 12 points, the ends and intersections of the line segments marked *a*, *b*, *m*, and *n* in Panel (a). There are additional nodes representing all of the segments and angles shown in the diagram. It is useful also to represent the abstract lines that are determined by the segments shown, and the half-lines (rays) that emanate in each direction from the various points that are given. The sides of angles are designated as the appropriate rays, rather than the segments involved,

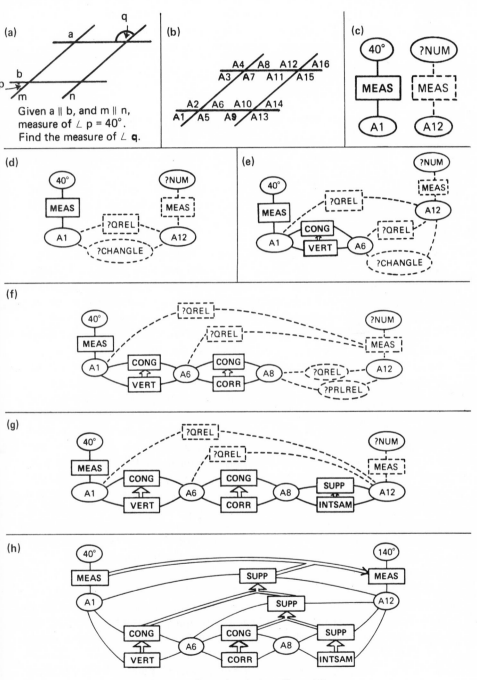

FIG. 1.1.   Stages in solution of a problem.

TABLE 1.2
Strategic Knowledge for Setting Goals Shown in Fig. 1.1

1. If the current goal is to find the measure of an angle, this can be achieved if you know the measure of another angle that is related to the unknown angle by some quantitative relation. If that is not true, set the goal of inferring a quantitative relation between the unknown angle and some angle whose measure is known.

2. If the current goal is to infer a quantitative relation between two angles, this is possible if a geometric relation is known between the two angles, or if the two angles are both related to a third angle by quantitative relations. If that is not true, set the goal of inferring a geometric relation between the angles.

3. If the current goal is to infer a geometric relation between two angles, set the goal of analyzing the features of the angles, using the procedure for pattern recognition.

4. If the current goal is to infer a quantitative relation between two angles, and it has already been determined that there is no geometric relation between the unknown angle and any angle with known measure, then set the goal of finding an angle that is spatially between the two angles and that is congruent to one of the angles. When that is accomplished, try to relate that angle to the other angle in the original goal, forming a chain of quantitative relations.

to avoid some ambiguities that arise regarding the segments. (For example, should the horizontal side of angle q be taken as the segment extending only to line m or the segment that extends from the vertex of q to the end of the segment shown?) The network also includes the relations of parallel lines that are given in the problem, with these represented as relations between the abstract lines rather than any of the various segments. The given information stating the measure of angle p is represented in the form shown in Panel (c) of Fig. 1.1, as a relation **MEAS** (for measure) between the angle denoted A1 and the number 40. The goal of the problem is also represented, shown in Panel (c), as a **MEAS** relation between the angle denoted here as A12 and a number that is not determined, denoted ?NUM. The fact that this is a goal, rather than a relation in the data structure, is indicated by dashed lines. In all the panels of Fig. 1.1, nodes represented as rectangles designate relationships and nodes represented as ovals designate objects in the problem such as angles and quantities. Single lines connecting a relation node with objects show which objects are connected by that relation. Goals are indicated by dashed lines. Double-line arrows are used to show inferences, where relations are added to the network because other relations have been identified.

The first step in solving the problem is shown in Panel (d) of Fig. 1.1. In Table 1.2, note that the first rule of strategy states that for a goal of finding the measure of an angle, an appropriate subgoal is to find a quantitative relation between that angle and some known angle. Because A1 is known, Perdix sets the goal of finding some quantitative relation (denoted ?QREL) between A12 and A1. Now the system tests for presence of a geometric relation that has been inferred (Rule 2 in Table 1.2), and since none has been inferred, the features of A1 and A12 are examined to see whether a known relation such as vertical angles, corresponding angles, etc., can be identified (Rule 3 in Table 1.2). That fails, so Rule 4 applies, and Perdix sets the goal of finding an angle that may be used in developing a chain of quantitative relations. This angle must be found in the diagram, and is designated ?CHANGLE.

When Perdix has the goal of finding a chaining angle, it forms a scanning line between the angles it is trying to relate and examines angles in order of proximity to that line.[1] In this case, A6 and A11 are on the scanning line, and of these, A6 is related to A1, the known angle, in a way that permits inference of congruence (**CONG**). The result is shown in Panel (e) of Fig. 1.1. The relation of vertical angles is identified by productions for perceptual pattern recognition, and that relation permits the inference of congruence through a propositional production.

When an angle congruent to A1 is found, the next goal is to analyze that angle to see whether it is related to A12. This goal is not achieved, so another chaining angle is needed. The nearest angle to the scanning path is A11, but this is not related to A6 in any way detectable by the pattern-recognizing productions. Angles A7 and A10 are next most proximal to the scanning line, but Perdix only accepts angles that are congruent to the base angle. The four angles A3, A8, A9, and A14 are equally proximal to the scanning line according to the calculations that Perdix uses. Any of these is congruent to A6; it happened in this example that A8 was considered first. The pattern recognizing productions identify the relation of corresponding angles, and the inferred relation of congruence is indicated in Panel (f).

The goal of relating A8 and A12 is set as shown in Panel (f). Perdix notes that A8 and A12 have sides that are parallel and other sides that are collinear (**CORR**). This feature is used to select a plan for achieving the goal of finding a quantitative relation called *PRLREL*, short for a relation based on parallel sides. The relation of interior angles on the same side, denoted **INTSAM**, and the inferred relation of supplementary angles (**SUPP**), are shown in Panel (g).

Next, the chain of relations is used to infer the relation of supplementary angles between A1 and A12. From this relation and the measure of A1, the measure of A12 is calculated, and the problem is solved. The final structure of relations derived during the solution is shown in Panel (h).

B. Comparisons With Student Performance

A major goal of the research program described here is to develop a model that solves geometry problems in a way similar to the way that students solve the problems. I have described a solution given by Perdix for the problem in Fig. 1.1. I will now consider the performance of some students on this same problem

---

[1]This scanning feature was not included in the version of the model described earlier and applied to this problem (Greeno, 1977b). In the earlier model, a chain of related angles was generated by seeking an angle with a specific relationship with the known angle. The present model is an improvement in that the scanning mechanism explains some features of student problem solving that were unexplained by the previous model.

and discuss the similarities and differences between the student protocols and Perdix' solution.

Table 1.3 shows the complete protocol given by one of the students in the group that was observed at regular intervals during their geometry course. At *1, the student read the problem. At *2, the student gave the answer and began giving reasons for the answer. I interrupted the student in order to have a sketch that I could use later to remember the sequence of steps. At *3, the student identified angle A5 as the first angle in a chain of relations. At *4, the student pointed to Angle A13 as the next angle in the chain, inferred its measure, and gave the reason. At *5, the student pointed to A12, gave the relation of congruence, justified it, and inferred the measure of A12, the unknown angle of the problem.

At *6, I asked the student whether there had been any memorable substages in finding the solution. As it turned out, the student reported a different solution than had been found initially and described that initial solution retrospectively. In this solution, the chain of angles found was A5, a vertical angle with A1, then A14, corresponding with A5, then A16, corresponding with A14, and finally A12, a linear pair with A16. This sequence was described in the comment at *8.

This subject's first solution, reported retrospectively, is one that Perdix would produce exactly. It differs from the one given in Fig. 1.1 at the step indicated in

TABLE 1.3
Student Protocol for Problem Shown in Fig. 1.1

*1	S:	Okay; a is parallel to b, m is parallel to n, the measure of angle, oh, the measure of angle p is 40. (Pause.)
	E:	What are you looking for?
*2	S:	Oh, well. I can tell you the answer. It'd be . . . angle p is supplementary to this angle, which is . . .
	E:	Okay, let me just draw that out, so I can follow what you're telling me. There's p down here . . .
	S:	Yeah.
*3	E:	And there's the one that you just pointed to there.
*4	S:	Right. Okay, that's going to be measurement 140.
	E:	Okay.
	S:	Because of corresponding angles of parallel lines.
	E:	Okay.
*5	S:	And that is going to be congruent to angle q.
	E:	Mm-hmm.
	S:	Because exterior angles of parallel lines are congruent. And then, so q is going to have the measure of 140.
*6	E:	Okay. Now, did you see that pattern in any stages? You looked at the diagram for awhile. Can you tell me how you put that together?
*7	S:	Oh, well, actually I didn't do it . . . the first thing I did was I looked across like this, because that's the line of your viewing, because you see pq.
	E:	Mm-hmm.
*8	S:	I saw that p and the vertical angle are congruent, and then I went across, then I went up, then I saw it was supplementary. I decided it would be . . . then I looked again, and I decided it would be faster to go across from p, from p to one.
	E:	You found a quicker way that had fewer steps in it. Okay. Good.

TABLE 1.4
Solutions by Student Subjects[a]

Step	Subject 1	Subject 2 (Initial Report)	Subject 2 (Retrospect)	Subject 3
1	(VERT A1 A6) (CONG A1 A6)	(LINPR A1 A5) (SUPP A1 A5) (MEAS A5 140°)	(VERT A1 A6) (CONG A1 A6)	(CORR A1 A3) (CONG A1 A3) (MEAS A3 40°)
2	(ALTINT A6 A3) (CONG A6 A3)	(CORR A5 A13) (CONG A5 A13) (MEAS A13 140°)	(CORR A6 A14) (CONG A6 A14)	(CORR A3 A11) (CONG A3 A11) (MEAS A11 40°)
3	(VERT A3 A8) (CONG A3 A8)	(ALTEXT A13 A12) (CONG A13 A12) (MEAS A12 140°)	(CORR A14 A16) (CONG A14 A16)	(LINPR A11 A12) (SUPP A11 A12) (MEAS A12 140°)
4	(INTSAM A8 A12) (SUPP A8 A12)		(LINPR A16 A12) (SUPP A16 A12)	
5	(SUPP A1 A12) (MEAS A12 140°)		(SUPP A1 A12) (MEAS A12 140°)	
6				

Step	Subject 4 (Initial)	Subject 4 (Revised)	Subject 5	Subject 6
1	(VERT A1 A6) (CONG A1 A6)	Initial Step 1	(ALTEXT A1 A8) (CONG A1 A8)	(VERT A1 A6) (CONG A1 A6) (MEAS A6 40°)
2	(?REL A6 A11) (CONG A6 A11)	(ALTINT A6 A3) (CONG A6 A3)	(INTSAM A8 A12) (SUPP A8 A12)	(ALTINT A6 A3) (CONG A6 A3) (MEAS A3 40°)
3	(VERT A11 A16) (CONG A11 A16)	(CORR A3 A11) (CONG A3 A11)	(SUPP A1 A12) (MEAS A12 140°)	(VERT A3 A8) (CONG A3 A8) (MEAS A8 40°)
4	(LINPR A16 A12) (SUPP A16 A12)	Initial Step 3		(LINPR A8 A4) (SUPP A8 A4) (MEAS A4 140°)
5	(SUPP A1 A12) (MEAS A12 140°)	Initial Step 4		(VERT A4 A7) (CONG A4 A7) (MEAS A7 140°)
6		Initial Step 5		(ALTINT A7 A12) (CONG A7 A12) (MEAS A12 140°)

Note. Adapted from "Process of Understanding in Problem Solving by J. G. Greeno. In N. J. Castellan, D. B. Pisoni, & G. R. Potts (Eds.), *Cognitive Theory* (Vol. 2). Hillsdale, N. J.: Lawrence Erlbaum Associates, 1977.

[a]Abbreviations of relations are as follows: MEAS, measure-of; CONG, congruence; SUPP, supplementary; VERT, vertical angles; ALTINT, alternate interior angles; INTSAM, interior angles on the same side of the transversal; LINPR, linear pair of angles; CORR, corresponding angles; ALTEXT, alternate exterior angles; ?REL, unspecified relation.

Panel (f) of that figure. At that point, Perdix happened to consider angle A8 first, of the four angles that are equally proximal to its scanning path. The subject who gave the protocol of Table 1.3 took angle A14 as the next step, but that is one of the angles that Perdix could as easily have chosen first. From angle A14, Perdix would consider either A11 or A16; if A16 happened to be first, Perdix would then generate the same solution as the one reported by the subject.

Table 1.4 shows, in brief form, the solutions found by six student subjects. Each line of the table corresponds to a relation between angles that would be constructed by Perdix in the course of solving the problem. In nearly all cases, the relation was mentioned by the subject. A few relations have been added to preserve uniformity in the detail of the solutions so that comparisons with Perdix' performance can be made.

The solution given by Subject 1 would be simulated by Perdix if A3 rather than A8 were considered first after the vertical angle A6 is noticed. Subject 2 is the student whose protocol is shown in Table 1.3. Subject 2's first solution, reported retrospectively, and Subject 1's solution are both among the solutions that Perdix could simulate exactly in its present form.

Subject 3's solution departs from performance that Perdix would give. First, angle A3 rather than A6 is the first angle found in the chain of related angles. If Perdix were programmed to choose A3 first, a different scanning procedure would be required from the one that forms a path between the vertices of the angles that are to be related and is now implemented. Choice of A11 as the second angle in the chain is consistent with the scanning process in Perdix. However, the protocol of Subject 3 departs from Perdix' performance in a way that would not be corrected by a modified scanning rule. Subject 3 inferred the measure of each angle in the chain before continuing the chain with an additional angle. In Perdix, the rule is: Find another angle that is congruent to the one you are working from, until you have an angle that has some quantitative relation with the unknown; then derive a quantitative relation between the unknown angle and the initially given angle. The strategic rule followed by Subject 3 is: Find the measure of another angle by relating it to the one you are working from, until you have an angle that has some quantitative relation with the unknown; then derive the measure of the unknown angle using the measure of the last angle you considered. The strategy used by Subject 3 corresponds to a program that is slightly more complicated than the one now implemented in Perdix because it returns to the goal of finding the measure of the unknown angle after each link in the chain is produced, rather than waiting for a quantitative relation to be found between the unknown and initially given angle.

Subject 4 made an interesting error in working on the problem that provides support for the hypothesis of scanning that is implemented in Perdix. After finding A6, the vertical angle, the subject mistakenly inferred a relation between A6 and A11. In fact, A6 and A11 are opposite interior angles of a parallelogram, and A11 could therefore be put in the chain if that theorem were available. However, theorems about parallelograms had not been studied at this point in the course. The student said, "There's a theorem that says that those two angles will be congruent." The student went ahead and completed a sketch of a solution, then said, "I can give you all the little theorems, except for that one." In doing this, the student accepted the "missing theorem" as a subproblem and solved it in the way shown in the solution labeled "Revised." Perdix would consider A11 at the point where Subject 4 put it in the chain but would avoid the error when the pattern-recognition system determined that A6 and A11 are not related in any known way. Subject 4 may have been misled by the apparent equality of the angles. In any case, angles A6 and A11 have features that do occur when angles are related. But the fact that the error occurred seems to support the hypothesis that a scanning process is an important component of the process of forming a chain of angles.

Subject 5 gave a solution that Perdix would not find and apparently used a more powerful strategy than the one that Perdix has. Perdix builds a chain of related angles by working forward from the given angle toward the unknown. In this procedure, an angle will be included in the chain if it is congruent with the angle Perdix currently is attending to. Subject 5's solution seems to require a process of searching for an angle that is related both to the given angle and the unknown angle, if one can be found. That more efficient strategy would not be difficult to add to Perdix' current strategic knowledge, but I have not done that because it seems to have occurred rarely in the sample of student protocols that I collected.

Subject 6's solution has the feature of Subject 3's in that measures are inferred at each step. The chain of angles that is constructed agrees with Subject 1's sequence through the first three steps. However, at Step 4, Subject 6 departs from Subject 1, and from Perdix, by failing to identify the relation between A8 and the unknown angle A12, which are interior angles on the same side of the transversal. The subject then departed from Perdix' strategy of using only congruent angles until the unknown angle is reached. However, Perdix' strategic policy would not be as plausible if the strategy were rearranged to provide for inferring a measure at each step. After taking Step 3, Subject 6's protocol includes the remark, "I was going to figure out if I could get this angle equal to q, and I figured out there's no way to do that, so I'm going to go by using supplementary angles." The subgoal of finding a supplementary angle with A8 would quite naturally be solved by finding A4, if the pattern-recognition system failed to identify the same-side interior relation. At that point, it is not clear why Subject 6 did not recognize the relation of corresponding angles between A4 and A12, although one could conjecture that the prior use of A8 interfered with the scanning process in some way.

Overall, Perdix' ability to generate solutions resembling these student solutions seems quite good. Of the six subjects, the solutions found first by Subject 1 and Subject 2 would be simulated by Perdix if angles were noticed in an appropriate order. Subject 5's solution would require a more powerful search strategy in which relations with both the given and unknown angle would be sought simultaneously. Subject 3's solution would require a change in strategy to provide inference of a measure at each step and a different scanning procedure. Subject 4's solution includes an error that appears to have arisen from a process consistent with Perdix' scanning process, but involved acceptance of a relationship when only a partial match of needed features was present. Subject 6 inferred a measure at each step and apparently failed to identify a relationship that was present between two angles. The existence of these discrepancies surely indicates that Perdix is not an exact replica of students' problem-solving processes. However, the nature of the modifications needed to simulate students' performance exactly in this problem seems to involve variations on a theme, rather than major structural changes. It seems a reasonable conjecture that the knowledge represented in Perdix is a fair approximation to the knowledge and strategy that students have acquired when they are successful in solving this class of problems.

IV.   PERCEPTUAL PATTERN RECOGNITION

In this and the following two sections, the knowledge structures that Perdix uses in solving geometry problems will be described in some detail. In this section, simulation of visual pattern recognition is described. To give a clear description of the pattern-recognition process, it is necessary to describe in detail the way in which information is represented in Perdix.

A.   Representation of Information in Diagrams

The information in a diagram is represented in Perdix as a network in which nodes represent points, line segments, angles, and other geometric objects, and links represent relations between those objects. The example in Fig. 1.2 shows much of the network representation of the simple diagram shown in the inset. Figure 1.3 labels the nodes of the diagram represented in Fig. 1.2. The nodes PNT159, PNT160, PNT161, and PNT170 represent the points labeled M, Q, N, and P, respectively. (The numbers included in the names of nodes have no significance other than to make the nodes distinctive.) Note in Fig. 1.2 that each node for a point is connected by a link to its label. The x and y coordinates of each point are also stored but are not shown in the diagram, and Perdix does not use these in solving problems. The nodes SEG166, SEG167, SEG169, and SEG174 represent the line segments that can be seen in the diagram. Each segment is connected to its label and also to each of its endpoints. The nodes RAY163, RAY164, RAY165, RAY168, RAY172, and RAY173 represent half-lines that are determined by segments in the diagram.

The slope of each half-line is calculated in a system similar to polar coordinates, except it is linearized to simplify calculation. A horizontal ray pointing to the right has slope 0.0, a vertical ray pointing upward has slope 1.0, a horizontal ray pointing to the left has slope 2.0, a vertical ray pointing downward has slope 3.0, and rays between these have intermediate values. The node for each ray is connected to its slope and to its endpoint. Thus, RAY163 is the half-line with endpoint Q that points downward in the diagram, and RAY168 is the half-line with endpoint Q that points upward. ANG175, ANG176, and ANG177 represent the angles that are formed by the intersecting half-lines. Each angle is connected to its vertex and to the two half-lines that are its sides. The quantity listed as the direction of each angle is the slope of the angle's bisector.

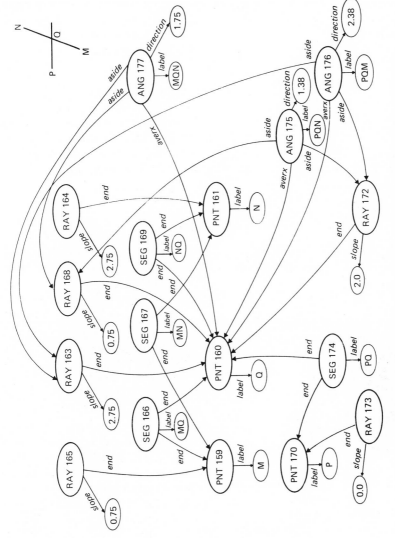

FIG. 1.2. Detailed illustration of representation in Perdix of information in a simple
diagram.

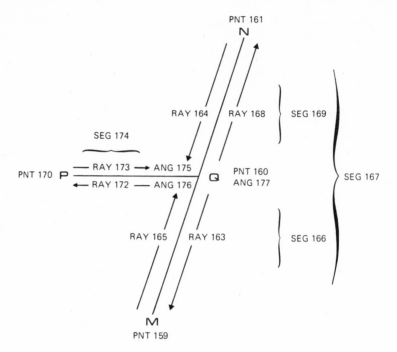

FIG. 1.3.   Labeled nodes of diagram represented in Fig. 1.2.

Two important components of the representation have been omitted from the diagram to keep it less unreadable. There are nodes in the network that represent names of categories: points, segments, rays, lines, and angles. The network contains links between these category names and their examples. Both the category name nodes and the membership links are omitted in Fig. 1.2. In addition, there are numerous links indicating part-whole relations that are not shown. For example, RAY163, RAY164, RAY165, and RAY168 are all parts of the whole line *M–N*, and the segments have part-of-relations with appropriate rays, SEG166 and SEG169 are both parts of SEG167, and so on.

B.   Simulation of Perceptual Pattern Recognition

Pattern matching is a basic component of all of Perdix' performance. The processing components that simulate perceptual pattern recognition are those in which Perdix' general pattern-matching processes are used in analyzing information in a diagram. Pattern recognition is performed in two ways. A simple pattern is identified in the condition of a single production; a more complex pattern recognition is accomplished using a set of related productions.

A pattern specified in a single production is a structure involving some specified links. An example is in Panel (a) of Fig. 1.4, which shows the pattern called *ANGLEPARTS*. When this pattern is included in the condition of a production, the system receives information about a specific angle; for example, it would be used to identify which point and half-lines are the vertex and sides of a specified angle. In the diagram, the central node designates an angle, linked through *averx* to the vertex, and through *aside* to the sides.

When a condition with this pattern is tested, there is a search of the network that represents the situation at that time. The search succeeds if there is a set of nodes in the situation that can be assigned to the open positions in the pattern with relations that agree with those specified.

When a pattern is included in a production, the positions in the pattern can be specified either as constants or variables and when the pattern is tested, some of the variables may already have values assigned. Suppose at some point that Perdix needed to find an angle with a specific segment as one of its sides. The condition of a production could be the pattern in Panel (b) of Fig. 1.4, stated with variables in all of its positions except the node labeled RAY, which is a

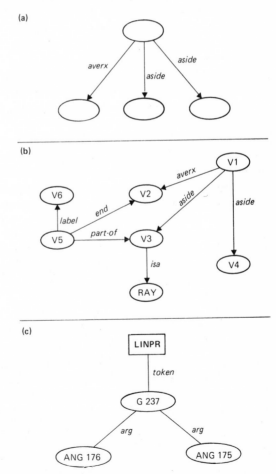

FIG. 1.4.   Examples of patterns recognized in single productions.

constant. To identify the segment that is to be on one of the sides, variable V6 could be bound to some specific label. Suppose the situation is the one shown in Fig. 1.2, and V6 has the value *MQ*. This means that to satisfy the condition, there must be nodes that can be assigned to V1, V2, V3, V4, and V5 that have the right relationships with *MQ* and RAY, as well as each other. As can be seen in Fig. 1.2, the pattern will be matched, V5 will be matched to SEG166, the node for which MQ is a label. SEG166 is a part of RAY163. RAY163 is in the category RAY, as required by the *isa* link, which denotes category membership. RAY163 also has the relation *aside* to an angle. Therefore, V3 will be matched to RAY163. An end of SEG166 in PNT160, which has the relation *averx* to an angle. PNT159 also is an end of SEG166, but PNT159 does not satisfy the requirement of having the *averx* relation. V2 will, therefore, be matched to PNT160. There are two nodes that could be matched to V1: ANG176 or ANG177; both have RAY163 as a side and PNT160 as the vertex. The system will match to one of them; which one is found depends on the order in which the angles were constructed in the initial representation. If V1 is matched to ANG176, then V4 will be matched to its other side, RAY172. However, if V1 is matched to ANG177, then V4 will be matched to RAY168.

For complex pattern recognition, Perdix uses sets of related productions corresponding to pattern-recognition systems. For problems involving parallel lines, a set of productions is used to identify the various relations between pairs of angles: vertical angles, linear pairs, corresponding angles, alternate interior angles, and interior angles on the same side of the transversal. These productions are organized in the manner of a decision net (Feigenbaum, 1963; Hunt, Marin, & Stone, 1966). When the pattern recognizing system is used, there is a series of tests. Each test determines whether some feature is present for the angles being considered. The feature tested next depends on the outcomes of previous tests. If an appropriate combination of features is found, the system identifies one of the relations that it knows.

As an example, consider the angles $\angle PQM$ and $\angle PQN$ shown in the inset of Fig. 1.2. The angles have the relation called a linear pair. The features needed to determine the relation are that the angles have the same vertex, they share a side, and their remaining sides are collinear. If Perdix had the goal of analyzing the relation between $\angle PQM$ and $\angle PQN$, the procedure would begin by noticing that the angles have the same vertex. Then the system would notice that one side of $\angle PQM$ is also a side of $\angle PQN$. Then the system would notice that the remaining sides of the two angles are collinear, but the line containing these sides and the line of the shared side are not perpendicular. Finally, Perdix would add information to the network indicating the relation of a linear pair between the angles.

One way to organize a system of productions to recognize patterns is in the form of a tree of decisions based on features (Feigenbaum, 1963; Hunt, Marin, & Stone, 1966). This decision-tree form has been used in Perdix, and an example is shown in Fig. 1.5. In the figure, the diamonds indicate tests that are performed. If the test is positive, the next step is indicated by the line marked yes.

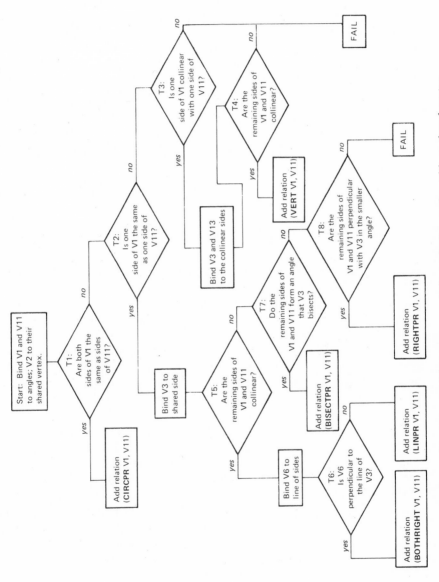

FIG. 1.5. Pattern-recognizing system used in analyzing angles with a shared vertex.

33

Rectangles are used to indicate actions performed by the system other than testing features.

The two kinds of action performed by these productions are the binding of values to variables and adding relations to the network that represents the situation. Binding a variable simply involves assigning a value to the variable and holding the assignment in memory. The decision-tree shown in Fig. 1.5 recognizes six different geometric relations that can be found between angles that have a shared vertex. The most frequent of these are vertical angles, denoted **VERT**, and a linear pair, denoted **LINPR**. The system also will recognize that two angles combine to form a complete circle (denoted **CIRCPR**); that two adjacent angles are both right angles (a special case of **LINPR**, denoted **BOTHRIGHT**); that two adjacent angles are formed by the bisection of another angle (denoted **BISECTPR**); or that two adjacent angles combine to form a right angle (denoted **RIGHTPR**). Perdix also includes another feature decision-tree test that is used to analyze pairs of angles that are formed by parallel lines and a transversal, such as corresponding angles, alternate interior angles, and interior angles on the same side of the transversal.

As an illustration of the pattern-recognizing system, I will describe the analysys of $\angle PQM$ and $\angle PQN$ shown in the diagram in Fig. 1.2. The procedure would begin with the nodes that represent these two angles assigned as values of variables V1 and V11. V1 would be bound to ANG176, the angle named by the label PQM, and V11 would be bound to ANG175, the angle named by the label PQN. The decision to use this set of productions would have been made by the planning procedures that Perdix has, and in this stage the variable V2 would be bound to the shared vertex, PNT160.

The first production to be tried is denoted T1 in Fig. 1.5. This production has a condition requiring that both sides of V1 are the same as the sides of V11. This fails; the sides of ANG176 are RAY163 and RAY172, and the sides of ANG175 are RAY168 and RAY172. The next production to be tried is T2. T2's condition is true if one side of V1 is the same as a side of V11. This succeeds, since RAY172 is a side of both angles, and RAY172 is assigned as the value of V3.

The next production to be tried is T5. The condition of T5 tests RAY163 and RAY168, the remaining sides of the two angles. The question is whether these are both parts of a single line. It happens they are: both are parts of LIN162. Thus, T5 succeeds, and LIN162 is assigned as the value of V6. Next, T6 is tried, and this involves testing whether LIN162 is perpendicular to LIN171, which is the line that contains RAY172. This condition is not met, so the final action is the addition of the relation **LINPR** to the network that represents the situation.

The action of adding relational information to the network represents the basic mechanism of making inferences in problem solving. Panel (c) of Fig. 1.4 shows the relational structure that is added as a result of the pattern-recognition analysis of $\angle PQM$ and $\angle PQN$. A distinctive token node is generated by the system and connected to **LINPR**, the name of ıe relation. This token node, shown as G237 in Fig. 1.4, is connected through links labeled *arg* (for arguments of the relation) to the nodes that represent the two angles that have this relation. The presence of this relation can later be recognized by productions whose conditions require specified kinds of relations between angles.

V.   PROPOSITIONS FOR INFERENCE

The second general kind of knowledge needed in geometry is inferential knowledge. Inferences in geometry are based on general propositions that are taught explicitly. Examples are: "Corresponding angles are congruent," "angles that form a linear pair are supplementary," and "the sum of the angles of a triangle is 180°." As in the previous section, I begin by describing the representation of propositional information in Perdix.

A.   Representation of Propositions

In addition to the kind of information shown in diagrams, there is information given in the form of verbal propositions, such as "angle p has a measure of 40°," or "line *a* and line *b* are parallel."

Information given in the form of verbal propositions is represented in a slightly more complicated form in Perdix than that shown earlier in Fig. 1.1. The difference is the addition of token nodes for each instance of a relation. These token nodes are needed because the system must distinguish between different relations of the same kind. For example, the proposition "vertical angles are congruent" states that if two angles are related by the relationship **VERT**, those same angles are also related by the relationship **CONG**. In Perdix, the representation of inferential propositions is very simple; each proposition is represented as a single production. The if ... then ... character of inferential productions corresponds directly to the form of productions. In each case, the condition of the production tests for the presence of the antecedent of the proposition. If the antecedent is present, the production is executed, and the action consists of adding the relation that is stated in the consequent of the proposition. An example is shown in Fig. 1.6. V1, V2, V3, and V4 are variables. If the pattern on the left is found, the pattern on the right is constructed, using the same nodes in the argument locations of the new structure as were found in the argument locations of the existing structure.

B.   Simulation of Propositional Inference

The knowledge used in making propositional inferences corresponds directly to the information that we usually think of as the content of geometry. At present, Perdix includes representations of the major propositions used in problems that involve parallel lines and in problems involving congruent triangles.

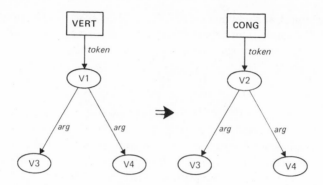

FIG. 1.6.   Representation of propositions.

The propositions of geometry are of two general kinds. One kind of proposition involves inference of a quantitative relation such as congruence or being supplementary. The other kind involves inference of a numerical measure.

The antecedents of propositions for inferring quantitative relations involve either geometric relations or other quantitative relations. For example, in Fig. 1.6, the antecedent of the inference is the relation of vertical angles. An example involving quantitative relations is a production in which the antecedent involves two angles that are congruent with one of them having some quantitative relation with a third angle. Then that quantitative relation can be inferred to hold between the other congruent angle and the third angle. For example, if $\angle A$ and $\angle B$ are congruent, and $\angle B$ is supplementary with $\angle C$, then the inference is made that $\angle A$ and $\angle C$ are supplementary. A third example is that angles or segments that are corresponding parts of congruent triangles can be inferred to be congruent.

Many propositions that infer the measure of an angle use general quantitative relations, such as congruence. For example, if $\angle A$ and $\angle B$ are congruent, and if the measure of $\angle A$ is $60°$, then the measure of $\angle B$ is also $60°$. Other productions are specific kinds of angles — for example, a right angle has a measure of $90°$, or the sum of angles in a triangle is $180°$.

The use of inferential productions is seen in Fig. 1.1. Inferences are indicated by double-line arrows. In Panel (e), the inference is made that A1 and A6 are congruent; the antecedent is that those angles are vertical angles. Similar inferences are shown in Panels (f) and (g). In Panel (h) inferences are shown that derive quantitative relations from other quantitative relations: For example, A12 and A6 are supplementary because A12 and A8 are supplementary and A8 and A6 are congruent. Panel (h) also shows an inference of quantitative measure. The final relation that is added by an inferential production is that the measure of A12 is $140°$. The condition found for the execution of that production is that A1 and A12 are supplementary and the measure of A1 is $40°$.

The information shown in Table 1.4 also illustrates the use of inferential productions. The table shows the sequence of relations that was inferred by each student subject in the process of solving the problem.

VI.   STRATEGIC KNOWLEDGE

Each step taken in solving a geometry problem involves inference of some new relation, based either on pattern recognition or on other relations stated in the problem or inferred earlier. The discussion in Sections IV and V has described the processes in Perdix that make these individual inferences. However, these elements of knowledge only enable the system to take individual steps. There must also be knowledge that organizes the individual's activity on the problem and produces the whole solution.

There are two closely related functions that provide organization for problem solving in Perdix. These functions are setting goals and planning. Knowledge for setting goals and planning is an essential part of the knowledge a student acquires in learning the subject of geometry. It is knowledge in the domain of skill involving knowing how to apply the information of geometry.

I begin this section by describing the basic processes in Perdix for setting goals and planning. Then I consider three substantive questions about the nature of stragetic knowledge in geometry that relate to general questions about problem solving. The first issue involves a more complex and flexible kind of goal structure than is in the system described in Section II. The second issue involves problem-solving sets and the process of selecting plans during problem solving. The third issue involves constructions in solving geometry problems and the general issue of completeness of the problem space that is given in the problem initially.

A.   Simulation of Goal Setting and Planning

Perdix has two general categories of goals which involve different kinds of actions that are called for in different situations. The two categories are goals to prove something and goals to find something (cf. Polya, 1962, 1965). A goal structure also includes a pattern that will be produced in the situation if the goal can be achieved. When the goal is to prove something, the pattern is the relational structure representing the proposition to be proved. If the action is to find something, then the pattern is incomplete, specifying the elements that are already present and indicating the kind of element that is needed to complete the pattern. As an example, suppose that the current goal is to prove that two angles are congruent. The action of this goal is to prove something rather than to find something. The pattern of the goal is a relation of congruence between the two specified angles. As another example, suppose that the current goal is to find a quantitative relation between two angles. Then the action of the goal is to find something, and the pattern is an incomplete structure, that includes the two angles and an indication that some quantitative relation is needed.

The knowledge that Perdix has for planning is similar in some ways to the system NOAH, developed by Sacerdoti (1975). Sacerdoti developed the idea of storing knowledge about various kinds of actions in a structure called a *procedural network*. The information stored about each action includes prerequisite features of the situation that are needed if the action is to be performed and consequences that are produced when the action is performed. This information is used in constructing a plan for solving the problem in which the various actions included in the plan have consequences that are compatible with the prerequisites of actions that will have to be performed later.

In Perdix, planning information is associated with the kinds of patterns that are included in goal structures. When the goal pattern involves the measure of an angle, possible plans include calculating the needed measure using the sum of angles in a triangle or calculating the unknown measure using some quantitative relation that the unknown angle has with some angle whose measure is known. When the goal pattern involves a quantitative relation between two angles, the possible plans include inferring the needed relation from geometric relations involving rotation, inferring the needed relation from geometric relations involving parallel sides and a transversal, proving that two triangles that contain the target angles are congruent, or constructing a chain of quantitative relations using other angles.

Each plan that Perdix knows about has prerequisites and to be selected, a plan's prerequisites must be present in the situation. The prerequisite features are not sufficient to guarantee that the plan will work, but they are sufficient to make it worth investigating the plan — they make the plan promising. For example, for the plan of inferring a quantitative relation from a relation of rotation between two angles, the prerequisite is that the angles must share the same vertex. For the plan of proving angles congruent by showing that triangles containing the angles are congruent, the prerequisite is that the angles be contained in triangles.

When a goal is set during problem solving, a set of planning productions for that goal are executed. In these planning productions, the conditions correspond to the prerequisites of the various plans that are available for that goal. The action of each production corresponds to a decision to adopt a specified plan. The effect of this is that the plan adopted must have its prerequisites satisfied, and whichever plan's prerequisites are noticed first will be the one adopted.

Goals and plans are represented in Perdix as network structures of the same general kind that are used to represent information in patterns and propositions. An example is in Fig. 1.6. The goal structure has an identifying token node G238, which is connected to the four nodes in the structure. These include the kind of action that the goal involves, the category of pattern that is to be

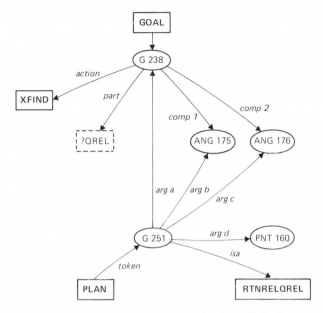

FIG. 1.7.   Representation of a goal and plan in Perdix.

achieved, and components that will be included in the pattern. In this case, the action is to find a relation, indicated as **XFIND**, the pattern is some quantitative relationship that is not specified, shown as ?QREL, and the components are two angles, ANG175 and ANG176.

Plan structures are represented using the general format of relational propositions. The specific plan is designated by a token node, G251. This particular plan involves an attempt to infer a quantitative relation from a relation of rotation between angles; this somewhat complicated category name is abbreviated **RTNRELQREL**. The nodes that are connected in the relational structure include the node that identifies the goal that the plan is for, the two angles that are to be related when the goal is achieved, and another object PNT160 that is relevant to the plan.

During the problem solving, when Perdix adopts a plan, the situation may permit the plan to be executed immediately. However, in most cases some further work must be done, and this requires Perdix to set a subgoal. Knowledge of subgoals that are useful in achieving plans is part of Perdix' planning knowledge. Usually the subgoal that is needed is obvious. For example, Perdix can execute the plan shown in Fig. 1.7 if the angles ANG175 and ANG176 are related by one of the relations of rotation such as vertical angles or the relation of linear pair. If the kind of relation that is needed is not represented in the situation, the subgoal is set to try to identify such a relation by using perceptual pattern recognition. The new subgoal replaces the earlier goal in current attention, but the previous goal is stored in memory to be retrieved when the new subgoal is either achieved or is determined to be impossible.

To illustrate the processes of goal setting and planning, return once again to Fig. 1.1. The goal that is given in the problem is taken as the main goal. The goal structure shown in Panel (c) is an abbreviation for a structure like the one shown in Fig. 1.7, where the action is to find something and the pattern is a measure of angle A12, indicated by an unknown number. Perdix tests the prerequisites of its two plans for finding a measure. The plan involving use of the sum of angles in a triangle is not applicable since there is no triangle in the diagram. Because angle A1 is known, Perdix adopts the plan of using a quantitative relation with A1 to derive the measure of A12 and sets the goal of finding such a measure. The goal of finding the measure of A12 is stored in memory, and the new goal of finding a quantitative relation of A12 with A1 becomes the current goal.

The goal of finding a quantitative relation requires planning, and Perdix examines the prerequisites of its available plans. These include containment of the angles in triangles, which fails. A second plan requires that the two angles have the same vertex, and this also fails. A third possibility is that the angles have two sides that are parallel and the other two sides along a transversal. Angles A1 and A12 have parallel sides, but their other sides are not collinear, so that plan also fails. At this point, Perdix adopts the plan of constructing a chain of congruent angles to link A1 and A12. The new goal of finding a congruent angle to go with A1 is adopted, and the goal of a quantitative relation between A1 and A12 is stored. This situation corresponds to Panel (d) in Fig. 1.1.

The attempt to find a congruent angle for a chain is governed by a process of perceptual scanning. A scanning path is constructed that connects the vertices of the angles to be related, and angles are considered in order of their proximity to the scanning path. Angles A11 and A6 are both directly on the scanning path, and the order of their consideration varies depending on accidental factors in the construction of the diagram. If A11 is considered first, it does not lead to a plan because it lacks prerequisite geometric relations with A1. When A6 is considered, the planning productions succeed since A1 and A6 have the same vertex. Pattern recognition is then executed, and it is found that A1 and A6 are vertical angles. This permits the inference that A1 and A6 are congruent, as required. A link in the chain has been constructed.

With the subgoal of finding a chaining angle achieved, Perdix sets the further subgoal of finding a quantitative relation between this new angle and the initial unknown angle, A12. Analysis of A6 and A12 is unproductive for the same reasons as in the case of A1 and A12. The subgoal of another chaining angle is set. This situation is shown in Panel (e) of Fig. 1.1.

In seeking a chaining angle between A6 and A12, the same scanning path is used as in the previous step. A11 is the closest angle, but it is not related to A6 in any of the required ways. (Note that it is at this step that Subject 4 in Table 1.4 erroneously identified a relation between A6 and A11. This student's planning procedure apparently contained a set of prerequisite features that were somewhat more general than they should have been. Furthermore, the student was sufficiently confident of the outcome of planning that the further step of verifying the specific relation involved was omitted.) Angles A7 and A10 are also close to the scanning path between A6 and A10, and they meet the prerequisites for relations involving parallel lines. However, when they are tested, it is found they are not congruent with A6, and congruence is required by Perdix for including an angle in a chain. Next, the angles A3, A8, A9, and A14 are all equally proximal to the scanning path, and whichever of these angles is examined first becomes the next link in the chain because they are all congruent with A6, either by corresponding or by alternate interior angles. In the example, A8 happened to be the angle examined first. This is followed by setting the subgoal of finding a relation between A8 and A12.

When A8 and A12 are considered by the planning productions for quantitative relations, the prerequisite conditions involving parallel sides and a transversal are satisfied. This causes Perdix to adopt the plan **PRLRELQREL**. Infer the quantitative relation from a relation based on parallel sides. The needed geometric relation is set as a subgoal, and the situation shown in Panel (f) is reached.

Relations based on parallel lines are found, if they are there, by the pattern-recognition system. This process is executed, and the relation of same-side interior angles is identified. With this subgoal satisfied, Perdix returns to the goal of finding a quantitative relation between A8 and A12. The plan of inferring that from a relation based on parallel sides now can be executed, and the inference of supplementary angles is made. This situation is shown in Panel (g).

Panel (g) also shows that the goals remaining in memory are a quantitative relation between A6 and A12, a quantitative relation between A1 and A12, and the measure of A12. The first of these can now be achieved since the congruence of A6 and A8, along with the fact that A8 and A12 are supplementary, permits the inference that A6 and A12 are supplementary. When that inference is made, the next subgoal can be achieved, giving the relation of supplementary angles between A1 and A12. Finally, Perdix returns to the main goal of the problem and the plan for its achievement, which involves using a quantitative relation between A12 and A1. That plan can now be executed, and the answer is obtained.

Indefinite Goal Structures.   Goal structures of the kind described in the preceding paragraphs are typical of the kinds of goals considered in most current theories of problem solving. At any time during problem solving, the problem solver has a goal consisting of a specific combination of features of the situation, and the problem-solving activity is directed toward constructing that combination of features.

In the next several paragraphs, I present an extension of that kind of theoretical representation. The extension permits representation of indefinite goals, which are goals that can be satisfied by several alternative combinations of features. The extension is required for a realistic theory of human problem solving in geometry, because an important class of problems are solved using this more flexible kind of goal structure. Evidence showing the need for the extended theory of goal representation was obtained in protocols given by high school geometry students, and this evidence will be described.

A kind of problem that is solved using indefinite goal structures is proof that triangles are congruent. Consider Fig. 1.8. The thin lines and the material written in the upper right-hand corner of the figure are the student's work on the problem. To solve the problem, use $\overline{PM} \perp \overline{QR}$ to show $\angle PMQ = \angle PMR$, use $\overline{PM}$ bisects $\angle QPR$ to show that $\angle QPM = \angle RPM$, and note that $\overline{PM} = \overline{PM}$. Thus, $\triangle PQM = \triangle PRM$ by angle-side-angle.

There are several different ways to prove that triangles are congruent. In addition to the angle-side-angle pattern used for this problem, congruence of triangles can be inferred if they have congruent parts in patterns of side-side-side, side-angle-side, angle-angle-side, and for right triangles, hypotenuse-leg.

It would be possible for a system like Perdix to solve problems involving congruence of triangles, using goal structures like the one shown in Fig. 1.7. To accomplish this, the system would be programmed to generate one of the congruence patterns as a subgoal when the main goal of congruent triangles was set. Side-side-side might be tried first; then when it was determined that there were not three sides that could be proved congruent, the system might try the side-angle-side pattern, continuing until one of the patterns was successfully proved. This strategy of working backward through specific subgoals would be relatively straightforward to program for Perdix, and it has been used in systems of artificial intelligence developed for solving problems in geometry (Gelernter, 1963; Goldstein, 1973; Ullman, 1975). The General Problem Solver (Ernst & Newell, 1969; Newell & Simon, 1972) has not been programmed specifically for solution of geometry problems, but its procedures for handling goals would lend

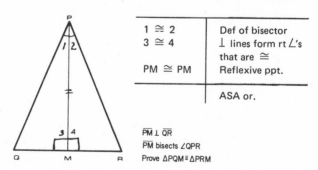

FIG. 1.8.   Additions to the diagram and steps of proof written by the student during solution described in Table 1.5. (Adapted from "Indefinite Goals in Well-Structured Problems" by J. G. Greeno, *Psychological Review*, 1976, *83*, 479–491. Copyright by the American Psychological Association, 1976. Reprinted by permission.)

TABLE 1.5
Student Protocol for Problem in Fig. 1.8

*1	S:	Okay; PM is perpendicular to QR, and PM bisects angle QPR. These two angles are equal, and prove this triangle is congruent to that one.
*2		That means that these two are equal, because this bisects it.
	E:	Mm-hmm.
	S:	And . . . would you like me to write out a formal proof?
	E:	Yeah, at least part of it.
	S:	Okay; well, then . . .
*3		the two right angles are right angles because . . . if I can just draw it quickly . . .
*4		all right, one and two.
	E:	Okay.
*5	S:	One is congruent to two because . . . PM bisects it.
	E:	Okay.
	S:	Well, if I'm going to write down a reason . . . well, that's kind of given. I'm trying to think if I know a reason. About bisecting. But, when . . . the definition of a bisector, I guess.
	E:	That would be fine.
*6	S:	Okay, and . . . make this three and four. Three is congruent to four because of perpendicular lines form right angles; right angles are congruent. . . .
*7		And then, PM is congruent to PM, because of the reflexive property. . . . And then I have angle-side-angle. Or, I could do it another way. I could say that . . . I have an optional.
	E:	Sure.
	S:	I could say that . . .
	E:	You can just tell me the optional.
*8	S:	Okay. Then you angle-side-angle, or, I could say that . . . these are right triangles because they contain a right angle, and then I could do the leg-angle.
	E:	Okay, fine. Now, when do you think you could tell that you were going to use angle-side-angle?
*9	S:	Well, I could just . . . I know that the . . . I was just looking for things I could prove were congruent. The one common side is congruent, and the bisector makes these two angles congruent, and I know that these angles are congruent, so . . . I just try to figure out what it is. I just try to prove what's congruent, and then I look at what it is, and then I write down what it is.
	E:	I see, okay.

Note. Adapted from "Indefinite Goals in Well-Structured Problems" by J. G. Greeno, *Psychological Review*, 1976, *83*, 479-481. Copyright 1976 by the American Psychological Association. Reprinted by permission.

themselves most easily to a process of involving definite subgoals and thus would be similar to the geometry problem solvers that have been constructed.

Table 1.5 gives an example of a solution to the problem in Fig. 1.8. The solution shows no evidence of the use of specific subgoals prior to finding a pattern that is sufficient for proving congruence. The protocol was given by one of the students whom I interviewed during the time they were taking geometry.

At *1 the student read the given information aloud. At *2 and *3 the student identified congruent pairs of components. At *4 the student labeled the angles numbered 1 and 2 in the diagram as shown in Fig. 1.8. At *5 the student wrote the first line of the proof, shown at the upper right in Fig. 1.8. At *6 and *7, the student labeled the angles numbered 3 and 4 and completed the statements in the proof. The student alluded to an alternative proof at *8, and at *9 the subject commented about an aspect of the sequence of steps that occurred.

The protocol in Table 1.5 shows no evidence for the use of definite subgoals prior to completing the angle-side-angle pattern. Evidence for such subgoals might have occurred early in the protocol, before *2, when the student might have said something like, "I'll start by looking for angle-side-angle." Less direct evidence could also have occurred had the student made a remark such as, "I need the sides congruent now to finish angle-side-angle," before the comment given at *7. A remark like this would have indicated that the student had thought of the pattern before noting the complete set of congruent pairs of components.

The protocol actually includes two rather definite indications that the student did not consider patterns specifically as subgoals. One indication is the remark made at *9, which shows the student's rather strong impression that the solution was found on the basis of a generalized search for congruent components rather than from attempts to find specific patterns corresponding to definite hypotheses. Another indication is that the student noted an alternative pattern to the one found. The comment at *8 includes reference to an optional statement of the pattern, which is specified at *9. If the student had been searching directly for the components of a specific pattern, it would be less likely that the student would notice that the components found also fit into another pattern.

The conclusion about Table 1.5 is typical. In the set of protocols that I obtained from high school students taking geometry, there were 24 protocols involving problems where congruence of triangles was proven (see Greeno, 1976, for details). Of these 24 protocols, only one showed definite evidence that a student thought of a specific subgoal at the beginning of work on the problem; only three showed definite evidence that a student thought of a specified subgoal at any time prior to haveing found a complete pattern of component congruent pairs. It appears that the typical approach to these problems involves generalized search for congruent components, with a monitor on the process that provides recognition of a complete pattern of congruent pairs when one appears. As one student described the process, "I was just letting this stuff, the given information, sort of soak through my head. ... I like to look at the information and just sort of let it, you know, run through my mind and make little guesses from here to there, you know."

The data support strongly the conclusion that in problems of proving that triangles are congruent, students conduct a general search for congruent pairs of components, rather than guiding their search by definite hypotheses corresponding to specific patterns. In order for Perdix to simulate this aspect of student performance, a significant extension of the theory was required. The general search was simulated by including a representation of the goal structure as a pattern-recognizing system capable of identifying any of several combinations of congruent components that might arise in a problem situation.

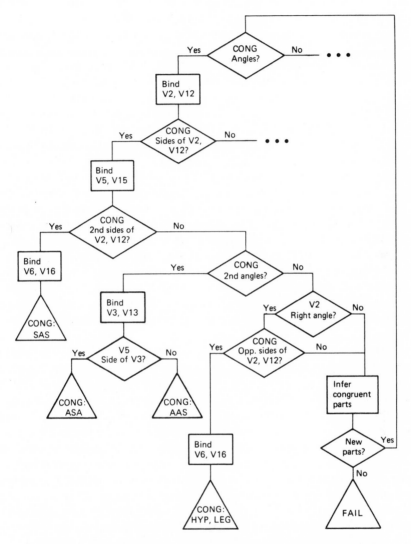

FIG. 1.9. Part of Perdix' goal structure for proving congruence of tri-angles, represented as a pattern-recognition system. (Abbreviations: CONG = congruent; SAS = side-angle-side; ASA = angle-side-angle; AAS = angle-angle-side; HYP, LEG = hypotenuse-leg.) (Adapted from "Indefinite Goals in Well-Structured Problems" by J. G. Greeno, *Psychological Review*, 1976, *83*, 479–491. Copyright by the American Psychological Association, 1976. Reprinted by permission.)

The general form of pattern recognition in Perdix was described in Section IV. The principles used are standard in recent theories of pattern recognition such as EPAM (Feigenbaum, 1963) and CLS (Hunt, Marin, & Stone, 1966). A pattern-recognizing system for representing a goal has a number of features that are tested, and the goal can be satisfied by several different combinations of features. Figure 1.9 shows about half of the nodes in the pattern-recognition network for identifying proofs of congruence between triangles. The system recognizes six different patterns, four of which are shown. Thirteen feature-testing nodes are included in the structure.

To see how the pattern-recognizing goal structure operates, suppose that the problem solver has found the pairs of congruent angles and the reflexive congruence of segment $\overline{PM}$ depicted in Fig. 1.8. Now notice the first test indicated in Fig. 1.9; it asks whether there is a pair of congruent angles in the two triangles being considered. There is such a pair — suppose that the system finds $\angle QPM$ and $\angle RPM$ first. These become the values of variable V2 and V12. Now the system tests whether sides of these angles are congruent. Segment $\overline{PM}$ is a side of both $\angle QPM$ and $\angle RPM$, and it is congruent to itself, so the test succeeds, and $\overline{PM}$ becomes the value of both V5 and V15. The next test in the sequence is whether the second sides of $\angle QPM$ and $\angle RPM$ are congruent. This involves segments $\overline{PQ}$ and $\overline{PR}$; these are not known to be congruent, so that test fails. The next test asks whether there is a second pair of angles known to be congruent. There is; these are $\angle PMQ$ and $\angle PMR$, and they become the values of variables V3 and V13. Finally, it is determined that segment $\overline{PM}$, which is the current value of V5, is a side of $\angle PMQ$, so the identified pattern is angle-side-angle (ASA).

In solving a problem such as Fig. 1.8, Perdix uses the pattern-recognizing goal structure, along with other productions for pattern recognition, inference, and setting of goals, as was discussed earlier. When Perdix begins work on this problem, the main goal of proving $\triangle PQM$ and $\triangle PRM$ congruent is known. This leads to a test using the pattern-recognition system for congruence. No pairs of components in the two triangles are known to be congruent, so the system sets a subgoal of inferring some congruent pairs of the triangles.

Inference of congruent parts is accomplished by a set of productions in which conditions correspond to patterns of features that imply congruence. In working on the problem of Fig. 1.8, the first production that succeeds identifies $\overline{PM}$ as a side of both triangles; in this condition, Perdix adds to the data structure the relation of congruence, applied reflexively to the segment labeled $\overline{PM}$. Then Perdix returns to the major goal and tests for congruence again using the pattern-recognition goal structure. A single relation of congruence involving sides is not sufficient, so the subgoal of inferring congruent parts is set again. The production that is executed this time has a condition involving the bisector of an angle, where the angles formed by the bisection are parts of the target triangles. The action performed is to infer the congruence of $\angle QPM$ and $\angle RPM$. Returning to the major goal, Perdix once again tests for a pattern that implies congruence of triangles, but there are not yet sufficient congruent components. The productions for congruent parts are once again tested, and this time the perpendicular lines are found, leading to the inference that $\angle PMQ$ and $\angle PMR$ are congruent. Now when the pattern recognizer is executed, the congruent features are sufficient for the angle-side-angle pattern to be recognized, and the problem goal is achieved.

B. Hierarchical Planning and Problem-Solving Set

Human problem solvers are often observed to work on a problem in an unsuccessful way, failing to recognize some feature of the situation that would make an easy solution possible. Luchins (1942) reported results of several experiments in which a solution method was practiced over a series of problems and then was used by subjects on problems that had a much simpler solution. Most of Luchins' experiments used problems involving water jars, requiring a series of pouring actions that result in a specified amount of water in one of the jars. In these well-known experiments, the method that was induced by practice consisted of a formula: Fill the second jar, pour out enough to fill the first jar once, and pour out enough to fill the third jar twice. Subjects were then given a problem that could be solved either with that formula or an easier one: Fill the first jar, and pour out enough to fill the third. Most subjects used the more complicated method, not noticing that an easier procedure was available. On a problem for which an easy solution was available but that could not be solved using the induced formula, many students were unable to find the solution at all.

Luchins also briefly reported results of a small study of geometry problem solving. He presented a series of four problems in which students proved the congruence of angles by proving that triangles containing the angles were congruent. Then in one condition, Luchins presented a problem that could be solved either through a proof that triangles were congruent or simply by noting that the angles were vertical angles. Of 10 students, 8 solved this problem by proving that the triangles were congruent. In another condition, Luchins presented a problem containing triangles that could not be proven congruent but that had a solution based on vertical angles. In this condition, 6 of 10 students failed to find a solution in the 2.5 minutes allowed. In contrast, the problem was solved easily by all of the 12 students given this problem without preceding problems to induce an inappropriate plan.

The kind of planning system implemented in Perdix provides an explanation of problem-solving set. As was mentioned at the beginning of this section, the planning knowledge simulated by Perdix includes a set of alternative ways of trying to solve a problem. When a goal of a certain kind is set, Perdix tests the situation for certain global features and selects a plan for which the appropriate prerequisites are present. Once a plan is adopted, Perdix carries out activities that are relevant to that plan until the plan either can be executed or it is determined that the plan is impossible.

The design of Perdix' planning procedure relates to the distinction between top—down and bottom—up processing in information processing. In top—down processing, there is a general concept or hypothesis that directs the system's activity. In bottom—up processing, the system is operating without any particular direction or expectation and makes decisions based on the information that is found in the situation. Realistic information processing systems are never exclusively top—down or bottom—up in nature, but systems do differ in the extent of control based on general concepts and expectations rather than specific information that is found in the problem situation.

When Perdix has set a goal, planning proceeds in a limited bottom—up manner. The selection of a plan depends on tests of features of the situation that are known to be required for the plan to be successful. Thus, selection of a plan depends on information from the situation more than it might. A completely top—down planning system would have a fixed order of trying plans without regard for features of the situation. On the other hand, the planning process only interrogates a limited set of features that are known to be relevant to the plans that are included in Perdix' set of alternatives, so the planning system is not completely bottom—up. Furthermore, the tests of features occur in a serial manner, with the test for prerequisites of one plan being tested at a time. The first plan in which the appropriate prerequisite features are found is the one adopted. After a plan is adopted, Perdix proceeds in a strongly top—down fashion, working on subgoals that are associated with that plan. Perdix has procedures for determining that the current plan cannot succeed, but it may take considerable work to reach the point of deciding to abandon a plan once it has been adopted. If a plan can be carried out successfully, Perdix will generally work on that plan until it is successfully achieved rather than look for alternatives that might be simpler or more efficient.

The performance that Perdix would give on Luchins' geometry problems would depend on the order of tests for prerequisites of plans. In Luchins' problems, the prerequisite features are present for two of the plans that Perdix has available. The angles to be proven congruent are parts of triangles, and this is the feature tested for the plan of congruent triangles. The angles also have a shared vertex, which is the feature tested for the plan of finding a relation based on rotation. Which of these plans is chosen depends simply on which is tested first. One might expect that the shared vertex might be tested first in most cases since it is a simple feature that probably has considerable perceptual salience. However, Luchins' data support the idea that recent experience in using a plan can cause its prerequisite features to become more salient and thereby bias the system toward choice of that plan rather than another, even if the other is simpler. A mechanism for changing the order of testing productions has not been programmed for Perdix, so Perdix does not provide a theory about the process of inducing a problem-solving set. However, different arrangements of Perdix' planning productions provide an explanation of the way in which a student with a problem-solving set differs from a student who does not have that set, and the difference is one that seems a plausible consequence of the experience that is known to induce a set.

C.   Problems Requiring Constructions

In order to solve many geometry problems, a student must add a line to the diagram of the problem or perform some other construction. Although most of the constructions required in geometry problem solving are quite simple, they present an interesting issue in the theory of problem solving. Most theoretical systems, including the version of Perdix described thus far, work on a problem by transforming materials that are already available. When a problem requires a construction, a component that is needed is not present and the student must create that component in order to solve the problem.

The need for constructions in some problems is related to the concept of a problem space, developed by Newell and Simon (1972). The problem space consists of the set of materials given in the problem, the ways that the problem solver has of making changes in the situation, the knowledge that the problem solver uses in choosing plans and selecting problem-solving operations, and the set of situations that can be created by the problem solver in the process of working on a problem. In a geometry problem, an important part of the problem space is the diagram that is given in the problem. The diagram provides a set of geometric objects — points, line segments, angles, triangles, and so on — that are to be analyzed in the problem. If the problem requires no construction, then the set of objects given initially in the problem space is complete for the problem. To solve the problem, a student must generate a set of relations among the objects, involving a good deal of constructive inference. But the student is not required to construct new objects. However, in a problem that requires a construction, the student must add to the set of objects that are given.

Problems requiring constructions are not well understood in current theories of problem solving. A major reason is that most theories represent problem solving as search for a solution, and the difficulty of search is much greater if the possibility of constructions is included. If the objects in a situation are fixed, then the number of possible actions at any time is limited to the number of different ways that the set of objects can be rearranged according to the rules given in the problem. However, if it is possible to add objects to the situation, the number of possible actions becomes very much larger because there are many different objects that one could add. As a consequence, procedures for making constructions have not been included in most systems, and problems requiring constructions are among the problems that existing systems are unable to solve (e.g., Ullman, 1975).

On the other hand, students are able to solve many problems requiring constructions quite easily. An example of a problem that is solved with a construc-

TABLE 1.6
Student Protocol for Problem Drawn in Fig. 1.10

	S:	Okay, so, I want to prove that angle A is congruent to angle B. Now, let's see. Do you want . . . ?
*1	E:	Yeah . . . why are you drawing that line?
	S:	I don't know yet. Okay, uhm . . . okay, then I could . . . if I drew a line . . .
	E:	Mm-hmm.
*2	S:	That would be the bisector of angle ACB, and that would give me . . . those congruent angles . . . no. (Pause.)
*3		Yeah, well that would give me those congruent angles, but I could have the reflexive property, so this would be equal to that. Okay, I got it.
	E:	Now, before you go ahead and write it all down, when you said you were going to draw the line . . .
	S:	Yeah . . .
	E:	And I said, why are you doing that, and you said you didn't know yet, what do you think happened to give you the idea of making it the bisector?
*4	S:	Okay. Well, I have to try to get this . . . I have to try to get triangle ACD congruent to BCD, because if I do that, then angle A is congruent to angle B because corresponding parts of congruent triangles are congruent.
	E:	So you were drawing the line to give yourself triangles, is that the idea?
*5	S:	No, to . . . to get a side that was in both triangles.
	E:	Okay.
	S:	And to get congruent angles.
	E:	So that's why you drew it as the bisector.
	S:	Yeah.

tion is the base-angles theorem problem for an isosceles triangle: Prove that if two sides of a triangle are congruent, then the angles opposite those sides are congruent.

Table 1.6 shows a protocol of a solution of this problem. The student began by drawing a triangle, labeling its vertices A, B, and C, and marking the congruent sides $\overline{AC}$ and $\overline{AB}$, and marking the angles at A and B, which were to be proven congruent, as shown in Fig. 1.10. At *1 in the protocol the student drew a line from C to the base of the triangle, labeling the point of intersection D. At *2 the student tentatively specified that $\overline{CD}$ would be the bisector of $\angle ACB$ and confirmed this at *3 when it was realized that $\overline{CD}$ is in both triangles and provides the needed second pair of congruent sides for the side-angle-side pattern of congruence of triangles.

This protocol provides an additional example of proving congruence of triangles using an indefinite goal structure rather than definite subgoals prior to

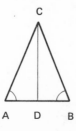

FIG. 1.10. Diagram drawn by student giving the protocol in Table 1.6.

finding a sufficient pattern of congruent components, a process discussed earlier in this section. It seems likely that if the student had an explicit subgoal such as side-angle-side, then the relation of segment $\overline{CD}$ to other components would have been specified when it was drawn.

Furthermore, the protocol illustrates a relatively indefinite process of generating constructions. The comments at *4 and *5 suggest that the student had the intention of forming two triangles containing the angles that were to be proven congruent and may have recognized the value of having a segment that would be shared as a side of both triangles. However, apart from this rather general intention, the student seems not to have had a specific plan in mind as to the way in which the segment that was added would be used in the proof.

Table 1.7 and Fig. 1.11 show another illustrative protocol involving the same problem — proving that the base angles of an isosceles triangle are congruent.

TABLE 1.7
Student Protocol for Problem Drawn in Fig. 1.11

	S:	Okay, what I do is I draw a line in here.
	E:	Okay.
*1	S:	That's not too good a line. I'd put one here. I'd put . . . drawn . . . probably, now, like, I can't overdetermine with this line. See, I couldn't call this . . . I would probably say that this is a median. Draw in AX; call it the median. The median of CB from A.
	E:	Okay.
*2	S:	And that's the definition of a median. Well, you know, it's just . . . an auxiliary line.
	E:	Okay.
*3	S:	I'll put my given down. AB equals AC is given.
	E:	Mm-hmm.
*4	S:	I could say that AX is congruent to AX.
	E:	Mm-hmm.
	S:	That's reflexive. So now I've got . . . let's see, this is congruent to itself, and this is congruent to this.
*5		Then I could say that because this is a median it bisects . . . meets at the midpoint of this segment. So I could say CX is congruent to BX.
*6		That would be definition of . . . here's your definition of a median.
	E:	Great.
*7	S:	And then I would say that . . . that triangle ACX is congruent to triangle ABX . . . that's, I would say, side-side-side. And then (6) would be angle C is congruent to angle B . . . corresponding parts of congruent triangles are congruent.
	E:	Okay, great. Now, let me ask you a little bit . . . when you first started, you decided to put a line down through there. Yeah. What were you thinking about when you . . .
*8	S:	Well, because I knew, when I first saw this . . . the only way, because you didn't give me anything in the given that talked about these angles, the only way that I was going to be able to prove them . . . if they could be corresponding parts of two triangles.
	E:	Okay.
*9	S:	That's the only way I could get two triangles out of it. . . split right down the middle. And also doing that I get a common side of two triangles.
	E:	Okay, great. Then when did you think about using the segments of that bottom side of the triangle?
	S:	Well, as soon as I drew that line, the first thing . . . the first thing I did after I put the given . . . I usually do this with all my proofs . . . is look for the common side.

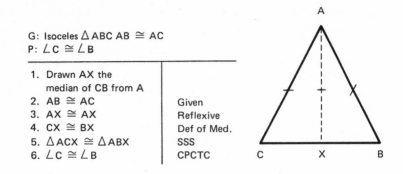

G: Isoceles △ ABC AB ≅ AC
P: ∠ C ≅ ∠ B

1. Drawn AX the median of CB from A	
2. AB ≅ AC	Given
3. AX ≅ AX	Reflexive
4. CX ≅ BX	Def of Med.
5. △ ACX ≅ △ ABX	SSS
6. ∠ C ≅ ∠ B	CPCTC

FIG. 1.11.   Drawing and writing by student giving the protocol in Table 1.7.

This student recognized the theorem as one already proven for isosceles triangles, and I explained that I would like to see the student work out the proof. The proof that had been given in the text used the angle bisector, rather than the median of the triangle, as this subject did. Thus, it seems clear that the proof was obtained by problem solving rather than being recalled from memory.

The student drew a triangle, labeled its vertices A, B, and C, wrote the two lines in the upper left corner of Fig. 1.11, and marked the two sides $\overline{AB}$ and $\overline{AC}$ as congruent. Then the subject drew segment $\overline{AX}$ and specified that it was the median of the triangle. Comments at *1 indicate that the subject did not have a definite use in mind for the constructed segment and selected the specification of a median quite arbitrarily. The comment at *2 refers to the comment "Def of Med.," which the student wrote down and then crossed out. This step probably was related to the student's concern to follow the formal requirement of writing a justifying reason for each step of a proof. At *3, the student wrote item (2) in the proof; at *4, the student wrote item (3), and at *5, the student wrote item (4), with the reason for (4) written at *6. At *7, the student finished writing the proof, putting down items (5) and (6).

The comments at *8 and *9 suggest that this subject, like the one whose protocol is in Table 1.6, had a rather general idea in mind when the auxiliary line was constructed. The student apparently wanted to form triangles containing the target angles and understood that the triangles would have a common side. The remainder of the protocol relates to the process of searching for congruent components for the proof that the triangles are congruent, including recognition at *10 that a different specification of the auxiliary line would have provided a different set of components. The component at *11 provides quite strong retrospective evidence against the hypothesis that the student might have had a specific plan in mind involving all the components of the diagram that would be needed for completing the proof.

An explanation of student performance such as that shown in Tables 1.6 and 1.7 is being developed as a set of procedures to be included in Perdix. There are two main ideas involved in the explanation. One is the idea of hierarchical planning described in the preceding set of paragraphs. A second idea, developed by Goldstein (1974), involves use of a cognitive schema that represents the features of a generic or ideal pattern along with procedures for changing a situation to agree with the schema. The theory of constructions now being developed uses a mechanism of hierarchical planning to decide that a construction is needed and uses a mechanism of schema-driven pattern completion to select a construction that changes the situation in an appropriate way.

Goldstein's program MYCROFT solves problems that occur when children write turtle programs in LOGO (Papert, 1971). Turtle programs are relatively simple procedures that direct objects to move about in space. In one kind of programming task, there is an electromechanical toy on wheels that moves about in ways that are determined by the program. Instructions in the program might include "FORWARD 50," instructing the turtle to move 50 units of distance, or "RIGHT 90," instructing the turtle to change direction by rotating 90° to the right. Another kind of programming task uses a graphical display instead of the toy turtle. In this task, the program determines the motion of a pointer that moves about on the display screen and draws a line as it goes producing a picture; for example, an appropriate set of instructions would produce a drawing of a stick figure of a person or a simple tree consisting of a triangle with a vertical line under the tree representing the trunk.

MYCROFT is a program that represents knowledge needed to correct errors in turtle programs that draw pictures. For example, a program might be written for the drawing of a tree, but it might be incorrect and have the triangle oriented incorrectly, or fail to have the trunk attached to the treetop, or make some other error. The knowledge that is represented in MYCROFT includes schematic descriptions of geometric figures. Each schema includes a list of the parts of the figure as well as they way in which the parts are related. MYCROFT can compare the figure produced by a turtle program with the schema it has of the intended figure. If there are discrepancies, MYCROFT has procedures for modifying the turtle program to make its output correspond to the features specified in the schema.

Performance such as that shown in Tables 1.6 and 1.7 can be simulated by a process that uses hierarchical planning of the kind programmed by Sacerdoti (1975) along with schema-driven pattern completion similar to that programmed by Goldstein (1974). First, recall that the students added auxiliary lines without knowing exactly how they would be used. This suggests that the planning process that precedes the making of constructions is hierarchical. In Perdix, the goal of proving that angles are congruent will lead first to checking whether the angles are in triangles, have a shared vertex, are formed by parallel lines and a transversal, or are arranged in a way that permits construction of a chain of angles. None of these prerequisite conditions is met in the diagram of the base-angles theorem problem, so none of the plans that Perdix has are promising. However, the decision to change the diagram to form triangles, rather than parallel lines or some other construction, seems to be made in the same way that Perdix and human problem solvers choose a general plan when construction is unnecessary. The general process probably involves three steps:

1. Test for prerequisites of available plans. If one is satisfied, adopt that plan.
2. Test for features that permit constructions to satisfy plan prerequisites. Choose a set of prerequisites that can be satisfied.
3. Carry out the plan whose prerequisites you have satisfied.

The protocols in Tables 1.6 and 1.7, which are typical for problems of this kind, indicate that step (2) is performed before step (3) is worked out in detail. This is consistent with the idea of hierarchical planning.

Second, the idea of schema-driven pattern completion that Goldstein developed provides a plausible hypothesis for the capability of students to produce the construction that is needed. The schema for a pair of triangles with a common side would include a list of two triangles, five segments, and four points as the main parts. If we denote the parts T1, T2, S1, S2, S3, S4, S5, P1, P2, P3, and P4, then the relations needed for the pattern could be denoted as a list of pairs indicating points that are the ends of the various segments [(P1, S1) (P1, S2) (P2, S2) (P2, S3) (P2, S5) (P3, S3) (P3, S4) (P4, S1) (P4, S4) (P4, S5)] and a list of pairs showing segments that are sides of triangles [(S1, T1) (S2, T1) (S5, T1) (S3, T2) (S4, T2) (S5, T2)].

Consider the problem in Panel (a) of Fig. 1.12. The proof requires a construction; the line needed is the diagonal $\overline{BD}$. Students solve this problem easily, typically putting in the diagonal quickly and with little apparent thought. A protocol is shown in Table 1.8, the construction was made at *1 and it is clear from later developments that the construction preceded working out details of the proof. Assume that the student has the schema described above and adopts

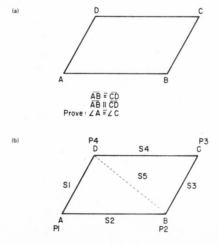

FIG. 1.12. Diagram for simple problem requiring a construction and correspondence of its parts with the schema described in the text.

TABLE 1.8
Student Protocol for Problem Shown in Fig. 1.12

	E:	I'll just ask you to prove a theorem, and you don't need to do all the steps in the proof. Just think it through and see how to get it. If two sides of a quadrilateral are congruent and parallel, then opposite angles of the quadrilateral are congruent.
	S:	Okay.
	E:	Think you can do it? How do you do it?
	S:	Well, you have a quadrilateral . . .
	E:	Yeah.
	S:	And . . . all right, I have two sides parallel and congruent, right?
	E:	Mm-hmm.
	S:	And so I want to prove opposite angles congruent?
	E:	Mm-hmm.
*1	S:	So I've got a line . . .
	E:	Okay.
	S:	And I'll put this . . . no, I want to prove this. This congruent to this.
	E:	Okay.
	S:	All right, so I . . . (pause) . . . these parallel lines . . .
	E:	Mm-hmm.
	S:	All right, so these are given. That's the definition of a quadrilateral. These are also, but I'm trying to prove the theorem that says the opposite angles.
	E:	Right.
	S:	Okay, so, I have . . . I'll mark angles.
	E:	Mm-hmm.
	S:	One, and two.
	E:	Mm-hmm.
	S:	I'll prove these congruent by . . .
	E:	Okay.
	S:	. . . alternate interior angles.
	E:	Okay.
	S:	Oh, I won't write the whole thing out. (Pause.)
	E:	Okay, great.
	S:	And then I have side-angle-side to prove that.
	E:	Right. That's great.
	S:	And then I have corresponding parts.
	E:	Right.

the plan of proving the angles congruent by proving congruence of triangles containing the angles. This requires that there be two triangles, and they contain the angles that are in the problem goal. This implies that one of the triangles has sides $\overline{AB}$ and $\overline{AD}$, and the other triangle has sides $\overline{BC}$ and $\overline{CD}$. The situation matches part of the schema with the following mapping: P1 is A, P2 is B, P3 is C, P4 is D, S1 is $\overline{AD}$, S2 is $\overline{AB}$, S3 is $\overline{BE}$, and S4 is $\overline{CD}$. Note that the connections required among S1, S2, S3, and S4 are satisfied. The situation lacks a component corresponding to S5, which should have endpoints B and D. The remedy is clear: Add a segment connecting B and D. This is depicted in Panel (b) of Fig. 1.12.

In the problem of proving congruence of base angles in an isosceles triangle, the mapping of the diagram onto the schema described here is slightly more complex. The initial diagram presents just three points with segments connecting them, rather than four. This means that the system must be able to divide the base of the triangle into two segments for the purpose of having sides for the two triangles that are needed. Apparently this trick presents little or no difficulty for human subjects. It is of interest to note that the proof generally considered more elegant, in which the triangles proved congruent are $\triangle ABC$ and $\triangle BAC$, was not found by any of the students who gave protocols in the study I conducted. I infer that the operation of dividing a segment into two subsegments may be more available to students than recognition that a single triangle can be viewed in different ways. In any case, if we adopt the labels shown in Fig. 1.11, the diagram maps onto the schema with C as P1, A as P2, B as P3, $\overline{AC}$ as S2, and $\overline{AB}$ as S3. The addition of Point X provides P4, as well as S1 ($\overline{CX}$) and S4 ($\overline{XB}$). Then the need for S5 ($\overline{AX}$) arises just as it does in the quadrilateral problem.

Two experiments have been conducted in which student subjects have solved geometry problems requiring simple constructions. The results are generally consistent with the ideas that I have presented here about the way that constructions might be produced in problem solving. One experiment shows that the process of generating a construction is easier when there is a relatively direct relationship between the features of a problem situation and the features of a cognitive pattern than it is when the relationship between the problem and the needed pattern is more complicated and less direct. The second experiment shows that the process of generating a construction is facilitated by recent use of a general plan that uses the same pattern as is needed to motivate the construction.

An experiment that Maria Magone and I have conducted compared the difficulty of two problems. Both problems use the diagram shown in Fig. 1.13. Point M is the center of the circle, and $\overline{BC}$ is a diameter. In the problem given to one group of subjects, the measure of arc $\overarc{AC}$ is given as 80°, and the goal is to find the measure of $\angle ABC$. A second group of subjects were given the measure of $\angle ABC$ as 40° and had the task of finding the measure of arc $\overarc{AC}$. The solution of either problem depends on making the construction $\overline{AM}$. This creates the central angle whose measure is the same as the arc it intercepts. The equality of the central angle and its intercepted arc is stated in the definition of the measure of an arc. Construction of $\overline{AM}$ also creates an isosceles triangle $\triangle MAB$ with congruent base angles whose sum equals the exterior angle formed at M.

This experiment's interest depends on the fact that most student subjects approach a problem by working forward from the given information rather than working backward from the goal. This means that when the measure of $\overarc{AC}$ is given, most subjects will try to find something in the diagram that they can relate to the arc; while when the measure of $\angle ABC$ is given, most subjects will try to find something in the diagram that they can relate to the angle. We reasoned

FIG. 1.13. Diagram for problems in experiment on constructions.

that the construction of $\overline{AM}$ would probably be more strongly elicited by information about the arc than by information about the angle. This is because the construction is part of the pattern of the central angle, and this is definitionally related to the measure of the arc. The angle can be related to the construction by thinking of an isosceles triangle, but there seems a much less direct connection between $\angle ABC$ and the pattern of an isosceles triangles than there is between $\overset{\frown}{AC}$ and the pattern of a central angle.

In our experiment, college student subjects were run in groups of up to six in size. The subjects were first given a review of geometric concepts needed to solve either problem, including the congruence of base angles of an isosceles triangle, the relation between an exterior angle and its opposite interior angles in a triangle, and the definitional equality of the measure of a central angle and the arc it intercepts on a circle. Figure 1.13 was presented, either with the arc given or the angle given, and the other quantity was to be found. The result was that the problem with the arc given was solved by .73 of the 52 subjects who received it, whereas the problem with the angle given was solved by only .47 of the 53 subjects who received that problem. The difference is reliable; the 95% confidence interval for the difference between the proportions was .26 ± .19. The result confirms our expectation that the angle-to-arc version would be harder than the arc-to-angle version. If our anlysis of the relationships between the two items of informatin and the relevant cognitive schemata is accepted, the result provides some supporting evidence that constructions are generated by a process of relating features of the problem to schemata that can be used as the basis of pattern completion.

Another experiment that Seth Chaiklin and I conducted involved the role of problem-solving set in problems requiring constructions. The theoretical analysis given for constructions depends strongly on the process that is assumed to perform planning in the system. It is assumed that the need for a construction is detected during the planning process, and the decision to perform a construction is made in the same top–down fashion that characterizes planning. It would be expected, then, that problems requiring constructions should be susceptible to the same kinds of effects of set as can be shown for other problems when the planning process is biased by the effect of recent experience.

Chaiklin and I arranged two series of induction problems. In one series, the problems were solved using relations among angles based on parallel lines. In the other series, the problems were solved using congruent triangles. Following these induction series, there was a problem that required a construction but could be solved in two different ways. One construction produced triangles that could be proven congruent, and the other construction produced angles related by parallel lines that could be used as a chain to solve the problem. The obvious hypothesis is that the subjects with induction for parallel lines would choose the construction that produced a chain of angles related through parallel lines, and the subjects with induction for congruent triangles would choose the construction that produced triangles that could be proven congruent. After the subjects finished with this ambiguous problem, each group received the problem that had been given last in the other group's induction sequence. To solve these problems, subjects were required to use a problem-solving plan different from the one they had been using. These problems did not require constructions, but gave a further opportunity to observe the biasing effects of problem-solving set at the level of general planning.

The subjects were college students. We gave each subject a series of review exercises that reintroduced them to the ideas involved in proving congruence of triangles and in proving theorems involving angles formed by parallel lines and an intersecting transversal. The induction sequences that followed the introductory problems were both 14 problems in length. Six subjects were run individually with each of the two sequences.

The fifteenth problem for each group was the problem shown in Fig. 1.12, except it was also given that $\overline{AD}$ and $\overline{BC}$ were congruent and parallel. Two quite easy solutions are available for the problem. The diagonal $\overline{BD}$ can be drawn, and then triangles $\triangle ABD$ and $\triangle CDB$ are congruent by side-side-side. Or side $\overline{AB}$ can be extended, $\angle A$ is congruent to the exterior angle by corresponding angles, and the exterior angle is congruent to $\angle C$ by alternate interior angles.

As mentioned earlier, each of the groups also had an additional problem that could not be solved using the general plan they had been practicing. The sixteenth problem is shown in Panel (a) of Fig. 1:14 and was given to the group that received induction of triangle congruence. The solution is easy using parallel lines: $\overline{AB}$ and $\overline{CE}$ are parallel; hence, $\angle CAB$ and $\angle ACD$ are supplementary. The sixteenth problem for the subjects who received induction of parallel lines is shown in Panel (b) of Fig. 1.14. The triangles are congruent by side-angle-side because of vertical angles. For each group, the fourteenth problem was the same as the one the other group received as the sixteenth problem.

The manipulation was strong enough to produce reliable differences, even with only six subjects per condition. In the problem of proving congruence of opposite angles of a parallelogram, five of the six subjects who received induction with congruent triangles solved the problem by constructing the diagonal and proving that the resulting triangles were congruent. Only one of the six subjects who received induction with parallel lines found this proof; the other five found proofs using relations between angles formed by parallel lines. (This is significant with $p < .02$ on a sign test, where the random event is agreement between the subject's solution and the induction sequence.)

The problem in Panel (b) of Fig. 1.14 must be solved by proving that triangles are congruent. In the group who were induced for congruence of triangles, all six subjects adopted a plan involving triangles initially. In the group induced for parallel lines, only two subjects initially worked with a plan for proving the triangles congruent; the other four subjects tried to use the relation of parallel lines. (This is also significant by a sign test, with $p < .02$.)

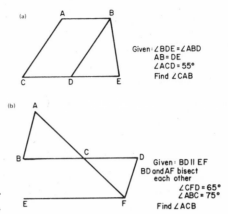

FIG. 1.14.   Problems used in experiment on constructions and set.

The problem in Panel (a) of Fig. 1.14 is solved using parallel lines. In the group where induction was with parallel lines, four of the six subjects used the plan involving parallel lines initially; the other two failed to see that parallel lines could be inferred but mentioned parallel lines as a subgoal. In the group where induction was with congruent triangles, three of the six subjects began with a plan involving congruent triangles, and only one used parallel lines; the other two subjects initially used a plan involving the sum of the interior angles of a quadrilateral. (Counting just those subjects whose initial plan was either congruence or parallel lines, the difference between the conditions was significant by a sign test, with $p < .04$.)

This experiment on set provides some support for the idea of a strong connection between the process of making constructions and the process of planning and, in addition, further illustrates the role of problem-solving set in the planning process. Work on the problem of constructions is still in progress. A simulation model of construction-making will be added to the present version of Perdix, and some further experimental work is being done. However, progress at this time seems promising for the prospect of achieving a relatively manageable explanation of the process of generating simple constructions in geometry problems based on concepts of hierarchical planning and schema-based pattern completion.

VII.   IMPLICATIONS FOR INSTRUCTION

The research that I have presented in this chapter has been descriptive and analytic, rather than prescriptive and developmental. I have attempted to understand and represent the knowledge that students acquire in their study of geometry, rather than to determine what should be taught or how instruction should be done. The results do not provide a basis for recommending any specific instructional practice. However, some issues concerning the content of instruction in geometry can be discussed in relation to the findings.

I discuss the three kinds of knowledge required for solving geometry problems in relation to the content of geometry instruction as it is represented in texts and, I presume, in most classroom instruction. The main point of this discussion is to note that whereas knowledge for pattern recognition and propositions for inferences are taught explicitly, strategic knowledge is not. I discuss some general features of strategic knowledge and distinguish the kinds of content-specific strategies that I have described in Section VI from more general problem-solving strategies that are sometimes considered. Finally, I mention some potential advantages and disadvantages that might result from increasing the amount of explicit instruction of problem-solving strategies in geometry courses.

First, consider the knowledge required for perceptual pattern recognition. Instruction in this skill is usually done primarily with diagrams and exercises that give practice in identifying the visual features and relationships that students need to recognize. For example, instruction about angles formed by parallel lines and a transversal usually includes a diagram such as Fig. 1.15. Students are required to identify various pairs of vertical angles, corresponding angles, alternate interior angles, and interior angles on the same side of the transversal. In most texts, instruction in this kind of pattern recognition uses very little verbal description. The visual patterns are illustrated in examples, and students learn the relevant features by selecting appropriate instances of the concepts.

Propositions used in making inferences during problem solving also are communicated through explicit instruction. Propositions such as "vertical angles are congruent" and "the sum of angles in a triangle equals 180°" are presented either as postulates or theorems and are stated explicitly.

Principles used in setting goals and forming plans are not mentioned explicitly in any text that I have examined. I suspect that rules for planning and setting goals such as those stated in Table 1.2 are generally thought not to be part of the content of geometry. Many people may consider that the content of the subject consists of the concepts and propositions that I have characterized as knowledge for pattern recognition and inference, and that what I have called strategic knowledge constitutes the students' abilities to apply the knowledge they are given. An alternative view is that concepts, propositions, and strategies are all forms of knowledge that students can acquire in their study of geometry, and that some students' difficulty in the subject may be due to their not having

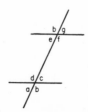

FIG. 1.15.   Diagram used for instructing pattern recognition.

TABLE 1.9
Student Protocol for Problem Drawn in Fig. 1.16

	S:	Okay. Given a and b is parallel to m and n.
	E:	No, now . . .
	S:	A is parallel to b. M is parallel to n.
	E:	That's right.
	S:	The measure of p equals 40. The measure of q. Uhm, I would name some of these angles.
	E:	Okay. Maybe the best thing to do is to draw a little copy, just a rough copy of the diagram, and then you can put in any names you want.
	S:	All right. I would put, like, p would equal one.
	E:	Okay.
	S:	And then, two.
	E:	Put in two there, right.
	S:	And then three. No, wait. Three and four, I guess.
	E:	Okay. Now why did you put two there?
	S:	Well . . . I don't know. It could have something to do with vertical angles.
	E:	Okay.
	S:	Wait. Do you want me to write out a proof?
	E:	No. Well, you can write out whatever you want to, but I'm just mainly interested in having you think through the problem.
*1	S:	Okay. All right, the first thing I guess I would try to do . . . I would try to find if there were any alternate interior or corresponding angles?
	E:	Okay.
	S:	Or any of those.
	E:	Mm-hmm.
	S:	I guess I would say that . . . well, wait a minute. I guess maybe I would put five there.
	E:	Okay.
	S:	I don't know if I would need this.
	E:	Okay.
*2	S:	These two are supplementary.
	E:	Right.
*3	S:	That doesn't help much. And then, the measure of angle five . . . would it equal the measure of angle one?
	E:	Well, you might have to work that out.
	S:	How . . . if this equals . . . this equals 40.
	E:	That's right.
*4	S:	Oh, all right. Wait, the measure . . . I can't, I don't know. I don't know how to do these.
	E:	Okay.

acquired the strategic knowledge they need to solve some of the problems they are given.

An example of the consequences of lacking strategic knowledge is shown in the protocol in Table 1.9. The student's drawing is shown in Fig. 1.16. The problem is the one shown in Fig. 1.1 and the successful solutions given by six students are given in Table 1.4. In the same interview session that included this problem, I asked a series of questions about the various relations among angles formed by a transversal and parallel lines. This student showed satisfactory knowledge of all the pairwise relations that might be needed in solving this problem. I infer that the student's failure to solve the problem was caused by absence of a strategy of constructing a chain of angles related by congruence. This component of strategy is shown in Rule 4 in Table 1.2. The comment at

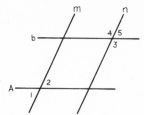

FIG. 1.16. Drawing made by the student giving the protocol in Table 1.9.

*1 in Table 1.9 seems to indicate that the student had the component of the strategy shown as Rule 2, involving an attempt to find a geometric relation between angles that would permit inferring a quantitative relation. The comments at *2 and *3 seem to indicate that the student had the strategy shown as part of Rule 2, involving inference of a quantitative relation between two angles if both of them are related by quantitative relations to a third angle. However, at *4 the student stopped working on the problem. The component strategy shown as Rule 4 would lead to finding some angle that is congruent by a known relation with $\angle p$, and the simplest interpretation of the student's failure is that the student's strategic knowledge did not include Rule 4.

The strategic knowledge needed for problem solving can be learned. Two weeks after the protocol in Table 1.9 was given, this student was able to solve a different problem requiring construction of a chain of congruent angles. A question of some theoretical as well as practical interest is how acquisition of strategic knowledge occurs in circumstances where strategies are not taught explicitly. A reasonable conjecture is that students are able to learn components of strategy by a process of induction from example problems that are given in the text and worked by the teacher. Some students may be able to generate strategies needed for problem solving without example problems from which to induce the rules that are needed, but it seems likely that many students depend on examples to acquire necessary strategic knowledge. Although principles for setting goals and forming plans are not included explicitly in the content of the geometry course, they are present in implicit form as properties of the examples that are given.

It may seem unusual to some readers that strategies, along with concepts and propositions, should be considered as a form of knowledge. Strategic knowledge is a form of skill, so knowledge of strategy is in the same category of knowledge as knowing how to prepare a meal or knowing how to sail a boat. It is natural to represent knowledge for skilled performance as a procedure, and that is sometimes thought to be different from knowledge of concepts and propositions. However, as Winograd (1972) showed, conceptual and propositional knowledge also can be represented in a natural way as procedures, and procedural representations are especially appropriate in the context of problem solving. Indeed, in Perdix the representation of concepts and propositions are in the form of procedures. Concepts are represented as procedures for pattern recognition, and propositions are represented as production rules for making inferences. Thus, strategic knowledge does not differ in a fundamental way from other forms of knowledge that are more commonly considered as the content of geometry instruction.

The strategic knowledge represented in Perdix for solving geometry problems is more specific than problem-solving strategies that are often considered. For example, Polya (1957) identified general strategic procedures such as identifying the unknown and given data of a problem and thinking of a simpler related problem if progress is not being made on the current problem. Another example is Landa's (1976) recommendation that students should think of all the ways in which components of a problem are related to one another. The strategies identified in the analyses presented here are more specific and utilize the specific content of geometry, the domain of the problems.

It may or may not be desirable to explicitly teach content-specific, problem-solving strategies; however, it should not be assumed that it cannot be done. The principles of strategy used in solving geometry problems are not mysterious. One version of the needed strategies is stated in explicit form in the model of problem solving that I have described in this chapter. Given an explicit statement of strategic rules, it becomes quite feasible to develop instructional materials that communicate those rules to students and give them practice in using the rules.

The major advantage of providing explicit instruction of domain-specific, problem-solving strategies would probably be improved performance on problems by students who have difficulty in the present instructional situation. A possibility of some interest is that a significant number of the students who fail to complete the geometry course or whose performance in geometry discourages them from continuing with further study in mathematics could achieve satisfactory performance if they received instruction in the strategies needed for solving problems in the domain of geometry.

A second advantage of giving instruction explicitly in problem-solving strategies would be a greater appreciation by students, and perhaps by teachers as well, of structural properties of problem solutions. Strategic principles show the purpose of problem-solving steps and thus provide a better understanding of the way in which different parts of a problem solution relate to one another and to the main problem-solving goal.

A disadvantage of including explicit teaching of problem-solving strategies might be to slow the pace of instruction. It is not clear whether the time now spent working example problems and thus presenting strategic principles implicitly would permit an explicit presentation of those principles. If it were the case that the time needed for each topic in geometry was increased as a result of instruction in strategies, a judgment would be required whether the additional understanding gained about the structure of problem solutions was sufficient to warrant covering less of the content of geometry during the time of the course.

A second possible disadvantage of explicit instruction in strategic knowledge might be an overly mechanical approach to problem solving, especially for those students who are now able to generate strategic principles themselves or induce them from examples. With instruction as it is now conducted, all students learn problem-solving strategies by the discovery method, if they learn them at all. It is not known whether the opportunity to discover strategic principles contributes in any important way to students' ability to use those principles and transfer them to new situations. However, this is a possibility. Perhaps the ideal way of including strategic instruction in the curriculum would be in the form of corrective instruction given individually to those students whose initial efforts to solve a category of problems did not lead to their discovering the strategies needed for the problems.

VIII.   IMPLICATIONS FOR GENERAL THEORY

The major goal of my research on problem solving in geometry has been to acquire new information about processes of problem solving and, I hope, to achieve a better understanding of the ways in which problem solving occurs. Some progress has apparently been made, leading to new theoretical developments in three areas. One issue in the general theory of problem solving is a distinction between well-structured and ill-structured problems. A clearer understanding of processes involved in solving ill-structured problems seems to be gained from the analyses of problem solving in geometry involving indefinite goal structures and constructions. A second issue of general theoretical interest is the process of understanding in problem solving, involving the distinction between merely solving a problem correctly and understanding the situation and solution that is achieved. The representation of problem solving as a process of pattern matching and pattern generation appears to provide a framework in which a number of aspects of the understanding process can be analyzed. Finally, geometry provides an especially suitable domain for studying relationships between perception and thought. The importance of perceptual processes in solving geometry problems is obvious, since the presentation of problems requires use of diagrams. The role of perceptual processes as components of the problem-solving process is beginning to be clarified by the analysis of planning that includes use of critical global features in the selection of a plan and the use of a perceptual scanning process in examining components of a figure.

A.   Well-Structured and Ill-Structured Problems

Most of the empirical studies of problem solving have involved relatively simple puzzles such as the Tower of Hanoi (Simon, 1975), water-jug puzzles (Atwood & Polson, 1976), and transportation puzzles (Greeno, 1974; Simon & Reed, 1976;

Thomas, 1974). All of these problems are well structured. There is a definite initial situation that is given, and there is a definite goal situation that is to be achieved. The operators that can be used to transform situations are specified, and the initial problem situation contains all the components that will be needed to produce the goal.

Many important problems do not fit into the category of well-structured problems, and an important question is whether the conclusions reached in studies of well-structured problems can be generalized to ill-structured problems. Some studies of ill-structured problem solving have been performed. Reitman (1965) studied a thinking-aloud protocol obtained as a composer worked on writing a fugue. Protocol studies and some experimental studies have been done with chess players (Chase & Simon, 1973; deGroot, 1966; Newell & Simon, 1972) and *Go* players (Reitman, 1976; Reitman & Wilcox, 1976). However, the analyses achieved in the studies of ill-structured problem solving have been much less complete than those obtained for well-structured problems, and it is an open question whether principles that operate in solution of well-structured problems also are significant in ill-structured problems and whether fundamentally different principles are needed for understanding the solution of ill-structured problems.

Problems in geometry are well structured, especially in comparison to problems such as composing music and playing chess. Generally the given information of the problem provides a definite initial situation; there is a definite statement to be proven or a specific unknown quantity to be found, and the operators that can be used correspond to the postulates and theorems that have been previously introduced and proven in the course. However, analyses of two important features of geometry problem solving seem to provide information about the kinds of processes that probably occur in less well-structured problem solving. Furthermore, the form in which these processes occur in geometry is relatively simple, and thus the nature of the processes involved seems especially easy to understand.

The features of geometry problems that seem to illuminate solutions of ill-structured problems are indefinite goal structures and constructions. These relate to two characteristics that occur quite generally in ill-structured problems. The goal of an ill-structured problem is often vague. For example, a chess player may decide to try to develop an attack on the opponent's queen side. A composer of music may begin work with decisions only about the form of the piece and the instrument or instruments that will play it, along with a few thematic ideas in mind. These are examples of goals that are highly indefinite. In contrast to well-structured problems, where the problem solver can compare the current situation with the goal at each stage of progress, an indefinite goal such as "attack the opponent's queen side" or "compose a fugue" does not provide a specific situation that can be used as a target of problem-solving activity.

Recall that geometry problems requiring proof of congruent triangles are solved by students using an indefinite representation of the goal. This performance is simulated by Perdix with a knowledge structure representing the goal in the form of a pattern-recognition system. It seems reasonable to conjecture that expert problem solvers in domains involving indefinite goals probably have complex systems of pattern recognition that permit evaluation of the complex situations that are produced during problem solving. There is substantial evidence for the importance of knowledge for pattern recognition as a factor in chess skill. DeGroot (1966) and Chase and Simon (1973) have shown that chess masters perform considerably better than experienced tournament players below the master level when they are asked to reproduce the pieces of a position that they are allowed to observe for just five seconds. It is inferred from this performance that chess masters have extraordinary knowledge for recognizing patterns of chess pieces (Simon & Gilmartin, 1973). There has not yet been a theoretical analysis showing how extensive pattern-recognition knowledge is used by chess masters in the problem solving they engage in during games. However, it seems a reasonable conjecture that pattern recognition is used in evaluating structural features of positions and identifying potential advantages for each player. Reitman and Wilcox' (1976) preliminary analyses of expert play in *Go* also places significant emphasis on pattern recognition as an important factor in influencing the player in setting goals during play of the game. The pattern-recognition system that represents the goal of proving congruence of triangles in geometry is a relatively simple case of pattern recognition in complex problem solving, but the generalization of the theory of well-structured problems to include pattern-recognition sytems for representing goals seems to involve a principle that seems likely to provide an important component of problem solving in many ill-structured problems.

A second feature, in addition to indefinite goals, that characterizes many ill-structured problems is incompleteness of the materials that are given in the problem. For example, at the beginning of work on a musical composition, the composer has only some general ideas about the components of the piece, perhaps including some thematic ideas that the composer had decided to try to use in the work. Much of the work of composing involves adding new musical material to the piece as it has been developed up to that point. One writer has remarked on the situation of a composer "who has just conceived a single musical thought and is facing the problem of how to go on, for this matter of 'going on' is the very heart of musical composition" (Abraham, 1949, pp. 4–5). This contrasts with well-structured problems, where there are a set of objects given in the initial situation, rules for changing the situation by rearranging the objects, and a goal situation that consists of some specific arrangement of the given objects. In musical composition, as in other problems of composition and design, the problem solver must generate substantial amounts of the material needed to obtain a solution, as well as determine how the materials are to be arranged.

The geometry problems that provide some information about performance with incomplete problem situations are problems requiring constructions. In these problems, the problem solver must supply components that are not initially given as part of the problem situation. The analysis of this process given in Perdix uses the idea of hierarchical planning, including knowledge of prerequisite conditions that must be met in order for a plan to be feasible, productions that detect discrepancies between the current situation and the prerequisite conditions that are needed, and procedures for producing the components that are found to be required. The idea of planning and pattern completion seems to agree with many features of the problem-solving process that Reitman (1965) observed when he studied a musical composer. As in the case of indefinite goal structures, a thorough analysis of performance in some ill-structured problems would be needed to establish the extent of analogy between constructions in geometry and productive processes in more complex situations. However, the general kinds of processes that seem to be needed appear to be similar to those that appear in simpler form in the domain of geometry problems.

Concerning the general issue of well-structured and ill-structured problems, the analyses of geometry seem to support a conclusion that problems differ along a continuum of definiteness of structure. Geometry problems seem to require some mechanisms that are more complex than those used in simple puzzles, but the extension of theory needed to account for geometry problem solving are quite modest. Furthermore, it seems reasonable to conjecture that mechanisms of pattern-recognizing goal structures, hierarchical planning, and schema-based pattern completion used in solving geometry problems may be simple forms of the kinds of mechanisms used in solving more complex ill-structured problems. Thus, while more complex processes are undoubtedly used in solving ill-structured problems than are needed for solving simple well-structured problems, there do not seem to be fundamental differences in the principles of problem solving found in these domains.

B. Understanding in Problem Solving

The process of understanding has not been a major topic in recent discussions of problem solving, although some recent work has provided important new analyses of the process of representing problems based on textual presentations (Hayes & Simon, 1974, 1977; Novak, 1976; Simon & Hayes, 1976). However, early work on problem solving by Gestalt psychologists emphasized the importance of understanding. Wertheimer (1959) was especially emphatic in emphasizing the distinction between solving problems by mechanical application of an algorithm and solving problems in a way that involves understanding of the structure of the situation.

The discussions given by Gestalt theorists such as Wertheimer were persuasive, but vague. The demonstrations of problem solving with understanding were largely anecdotal and were not supported by analysis of cognitive processes that brought about the understanding that was achieved. A goal of the research on geometry described in this chapter has been to develop a theory in which understanding is represented in a significant way. Recent analyses of understanding language have included the development of language understanding systems that construct integrated representations of statements, paragraphs, or stories. In these systems, understanding is implicitly defined as the process of apprehending relations among components of a message and constructing a representation that includes those relations.

An example of the kind of representation that is achieved by a language understanding system is shown in Fig. 1.17. The representation is constructed by the computer system developed by Norman and Rumelhart and the LNR Research Group (1975). The specific sentence whose representation is in the pic-

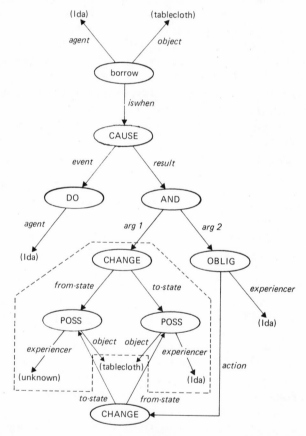

FIG. 1.17.   Representation of "Ida borrowed a tablecloth" constructed by a language understanding system. (Adapted from "Evidence for the Psychological Reality of Semantic Components: The Verbs of Possession" by D. Gentner. In D. A. Norman & D. E. Rumelhart, *Explorations in Cognition.* San Francisco: Freeman, 1975. Copyright 1975 by W. H. Freeman and Company. Reprinted by permission.)

ture is, "Ida borrowed a tablecloth." The specific components involved in this sentence and other sentences involving verbs of possession were worked out by Gentner (1975). The system receives the string of words "Ida borrowed a table-cloth," as input. A parsing procedure is performed, resulting in identifying "Ida" as the subject of the sentence, "borrow" as the central relation, and "tablecloth" as the object of the relation. A schematic representation of "borrow" is stored in the system, and using this schema, the system constructs the representation showing that Ida is the agent of the action, and the tablecloth is the object that is borrowed. In addition to these basic relations among Ida, borrowing, and the tablecloth, understanding the meaning of the sentence includes further information that is also represented. The representation includes the information that an action performed by Ida caused a change in the possession of the tablecloth, that the one who possessed the tablecloth after the borrowing was Ida, and that Ida also then had an obligation to change the possession of the tablecloth back to whomever it was she borrowed it from.

The specific content of representations such as Fig. 1.17 can be debated, but the specific set of relations included is less important than some general properties of the language understanding theory. What investigators working on language understanding have discovered in recent years is a set of general principles about the kind of process that is required for representations of this general character to be constructed. The major kind of knowledge used in Norman and Rumelhart's system is the schematic representation of the meanings of verbs, because the system proceeds by assigning the various concepts mentioned in a sentence as the arguments of the verb that represents the main action or relationship stated in the sentence.

The model of problem solving described in this chapter provides a representation of understanding in problem solving analogous to the representation of language understanding given in systems such as Norman and Rumelhart's. This is because in the process of solving a problem, Perdix constructs a pattern of relations among the components of the problem that are used in the solution. Recall Fig. 1.1, where Panel (h) shows the representation constructed when the problem has been solved. The representation is similar in form to Fig. 1.17, though this is not very significant because both representations simply are networks with labeled arcs, a very general form of representation. The significant fact is that the representation in Fig. 1.1 was generated as part of the process of solving a problem, and thus represents a process of understanding as a part of the process of problem solving. The fact that Perdix generates structures similar to those constructed by language understanding systems is not accidental. The framework in which Perdix is programmed is a version of the ACT programming system, developed by Anderson (1976) for the purpose of analyzing language processing and language acquisition.

The representation of a problem that Perdix generates includes relevant relations among components of the problem situation. Another question sometimes raised about a problem solver is whether it understands what it does in solving a problem. This question concerns relations among the various component actions that are performed during problem solving, rather than relations among the various components of the problem situation.

There are two ways to consider the understanding of a set of actions. One way involves consideration of the goals that the actor has in performing the various components of the action. This may be called the *functional* or *intentional mode of understanding an action* since the representation of the action shows what each component of the action was for or what the actor was trying to accomplish by performing each component. The second way involves representing the justification of the steps of the action. This may be called an *explanatory mode of understanding an action*, because the representation shows why each component could be accomplished and, in that way, shows how the action worked.

The representation shown in Fig. 1.1 provides a partial explanatory understanding of the action of solving the problem. Each main step involves inference of a quantitative relation between angles or inference of the measure of an angle. Each of these steps is justified by some other relations that have been inferred earlier. Understanding is achieved by representing the connections between the various relations, showing which relations provide a justification for the inference of which other relations.

The information needed for functional or intentional understanding also is represented in Perdix' solution of a problem. At each step, Perdix' action is related to a goal that is represented in the system; these are shown in Fig. 1.1 enclosed by dashed lines. The goals are ordered, with lower-level subgoals related to the higher-level goals to which they are subordinate. The system achieves an intentional understanding of its solution of a problem by keeping a record of the higher-order goal for which each subgoal was established. This kind of representation of the problem solution as a goal tree has been a means of representing knowledge used in solving problems in several theoretical systems (Ernst & Newell, 1969; Winograd, 1972).

C.   Processes of Perception and Thought

Geometry problems are presented in diagrams. Many of the principles that are used in solving the problems are learned as verbal propositions. It seems that an analysis of the process of solving geometry problems should provide useful information about the interaction of processes of visual perception and thinking based on verbal principles.

There are two issues about the interaction of perceptual and thinking processes about which information has been obtained in these analyses. One issue is a general theoretical question about the compatibility of forms of information. It might be thought that the information found in a diagram and the information represented in verbal propositions would be incompatible in some significant ways, so that elaborate translation procedures would be needed for a single problem-solving system to make effective use of both kinds of information. The analyses conducted thus far have not revealed any significant difficulty along these lines, and thus suggest that pictorial and verbal information might have cognitive representations in essentially the same form. A second issue involves the way or ways in which the problem-solving system utilizes information from a diagram in the process of solving a problem. The analyses conducted thus far suggest that there are three general ways in which spatial information is used: one involving simple pattern recognition to identify relationships that are required for specific inferences, one involving identification of global features in selecting plans, and one involving detecting discrepancies between diagrams and spatial schemata that are then corrected by the addition of constructions.

Regarding the first issue concerning compatibility of representations, the major finding is that the information from diagrams needed in solving geometry problems is easily represented in a labeled network. It has been noted by a number of investigators (Palmer, 1975; Winston, 1975) that a network provides a convenient way of representing many kinds of information found in pictures. In retrospect, it is not surprising that this format provides a sufficient representation of the information used in solving geometry problems. However, the consequence of representing pictorial information as a network is that no translation between pictorial and verbal information is necessary in the system. It should be recognized that the simulation performed by Perdix begins with information represented in networks. A human problem solver must extract information from pictures and from verbal text, and these translation processes are not represented in Perdix. However, the complete compatibility of the two kinds of information in a single network representation suggests that it is at least possible that human perception of both pictures and verbal text results in an abstract representation of elements and their relations, and that problem solving involves manipulation of these abstract relations that are in the same form, regardless of the origin of the information.

The second general issue concerns ways in which pictorial information is used during problem solving. One use of pictorial information is simple pattern recognition. When the current problem-solving plan requires information about the relationship between two angles or other components of a diagram, the pattern-recognition productions are executed and the information is obtained.

A second use of information from a diagram is in planning. The various plans that are associated with a goal generally use different global features of the situation. For example, one plan for finding a quantitative relation between angles uses relations based on parallel sides, while another uses congruent triangles. The planning system uses these global features to select the plan whose prerequisite features are present. In some situations, where there are many optional elements that could be examined in relation to a goal, the planning system uses a scanning procedure, fixing a line in the diagram and examining elements of the diagram in order of their proximity to the scanning lines.

A third use of spatial information arises in problems that require constructions. In the analysis proposed here, spatial information is processed in relation to schematic representations that specify components and relations needed to achieve certain goals using certain plans. The processing system is able to detect discrepancies between the diagram and the schemata and is able to make diagrams correspond to the schemata by making construction.

IX.   SUMMARY AND CONCLUSIONS

In this chapter I have presented a model of problem solving in the domain of high school geometry. The model is in the form of production system that tests for the presence of patterns in a data structure and adds new relational material to the situation.

The main findings of the study involve identification of the kinds of knowledge that apparently must be acquired by students in order to solve the problems they are given. The required components of knowledge are in three general categories: knowledge for perceptual pattern recognition, knowledge of propositions for making inferences, and strategic knowledge for setting goals and adopting plans.

Knowledge for pattern recognition and for propositional inferences are represented in a straightforward way using concepts that are standard in current theories of problem solving. Modeling students' stragetic knowledge presented somewhat more interesting problems and required use of a pattern-recognition system for representing an indefinite goal structure, a hierarchical planning system, and a schema-based pattern completion system for making constructions. The model gives a reasonably accurate simulation of student performance, including an explanation of effects of problem-solving set.

The main implication of the analysis regarding instruction is in regard to strategic knowledge. Knowledge for pattern recognition and propositions to be used in making inferences are taught explicitly as part of the content of the geometry course. Strategic knowledge for setting goals and choosing plans is not a part of the explicit content of the course, although it seems likely that many students acquire strategic knowledge by induction from example problems that present strategic principles implicitly. The idea of increasing the explicit instruction given for content-specific problem-solving strategies has some appeal, although it would probably have some disadvantages as well.

The analyses have contributed some concepts to the general theory of problem solving. Geometry problems have some features that have been thought to characterize ill-structured problems, and the analyses of indefinite goals and constructions in geometry problems have clarified the relationship between processes used in solving well-structured and ill-structured problems to some extent.

The representation of problem solving as a process of pattern construction provides a way of representing problem solving as a process of understanding. Finally, the analysis shows that the information from diagrams and information presented as verbal propositions are entirely compatible and shows some of the ways in which pictorial information is apparently used in the solution of geometry problems.

The most general conclusion of this work is that the concepts and methods of contemporary cognitive psychology and artificial intelligence apparently can be applied in the analysis of school tasks. The use of these methods has apparently succeeded in giving a reasonably accurate characterization of a number of features of problem-solving performance in high-school geometry. Furthermore, the study of this problem-solving performance has also led to some progress in understanding some issues in the general theory of problem solving.

ACKNOWLEDGMENTS

This research was supported by Grant No. 7R01MH29315-01 from the National Institute of Mental Health. I am grateful to Alan Lesgold, Robert Glaser, and Joan Jewell for comments on the first draft of this chapter.

REFERENCES

Abraham, G. *Design in music*. London: Oxford University Press, 1949.

Anderson, J. R. *Language, memory, and thought*. Hillsdale, N.J.: Lawrence Erlbaum Associates, 1976.

Atwood, M. E., & Polson, P. G. A process model for water jug problems. *Cognitive Psychology*, 1976, *8*, 191–216.

Bourne, L. E., Jr., Ekstrand, B. R., & Dominowski, B. R. *The psychology of thinking*. Englewood Cliffs, N.J.: Prentice-Hall, 1971.

Chase, W. G., & Simon, H. A. Perception in chess. *Cognitive Psychology*, 1973, *4*, 55–81.

deGroot, A. D. Perception and memory versus thought: Some old ideas and recent findings. In B. Kleinmuntz (Ed.), *Problem solving: Research, method, and theory*. New York: Wiley, 1966.

Duncker, K. On problem solving. *Psychological Monographs*, 1945, *58*(Whole No. 270).

Ernst, G. W., & Newell, A. *GPS: A case study in generality and problem solving*. New York: Academic Press, 1969.

Fahlman, S. E. A planning system for robot construction tasks. *Artificial Intelligence*, 1974, *5*, 1–49.

Feigenbaum, E. A. The simulation of verbal learning behavior. In E A. Feigenbaum & J. Feldman (Eds.), *Computers and thought*. New York: McGraw-Hill, 1963.

Gelernter, J. Realization of a geometry-theorem proving machine. In E. A. Feigenbaum & J. Feldman (Eds.), *Computers and thought*. New York: McGraw-Hill, 1963.

Gentner, D. Evidence for the psychological reality of semantic components: The verbs of possession. In D. A. Norman & D. E. Runelhart, *Explorations in cognition*. San Francisco: Freeman, 1975.

Goldstein, I. *Elementary geometry theorem proving* (Artificial Intelligence Memo No. 280). Cambridge, Mass.: Massachusetts Institute of Technology, 1973.

Goldstein, I. P. *Understanding simple picture programs* (Artificial Intelligence Laboratory Report TR-294). Cambridge, Mass.: Massachusetts Institute of Technology, 1974.

Greeno, J. G. Hobbits and orcs: Acquisition of a sequential concept. *Cognitive Psychology*, 1974, *6*, 270–292.

Greeno, J. G. Indefinite goals in well-structured problems. *Psychological Review*, 1976, *83*, 479–491.

Greeno, J. G. Natures of problem-solving abilities. In W. K. Estes (Ed.), *Handbook of learning and cognitive processes*. Hillsdale, N.J.: Lawrence Erlbaum Associates, 1977. (a)

Greeno, J. G. Process of understanding in problem solving. In N. J. Castellan, D. B. Pisoni, & G. R. Potts (Eds.), *Cognitive theory* (Vol. 2). Hillsdale, N.J.: Lawrence Erlbaum Associates, 1977. (b)

Hayes, J. R., & Simon, H. A. Understanding written problem instructions. In L. W. Gregg (Ed.), *Knowledge and cognition*. Hillsdale, N.J.: Lawrence Erlbaum Associates, 1974.

Hayes, J. R., & Simon, H. A. Psychological differences among problem isomorphs. In N. J. Castellan, Jr., D. B. Pisoni, & G. R. Potts (Eds.), *Cognitive theory* (Vol. 2). Hillsdale, N.J.: Lawrence Erlbaum Associates, 1977.

Hunt, E. B., Marin, J., & Stone, P. I. *Experiments in induction*. New York: Academic Press, 1966.

Hunt, E. B., & Poltrock, S. E. The mechanics of thought. In B. H. Kantowitz (Ed.), *Human information processing: Tutorials in performance and cognition*. Hillsdale, N.J.: Lawrence Erlbaum Associates, 1974.

Klahr, D., & Wallace, J. G. *Cognitive development: An information-processing view*. Hillsdale, N.J.: Lawrence Erlbaum Associates, 1976.

Köhler, W. *The mentality of apes*. New York: Harcourt Brace, 1927.

Landa, L. N. *Algorithmization in learning and instruction*. Englewood Cliffs, N.J.: Educational Technology Publications, 1974.

Landa, L. N. *Instructional regulation and control: Cybernetics, algorithmization and heuristics in education*. Englewood Cliffs, N.J.: Educational Technology Publications, 1976.

Luchins, A. S. Mechanization in problem solving. *Psychological Monographs*, 1942, *54*(Whole No. 248).

Newell, A. A theoretical exploration of mechanisms for coding the stimulus. In A. W. Melton & E. Martin (Eds.), *Coding processes in human memory*. Washington, D.C.: Winston, 1972.

Newell, A. You can't play 20 questions with nature and win: Projective comments on the papers of this symposium. In W. G. Chase (Ed.), *Visual information processing*. New York: Academic Press, 1973.

Newell, A., & Simon, H. A. *Human problem solving*. Englewood Cliffs, N.J.: Prentice-Hall, 1972.

Norman, D. A., Rumelhart, D. E., & LNR Research Group. *Explorations in cognition.* San Francisco: Freeman, 1975.

Novak, G. S., Jr. *Computer understanding of physics problems stated in natural language*. University of Texas: Department of Computer Science Technical Report, NL-30, 1976.

Palmer, S. E. Visual perception and world knowledge: Notes on a model of sensory-cognitive interaction. In D. A. Norman & D. E. Rumelhart (Eds.), *Explorations in cognition*. San Francisco: Freeman, 1975.

Papert, S. A. *A computer laboratory for elementary schools* (Artificial Intelligence Memo No. 246). Cambridge, Mass.: Massachusetts Institute of Technology, 1971.

Polya, G. *How to solve it*. Garden City, N.Y.: Doubleday-Anchor, 1957.

Polya, G. *Mathematical discovery: On understanding, learning, and teaching problem solving* (Vol. 1). New York: Wiley, 1962.
Polya, G. *Mathematical discovery: On understanding, learning, and teaching problem solving* (Vol. 2). New York: Wiley, 1965.
Reitman, J. S. Skilled perception in *Go*: Deducing memory structures from inter-response times. *Cognitive Psychology*, 1976, *8*, 336–356.
Reitman, W. R. *Cognition and thought*. New York: Wiley, 1965.
Reitman, W., & Wilcox, B. *A program for playing Go: Interim report*. Ann Arbor: University of Michigan, 1976.
Resnick, L. B. Task analysis in instructional design: Some cases from mathematics. In D. Klahr (Ed.), *Cognition and instruction*. Hillsdale, N.J.: Lawrence Erlbaum Associates, 1976.
Resnick, L. B., & Glaser, R. Problem solving and intelligence. In L. B. Resnick (Ed.), *The nature of intelligence*. Hillsdale, N.J.: Lawrence Erlbaum Associates, 1976.
Sacerdoti, E. D. *A structure for plans and behavior* (Artificial Intelligence Center Technical Note 109). Stanford, Calif.: Stanford Research Institute, 1975.
Simon, H. A. The functional equivalence of problem solving skills. *Cognitive Psychology*, 1975, *7*, 268–288.
Simon, H. A., & Gilmartin, K. A simulation of memory for chess positions. *Cognitive Psychology*, 1973, *2*, 29–46.
Simon, H. A., & Hayes, J. R. The understanding process: Problem isomorphs. *Cognitive Psychology*, 1976, *8*, 165–190.
Simon, H. A., & Reed, S. K. Modeling strategy shifts in a problem-solving task. *Cognitive Psychology*, 1976, *8*, 86–97.
Sussman, G. J. *A computational model of skill acquisition* (Artificial Intelligence Laboratory Report TR-297). Cambridge, Mass.: Massachusetts Institute of Technology, 1973.
Thomas, J. T., Jr. An analysis of behavior in the hobbits-orcs problem. *Cognitive Psychology*, 1974, *6*, 257–269.
Ullman, S. *A model-driven geometry theorem prover* (Artificial Intelligence Memo No. 321). Cambridge, Mass.: Massachusetts Institute of Technology, 1975.
Wertheimer, M. *Productive thinking*. New York: Harper & Row, 1959.
Winograd, T. Understanding natural language. *Cognitive Psychology*, 1972, *3*, 1–191.
Winston, P. H. Learning structural descriptions from examples. In P. H. Winston (Ed.), *The psychology of computer vision*. New York: McGraw-Hill, 1975.

2

Knowing When, Where, and How to Remember: A Problem of Metacognition

Ann L. Brown
Center for the Study of Reading
University of Illinois

I. INTRODUCTION

A. Another Memory Development Chapter?

I would like to begin by sympathizing with those whose initial reaction to this chapter is, "Do we really need another memory development chapter?" During the past decade, research interest in the development of memory has intensified, and currently there exists a copious literature consisting of books, projected books, and review chapters too numerous to mention. More are threatened in the near future, and the task of keeping abreast of this burgeoning literature is formidable. In view of the plethora of information sources, a complete review of the literature would clearly be redundant, and this chapter is not intended to provide an overview. Rather, the concentration is focused more narrowly on the development of certain general problem-solving skills that are subsumed under the heading of metacognition. Althought the focus is primarily on metamemory development, this reflects the state of the art rather than any conviction that the metacognitive skills involved in intelligent control of one's actions while memorizing are necessarily different from those involved in any other problem-solving situations, whether experimentally induced or naturally occurring.

Even within the restricted domain of metamnemonic development, this chapter is not intended as a complete review, because an excellent summary already exists (Flavell & Wellman, 1977). The review section of this chapter (Section III) represents an idiosyncratic selection of pertinent literature centered around research findings from our own laboratory. The main emphasis is on the efficiencies and limitations of both spontaneous and induced problem-solving skills in slow-learning children.

The particular problem-solving skills selected for review are those attributed to the executive in many theories of human and machine intelligence: predicting, checking, monitoring, reality testing, and coordination and control of deliberate attempts to learn or solve problems. I believe that these are the basic characteristics of thinking efficiently in a wide range of learning situations. Thinking efficiently is a good definition of intelligence, and the focus of this chapter is on intellectual development. The selection of memory processes reflects the extensive literature that predates this chapter. Quite simply, a great deal is known about the normal course of mnemonic development, and a reasonable picture of the development of metamemorial awareness is beginning to be constructed. Therefore, this information can be used to help us understand aberrant development. But this emphasis on traditional memory skills should not be taken as an indication of belief in a separate memory system that is somehow independent of the general operations of the intellect. To reiterate Reitman's (1970) cogent observations, "memory behavior does not depend solely upon a memory subsystem; it reflects the activity of the human cognitive system as a whole [p. 490]." In fact, the terms *memory* and *metamemory* are used only as a matter of convenience to identify a traditional subset of operations. The inseparability of memory from any other aspect of cognition has long been established as an article of faith of modern cognitive psychology (Bartlett, 1932; Jenkins, 1973; Neisser, 1967, 1976; Norman, 1973; Piaget & Inhelder, 1973), and it is a reflection of this bias that throughout the chapter thinking, problem solving, learning, etc., are often referred to interchangeably with remembering. Furthermore, the concentration is on the metacognitive skills of intelligence that apply to a wider range of activities than traditionally treated under the rubric "memory."

B. Organizational Scheme

Again, I sympathize with those whose second reaction to this chapter is "If we must endure another memory development opus, does it have to be this long?" Obviously not, but it is, and therefore, I would like to provide some hints on which sections can be selected for readers with different purposes. Section II provides a very brief introduction to the term *metacognition* and the reasons why interest is now focused on the various "metas" of developmental cognition. Section III is a relatively long review of data gathered in our laboratory couched in a framework of the basic metacognitive skills that are emphasized in this chapter. For those not primarily interested in the details of our ongoing research program, this section can easily be skimmed without vitiating attempts to understand subsequent sections. Section IV reflects a concern with the types of questions being addressed in current research programs addressed at metamnemonic development, with particular emphasis on programs where intervention or remediation are at least implicitly of main concern. Finally, in Section V, the cultural relativity of many of the traditional memory skills investigated in the laboratory and legitimized in tests and definitions of intelligence is examined. The particular problems of the disadvantaged child are also discussed in Section V, together with the implications for future research in the area of metacognition in developmentally delayed children.

II. METACOGNITION: AN EPIPHENOMENON?

I empathize with those who express confusion at the proliferation of "metas" in the current literature on developmental cognition, and indeed, there has been some serious concern that "metacognition" is an epiphenomenon recently elevated and dignified with a new title, but really the stuff that the problem-solving literature has been concerned with all along. When faced with terms such as *metalearning, metamemory, meta-attention, metacomprehension, metalinguistics,* etc., the dubious reader may wonder why the meta need be added. The addition can be defended, if at all, only if it reflects a real change of emphasis – which I believe it does. My bias is that the processes described as metacognitive are the important aspects of knowledge, that what is of major interest is knowledge about one's own cognitions rather than the cognitions themselves. Just as fever is a secondary symptom, an epiphenomenon of disease (*Oxford English Dictionary*), so the outcome of intelligent evaluation and control of one's own cognitive processes are secondary symptoms of the basic underlying processes of metacognition. This is not to say that conscious control of one's own activities is essential for all forms of knowing, and indeed, I have concentrated elsewhere on incidental learning as a function of active interactions with a meaningful environment (Brown, 1975); but in the domain of deliberate learning and problem-solving situations, conscious executive control of the routines available to the system is the essence of intelligent activity – the underlying force that the observed routines reflect, are symptomatic of, and are epiphenomenal to.

Before proceeding with this section, it would be helpful to define what is meant by metacognitive skills, and in order to incriminate another in the proliferation of "meta" terms, I quote John Flavell (1976b), who, more than any other developmental psychologist, has been responsible for the current interest in research in this area:

"Metacognition" refers to one's knowledge concerning one's own cognitive processes and products or anything related to them, e.g., the learning-relevant properties of information or data. For example, I am engaging in metacognition (metamemory, metalearning, metattention, metalanguage, or whatever) if I notice that I am having more trouble learning A than B; if it strikes me that I should double-check C before accepting it as a fact; if it occurs to me that I had better scrutinize each and every alternative in any multiple-choice type task situation before deciding which is the best one; If I sense that I had better make a note of D because I may forget it. .... Metacognition refers, among other things, to the active monitoring and consequent regulation and orchestration of these processes in relation to the cognitive objects on which they bear, usually in the service of some concrete goal or objective [p. 232].

The skeptic will be pleased to note the similarity between these activities and the activities traditionally considered under the heading "study-skills" (Brown & Smiley, 1977a; Robinson, 1941). The area of metacognition is not as new as it would appear.

Klahr (1974) raised the question of whether the distinction between knowledge is a viable one:

Should we not consider instead two forms of knowledge: (a) knowledge of the thing itself, and (b) knowledge of its appropriate use? Certainly one of the things I know about K is about it per se, such as how to multiply. Another thing I know is a set of appropriate conditions under which to apply that knowledge. It seems that an increase in either is an increase in my understanding of K [pp. 295–296].

This quote illustrates the essential interdependence of the metas with their content area; this interdependence is discussed in a later section (IV.D). There are three main points I would like to make here. First, the difference between knowledge and the understanding of that knowledge (in terms of appropriate use) appears to be a real one with great heuristic value for those interested in what develops. Educationally, the traditional distinction between knowing what and knowing how (Broudy, 1977) is still a viable one with important implications for educational practices (see Sections IV.F, IV.G, and V.D). Second, although there is obviously an incestuous relationship between metacognitions concerning a certain process area and the processes themselves (e.g., metamemory and memory), many skills currently being studied as skills of metacognition are trans-situational (i.e., they apply to many forms of problem-solving activity). Finally, if one is interested in the "ecological validity" of the processes selected for study, the skills of metacognition do appear to have recognizable counterparts in "real-world, everyday-life" situations. Checking the results of an operation against certain criteria of effectiveness, economy, and common-sense reality is a metacognitive skill applicable whether the task under consideration is solving a math problem, memorizing a prose passage, following a recipe, or assembling an automobile. Self-interrogation concerning the current state of one's own knowledge during problem solving is an essential skill in a wide variety of situations, those of the laboratory, the school, or everyday life.

In summary, the isolation, however artificial, of metacognitive skills for intensive study is a viable separation that will help us focus on the similarities rather than the differences among traditional cognitive domains (Flavell, 1976a). Furthermore, because metacognition demands the ability to introspect about one's own performance and to differentiate one's own perspective from that of others, related areas of study such as social cognition, role-taking, and communication become directly relevant. In addition, because self-evaluation of one's own performance cannot be objective — such self-interrogation is contaminated by one's own feelings of competence — some previously separate areas of personality development are again of obvious relevance (e.g., fear of failure, need for achievement, external vs. internal control, learned helplessness, and level of aspiration). By concentrating on metacognitive development, not only will artificial separations between traditional cognitive domains be weakened, but also boundaries across various distinct areas of inquiry in developmental psychology may be questioned. This realigning of boundaries cannot help but be beneficial if we are seriously concerned with the developing child as a whole person rather than as the repository of certain interesting fragmentary skills in various stages of development.

III. METAMEMORY: A SELECTED REVIEW
OF THE LITERATURE

Most empirical research in metacognition has centered around metamemory — knowledge concerning one's own memory abilities and strategies. The term was introduced by John Flavell (1970) who, together with his students, has provided a rich source of data concerning the development of metamemorial knowledge. An excellent review of this literature predates this chapter (Flavell & Wellman, 1977) and will not be reiterated here. In this section, therefore, some recent research from our laboratory concerned with metamemorial knowledge in slow-learning children will be introduced.

In addition, the section will focus on a general problem with the developmental research to date; that is, that the particular forms of metamemory selected for study have encouraged an underestimation of the complexity of the operations involved. The primary concentration has been on isolated fragmentary introspections concerning metamemorial knowledge rather than on the complex ongoing interaction of person, task, and strategy variables (Flavell & Wellman, 1977) that are called into play during an actual attempt to deliberately retain information. The issue of the level of difficulty of the introspection required has not been examined adequately. Thus, a quick perusal of the existing developmental literature might suggest that metamemorial knowledge is quite mature by third grade (see Section IV.C). However, I will argue that this is an illusion created by the simple types of metamemorial skills that have been examined.

Some idea of the complexity of the metacognitive abilities demanded of the fully mature memorizer can be gleaned by considering the operations attributed to the central processor, interpreter, or executive, introduced as the overseer in many current models of memory. Being capable of performing intelligent evaluation of its own operations is an essential characteristic of the central mechanism favored by many current theories; some form of self-awareness or explicit knowledge of its own workings is critical for an efficient problem-solving system (Becker, 1975; Bobrow, 1975; Bobrow & Norman, 1975). The basic requirements of such an executive demonstrate the complexity of the issue. It must include the ability to: (1) predict the system's capacity limitations; (2) be aware of its repertoire of heuristic routines and their appropriate domain of utility; (3) identify and characterize the problem at hand; (4) plan and schedule appropriate problem-solving strategies; (5) monitor and supervise the effectiveness of those routines it calls into service; and (6) dynamically evaluate these operations in the face of success or failure so that termination of strategic activities can be strategically timed. These forms of executive decision making are perhaps the crux of efficient problem solving because the use of an appropriate piece of knowledge or routine to obtain that knowledge at the right time and in the right place is the essence of intelligence.

Obviously, whether knowledge of his own memory or problem-solving processes will be attributed to a child will depend on the level of complexity of the judgment required. For example, the seemingly mature understanding displayed by third graders in metamemory studies to date is not apparent if more complex coordination and predictions are examined (Brown, 1977a; Brown & DeLoache, in press; Butterfield & Belmont, 1977). In the following selected review, we have attempted to consider the current literature in the light of the degree of complexity of the judgment required.

A. Secondary Ignorance: On Not Knowing When or What You Know

A very basic form of self-awareness involved in all memory and problem-solving tasks is the realization that there is a problem of knowing what you know and what you do not know (Brown, 1975). We are indebted to Joan Sieber (1968) for bringing the problem of "secondary ignorance" to our attention even though it took some time before we appreciated the importance of the observation. Sieber used the term for that state beyond ignorance when one is aware that one is in a state of ignorance. An astute observation by Holt in his book *How Children Fail* (1964) illustrates this situation well:

> Part of being a good student is learning to be aware of one's own mind and the degree of one's own understanding. The good student may be one who often says that he does not understand, simply because he keeps a constant check on his understanding. The poor student who does not, so to speak, watch himself trying to understand, does not know most of the time whether he understands or not. Thus the problem is not to get students to ask us what they don't know; the problem is to make them aware of the difference between what they know and what they don't [pp. 28–29].

1. *Metacomprehension.*   The problem of ascertaining the state of one's own ignorance or enlightenment is one of metacomprehension. Understanding instructions would be a case of comprehension of a message, while knowing that one has or has not understood would be an example of metacomprehension. Holt's (1964) lucid description of children's mystification over school problems includes many instances of metacomprehension failures. For example, one child faced with the task of listing verbs that end with a "p" became upset repeating, "I don't get it," but was totally unable to say why she failed to understand. Holt then asked the child if she knew what a verb was and gave her some examples. Relieved, the child went to work. Holt (1964) believes that this child did not ask what a verb was simply because:

> She did not know herself that she did not know. All she knew was that she had been told to start doing something and she didn't know what to do. She was wholly incapable of analyzing the instructions, finding out what part of them made sense and what did not, where her knowledge ended and her ignorance began [p. 145].

Although Holt's charming book contains many anecdotes concerning the child's difficulty in evaluating his or her own state of knowledge, controlled experimental tests of this developmentally related phenomena are rare. In a recent series of experiments, Markman (1977) examined the insensitivity of young children to their own failure to comprehend. Children from Grades 1 through 3 were asked to help the experimenter to design instructions for new games (e.g., card games) to be taught to other children of their age. The instructions were obviously incomplete and the measure of whether the child realized he had not understood was his request for more information. For example, the experimenter and the child each received four alphabet cards and the child was given these instructions. "We each put our cards in a pile. We both turn over the top card in our pile. We look at cards to see who has the special card. Then we turn over the next card in our pile to see who has the special card this time. In the end the person with the most cards wins the game." No mention was made of what the special card could be. Not only did the younger children require many additional prompts before they indicated incomprehension, but it also appeared that they needed to repeat the instructions or even to attempt to execute the task before they became aware that they did not know how to play the game. Because the ability to monitor one's own understanding of instructions and messages, whether spoken or written, is an essential prerequisite for all problem-solving activity, further research on this topic would be welcomed.

2. *The Lack of Knowledge Inference.*   Although it would seem that being aware of what it is you know or do not know is a primitive precursor of more complex forms of metacomprehension, the difficulty of this introspection is an important issue because under certain conditions, even college students may

have problems estimating the state of their own knowledge. Identifying what you do not know, or could not know, can involve quite complex forms of reasoning. Mature problem solvers not only have a reasonable estimate of the accessibility of their known facts, they are also cognizant of which facts cannot be known and which can be deduced on the basis of what they already know. Adults realize immediately that they cannot know Charles Dickens' phone number (Norman, 1973), but they arrive at this conclusion by inferential reasoning concerning other aspects of their knowledge. Not only do children know less than adults and often have poorly organized, incomplete, and inconsistent knowledge, but they also lack the complex systems of inferential reasoning used by adults to infer information from incomplete and contradictory knowledge bases. Collins (1977) has shown that college students use a variety of inferential reasoning strategies to assess the probability that an assumption is true given the information they already have. The full flavor of Collins' work cannot be given here, but the types of inferences described are many, and I would refer the reader to the protocols from his Socratic dialogues as particularly rich examples of the complexity of such skills.

3. *The Expert.*   The problems of metacomprehension can range from the awareness that one is not understanding to the strategic monitoring of awareness in order to ascertain that one has the optimal information for attacking a particular task. Consider the problem of a deliberate memorization task. The memorizer must recognize this class of problems and realize that they call for suitable actions on his or her part. Merely identifying the class of problems requiring deliberate remembering can pose a considerable burden on the metacongitive powers of the very young. How then would an expert memorizer go about the task of identifying the problems involved in a specific memorization task?

> No self-respecting memory expert would put up with the way psychologists run most memory experiments. Experts would ask questions like "What must I remember?", "How many items?", "How much time will there be?":, "What's the nature of the tests?", etc. They would know what they needed to know in order to perform optimally – and would settle for nothing less [Bransford, Nitsch, & Franks, 1977, p. 38].

Binet's pioneer work with "lighting calculators," "outstanding mnemonists," and chess players (Binet, 1894; Reeves, 1965) also illustrates that the expert not only needs to identify fully all the facets of a problem before proceeding, but also prefers to structure the input in an optimal manner to achieve efficiency. Identifying the exact nature of a problem can be a complex act.

Thus, the task of deliberate memorization may involve complex metacognitive introspection that can tax even college students' ingenuity (Brown & Smiley,

1977a). But let us return to our embryonic expert, the preoperational child. What evidence do we have that the child knows anything about what he knows concerning even "simple" memory tasks? One method of obtaining this information is to ask children how sure they are that their answers are correct (i.e., obtain confidence ratings).

4. *Confidence.* A feature of many memory paradigms is that it is possible to ascertain how confident the subject is that his or her response is correct. Thus, in continuous recognition memory paradigms, one can consider the hit rate (items correctly recognized) in comparison to the false alarm rate (items incorrectly recognized). A conservative response bias refers to the case where the subject has a very low false alarm rate; if the subject designates an item as one seen before (old) it was seen before. Young children have a very conservative response bias (Brown & Campione, 1972; Brown & Scott, 1971), suggesting that they reserve their identification of "old" to items they are sure they have seen before. This is a very crude measure of confidence, and d' measures have typically been introduced to separate out retention-based components of recognition performance to separate our retention-based components of recognition performance from criterion- or decision-based components Using a d' measure, Perlmutter and Myers (1974) and Berch (1975) also concluded that very young children employ a conservative response bias in recognition performance. Alternatively, it is possible to approach the problem directly and require the subject to rate the confidence his response of "old" or "new" with respect to a specific scale. Berch and Evans (1973) used this procedure successfully with children as young as 6 years old. Although 9-year-olds were better than 6-year-olds at gauging the accuracy of their recognition performance, younger children were capable of assessing the accuracy of their response to some extent. The lower the child's level of confidence in judging an item as old, the lower the probability that the item actually was old.

The feeling-of-knowing experience in children will be considered fully in the next section however, one factor concerning confidence ratings emerged in a study by Brown and Lawton (1977) and is of interest here. Educable retarded children, whether or not they could predict their feeling of knowing *prior* to a recognition choice, were able to assess the accuracy of their response *after* it had been made. Accuracy of recognition attributed to "sure" and "not sure" judgments are given in Table 2.1. The difference between categories is lower for the younger group, but even here, it is reliable.

This difference between predicting potential accuracy prior to performance and confidence in accuracy following performance was also reported by Moynahan (1976). First and third graders were given eight-item lists to learn. Following recall attempts, they were asked to indicate how many items they had recalled. A similar study was conducted in our laboratory with educable retarded children. All subjects were almost errorless when estimating how many items they had

TABLE 2.1
The Relation of Accuracy to Confidence Judgments Concerning
Recognition Choices in a Feeling-of-Knowing Experiment

Subjects	Young (MA 6)	Medium (MA 8)	Old (MA 10)
N	17	15	27
Sure	.54	.71	.66
Not sure	.34	.34	.28
Difference	.20	.37	.38

Note. Adapted from "The Feeling of Knowing Experience in Educable Retarded Chil-dren" by A. L. Brown and S. C. Lawton, Developmental Psychology, 1977, 13, 364-370. Copyright 1977 by American Psychological Association. Reprinted by permission.

recalled, although children of this age are unable to predict their span *prior* to recall attempts (Brown, Campione, & Murphy, 1977). In addition, the educable children in our study were asked to indicate which specific items were recalled. Again, the children were virtually errorless at the task, correctly identifying 95% of their recalled items. Apparently, even young children can gauge accurately the success of their prior recognition accuracy and recall performance. They know when and what they know if the situation is a relatively straightforward recognition memory task.

B. Prediction

The ability to accurately assess performance after a response is made contrasts sharply with the ability to predict accuracy prior to a retrieval attempt. Moyna-han (1976) and Brown and Lawton (1977) attribute the greater difficulty of prediction to the degree of abstraction involved. Predicting in advance of responding requires the ability to imagine cognitive acts that have not yet occurred. There is considerable evidence that such acts of imagination are more difficult for the young child.

1. *The Feeling of Knowing.* Consider first the feeling-of-knowing experience. As with the lack-of-knowledge inference (Collins, Warnock, Aiello, & Miller, 1975), it is necessary to distinguish between the recognition that a gap in knowl-edge exists and the active strategic attempts that might be instigated to fill "the gap that is intensely active" (James, 1890). This type of active attempt at re-trieval has been considered in tip-of-the-tongue experiments (Brown & McNeill, 1966; Yarmey, 1973). For adults, the tip-of-the-tongue phenomenon consists of first, a "feeling of knowing" (Blake, 1973; Hart, 1967) that the sought-after information is known and merely awaits the appropriate accessing, followed by

active strategic attempts to facilitate retrieval of the temporarily inaccessible but putatively available material (Tulving & Pearlstone, 1966).

Brown and Lawton (1977) conducted two studies on the feeling-of-knowing experience in educable retarded children of varying levels of cognitive ability (MA 6–10). The first study was similar to the paradigm used with adults. Children were pretrained to bet one to three tokens that they would recognize a familiar picture that they had failed to recall. Because a large proportion of older children recalled accurately, only the younger subjects could be examined for feeling of knowing. In addition to a large drop-out rate due to accuracy, the data from a considerable number of the remaining children were suspect as they appeared to use the betting procedure inappropriately. These children wagered three chips on almost all the tests and were always correct. Subsequent interrogation revealed that they deliberately "failed" to recall familiar pictures so that they could enjoy the excitement of the betting procedure. Furthermore, several of them were unaware that if they recalled correctly, they were sure of three chips and would always get at least as many if not more from a correct recall. It was their impression that if they bet three and won three, they had somehow gained six. The suspected data were not included in the subsequent analysis, leaving only 13 MA 6 children and 14 MA 8 children of an original pool of 67 subjects.

Considering only the "acceptable" data, the conditional probabilities of a correct recall given that the subject bet one, two, or three chips are presented in Fig. 2.1. Older children did recall more when they wagered more. Younger children did not appear to differentiate between a bet of one or two chips, but their probability of correct recognition given a bet of three, $P(C/3)$, was high, indicating some feeling-of-knowing sensitivity in the younger children.

The problem experienced with the betting procedure and the high-recall success rate of the older children led to an unacceptably large drop-out rate and interpretation of these results must be tempered with caution. For these reasons, the first experiment was replicated, using as measures of prediction something less attractive than the betting procedure. Three groups of educable retarded children, MA 6 ($N = 17$), MA 8 ($N = 15$), and MA 10 ($N = 27$), were shown a pool of 100 pictures of famous characters and asked to give the correct names. Any picture a child could not name was recorded and used in his feeling-of-knowing test. On each feeling-of-knowing trial, the subject viewed a character he had not named previously and was asked to indicate whether he or she would recognize the name (yes response), would not recognize the name (no response), or might recognize the name (maybe response). After this, four names were read: the correct name, a totally impossible name, and two names from the same category as the target. For example, if Richard Nixon were the target, the three three distractors would be John Kennedy, Abraham Lincoln, and Ronald McDonald.

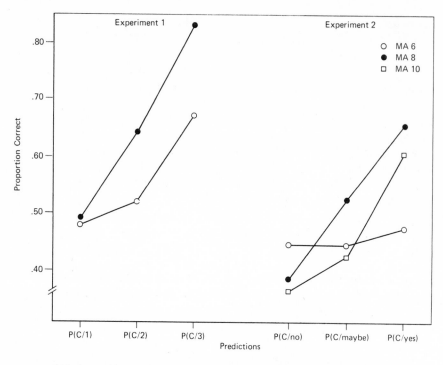

FIG. 2.1.   The probability of a correct recognition given a wager of 1, 2, or 3 tokens in Experiment 1, or given a judgment of yes, maybe, or no in Experiment 2. (Adapted from "The Feeling of Knowing Experience in Educable Retarded Children" by A. L. Brown and S. C. Lawton, *Developmental Psychology*, 1977, *13*, 364–370. Copyright 1977 by the American Psychological Association. Reprinted by permission.)

The conditional probabilities of a correct response given that the subject predicted he would, P(C/yes), would not, P(C/no), or might, P(C/maybe), recognize the name are presented in Fig. 2.1 together with the data from the first experiment. The youngest group did not predict their subsequent ability to recognize the name, but both the MA 8 and MA 10 groups did identify more items when they predicted they would be able to recognize them.

Consideration of the data from both experiments indicates a developmental trend in the ability to predict recognition accuracy when recall fails. The point of confusion lies in the estimation of the sensitivity of the youngest children. In the first experiment, they did show some ability to predict their recognition accuracy for they were reliably better on those trials where they bet three items. In the second experiment, however, the more representative sample of younger children did not recognize more items when they predicted that they would recognize the names. This cross-experimental difference illustrates the problem with assessing children's metamemorial ability within only one task; a more accurate picture of their capabilities might be gleaned from considering their performance across a variety of tasks and situations (see Sections IV.E and V.A).

2. *Span-Estimation.* Another form of prediction which has received considerable attention is the ability of young children to estimate (predict) their own memory capabilities. Flavell, Friedrichs, and Hoyt (1970) asked children from second and fourth grades, together with nursery and kindergarten children, to estimate their recall span. From one to ten pictures were exposed incrementally, and the child's task was to indicate at each list length whether he or she could still recall a list that large. Whereas only a few of the older children predicted they could recall all ten pictures, over half the nuresry and kindergarten children predicted in this manner. If we take estimation of ±2 of the actual span as a measure of realistic estimation, the group means met this criterion at the second- and fourth-grade level, but this was not true for the younger children.

Markman (1973) and Yussen and Levy (1975) replicated these findings as did Brown et al. (1977) with educable retarded children. All three studies included a training component which we will consider later (Section IV.F). Of interest here is a problem encountered in the Brown et al. study; instead of halting the proceedings when subjects indicated a list length was beyond their span, the experiments continued to expose items incrementally until all ten had been exposed. This minor change in procedure resulted in three groups of subjects: those judged realistic (±2 of span), those judged unrealistic as in previous studies, and a third group (32%) called inconsistent. These children indicated that a particular list length was too difficult for them, but then proceeded to estimate that at least one longer list was within their capacity. Allowing subjects to demonstrate inconsistent responding markedly changed the pattern of results obtained; and there is no way of knowing how many "realistic" subjects in the previous studies would have produced inconsistent patterns of responses if given the opportunity. For example, 80% of the MA 6 inconsistent subjects in our study would have been judged realistic if we had stopped at their first "too difficult" response, the procedure used previously (Flavell et al., 1970; Markman, 1973). Of the total population, this would have led to an estimation of 28% of MA 6 subjects judged realistic, a figure not unlike those found by Markman and Flavell et al. (22% and 36% for kindergartners). This finding illustrates a problem with accepting a young child's verbal response as a true estimate of his metamemorial capabilities, a difficulty we will also return to later (Section IV.E).

3. *Estimating Task Difficulty.* Several sources of information are available concerning the young child's awareness of task difficulty. We will consider first the questionnaire data provided by Kreutzer, Leonard, and Flavell (1975). Kreutzer et al. asked children many questions about the state of their knowledge concerning the memory processes of themselves and others. We used the same questions (slightly modified) with educable retarded children as a measure of the

general effectiveness of two years of consistent training in metamemory tasks (experiences vs. naive subjects). We will return to the training aspect later (Section III.E) but will include the retarded children's data here when appropriate. We selected three of the Kreutzer et al. items as particularly good tests of the child's awareness of task difficulty: the story-list problem, the opposite-arbitrary item, and the rote-paraphrase question.

The story-list problem was designed to test whether children had any knowledge of the beneficial effects of embedding a series of to-be-remembered items within a narrative context. The data are presented in Table 2.2. There was a marked developmental difference in the type of response given by normal children. Only 50% of kindergarten children realized the greater ease of the embedded condition, but all third graders were aware of this fact. In addition, 70% of the older children gave adequate justification of their choice, but only 15% of the younger ones did.

The opposite-arbitrary item is another example of predicting task difficulty. Here, children were asked to judge the relative difficulty of learning a list of words consisting of randomly paired items or lists of pairs based on common associates (opposites). These data are presented in Table 2.3. The younger normal children had difficulty predicting accurately, but by third grade, almost perfect prediction was obtained. Only half the MA 8 children could predict accurately. A consideration of justifications given for a choice further illustrates the younger child's difficulty since only a few normal kindergartners and MA 6 retardates could give a reasonable justification.

The third question selected was the rote-paraphrase item. Kreutzer et al.'s scoring and tabulation of this item was extremely complex, and we have selected only certain salient features for inspection. The children were asked questions

TABLE 2.2
Story List Item:[a] Proportion of Subjects Making Each Choice
and Justifying Their Choice[b]

| Subjects | N | Story Format | | | Adequate Justification |
		Easier	Harder	Other	
Six-Year-Olds (MA)					
Normal Kindergarten[c]	20	.50	.25	.25	.15
Naive Educable	21	.81	.19	.00	.05
Experienced Educable	40	.78	.18	.03	.20
Eight-Year-Olds (MA)					
Normal Third Grade[c]	20	1.00	.00	.00	.70
Naive Educable	28	.75	.04	.21	.04
Experienced Educable	30	.80	.20	.00	.40

[a]From Kreutzer et al. (1975) questionnaire.
[b]Interrater reliability = .96.
[c]The data for normal children are from Kreutzer et al. (1975).

TABLE 2.3
Opposite-Arbitrary Item:[a]
Proportion of Subjects Making Each Choice[b]

Subjects	N	Opposites Easier	Arbitrary Easier	Same	Adequate Justification
Six-Year-Olds (MA)					
Normal Kindergarten[c]	20	.30	.50	.20	.10
Naive Educable	21	.43	.57	.00	.10
Experienced Educable	40	.31	.69	.00	.12
Eight-Year-Olds (MA)					
Normal Third Grade[c]	20	.90	.10	.00	.65
Naive Educable	28	.57	.39	.04	.42
Experienced Educable	30	.48	.52	.00	.40

[a]From Kreutzer et al. (1975) questionnaire.
[b]Interrater reliability = 100%.
[c]The data for normal children are from Kreutzer et al. (1975).

concerning the ease of learning a recorded story to see whether they understood the differential study and recall requirements of gist vs. verbatim recall. A summary of the main results is given in Table 2.4. A model child was observed asking the experimenter whether or not recall was to be in her own words or just like in the story. All experimental subjects were then asked the following questions: Question 1 was "Why do you think she asked that question?" The number

TABLE 2.4
Rote Paraphrase Item:[a]
Proportion of Subjects Making Each Choice[b]

Question Number		1	2	3 & 4	5	6
Subjects	N	Appropriate Response	Yes Response	Appropriate Activity	Own-Words Easier	Adequate Justification
Six-Year-Olds (MA)						
Normal Kindergarten[c]	20	.05	.50	.20	.55	.10
Naive Educable	21	.00	.90	.00	.76	.00
Experienced Educable	40	.05	.95	.05	.82	.08
Eight-Year-Olds (MA)						
Normal Third Grade[c]	20	.55	.75	.70	.90	.75
Naive Educable	28	.21	.82	.18	.64	.28
Experienced Educable	30	.20	.83	.30	.73	.20

[a]From Kreutzer et al. (1975) questionnaire.
[b]Interrater reliability = .96.
[c]The data for normal children are from Kreutzer et al. (1975).

of responses indicating awareness of the greater difficulty of verbatim recall are shown in column 1 of Table 2.4. Question 2 was "Would it help her to know the answer?" Yes responses are given in column 2. Questions 3 and 4 basically required the child to indicate what he or she would do if told to learn word for word or to acquire the gist. Any answers indicating appropriate activity are entered in columns 3 and 4. In questions 5 and 6, the child was asked which would be easier, gist or verbatim recall. Answers indicating that recall in one's own words would be easier are given in column 5 and adequate justifications in column 6. The predictions were somewhat more difficult than in the previous two items; however, the same trends are apparent. The majority of the children indicated that it would be easier to recall in one's own words; however, the majority of younger normal and educable retarded children could not justify their response, nor could they indicate appropriate study activities for each recall demand.

These questionnaire data indicate that children become more aware of task difficulty as they mature. Although normal 8-year-olds are quite sensitive to the problems of task difficulty examined here, progress is not so dramatic for educable children. Of interest is that both groups are easily misled in this game; 60% of normal 6-year-olds and 55% of normal 8-year-olds believed colored pictures to be easier to learn that black and white items. This misconception was shared by the educable children; 70% of the MA 6 and 55% of MA 8 children were similarly misled.

The efficiency with which children can judge task difficulty obviously depends on the type of task they must judge. In the questionnaire study, almost all the retarded children realized that recognition was an easier task than recall, while almost none had any appreciation of retroactive interference. Again, this points to the interaction of awareness and the level of difficulty of the judgment to be made. Young children are not simply aware or unaware of task difficulty. Some types of problems are readily apparent to them, whereas others are completely beyond their comprehension.

This effect of the complexity of the task judgment is revealed in empirical studies as well as in the questionnaire data. First, consider studies on estimating the difficulty of lists of items to be rote learned. Tenney (1975) asked kindergarten, third, and sixth graders to compose lists of words that would be easy for them to recall. Organizational strategies were assessed by comparing lists designed for recall with free association lists. The younger children made up essentially the same lists under both conditions, but the older children tended to provide category organization.

As part of our longitudinal studies of metamemory in educable children, we replicated the Tenney study with MA 6 and MA 8 children together with children from regular classes, matched for CA and MA with the educable sample. As in the Tenney study, children produced units that contained four items: the key word and three words that they judged to be easy to recall with the key word.

TABLE 2.5
Classification of Student-Produced Lists for Recall

Subjects	N	Taxonomic	Thematic	Rhymes/Sound-alikes	Random
Normal					
CA 6	20	.21	.37	.14	.28
CA 8	20	.72	.26	.01	.01
CA 10	20	.68	.30	.00	.02
Educable					
MA 6	27	.38	.27	.10	.29
MA 8	31	.42	.23	.12	.23

Details of the types of structures built into the units are given in Table 2.5. The three classes of organization that occurred often enough to score were taxonomic category, thematic category (i.e., grouping together objects around a theme: baby, crib, rattle, diaper), and rhymes and sound-alikes. All other responses appeared to be random. Within the normal population, the incidence of random responding decreased with age as did sound responding, and there was a corresponding increase in categorization. Educable children did not improve with increasing MA and also produced many random units. Of interest is the high incidence of thematic responding. Although Denney and Ziobrowski (1972) found that young children clustered more by thematic than taxonomic category, Tenney (1975) did not find significant thematic responding in any of her groups. If we consider the proportion of all classified responses (omitting random responses), there was a high incidence of thematic responding in all groups (normal subjects: CA 6 = 51, CA 8 = .26, and CA 10 = .31; educable subjects: MA 6 = .36 and MA 8 = .30). The thematic responding accounts for half of all categories used by the normal kindergarten children; all other groups used this type of response for approximately one-third of the units that were organized.

   Another measure, adapted from Tenney, that illustrates the child's understanding of the task is whether the categories that are produced are broad or narrow. A narrow category is one in which the internal organization of the unit can serve as an additional retrieval cue. For example, Monday, Saturday, Thursday, Tuesday would be a taxonomic broad response, and Monday, Tuesday, Wednesday, Thursday would be a taxonomic narrow response. Obviously, narrow responses (like 1, 2, 3, 4) are much better examples of an easy list, and, therefore, we looked at the proportion of categorical responses classified as broad or narrow. These data are given in Table 2.6. Again, the developmental trend is apparent. The number of narrow categories increases as the CA of the normal children increases. Educable children also show a slight improvement, but per-

TABLE 2.6
Proportion of Categorical Responses Classified As Broad and Narrow

		Classification	
Subjects	N	Broad	Narrow
Normal			
CA 6	20	.62	.38
CA 8	20	.25	.75
CA 10	20	.18	.81
Educable			
MA 6	27	.67	.33
MA 8	31	.49	.51

form more like normal kindergarten children than any other normal group. This developmental pattern is rendered clearer if one considers the proportion of all responses that are narrow categories, the most strategic form of responses. For normal children, the range is .27, .75, and .80 for CA 6, 8, and 10; for educable children, it is .21 and .33 for MA 6 and 8, respectively. The large majority of normal 10-year-olds "catch on" and give narrow categories as lists, while this efficient response type is much less frequent in developmentally less mature individuals.

Other studies that have considered the child's estimation of task difficulty have been those of Moynahan (1973) and Salatas and Flavell (1976) where children were asked whether categorized or noncategorized lists would be easier to recall. These studies will be considered in a subsequent section concerned with the relationship between prediction and performance (Section IV.D). Here, it is sufficient to point out that a similar developmental trend was found. Younger children had more difficulty than older children, but almost perfect prediction was shown by third grade. Retarded children perform like normal kindergarten children (Brown et al., 1977).

We would like to describe one further study in this section (Brown & Smiley, 1977b) because it illustrates that the developmental trend in task prediction is apparent at a much later age if more complex materials are used. The procedure was based on a study by Johnson (1970) who devised an objective method for dividing prose passages into idea units. After the passages had been so divided, independent raters judged the importance of the units to the story theme. Subsequently, it was found that recall scores of further independent samples of college students were determined by the rated importance of the units. The Johnson procedure is particularly suitable for use with children because it provides both a method of quantifying what is recalled from prose passages and a measure of metacomprehension. Not only is it possible to ascertain whether children's recall is similar in pattern to adults, but it is also possible to see whether the child has sufficient knowledge of text materials to determine what are the important units.

Students between 8 and 18 years old were given folk tales to rate or recall. All stories rated and recalled had previously been rated for importance units by independent groups of college students. The procedure for 12- and 18-year-olds was similar to that used by Johnson with adults. The subjects were seen in groups and first listened to a tape recording of the story as they simultaneously read the passage through. The stories were printed with one (previously identified) idea unit on each line. After a second reading, the subjects were told that the individual units differed in their importance to the whole story, and some of the less important units could be eliminated without destroying the main theme of the story. They were first instructed to eliminate approximately one-fourth of the units that they judged to be the least important by crossing them through with a blue pencil. They were then requested to eliminate another quarter crossing them with a green pencil. Finally, they were asked to remove a further quarter of the items by crossing through them with a red pencil, thus leaving one-fourth of the original units exposed. This procedure resulted in four levels of judged importance with the items eliminated first (the least important) given a rated importance score of 1 and those left exposed at the end (most important) given a score of 4. The procedure for young subjects was essentially the same except they were seen individually and received considerable pretraining in the rating procedure (for details, see Brown & Smiley, 1977b).

The mean importance ratings of the four experimental groups were compared with the previously acquired college students' rated importance. These data are presented in Table 2.7. A strong developmental trend was apparent with a gradual

TABLE 2.7
A Comparison of Mean Importance Ratings of Four Experimental
Groups on Prejudged Levels of Importance

Subjects	Importance Level			
	1 (Least)	2	3	4 (Most)
Eight-Year-Olds	2.41	2.52	2.51	2.56
Ten-Year-Olds	2.42	2.35	2.46	2.76
Twelve-Year-Olds	2.02	2.36	2.58	3.05
Eighteen-Year-Olds	1.61	2.09	2.78	3.52
Total	2.12	2.33	2.58	2.97

Note. Adapted from "Rating the Importance of Structural Units of Prose Passages: A Problem of Metacognitive Development" by A. L. Brown and S. S. Smiley, *Child Development*, 1977, *48*, 1-12. Copyright 1977 by the Society for Research in Child Development, Inc. Reprinted by permission.

improvement in the sensitivity to degree of rated importance emerging over the entire age range studied. Only 18-year-olds reliably distinguished all four levels of importance; 12-year-olds did not differentiate the two intermediate levels of importance. The greater range of mean scores across the four importance levels shown by the 18-year-olds also suggests that sensitivity to fine degrees of importance continues to be refined in the high school years. Eight-year-olds made no distinction between levels of importance in their ratings, and even 10-year-old students could only distinguish the highest level of importance from all other levels. Thus, there was considerable agreement between independent groups of college students and even 12-year-olds concerning the importance of constityent idea units of a text passage, but 8- and 10-year-old subjects were unable to differentiate units in terms of their relative importance to the text.

All children recalled passages as well as rated them. The recall scores for all ages were extremely sensitive to the importance level of the units as rated by adults. These data are presented in Table 2.8. Although older subjects recalled more than younger children, the general pattern of results was consistent across the age range of 8 to 18 years, the least important units were recalled less frequently than all other units, and the most important units were most often recalled. We have some additional pilot data that suggest that this effect of structural importance is also found with much younger children. A group of 37 nursery-school children and 20 kindergartners were also given the same stories to recall under a variety of conditions which need not concern us here (Brown, 1976a). Although we had considerable difficulty extracting satisfactory recall protocols, and the total number of units recalled was small, we did find the same

TABLE 2.8
Mean Proportion Correct Recall as a Function
of Age and Structural Importance

| Subjects | Importance Level | | | | |
	1 (Least)	2	3	4 (Most)	Total
Eight-Year-Olds	.17	.22	.38	.61	.35
Ten-Year-Olds	.23	.32	.48	.68	.43
Twelve-Year-Olds	.28	.39	.51	.75	.47
Eighteen-Year-Olds	.27	.39	.54	.74	.48
Total	.23	.33	.48	.69	

Note. Adapted from "Rating the Importance of Structural Units of Prose Passages: A Problem of Metacognitive Development" by A. L. Brown and S. S. Smiley, *Child Development,* 1977, *48*, 1-12. Copyright 1977 by the Society for Research in Child Development, Inc. Reprinted by permission.

pattern of sensitivity to level of importance as rated by college students. Considering the 32 protocols where at least 15% of the units were recalled, the mean number of units recalled was .12, .08, .22, and .42 respectively for the four levels of importance. The differences between levels 2 and 3 and levels 3 and 4 were reliable. Again, there is some evidence that the least important units (levels 1 and 2) are seldom, if ever, recalled while the most important units dominate recall attempts. Our data are consistent with those reported by Yendovitskaya (1971) and Christie and Schumacher (1975); even preschool children favor the central theme when recounting stories and disregard minor nonessential details.

Thus, although children's recall does reflect an adult pattern in that important units are recalled more readily than unimportant items, young children are unable to predict in advance the importance of units of text material. This suggests that the same problems experienced by 6- to 8-year-olds in predicting item difficulty in list-learning tasks would also be experienced by 8- to 12-year-olds in predicting unit difficculty in learning from texts. Children who have difficulty determining the key points of a passage would hardly be expected to strategically select them for intensive study (Brown & Smiley, 1977a).

4. *Predicting the Outcome of Strategic Activity.* In the previous section, we examined children's understanding of task difficulty. Here, we are concerned with children's appreciation of strategic intervention in memory tasks – their own or that of another memorizer. The Kreutzer et al. questionnaire contained an item that we judged a good example of the child's ability to predict the outcome of strategy usage, the study-time item. The children were given 20 colored pictures and told that two children had already seen the pictures and been asked to learn them. One child studied for 5 minutes, the other for 1 minute. The children were asked to predict which child remembered more and to jusitfy their answer. They were further asked to indicate how long they personally would study, 1 or 5 minutes. The data from both normal and retarded children are given in Table 2.9. The majority of all children predicted that studying for five minutes would be a better strategy, but younger normal children and educable retarded children were less able to justify their choice. In addition, the MA 6 children did not always indicate that they would study for 5 minutes themselves, even if they indicated the longer time to be beneficial.

In a study currently underway in our laboratory (Brown, Campione, Barclay, Lawton, & Jones, work in progress), we are investigating the ability of normal and retarded children to appreciate the utility of strategy usage during study for free recall. Children are asked to view a video tape of a 12-year-old child performing four different study activities, while attempting to learn a 12-item list of pictures. The four activities modeled are categorizing, rehearsing, labeling, and looking. After the child views the four activities, he or she is asked to indicate which one will lead to better performance. The entire prediction procedure is repeated to obtain reliability scores. Following the second prediction, the child

TABLE 2.9
Study-Time Item:[a] Proportion of Subjects Selecting 1 or 5 Minutes[b]

Subjects	N	Predicted Time for Remembering Most		Adequate Justification	Subject's Choice	
		5 min.	1 min.		5 min.	1 min.
Six-Year-Olds (MA)						
Normal Kindergarten[c]	20	.75	.25	.35	.65	.35
Naive Educable	21	.81	.14	.29	.71	.29
Experienced Educable	40	.85	.15	.56	.69	.31
Eight-Year-Olds (MA)						
Normal Third Grade[c]	20	1.00	.00	1.00	.95	.05
Naive Educable	28	.86	.14	.57	.93	.07
Experienced Educable	30	.93	.07	.70	.93	.07

[a]From Kruetzer et al. (1975) questionnaire.
[b]Interrater reliability = .99.
[c]The data for normal children are from Kreutzer et al. (1975).

is given the same stack of pictures and told to study them in any way he wishes in order to learn as many as possible.

The prediction data for those subjects showing a consistent preference for an activity are presented in Table 2.10. Fourteen normal nursery-school children, 11 MA 6 and 6 MA 8 educable children were not considered as they were inconsistent in their prediction. Consider first the educable retarded children. Both the MA 6 and MA 8 groups predicted that the two appropriate strategies, categorization and rehearsal, would lead to better performance. No child predicted that labeling or looking strategies were appropriate. The normal 4-year-olds, however, were relatively evenly (randomly) divided across all four activities in their predictions. Whereas the MA 6 to 8 retardates appreciated the value of an active strategy, the young CA 4 children did not. But by third grade, the majority

TABLE 2.10
Proportion Predicting Which Activity Will Lead to Best Performance

Activity	Categorize	Rehearse	Label	Look
Preschool (CA 4)	.24	.33	.13	.28
First Grade	.44	.25	.09	.22
Third Grade	.35	.46	.19	.00
Educable (MA 6)	.64	.36	.00	.00
Educable (MA 8)	.38	.62	.00	.00

Note. Adapted from "Predicting the Outcome of Strategy Intervention" by A.L. Brown, J. C. Campione, C. R. Barclay, S. C. Lawton, and R. Jones, work in progress, Center for the Study of Reading, University of Illinois at Urbana Champaign.

TABLE 2.11
Proportion Predicting Categorization or Rehearsal
as Superior and Adopting That Strategy

Subjects	N	Predict Superior	Strategy Performed	P(Perform/Predict)[a]
Preschool (CA 4)	46	.58	.13	.22
First Grade	32	.69	.25	.36
Third Grade	26	.81	.62	.77
Educable (MA 6)	14	1.00	.36	.36
Educable (MA 8)	21	1.00	.19	.19

Note. Adapted from "Predicting the Outcome of Strategy Intervention" by
A. L. Brown, J. C. Campione, C. R. Barclay, S. C. Lawton, and R. Jones, work in
progress, Center for the Study of Reading, University of Illinois at Urbana Champaign.
[a]P(Perform/Predict) = probability that the subjects will perform the strategy
they predicted as the most suitable.

of normal children predicted that an active strategy was the best activity to adopt
for the purposes of remembering.

Although we will consider the relationship between performance and prediction in a later section, the actual performance of children following the prediction task will be included here for closure. The data were collapsed across the
two "appropriate" strategies, categorization and rehearsal. Of interest were the
proportion of subjects who predicted that an active strategy would be superior
and those who adopted one of those strategies themselves. These data are presented in Table 2.11. Although the ability of the educable children to predict
the superiority of active strategies was impressive, their actual performance was
less so. All educable children predicted that categorization or rehearsal would lead
to better performance; yet, when faced with the identical task and stimuli
immediately after viewing the tape, only 28% actually adopted one of the
activities predicted to be superior. In terms of actual performance, the educable
children did not differ from normal preschool or first-grade children. Third-graders
tend to adopt the strategy they predict would be superior; but even for these
children, the relationship between prediction and performance is not perfect.
We are currently obtaining data from a fifth-grade sample. Initial inspection of
these data indicates that even the fifth-grade children do not routinely adopt the
active strategy that they predict to be superior.

C. Planning

The child's ability to plan ahead and his knowledge about the efficiency of such
planning are part of his repository of metamemorial information. This knowledge
has been examined both by questionnaire surveys and in experimental situations.
We will consider the questionnaire material first.

1. *Questionnaire Data.* Several of the Kreutzer et al. items were addressed directly to the question of planning ahead in memorization situations. We have selected two items as particularly appropriate, the immediate-delayed item and the study-plan item. In the immediate-delayed item, children were asked whether, after having been told their friend's phone number, they would prefer to phone right away or get a drink of water first. They were then asked what they did when they had to remember a phone number. A summary of the replies is given in Table 2.12. By third grade, 95% of normal children indicated that they would phone first or demonstrated that they were aware of the problems entailed by waiting; only 40% of kindergartners showed similar awareness. Educable children performed somewhere in between these two levels. Many children indicated that they would write down the phone number if they were required to remember it. All of the third graders gave some evidence of planfulness, but 40% of kindergartners did not. Generally, it appears that many of the educable children and the normal kindergartners could not indicate a plan for remembering.

The study-plan item was designed to test the child's awareness of strategies for studying a list of categorized pictures. In Table 2.13, the child's chosen activities have been divided into strategy responses and no strategy responses. If a child indicated he would employ either categorization, association, rehearsal, or external storage, this was designated a strategy response. A no strategy response was scored if the subject indicated that he would look at, or randomly rearrange the items, or would do nothing at all. Normal children outperformed retardates. Again, by third grade, almost all children indicated a planful behavior on this task.

TABLE 2.12

Immediate-Delayed Item:[a] Proportion of Subjects Making Each Choice[b]

Subjects	N	Phone First or Aware of Problem with Delay	Activity to Remember			
			Write Down	Rehearse	Other	None
Six-Year-Olds (MA)						
Normal Kindergarten[c]	20	.40	.55	.00	.05	.40
Naive Educable	21	.65	.30	.00	.00	.70
Experienced Educable	40	.46	.46	.00	.00	.54
Eight-Year-Olds (MA)						
Normal Third Grade[c]	20	.95	.80	.10	.10	.00
Naive Educable	28	.75	.96	.00	.04	.00
Experienced Educable	30	.67	.63	.00	.03	.23

[a]From Kreutzer et al. (1975) questionnaire.
[b]Interrater reliability = .93.
[c]The data for normal children are from Kreutzer et al. (1975).

TABLE 2.13
Study-Plan Item:[a] Proportion of Subjects Making Each Choice[b]

Subjects	N	Planning a Strategy	Not Planning a Strategy
Six-Year-Olds (MA)			
Normal Kindergarten[c]	20	.45	.55
Naive Educable	21	.24	.76
Experienced Educable	40	.21	.80
Eight-Year-Olds (MA)			
Normal Third Grade[c]	20	.90	.10
Naive Educable	28	.25	.75
Experienced Educable	30	.20	.80

[a]From Kreutzer et al. (1975) questionnaire.
[b]Interrater reliability = .93.
[c]The data for normal children are from Kreutzer et al. (1975).

2. *The Differentiation Hypothesis.* Planning for future recall can involve simple behaviors that fall within the competency of the preschool child, but such planning can also involve complex coordinated patterns of strategic activity. Consider first a simple form of planning within the confines of a typical memorization paradigm. Can young children differentiate between situations where they must actively attempt to remember and those where memorization is not required? Early studies concerned with this differentiation hypothesis suggested that it was not until first grade that children behaved differently when instructed to remember vs. just to look at pictures (Appel, Cooper, McCarrell, Sims-Knight, Yussen, & Flavell, 1972). However, the task used confounded the child's lack of knowledge of how to remember in such situations with his awareness of memorization demands per se. If the only measure of active intervention is some indication of a strategy not yet in the child's repertoire, it is difficult to imagine how one could expect the child to demonstrate awareness of the meaning of instructions to remember. Although children may be perfectly aware of the difference between remembering and looking, if they do not know how to rehearse, categorize, etc., in a study period, they cannot be expected to outperform children not required to memorize.

Subsequent studies confirmed this diagnosis for when just looking longer was taken as a measure of differentiation, children as young as 4½ years old behaved differently under instructions to remember (Yussen, 1974). However, even looking-time measures are sensitive to the complexity of the metamemorial judgment involved. Rogoff, Newcombe, and Kagan (1974) told 4-, 6-, and 8-year-old children that they would be tested for recognition of a series of 40 pictures after a delay of a few minutes or one or 7 days. Only 8-year-olds adjusted their inspection time according to the anticipated length of delay; the younger children did not exhibit this sign of planfulness.

If the task is sufficiently simple, however, evidence of planful behavior can be seen in children as young as 3 years old. Wellman, Ritter, and Flavell (1975) investigated a very simple memory situation that did not depend on the possession of skills of rote-memorization as did the Appel et al. study. Nursery school children watched an experimenter hide a toy under one of a series of identical cups. Before leaving the room for 45 seconds, the experimenter told half the children to "wait here with the toy," and the remaining children were told to "remember where the toy is." Children asked to remember the location exhibited deliberate attempts to retain the information, such as touching the correct box or making it distinctive in some way. One delightful example of "visual rehearsal" was a little girl who sequentially pointed to the cups and shook her head negatively to all nonbaited cups, and nodded affirmatively to the baited cup. The group that was asked to remember recalled the location better than the wait group; note that the children were 3 years old.

In situations that do not require rote recall but retention of spatial location, young children do have some concept of what it means to remember (Acredolo, Pick, & Olsen, 1975). Identifying the location of objects is a meaningful task even for toddlers (Huttenlocher, 1976), but rote recalling a list of items is not usually a common task encountered by the child before the onset of formal schooling (Brown, 1975). It is hardly surprising, therefore, that children cannot benefit from instructions to remember when they lack the prerequisite skill to set deliberate memorization routines into motion. This series of studies provides a cautionary example of the problem of diagnosing lack of metacognitive skills from one specific situation. Whether or not a subject, child or adult, will be attributed with metacognitive insights will be determined by the level of difficulty of the task and the match between the task demands and the subject's extant cognitive skills (Brown & DeLoache, in press; Chi, 1977).

3. *Study-Time Apportionment.* Faced with the common task of attempting to commit to memory a set of material when time limitations or other restrictions impede leisurely study, how do we plan our time for most efficient results? The task can involve very fine degrees of metamemorial judgment as any student can attest (Brown & Smiley, 1977a). A relatively simple experimental analogue was introduced by Masur, McIntyre, and Flavell (1973). First- and third-grade children, together with college subjects, were given a multitrial, free-recall task. On all trials but the first, the subjects were allowed to select for further study only half of the total set of items. Strategic behavior was thought to be selection of those items that had previously not been recalled. Masur et al. found that both third-grade and college students did select previously missed items for extra study, but this was not true of first-grade children who appeared to select ran-

domly. The authors concluded that "the strategy of deliberately concentrating one's study activities on the less well-mastered segments of materials to be learned, like other elementary memory strategies (e.g., rote rehearsal), cannot automatically be assumed to be part of a young child's repertoire of learning techniques" (Masur et al., 1973, p. 237).

One interesting feature of the Masur et al. study was the relationship between adoption of an identified "good" strategy and efficient leaning. Although the relationship between strategy usage and performance was reasonably clear for the college sample, the utility of the strategy was not so clear for third graders, and even less clear for the youngest children. First graders seem to benefit equally from selecting recalled items or from selecting missed items, the supposedly optimal strategy. Even the third graders appear to gain only slightly by selecting the missed items. One explanation of this lack of relationship between strategic selection and good performance lies in the demands of the study situation. In order to perform efficiently, the subject would need to: (1) identify the missed items — Masur et al. have shown that this is not a difficult task even for young children; (2) select these items for additional study; and (3) while studying the previously missed items, keep alive the previously recalled items, presumably by rehearsal. We suspect that the problem lies in (3). Although the young child may recognize the missed items and may even be aware that he should select them for more intensive study, the strategy would only be effective if he could also keep alive the nonselected, previously recalled items. Without rehearsal, known to be difficult at first grade and less than optimal by third grade, this third-demand of the task would be impossible, thus mitigating any positive effects of strategic selection.

Brown and Campione (1977) attempted to replicate the Masur et al. study with educable retarded children. The main feature of the study was its training feature where several strategies were examined. Of interest here is the pretest data. No group of subjects showed above chance strategic selection of missed items; however, when the data from individual subjects were considered, approximately one-third of all children selected previously missed items. This selection, however, was not accompanied by an improvement in recall accuracy. Thus, the pretest data essentially confirm the pattern found with young normal children (Masur et al., 1973). The majority of educable children do not select strategically, and even those that do concentrate on previously missed items do not benefit from this foresight.

Strategic study-time apportionment can involve tasks other than rote learning a list of unrelated items. Of particular interest educationally is learning from texts. Although we are beginning to identify effective strategies used for comprehending and remembering prose by adults (Anderson & Biddle, 1975; Frase, 1975), we know little about the development of these abilities in children (Brown, 1977b; Brown & Smiley, 1977a). We know even less about the self-awareness needed for efficient control of such comprehension strategies. It is by no means certain that spontaneous use of a general classs of mathemagenic skills (Rothkopf, 1972; Smiley, 1974) for enhancing recall is a reliable feature of study behavior even in high school and college students who have not been specifically trained in their use. Yet, it is a common educational practice to instruct children to make outlines of study materials and concentrate on the main events to the exclusion of nonessential material. As we have seen, children have difficulty isolating the main events of complex prose passages (Brown & Smiley, 1977a, 1977b; Smiley, Oakley, Worthen, Campione, & Brown, 1977); thus, they would not find such instructions overly informative (Brown, 1977b).

D. Checking and Monitoring

In the sections on prediction and planning, we were particularly concerned with the child's ability to consider certain task-relevant aspects prior to attempting to solve a problem. In this section, the ability to check and monitor the outcome of an attempt to learn or remember is examined. As in previous sections, many of the examples come from the problem-solving literature since there are few studies of checking and monitoring in memory research. In considering material for inclusion here, I was again struck by the prevalence of this "metacognitive problem" over a wide age range; for it is not that young children are bad and adults good at checking the adequacy of their performance, but that inadequate checking will be manifested at any age if the subject does not fully comprehend the nature of the task.

1. *Internal Consistency.*   One example of inadequate checking is the child's apparent willingness to live with contradictory answers. Examples of internal inconsistency are numerous within the literature on Piagetian conservation tasks, and it has been suggested that one measure of true conservation is the child's awareness that the correct answer can be checked in many ways and that the results of all such checks must agree (Schaeffer, Eggleston, & Scott, 1974). Yet, young children are less disturbed by their own contradictions than are more mature problems solvers. Consider this example from one of our studies on sequence reconstruction (Brown, 1976b). Children were asked to reconstruct a previously seen picture sequence corresponding to a narrative story. They were required to select four pictures from a possible eight. Four of the pictures had been part of the original story. Two of the distractors were obviously incorrect, and the remaining two pictures were consistent with the sequence of events, but had not actually occurred as part of the original. Of the preschool children who could attempt the task, 41% selected all six possible pictures and sequenced them correctly. They refused to indicate which of the six pictures they had seen themselves. A typical dialogue was as follows:

Experimenter: "Which pictures of the story did you see?"
Subject: "These ones" (indicating the six items of their reconstructed story).

Experimenter: "How many are there?"
Subject (counting): "Six."
Experimenter: "How many did you see?"
Subject: "Four."
Experimenter: "So which ones did you see — pick the four."
Subject: "I see all of them."

These young children were not at all discomforted by their incompatible answers. By kindergarten, this pattern of results had disappeared.

Although we have evidence that children as young as second grade do check their answers for internal consistency and, for example, will not accept meaningfully inconsistent sentences as part of the same story (Thieman & Brown, 1976), there are certain situations where inconsistencies will be accepted. Apparently, school arithmetic problems provide just such situations as the number of examples given by Holt (1964) would confirm. Consider the following example. Two fifth-graders were given the problem 256 + 327 and, together with the teacher, worked through each step and arrived at the correct answer of 583. Then, with this sum in clear view, the teacher wrote the next problem 256 + 328 on the board and pointed out that in both cases, they were adding something to 256; "instead of adding 327, we are going to add 328," hoping that the children would recognize that the answer would need to be one larger. No luck; the children laboriously worked the problem out from scratch. The teacher wrote a new problem and went through it step by step until the children were satisfied it was correct. Then, right beside it, he wrote *exactly the same problem.* The children again worked through the problem from scratch and came up with the wrong answer. On the board now, side by side, were two problems and their answers, 245 + 179 = 424 and 245 + 179 = 524. The children were quite satisfied with these solutions and sure both were correct, even though, on the basis of internal consistency alone, they must reject one solution.

   2. *Reality Testing.*   Holt makes a strong case that children do not expect mathematics to "make sense," and, therefore, it is not surprising that they often fail to employ another valuable checking device, reality testing, or an "error-noticing, nonsense-eliminating device." Indeed, several of Holt's fifth-graders were characterized as pathologically deficient in this regard. Holt (1964) describes one child as "emotionally as well as intellectually incapable of checking her work, of comparing her ideas against reality, or of making any kind of judgment about the value of her thoughts [p. 48]." That Holt's more striking examples come from elementary mathematics classes might not surprise the college teacher of elementary statistics faced with comparable symbol-shock symptoms in apparently intelligent adults. College students are by no means free of prejudice against reality testing; negative probabilities or variances are readily accepted as solutions if the student believes the formula was followed correctly!

If children do not realize that a subject, particularly mathematics, is supposed to make sense, checking answers on the basis of common sense must be ruled out. Consider the following fifth-grader:

> One boy, quite a good student, was working on the problem "If you have 6 jugs, and you want to put 2/3 of a pint of lemonade into each jug, how much lemonade will you need?" His answer was 18 pints. I [Holt] said "How much in each jug?" "Two-thirds of a pint." I said, "Is that more or less than a pint?" "Less." I said, "How many jugs are there?" "Six." I said "But that doesn't make any sense." He shrugged his shoulders and said, "Well that's the way the system worked out." (Holt, 1964, p. 18)

How does the general notion of reality testing apply to the realm of the problem? Although there are few examples of reality testing in the memory literature, this is not because the problem does not exist, but because it has not been examined. Yet, the general notion of checking a procedure against common sense criteria is as applicable to memory tasks as to any other form of problem solving. When applying a memorization strategy, are children capable of evaluating the appropriate nature of the routine they are using by asking such questions as: " Does it make sense to use, e.g., rehearsal?" "Does it pay off in terms of the type of recall needed?" "Is the amount of effort required reasonable?" Studies concerned with the child's awareness of memory routines, not as overlearned recipes for performing, but as valuable tools for thinking are badly needed.

3. *Blind-Rule Following.* The next set of examples are also taken from the literature dealing with mathematical problem solving in children. In all cases, the materials used are variants of those designed especially to provide a concrete means of checking solutions, operations, etc. Holt used cuisinaire materials; briefly, these consist of rods of 1 cm. wide and 1 cm. high that vary in length from 1 cm. to 10 cm. Each size is of a consistent color. All color-length correspondences are overlearned by first-grade children who later used the materials to aid them in mastering increasingly complex operations — or do they?

Consider Edward, one of Holt's fifth graders who has learned a rule for counting. Edward was given 15 10-cm. rods and 1 4-cm. rod and asked how many single units he would need to make that many. (The answer is 154.) First, he lined up the 10-cm. rods and put the 4-cm. rod on the end. Then, he began to count the rows, reciting 10, 20, 30, etc., until he reached 100, where he proceeded to touch the remaining six rods, reciting 200, 300, 400, 500, 600, 604 — with 604 as his solution. Asked to try again, he realized that something must be wrong, and the second time he proceeded correctly to 100 as before and then began reciting 101, 102, 103, 104, 105, 109 — with a solution of 109. Remember that all 15 10-cm. rods are exactly the same height and color and that Edward has been using them foryears. Intervention was tried and the material was split into two sections, the first containing 100 (the first 10 10-cm. rods), and the second containing 54 (the last 5 10-cm. rods and the 4-cm. rod). Now, Edward could answer correctly with no hesitation. The two sections were then pushed together in front of him and Edward was asked the original question. He proceeded through the original routine and again came up with 604. Edward is consistent at least.

Another training device was then introduced. Edward was given 100 (10 10-cm.) rods and asked how many there were, an overlearned task readily complied with. Then separate white units (singles) were added, one at a time, and Edward correctly counted 101, 102, 103, up to 109, as each unit was placed on top of the last. However, when the last unit was placed on top so that there were exactly 11 rows of 10 units, Edward replied 200. What was Edward's problem? He had learned to change the unit of counting when a turning point was reached, but not why or how to change. He had certainly not learned that the task was meant to make sense.

The origins of this blind-rule learning were easily seen in first graders beginning to use the rods. Each child had learned the name and color of the rods from one to ten and was beginning to use the rods for computation; they could count to 100 and deal with concepts such as tens and units, etc. Although they could perform such operations in set situations, Holt demonstrated that they did not understand the basic principles underlying the rods. He asked first graders "If we started at the edge of the desk, how far across would a row of 38 whites (ones) reach?" One child immediately took out three orange rods (tens) and a brown rod (eight) and lined them up. All the remaining children tried to line up 38 separate whites units, usually losing count several times in the process. This is a fine example of the arbitrary use of the labels for the child who, while perfectly capable of rote learning that the orange rod is a 10, does not grasp that it is in every way equivalent to 10 white units. "Six is just the name that the dark green rods happens to have, it has nothing to do with its size in relation to some other rod" (Holt, 1964, p. 131).

Resnick and Glaser (1976) also report a striking example of blind-rule following. Children from 5 to 6 years of age were taught to use blocks for finding the area of a rectangle. Then they were asked to find the area of a parallelogram. This is a version of Wertheimer's parallelogram problem, and the correct solution is to remove the area to the left of a perpendicular, dropped from the top angle to the base, and move it over to the right side of the figure, thus creating a rectangle. Resnick and Glaser found little evidence of such creative solutions. Of more interest to this section, they found quite dramatic examples of checking failures. Many children tried to apply the well-learned rule and attempted to superimpose the blocks onto the parallelogram, ignoring the absence of right angles. Thus, blocks were hanging over the edges. The children proceeded as if there were no difficulty at all (Resnick & Glaser, 1976).

Holt has argued that training children on rules or recipes for problem solutions, without at the same time making them aware of the rationale behind the rule, leads directly to blind problem-solving routines like Edward's. A case could be made that such an outcome could very well follow attempts to inculcate deliberate memorization strategies. It has been suggested (Brown, 1975) that there is a danger that facility with a strategy of rote learning might blind the child to possibilities of higher-level interactions with the to-be-remembered material. For example, if a child is trained to rote rehearse series of digits such as 4 9 2 6 1 8 or 9 1 7 3 4 2, he may also attempt to rehearse the series 2 3 4 5 6 7, failing to realize that rehearsal is not needed for such a meaningful set. The analogy here is to problem-solving tasks such as the Luchins' water jar problem (Luchins, 1942) where facility with a successful complex solution, applied over a series of problems, leads the subject to adopt the complex rule even when a far simpler solution could be used. Thus, subjects trained to rote rehearse may also be less likely to notice and use redundancies (Spitz, 1973) in digit sets (such as 425, 425) than subjects not pretrained in the rehearsal strategy.

We have some evidence of blind-rule following in a memory task, but it is indirect and coming from the less mature children in a study of recall readiness (Brown & Barclay, 1976). Educable retarded children were trained on a recall-readiness task similar to that introduced by Flavell et al. (1970). On each trial, the child was presented with a list of pictures (1½ times his span) and required to continue studying the items until he was sure he could remember all of them in order. One-third of the children were trained to rehearse cumulatively, one-third to anticipate the next item, and the remaineder served served as a control group, instructed merely to label an activity that did not require self-testing. The success and limitations of the training will be considered later. Of interest here is the behavior of the younger (MA 6) children. Training on a specific self-testing strategy was sufficient to lead to long-term improvement in their strategy production; children trained to rehearse continued to do so, but this did not lead to a concomitant improvement in their ability to monitor. Two weeks after training, the younger children were rehearsing or anticipating as trained, but this did not lead to perfect recall (or even near-perfect recall), the measure of adequate monitoring of a mnemonic activity. Our explanation for the outcome is that the children were following the "blind-rule" procedure. Told to rehearse, they rehearsed, but the reason why such an activity would help them meet the recall-readiness task demands was not apparent to them.

4. *Insight.* Insight, the opposite of blind-rule following, has traditionally been a major concern for psychologists interested in problem solving and intervention (Resnick & Glaser, 1976). Evidence of insightful solutions in young children's problem solving is rather rare and, awkward as it may be for educationalists, such solutions often occur when children have not been taught a rule. Holt's examples of fifth-grade arithmetic problem-solving situations are largely negative. There appeared to be only three compelling examples of insight among them, the first-grader who used the 10 and 8 rods to measure her desk and the following examples: Faced with the problem 2/4 + 3/5, one child immediately

said that the answer must be one or more. "You need two more fifths to make 1, and 2/4 is more than 2/5 so the answer is bigger than 1" (Holt, 1964, p. 114). Similarly, another child realized immediately that 1/2 and 1/3 = 3/4 was incorrect. "No, 1/3 isn't the same as 1/4. It took me (Holt) a second or two to see what she meant. Since 1/2 + 1/4 = 3/4, 1/2 + 1/3 cannot equal 3/4" (Holt, 1964, p. 113).

We know of only two experimental illustrations of intelligent use of a memory rule by children, but this is also an area where little attention has focused. In the Brown and Barclay (1976) recall-readiness task just described, the older children (MA 8) did show intelligent use of the trained strategy. Taught to anticipate or rehearse, they not only maintained the trained strategy, but their ability to judge their recall readiness also improved dramatically. (These data are presented in Fig. 2.2, which is discussed in the next section.) The older subjects in both the rehearsal and anticipation groups dramatically improved their performance — an improvement that was maintained for at least one year after training. This example provides some indirect evidence of intelligent rule use as the children were not explicitly instructed in how to use the strategy to ensure that recall readiness was achieved. Merely training in a task-appropriate, self-testing routine was sufficient. The decision to continue using that activity until the task demands had been met was entirely the child's responsibility.

A more direct example of intelligent strategy used has been provided by Butterfield and Belmont (1977), who were concerned primarily with changes in the employment of a strategy as a function of task difficulty. That is, they were concerned with the flexibility with which an initial choice of a strategy could be made and the efficiency with which individuals abandoned a strategy when it was no longer necessary and subsequently reinstated it when its use again became appropriate. The basic procedure consisted of presenting a number of different lists of items for recall and observing the amount of time required for selection of a stable rehearsal strategy. Then, without warning, one list is re-presented for a number of successive trials, at which time an individual no longer needs to work actively on the items. Finally, new lists are introduced unannounced, and the individual must again begin using his or her chosen strategy to deal with the information. Younger children, as compared with older children and adults, take longer to: (1) select a strategy initially; (2) abandon it when it is no longer necessary; and (3) reinstate it when its use is again required.

The Butterfield and Belmont studies (1977) provide nice examples of the increasing intelligence and flexibility that adults come to use when applying even a simple rote learning skill. As far as we know, there are few such experimental examples of intelligent strategy use in the literature; most of the existing examples are anecdotal accounts such as our report of college students' rapid abandonment of inappropriate strategies in a judgment of recency task (Brown, 1973a). What is needed in this area is systematic research concerned with when and where children will apply a strategy and whether this is influenced by training. In addition, we know of no examples where intelligent choice between two or more competing strategies has been examined, surely a more realistic analogue to real-life memorization situations.

Another neglected research area is the creative modification a subject might make applying a well-learned strategy to a new task. Although the difficulty in working with such problems is appreciated, we are surprised at the lack of research interest in such topics. One interesting avenue that could be profitable was suggested by Bransford et al. (1977). Obtaining protocols from expert memorizers might shed light on the operations they employ in order to learn. Such insights concerning efficient performance could then be used to guide instructions of the less advanced memorizer.

E. Training Studies

Although considerable ingenuity and effort has been expended in attempts to inculcate specific memory strategies in those who would not think to use them unaided, the notion of training metamemorial awareness is a new departure. With the exception of a study by Markman (1973), all major training attempts directed at the child's self-consciouness as a memorizer have been conducted in our laboratory and have been directed at an educable retarded population (IQ = 60–75). Anyone who has read the preceding sections will be aware by now that these children have a great deal of difficulty coping with even simple tests of metamemory. One explanation of their relative passivity in memorization tasks could be that this is the direct result of their lack of awareness concerning themselves as agent in the learning process. Thus, some of the main resons for initiating the series of training studies was to see whether: (1) metamemory could be improved in educable children; (2) any improvement would be durable and generalizable; and (3) any improvement would lead to a concomitant improvement in the general use of stragegies for remembering.

The general rationale for such training studies with slow-learning children follows from a controversy concerning the utility of training *specific* mnemonics in order to effect any worthwhile or lasting improvement in memorization skills (Brown, 1974; Butterfield, Wambold, & Belmont, 1973). The problem lies in the dubious success so far achieved by attempts to train common memory skills. The general picture to emerge is that educable mentally retarded children readily respond to appropriate training and evidence a variety of trained mnemonic skills accompanied by a satisfying improvement in recall performance (Belmont & Butterfield, 1971; Borkowski & Wanschura, 1974; Brown, Campione, Bray, & Wilcox, 1973). Furthermore, it appears that following well-designed and extensive training, maintenance of the effects of this experience can be detected over a reasonable time period (Brown, Campione, & Murphy, 1974). Unfortunately, evidence for generalization to new situations is hard to find (Brown, 1974; Campione & Brown, 1974, 1977). The problem of generalization is not a new one, particularly in the context of training retarded individuals. Both American and Soviet psychologists have suggested that one of the main difficulties in training mildly retarded children is that they tend to acquire information that is "welded" to the form in which it was acquired (Shif, 1969). A spate of recent studies has provided impressive experimental documentation concerning this problem of generalization following training (Brown & Campione, in press; Campione & Brown, 1977).

The lack of convincing evidence of broad generalization of a trained mnemonic strategy indicates a poor prognosis for obtaining educational benefits from such exercises and has led some investigators (Brown, 1974; Butterfield et al., 1973; Butterfield & Belmont, 1977) to advance the view that training efforts should be directed at general determinants of performance rather than specific skills or strategies. Rather than training only one domain-specific heuristic, they suggest that it would be more profitable to direct training attempts at the development of knowledge concerning strategies in general. If we are interested in effecting improvement in the child's general performance on a variety of similar tasks, then we must consider both the specific gains from training (strategy use) and the general benefits (improved knowledge concerning memory tasks).

To examine this point, we have conducted a series of training studies concerned with metamemorial knowledge in retarded children. As is the case with any training study, whether directed at specific strategies or knowledge concerning memory in general, the effectiveness of training must be considered against two criteria which we have called maintenance and generalization (Brown, 1974; Campione & Brown, 1977). As a first index of successful training, it is obviously desirable to show that what has been trained can be detected after a reasonable time period has elapsed. This is particularly necessary because there is considerable evidence that the developmentally young tend to abandon a trained behavior when no longer specifically instructed to continue it (Brown, 1974; Flavell, 1970). The second and more important index of successful training is that of generalization to new situations; for without evidence of breadth of transfer, the practical utility of any training program must be called into question (Brown, 1974; Brown & Campione, in press; Brown & DeLoache, in press).

1. *Maintenance.*

(a) *Recall readiness.* In the initial training study conducted in our laboratory (Brown & Barclay, 1976), recall-readiness estimations were examined. The main results of this training procedure were described in the preceding section (III.D.3). In brief, educable children were trained in one of two self-testing strategies, rehearsal or anticipation, or were assigned to a control group instructed to label the items, a procedure that does not require self-testing. Following training, four posttests were given – a prompted posttest (one day after training) on which individuals were instructed to continue the trained strategy and three unprompted posttests given one day, approximately two weeks, and approximately one year later. The main results are shown in Fig. 2.2, which gives the percentage of correct recall. As can be seen, both the younger and older children in the anticipation and rehearsal groups performed significantly better on the prompted posttest (posttest 1) than on the pretest. Additionally, in the anticipation and rehearsal groups, 13 of 18 younger subjects recalled perfectly on at least one trial, compared with 0 of 18 on the pretest; the corresponding figures for the older subjects are 24 of 26 on posttest 1, compared with 2 of 26 on the pretest. Thus, training the useful self-testing strategies resulted in both enhanced performance (percent recall data) and improved monitoring (data on number of perfect recalls). Note that the labeling group (control) did not show this improvement.

The MA 6 and MA 8 groups differed considerably on the last three (unprompted) posttests. For the younger group, performance on posttests 2, 3, and 4 was not significantly different from the pretraining level, whereas for the older children in the anticipation and rehearsal groups, performance on all posttests differed significantly from the pretraining level. Thus, as in previous studies concerned with direct training of a strategy, training facilitated performance, with the effect being somewhat durable for the older children, but transitory for the younger ones.[1]

The younger child's dependency on continual prompting was particularly well illustrated on the one-year follow-up test, which consisted of 4 days of testing. On the 2 initial days, the children were given unprompted posttests identical to the previous unprompted tests. On the third day, the experimenter reverted to the prompting procedure, demonstrating and reminding the children of their trained strategies and urging their continued use. The fourth day of the one-year follow-up was a further unprompted posttest. These data are included in Table 2.14. Note that both the younger and older children benefited from the prompting, although the effect is less dramatic for the older children who were performing quite adequately without the prompts. Of main interest is the failure of the younger children to maintain their enhanced performance on the final nonprompted test. Without continual prompting, the younger children show little evidence of the effects of intensive training.

(b) *Study-time apportionment.* In our next training study, we considered strategic study-time apportionment (Brown & Campione, 1977). The pretest data from this study has been discussed previously (Section III.C.3). During pretesting, on each trial but the first of a multi-trial, free-recall procedure, educable retarded subjects were allowed to select half (6/12) of the to-be-remembered

---

[1]Preliminary data suggest that successful maintenance of recall readiness was followed by generalization to a prose learning situation. This study is still underway (Brown & Campione, in press).

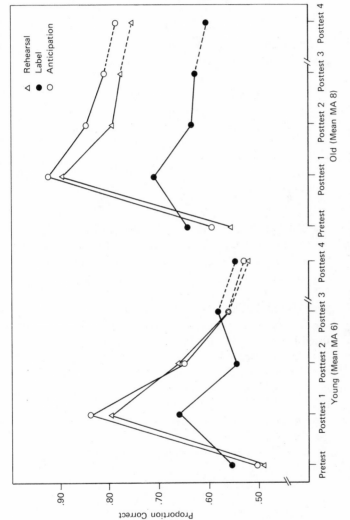

FIG. 2.2. Proportion of correct recall as a function of mental age, training condition, and test phase. (Adapted from "The Effects of Training Specific Mnemonics on the Metamnemonic Efficiency of Retarded Children" by A. L. Brown and C. R. Barclay, *Child Development*, 1976, *47*, 71–80. Copyright 1976 by the Society for Research in Child Development. Reprinted by permission.)

113

TABLE 2.14
Proportion Correct on Recall-Readiness Posttests

			Posttests						
			Original Data			One Year Follow Up			
Group	Condition	N[a]	No Prompt	No Prompt	No Prompt	No Prompt	No Prompt	Prompt	No Prompt
	Anticipation	8	.82	.62	.52	.50	.48	.81	.57
MA 6	Rehearsal	7	.77	.61	.49	.46	.50	.90	.63
	Label	6	.60	.56	.55	.46	.58	.78	.54
	Anticipation	12	.92	.84	.81	.80	.72	.95	.85
MA 8	Rehearsal	12	.89	.82	.81	.74	.73	.84	.83
	Label	11	.74	.65	.63	.60	.61	.67	.63

[a]Included are data from those children who were available for all phases of the experiment.

items to see if they would strategically select missed items for extra study. Following pretesting, subjects were divided into three groups for training where the experimenter selected study items for the children. For the first group of children (standard strategy), the experimenter's selection followed the strategy diagnosed as mature (Masur et al., 1973); that is, she returned to the child those items he had missed on his prior free-recall attempt. Another type of systematic selection was adopted for the second group. Here, the experimenter returned to the subject the items he had recalled plus one new item (creeping strategy). The rationale behind this was that if immature subjects cannot benefit from additional study time on missed items because they fail to keep previously recalled items alive, then the utility of the standard strategy for them is dubious. The creeping strategy would enable them to add just one extra item per trial, while permitting them to continue to review the previously recalled items. Thus, they would gradually *creep* up to a better level of performance. The third group of subjects received randomly selected items for review on each study trial. Following training, the children received posttests where they were again free, as on the pretest, to select whichever items they wished for study, with the restriction that they must not choose more than six.

Both the mean proportion correct and the standardized selection scores (the higher the score, the greater the tendency to select previously unrecalled items for further study) were considered on the pre- and posttests (for details, see Brown & Campione, 1977). The mean proportion correct recall on the pre- and posttests are presented in Fig. 2.3. There appears to be no change between pre- and posttests as a function of any training condition for the younger subjects. For older subjects, the proportion recalled by subjects forced to study missed items during training (standard procedure) rises dramatically on the posttest. The other two conditions do not seem to change between the pre- and posttests.

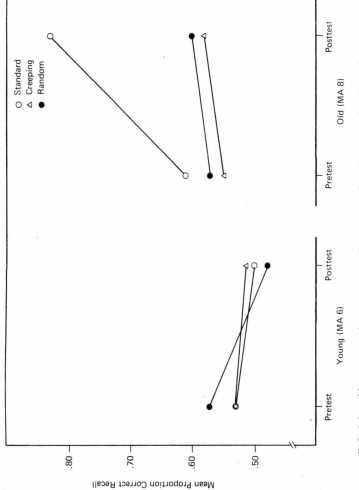

FIG. 2.3. Mean proportion correct recall on pre- and posttests as a function of age and training condition. (Adapted from "Training Strategic Study Time Apportionment in Educable Retarded Children" by A. L. Brown and J. C. Campione, *Intelligence*, 1977, *1*, 94–107. Copyright 1977 by Ablex Publishing Corporation. Reprinted by permission.)

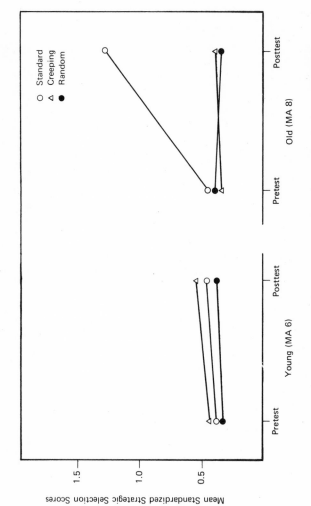

FIG. 2.4. Mean standardized strategic selection scores on pre- and posttests as a function of age and training condition. (Adapted from "Training Strategic Study Time Apportionment in Educable Retarded Children" by A. L. Brown and J. C. Campione, *Intelligence*, 1977, *1*, 94–105. Copyright 1977 by Ablex Publishing Corporation. Reprinted by permission.)

Thus, the only evidence for improvement on the posttest occurred in the older children who were forced to study missed items in training. The mean standardized selection scores are presented in Fig. 2.4, together with the comparable scores from the pretest. The same pattern appears here as was seen for the recall scores. Only the older children from the standard condition show any change between the pre- and posttests.

Was this failure to find a pretest-posttest difference in all but one group a failure of training or transfer? To answer this question, we must consider the training data that are presented in Table 2.15. Only recall data are available in training because the experimeter selected these items for study. Younger subjects improved reliably across trials and trial blocks in the creeping condition and showed very little improvement in the other two conditions. Older subjects improved reliably in the standard condition, across both trials and trial blocks, and showed no improvement in the random condition. Note, however, that there is some improvement across trials, although not across trial blocks, for older subjects in the creeping condition. Evidence for improvement was found then in both younger and older children in the training phase, and, therefore, the lack of a posttest improvement in the younger children can be attributed to a transfer failure.

A summary of the training results would be that younger children benefit from an imposed creeping strategy, but not from an imposed standard (Masur

TABLE 2.15
Mean Proportion Recalled in Training as a Function
of Age and Training Condition

Subjects	Young (MA 6)		Old (MA 8)			
Trial Blocks[a]	1	2	1	2		
Training Condition						
Creeping	.36	.46	.46	.44		
Standard	.34	.33	.50	.59		
Random	.29	.28	.41	.42		
	Young (MA 6)			Old (MA 8)		
Trials[b]	1	2	3	1	2	3
Training Condition						
Creeping	.34	.40	.48	.41	.43	.51
Standard	.32	.33	.35	.46	.55	.62
Random	.27	.28	.31	.41	.40	.43

Note. Adapted from "Training Strategic Study Time Apportionment in Educable Retarded Children" by A. L. Brown and J. C. Campione, Intelligence, 1977, 1, 94-107. Copyright 1977 by Ablex Publishing Corporation. Reprinted by permission.

[a] The children received four lists a day. These were collapsed into two trial blocks.
[b] For each list the subject attempted four recalls; the last three, which are the trials followed item selection.

et al., 1973) strategy. Older children benefit most from an imposed standard strategy and little from the creeping strategy or the random selection. This pattern of results appears to confirm that strategies, to be successful, must be compatible with the cognitive competency of the child. Forcing children to study according to an adult strategy (standard) only helps older children who can meet (to some extent) the demand characteristic of that strategy.

(c) *Span estimation.*   At this point, we decided that, at least for very immature subjects, a good research strategy would be to concentrate on direct training of metamnemonic behavior rather than the indirect approach adopted by Brown and Barclay (1976) and Brown and Campione (1977). Another change of focus was a shift away from monitoring of strategy utilization, the subject of both the Brown and Barclay and the Butterfield and Belmont studies. Concurrently applying a task-relevant mnemonic and monitoring its success or failure appears to involve a complex coordination of introspection and overt behavior, a coordination that is late developing in both normal and retarded populations. In light of our prior failures, we decided to consider a simpler form of metamemorial awareness, the ability to estimate one's own span, which seems to underlie any subsequent attempts to introduce and control specific strategies (Brown et al., 1977). If children are not aware of the extent of their memory limitations, they can scarcely be expected to introduce steps to remedy their shortcomings.

The span-estimation task was also chosen because it has been the subject of prior training attempts, with somewhat contradictory results. Whereas Yussen and Levy (1975) found preschool children remarkably impervious to feedback from a practice trial revealing their recall inadequacies, Markman (1973) found that 62% of kindergarten children responded to 10 explicit training trials. Both age and extent of explicit training could be responsible for these differences. As both explicit and extended training is usually needed to effect an improvement in retardates' use of specific memory skills (Butterfield & Belmont, 1977; Campione & Brown, 1977; Rohwer, 1973), we decided to provide extensive explicit training on the metamemory task. In short, we hoped to provide an optimal training experience in order to assess whether such training could lead to long-term improvement of younger children's knowledge concerning their own memory limitations.

Two groups of naive educable children (MA 6 and 8) were shown arrays of 10 pictures (exposed simultaneously) and asked to predict how many they would be able to recall. [Throughout the study, half the pictures were categorized and half were uncategorized. This variable was included so that students would not learn that they should say a particular number (e.g., 6) when asked to predict the number they would recall. An appropriate response would indicate a higher number for an organized list and this was found.] The children's predictions were then compared with their (subsequently determined) actual recall. Individuals whose estimates were within two items (±2) of their actual recall were termed realistic estimators; those whose guesses were more than two items in error were termed unrealistic estimators. Only 31% of the older children and 21% of the younger ones could be classes as realistic, with the remainder overestimating their performance levels (most predicted they could recall all 10 pictures).

All children were then given a series of 10 training trials on which they were required to estimate their performance and then to recall. For half the participants at each MA level, explicit feedback was provided in which children were reminded of their prediction and shown visually and orally the number of items they had actually recalled. This feedback followed each estimation-recall series. The remaining children predicted and recalled, but no explicit feedback was provided. After training was completed, three posttests were given – the first, 1 day after training, the second, 2 weeks after training, and the third, approximately 1 year after the original posttests.

The data of major interest are shown in Figs. 2.5 and 2.6. In Fig. 2.5, the proportion of realistic estimators are shown, separately for the two MA levels on the pretest and on each of the subsequent posttests. In general, the younger children showed some improvement on the first posttest (one day after training) but were back to baseline levels following 2 weeks. For the older children, the initial improvement was more dramatic and was better maintained over time. Even 1 year later, the proportion of realistic estimators (56%) was considerably larger than it was prior to training 31%).

In Fig. 2.6, the data of only the originally unrealistic estimators are considered; further, the results are broken down in terms of both MA level and the feedback variable. Students classes as realistic initially remained so throughout the experiment. Luckily, our training did not cause them to regress. Considering the first posttest of the originally unrealistic children, 65% of the older individuals became realistic independent of the feedback condition. Of the younger trainees, 62% of those given feedback became realistic, whereas only 9% of those not given feedback improved to the point of being realistic. Looking at the data from posttest 2, the older individuals remained unchanged; 60% were still realistic, and there was no effect of the feedback variable. However, for the younger children, only 18% of those given feedback remained realistic, and no children in the no-feedback group could be classed as realistic. Thus, considering only the first two posttests for the older children, training with or without explicit feedback was sufficient to bring about realistic estimation and the effect was durable. The pattern obtained with the younger students contrasted sharply; there was significant improvement on the first posttest only when explicit feedback was provided during training; even in this case, the effects were not lasting as the proportion of realistic estimators dropped from 62% on posttest 1 to 18% on posttest 2. The effect of providing explicit feedback for the older children was

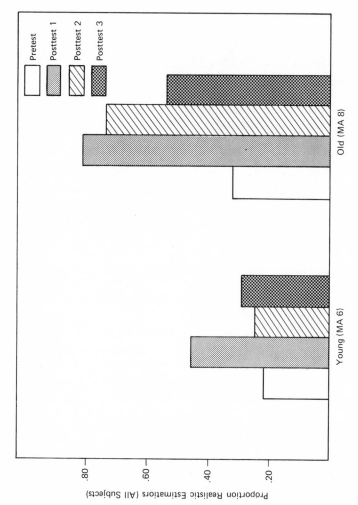

FIG. 2.5. The proportion of realistic estimators as a function of mental age and test phase. (Adapted from "Maintenance and Generalization of Trained Metamnemonic Awareness in Educable Retarded Children" by A. L. Brown, J. C. Campione, and M. D. Murphy, *Journal of Experimental Child Psychology*, 1977, *24*, 191–211. Copyright 1977 by Academic Press, Inc. Reprinted by permission.)

120

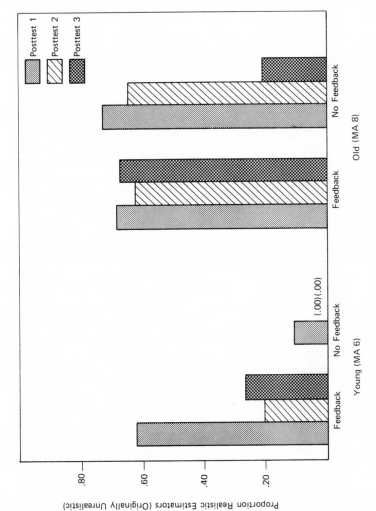

FIG. 2.6. The proportion of realistic estimators (considering only those who were orignally unrealistic) as a function of mental age, feedback condition, and test phase. (Adapted from "Maintenance and Generalization of Trained Metamnemonic Awareness in Educable Retarded Children" by A. L. Brown, J. C. Campione, and M. D. Murphy, *Journal of Experimental Child Psychology*, 1977, *24*, 191–211. Copyright 1977 by Academic Press, Inc. Reprinted by permission.)

noticed only on the final posttest. The proportion of realistic estimators remained unchanged in the feedback condition, whereas for those not given feedback during training, only 20% remained realistic approximately one year after training.

(d) *Summary.*   The results of these initial experiments indicate that mildly retarded children have problems estimating their own performance, both prior to and during the time they are performing on a task. It also seems clear that, for the younger children, information about their performance needs to be explicit before it will have any effect and continual prompting may be necessary to maintain performance. Also, in all three experiments, a clear developmental trend was found regarding the durability of training effects. Whereas training had a relatively durable effect with the older children, the effects with the younger ones were extremely short-lived.

2. *Generalization.*   The limited success of our attempts to find maintenance of training had the effect of dampening our enthusiasm for tests of generalization. However, as the older children in all studies did show adequate maintenance, we did include specific tests of generalization in the Brown et al. (1977) study, and we are currently looking at recall-readiness generalization in the older children (Brown & Campione, in press). In addition to tests of specific skill generalization, we have also considered a more general transfer phenomenon; that is, are there any differences between the children who have participated in several memory and metamemory training studies and comparable naive populations, either in terms of general improvement on each new task or on a questionnaire investigation of general metamnemonic awareness?

Before continuing to describe our general and specific transfer data, we should make clear what our criteria for generalization are. Many studies that have claimed generalization we would regard as measuring maintenance, for they involved only the use of a new stimulus list on the generalization task. We use new stimuli throughout our studies and assume that continuing the trained activity on new lists to be a test of maintenance. Generalization tests involve not only new stimuli but some other change as well, however minimal that change might be. We will return to the question of adequate criteria for generalization later (Section IV.F).

(a) *Specific generalization.*   The only completed study in which we included specific tests of generalization of training was the span-estimation training study of Brown et al. (1977). For pre-, post-, and training tests, a modified version of the span-estimation task was used. That is, on each trial, the child was confronted with a large card containing 10 small pictures and then was asked to estimate how many he or she would recall. On the pre- and posttests, the seriated task used by Flavell et al. (1970) was also included. Here, the items were exposed incrementally (1, then 2, then 3, up to 10), and on each exposure, the child must indicate if he or she can recall a list length that large. The proportion of realistic estimators on the seriated sets was low for both groups and varied little as a function of time of test (.18, .18, .20, .15 for older subjects on the pretest and three posttests, compared with .03, .07, .03, .05 for younger children). Even though there was an improvement, particularly among the older children as a result of training on the 10-item task, this improvement did not generalize to the very similar seriated test.

An additional generalization test was given on the day following the second posttest. The subjects were shown 20 10-item cards each containing the numbers 1 to 10. Ten of the cards contained the numbers in numerical order starting with a number other than 1; the remaining cards contained the numbers in a randomized order. The subjects went through the 20 cards and indicated how many they would be able to recall on each. Next, actual recall was assessed on both types of materials. Finally, the cards were paired, one random and one organized, and the subjects were asked which set would be easier to recall and why. Thus, two sets of cards were used, organized and disorganized. Predicting 10 items on an organized list (e.g., the numbers in serial order) would be a realistic estimate, whereas predicitng this way would be unrealistic for the random lists. For this reason, we considered the two list types separately. The data from random lists only are presented in Table 2.16. Consider first the originally unrealistic subjects. Apparently, there is no evidence of generalization following training on the highly similar 10-item picture task. The proportion of realistic subjects is low for both young and old subjects, and the number of children guessing 10 is

TABLE 2.16
Proportion of Realistic Judgments on Number Generalization Test

	Originally Realistic		Originally Unrealistic			
			No Feedback		Feedback	
	Young (MA 6)	Old (MA 8)	Young (MA 6)	Old (MA 8)	Young (MA 6)	Old (MA 8)
N	6	12	11	14	12	12
Mean difference score	2.83[a]	1.08	5.09	3.64	5.00	4.42
Proportion realistic	.67	.75	.09	.28	.08	.25
Proportion 10 guessers	.17	.17	.73	.43	.67	.50

Note. From "Maintenance and Generalization of Trained Metamnemonic Awareness in Educable Retarded Children by A. L. Brown, J. C. Campione, and M. D. Murphy, *Journal of Experimental Child Psychology*, 1977, *24*, 191-211. Copyright 1977 by Academic Press, Inc. Reprinted by permission.

[a]This figure is misleading. There are only six subjects in this cell, four realistic and two unrealistic. The mean difference score for the four realistic subjects was 1.75. Both the remaining subjects overestimated their span by 5.

TABLE 2.17

Easier to Recall Judgments on the Number Generalization Test[a]

	Originally Realistic		Trained Realistic		Unrealistic	
	Young (MA 6)	Old (MA 8)	Young (MA 6)	Old (MA 8)	Young (MA 6)	Old (MA 8)
Organized Easier	.66	.75	.14	.26	.19	.12
Unorganized Easier	.00	.00	.14	.11	.13	.12
Inconsistent	.33	.25	.71	.63	.67	.75

Note. From "Maintenance and Generalization of Trained Metamnemonic Awareness in Educable Retarded Children by A. L. Brown, J. C. Campione, and M. D. Murphy, *Journal of Experimental Child Psychology,* 1977, *24,* 191-211. Copyright 1977 by Academic Press. Inc. Reprinted by permission.

[a]Entries are the proportion of subjects falling into each category.

very high. Consider next the originally realistic subjects (collapsed across feedback conditions). Here, the picture is quite different. The mean difference scores (predicted vs. actual) for both young and old subjects fall within the realistic range (±2). Approximately two-thirds of the originally realistic subjects are realistic on the number generalization tests, and the number of 10 guessers is low.

Turning to predictions on the organized lists, a similar pattern emerges. The proportion of subjects who accurately predict they will recall 9 or 10 items (e.g., appreciate the organization of the lists) is .67 and .58 for the young and old originally realistic subjects. No originally unrealistic young child does this, and only .26 of the older children predict 9 or 10 items.

Finally, the children were given 10 forced-choice trials, in which an organized card was paired with a random card, and asked which would be easier to recall. The number of subjects indicating that organized sets of numbers would be easier to recall than random sets (i.e., predicted organized > randomized on 8/19 trials) are included in Table 2.17. Again, approximately two-thirds of the originally realistic subjects predict that the organized cards will be easier to recall whereas the trained realistic do not seem to differ from the unrealistic subjects.

Thus, our one systematic attempt (completed so far) to find generalization of specific training was less than encouraging for there was little evidence of generalization as a function of training. Those subjects originally realistic on the training task did show transfer to all the generalization tasks, which suggests that the tasks themselves were adequate tests of transfer for efficient subjects; however, the trained realistic subjects were not so flexible. It should be noted that the generalization tasks were highly similar to the training task; in all, the basic requirement was to estimate one's own span for a 10-item list. The seriated method included the same type of stimuli, but the task format changed slightly. In the number estimation problem, the task format (10 items) was preserved, but the stimulus type changed. Both are very minor changes and both have been suggested as excellent first steps to provide an optimal situation for generalization (Brown, 1974; Campione & Brown, 1974). Yet, none was found even in the older subjects. Maybe the dismal failure of this training program lies in the fact that training took place on one task only and the information gained was truly "welded" to that specific task (Shif, 1969). If this is true, then the next step must be to provide training in a variety of similar tasks, all requiring the same strategy, and then to look for generalization to new tasks that fall within the same class as the training tasks. A second reason for failure to find generalization is that no training or explicit mention of generalization was given to the child (see Section IV.F). In any event, considerable time and effort will be needed in the search for the elusive evidence of generalization of cognitive training in retarded children.

(b) *General transfer.* Our initial attempt to inculcate generalization of training was not encouraging. Our other indices that educable children do not show generalization very readily stem from our comparison of experienced and naive subjects. First, we have never *found* reliable differences between experienced and naive subjects entering a new experiment (Brown & Barclay, 1976; Brown & Campione, 1977; Brown et al., 1977; Brown & Lawton, 1977). Whatever the effects of training, they certainly are not sufficiently robust to contaminate our suject population for further studies — nor to educate them!

In an attempt to examine generalization systematically, we used the Kreutzer et al. (1975) questionnaire of general metamnemonic awareness. This was administered to four groups of children all from the same school district: MA 8 naive (*N* = 28), MA 8 experienced (*N* = 30), MA 6 naive (*N* = 21), and MA 6 experienced (*N* = 40). The experienced children had taken part in at least two metamemory training studies and, in some cases, other problem-solving and memory experiments. The naive children had never served as experimental subjects to our knowledge. The idea was to see if experienced subjects exhibited greater general awareness than did the naive children on the wide-ranging questionnaire items.

Some of these data have already been presented (Tables 2.2, 2.3, 2.4, 2.9, 2.12, and 2.13), and the observant reader will have noted the dramatic lack of an effect due to experience. No consistent patterns emerged. Experienced subjects did not show more awareness than naive children even on those subtests that were relevant to specific training they had received (i.e., children trained to rehearse did not indicate that rehearsal would be a reasonable activity to employ or would result in better performance). There was some slight evidence that experienced children were more able to give adequate explanations of their responses, but they also produced more explanations and this was thought to be the result of their greater familiarity and ease in talking to the experimenter who conducted all prior studies with the population. The only reliable difference to emerge in the entire study occurred on the initial item where the children were asked whether they were good at remembering; many more of the experienced subjects believed that they were not (MA 6, niave = .24, experienced = .46; MA 8, naive = .46, experienced = .64). Thus, the only tangible effect of two years of training was to alert the children to their own memory deficiencies, but not to possible methods of overcoming them, a less ·positive outcome than we would have wished.

IV.   METAMEMORY:
NEW THOUGHTS AND OLD PROBLEMS

When the original studies of metamemory in children first appeared, the general response was one of excitement; here was surely a more intelligent way of studying memory development! The appearance of such studies reflected an apparent shift of emphasis away from a concentration on the child's rote-learning skills toward a consideration of the child as an active agent in knowing — furthermore, an active agent influenced by a variety of hitherto unconsidered forces. The development of memorization skills and knowledge concerning memory began to be considered, not as separate phenomena, but as integral parts of the cognitive development of the child seen in a cultural context. Although we would argue that this shift in emphasis was an exciting and fruitful development, we have some hesitations concerning the direction the field appears to be taking. Now that the study of metamemory development is over five years old, it seems reasonable to stress these reservations and consider problems that seem common to the area. We would like to point out that many of the criticisms apply to our own work at least as much, if not more, than to any other research.

A.   Beyond Demonstration Studies

The history of developmental research into aspects of memory is relatively short, and such endeavors did not become part of the mainstream of research with children until the 1960s. During this decade and on into the 1970s, we witnessed an upsurge of interest centered around the young child's ability to use active strategies of learning. The majority of these studies concerned rote-learning skills, particularly those of rehearsal and categorization, which were used to ensure reproductive recall of isolated lists of materials (Brown, 1975). Interest in this topic resulted in literally hundreds of studies showing that the developmentally young: (1) were deficient in the use of such skills; (2) could readily be trained to use strategies; and (3) tended to abandon the trained skills unless explicitly prompted to continue.

In the late 1960s and early 1970s, the first batch of metamemory studies appeared. These also focused primarily on the child's knowledge concerning basic rote-learning skills — in fact, the same two: categorization and rehearsal. Here, too, history is beginning to repeat itself, for we are seeing an increasing number of demonstration studies showing that the same population that was deficient in the use of basic mnemonics is also less than well infomed concerning the utility of such strategies. We anticipate, pessimistically, a similar spate of spin-off demonstration studies over the next few years aimed at making this point crystal clear. We have contributed to this proliferation in the past and will probably continue to do so in the future.

Although demonstration studies add to our growing knowledge of the memory deficiencies of immature thinkers, and the initial studies in this area must be regarded as extremely important contributions to that knowledge, the value of a proliferation of such demonstrations must be doubted. Do we really need many more studies showing that young children do not often think about thinking, remember much about remembering, or have not learned much about learning? What is needed is the development of a theory that would enable us to direct empirical research intelligently, to confine our demonstration studies to areas where they are still needed, and advance forward, rather than sideways, in our attempt to understand the development of thinking. We realize that the development of such a theory is not something that can be accomplished overnight. Developmental theories, in general, suffer from several characteristic faults: for example, they are so general that there is no means of refuting them or so specific that their range of generality is limited; they concentrate on developmental issues to the virtual exclusion of the processes that are the subject of the development, or they concentrate on process and ignore the thorny problem of development. The call for theory is not a minor one.

On a more practical plane, isolated demonstration studies can be discouraged in favor of more in-depth and detailed analyses of the particular paradigms employed. Again, we would not like to encourage a spate of research on paradigms; the literature is too full of examples of questions being lost in favor of detailed analyses of the tasks employed. However, a middle ground does seem to be needed. For example, there are only two metamemory paradigms that have been investigated more than once, recall-readiness and span-estimation, two of the initial tasks introduced by Flavell et al. (1970). Both were found to have interesting procedural flaws leading to an overestimation of the child's metacognitive skills. Increasing the list length beyond span drastically limits performance on the recall-readiness task (Brown & Barclay, 1976; Markman, 1973). On the span-estimation task, the procedure of stopping at the child's first indication that his capacity was overreached may also have produced an overoptimistic picture of metamemory in young children (Brown et al., 1977). Uncritical acceptance of an isolated demonstration study, without a firm understanding of the task demands, can be a dangerous pastime.

B. Metamemory or Meta Rote Learning?

Not only have studies in metamemory been largely restricted to isolated demonstration studies, but they have concentrated almost exclusively on the child's knowledge and control of a few simple rote-learning skills. A notable exception to this statement must be Flavell's interest in realistic search behavior, both internal and external (Drozdal & Flavell, 1975; Flavell, 1976b). It is currently fashionable to deplore the undue concentration on skills of rote learning for reproductive recall, particularly of meaningless, isolated lists of materials (Brown, 1975; Jenkins, 1973), but this criticism is rarely raised in conjunction with the metamemory literature. Yet, a child's knowledge of his ability to rote learn laboratory materials is not the only form of metamemory. Indeed, one could argue that the utility of such knowledge would have a limited range of applicability (Brown, 1975, 1977b). For much of what we must learn requires gist recall of connected discourse, where common mnemonic techniques used to ensure rote recall of word lists may no longer serve a useful function.

If demonstration studies of metamemory are to proliferate, they may concentrate more fruitfully on areas where we lack even basic information. For example, examinations are needed of the child's knowledge of his ability to retain the essential ideas of a written or spoken communication, to understand instructions, to distinguish between situations where recall must be reproductive or reconstructive and between situations where deliberate memorization is needed or not needed, or on any of a host of other intelligent activities that are involved in remembering (see Section IV.F and V.D.).

One reason why we have limited information concerning such metamemory in children, or adults for that matter, is because we know little about the way mature thinkers solve such problems. Knowing a fair amount about rehearsal and taxonomic organization, we can safely ask does the child know too. Knowing little or nothing about more complex memorization skills, it is hard to define what the child should know. Collins et al. (1975) have provided glimpses of the rich repertoire of cognitive pyrotechnics graduate students can bring to their Socratic dialogue game. What is needed is a similar set of protocols from coherent adults and bright children faced with a variety of memory situations (Brown, 1977b). A good starting point would be study skills, for every student is required to attempt them, every student must be aware of the strengths and limitations of certain activities and the end goal (Brown & Smiley, 1977a). Knowing more about such awareness in adults, we may be in a better position to assess what it is that the less mature learner does not know, needs to know, and possibly could be trained to know.

C. Developmental Trends

The restriction of attention to the child's knowledge concerning (1) basic rote-learning strategies, (2) the distinctions between memorization and perceiving, and (3) his less-than-perfect capacity for rote remembering has led to the impression that metamemorial development is rapid and functionally complete by the third grade. This is not to say that anyone believes that development is complete by this time, and it is encouraging that there is a consistency in the age at which children acquire knowledge of the particular subset of skills that have been studied. In the study using the Kreutzer et al. (1975) questionnaire, there is impressive evidence of a ceiling in performance at around third grade for the majority of problems set. In addition, most of the empirical studies indicated that third grade or before is the point at which awareness is attained by the majority of children. Thus, both recall readiness and span estimation improve little after second grade (Flavell et al., 1970; but note objections cited earlier). On the study-time apportionment task, there is improvement between first and third grade, but third graders behave very much like college students (Masur et al., 1973). Moynahan (1973) found little difference between third and fifth graders in predicting task difficulty for categorized and uncategorized lists. Indeed, if one were to exclude the youngest group in many of the existing metamemory studies (e.g., the kindergarten or first-grade sample), one would be left with no reliable developmental differences! The pattern seems fairly consistent across tasks; by third grade, children know a fair amount about rote memorization of lists.

When a task is more complex, however, as in judging the difficulty of prose passages or the importance of various aspects of texts (Brown & Smiley, 1977a, 1977b), a much later age would be suggested for efficiency. Throughout the review of the literature, we have attempted to illustrate the importance of the effects of task difficulty. Whether or not children will be judged aware or unaware or will be attributed with metacognitive insights depends on the level of difficulty of the task and the match between the task demands and the child's existing cognitive skills (Brown, 1975; Brown & DeLoache, in press). A child who knows a great deal about organization, when the basis of that organization is taxonomic categorization, may know little or nothing concerning organizational principles underlying text materials.

Two other points concerning developmental trends will be treated more fully later and will be mentioned only briefly here. First, Kreutzer et al. (1975) raised an important issue when they suggested that the knowledge middle-school children may have about certain facets of memorization may have little to do with how they will perform on such tasks. For example, Danner (1974) pointed out that knowledge concerning important organizational features of texts considerably precedes the ability to select suitable cues for retrieval purposes. Similarly, knowing that an active strategy will aid recall does not necessarily mean that a child will elect to use that strategy himself (Brown et al., work in progress). Later development may be characterized by an increasing coordination between what one *knows* about memory and what one does about memorizing. We will return to this in the section concerned with predictions and performance.

Second, research to date on the development of metamemory has been characterized by an emphasis on the early signs of cognitive self-knowledge and the emergence of primitive precursors of metamemory. This is reflected in the push to find evidence of metacognition at as young an age as possible, and, in good hands, this has resulted in some exciting and ingenious work (Wellman, Ritter, & Flavell, 1975; Wellman, in press). Such work is encouraged and will continue to be encouraged by the pervasive influence of "anti-structuralism" (Belmont & Butterfield, 1977) in American developmental psychology. In an effort to prove contrary to (a misinterpretation of) Piaget that preschool children can perform rationally and, contrary to (a misinterpretation of) mediational learning theories that preschool children can think, demonstrating evidence of such intelligence in preschool children has become an end in itself. Thus, the "game" for many neo-Piagetians is to show evidence of concrete operations at a younger and younger age. However, there is less emphasis on attempts to define the limits of this early awareness by employing stringent criteria of mature comprehension. The child's response(s) are taken at face value as indicative of intelligent understanding of he concept studied before a realistic appraisal is made of the robust nature of that understanding (Brown, 1976a). The same approach dominates the emergent metamemory literature and, therefore, more emphasis on the "testing of the upper limits approach" should be made, as the "how young can they do it" school is fairly represented.

D. Predictions and Performance

One of the most persuasive arguments in favor of studying metamemory develop-
ment is that there must be a close tie between what one knows concerning memory and how one goes about memorizing. If it can be shown that the child does not appreciate the utility of rehearsing a telephone number, the fact that he does not choose to rehearse would not be surprising. Similarly, if the child could be made aware of the importance of strategic intervention, then he would sup-posedly choose to behave strategically. Evidence for this close correspondence is notably lacking. Admittedly, there have been few attempts to study this tie between memory and metamemory systematically. What evidence we have comes largely from post hoc examinations from studies that were never intended to address prediction and performance, and so far these have provided less than impressive support for a close tie.

Consider first the limited data we have. Salatas and Flavell (1976) and Moyna-han (1973) examined knowledge concerning categorization and recall. Both failed to find a direct link. Moynahan found that awareness of the effects of categorization was not related to actual performance on categorized vs. uncate-gorized lists. Similarly, Salatas and Flavell (1976) found that first graders who had not categorized were as likely as those who had categorized to indicate that categorization would aid recall. A complete separation between prediction and performance, however, was not suggested by either study. Salatas and Flavell did find that children instructed to remember gave more correct answers on metamemory questions, and Moynahan (1973) found better responses to meta-memory questions after rather than before active attempts at remembering. Experience with remembering does have some effect on metamemorial awareness, but not the direct influence that one would like.

The absence of a direct link between predictions and performance was well documented in young normal and educable retarded children (Brown et al., work in progress; see Section III.B.4, this volume). Asked to predict which modeled activity would result in superior recall, all the MA 6 and MA 8 children indicated the superiority of an active strategy (in contrast to preschool and first-grade normal children who were not so sensitive). Given the exact task to perform themselves, immediately after viewing the model, only a minority actually performed the efficient strategy themselves (see Table 11). By third grade, the majority of children elected to perform the strategy they had predicted to be most efficient, but even for these older children, the relationship was less than perfect. Items from the Kreutzer et al. (1975) questionnaire also show this pattern. Children who predicted that studying longer and more actively will lead to better recall do not necessarily say that they would act this way themselves.

Flavell and Wellman (1977) point out that there are many reasons why the ideal relation of metamemory and memory may not be found:

> Suppose a person judges that categorized stimuli are easier to recall than noncategorized ones. Would he inevitably use categorization as a storage strategy, given obviously categorizable stimuli? Not at all. He may know about categorization but think that something else might be better yet in this situation. He may think the list easy enough to use simple inspection for storage. He may have enough knowledge to judge that categorization would be a good strategy, if asked about it, but not enough to think to utilize such a strategy on his own. Lastly, there are undoubted gaps between metamemory and memory behavior attributable to Original Sin. Moral action does not always accord with moral beliefs, and similarly, we do not always try to retrieve information or prepare for future retrieval in what we believe to be the most effective ways [pp. 27–28].

Like Flavell and Wellman (1977), we believe that there should be "a development of metamemory judgment, of memory behavior, and a developing coordination between the two." Yet, we know of little evidence to support this statement. All the actual data cited above were gathered from children with MAs of eight years or below. Here, the relation of metamemory and memory is weak. In our modeling study (Brown et al., work in progress), we did note an increase in older children in the desired correspondence, but further investigations of the development between growing metamemory awareness and improvement in actual memorization behavior are still needed.

To reiterate another point made by Flavell and Wellman (1977): "the causal chain may be more clearly and exclusively metamemory → memory behavior later in development." Yet, how does this development progress? Does the dawning awareness of metamemory precede improved efficiency of memory behavior (metamemory → memory behavior)? Does increasing experience with memorization lead to metamemorial awakening (memory behavior →metamemory)? Or is the process a complex cross-fertilization of the two (memory behavior → metamemory)? Everything we know about cognitive development would point to the third alternative, since one can scarcely expect the child to become enlightened with metamemorial knowledge by divine intervention, prior to repeated experience with a variety of memorization tasks. The coordination of knowledge and actions concerning memory may be the essence of development after the early school years. Investigations of the hypothesized increased coordinations have barely begun.

Of both theoretical and practical importance is the nature of the experiences that would effect such cognitive growth. Flavell and Wellman (1977) suggests that general experience with school and school tasks would provide the impetus for this development, but the lack of sophistication of high school children at assessing their own capacity would suggest that such indirect influences might not be too efficient (Brown, 1977b; Brown & Smiley, 1977a, 1977b). Indeed, it may be the case that such general improvement in intelligent understanding cannot be taught explicitly. Yet, for those interested in instructional psychology, the field is wide open to attempts to identify essential experience that might effect improvement. This is particularly important if one is interested in the slow-learning child who may never acquire such insights unless explicitly directed.

E. Measurement and Criteria of Awareness

Because the study of metacognition is in its infancy, it is not surprising that refined measures for assessing metamemorial awareness have yet to be developed. But there are examples of the growing pains experienced in other related fields, and it is economical to attempt to benefit from others' mistakes. We know from related areas of cognitive development of the problems associated with accepting a child's verbal responses as an index of what he knows. What a child says he has done, or will do, is not necessarily related to what he does. Reliance on verbal responses and justifications is a risky venture when the advocate is a child. As the majority of hard (soft) data in the metamemory area consist of just such verbal self-reports, the problem of the criteria for evaluation of data is a crucial issue.

The problem of measuring metamemorial judgments is a sensitive one for we are concerned not with what the child is doing, but with what he thinks he is doing and why. A direct method of inquiring into what a child knows is to ask him. Some examples of the problems of this approach may prove illustrative.

One experimenter responsible for running the modeling study (Brown et al., work in progress) asked her 7-year-old son how he would study the pictures (after he had seen the video-tapes). He replied, without hesitation, that he would look at them; he always did that if he had to remember. Given the list, he carefully put all the pictures into taxonomic categories, spatially separated the categories, and proceeded to scan them systematically. Asked what he had to remember, he replied that he just looked at the pictures just like he said he would.

Less anecdotal examples of the pitfalls of taking a verbal response at face value have been reported throughout the literature review. Perhaps the most illustrative is the difference in span estimation obtained by Brown et al. (1977) when the index of awareness was the child's first indication that his capacity was overreached, or when the child was allowed to continue estimating up to the maximum list length of 10 items. Many of the children who would have been judged realistic if we had stopped at the first response were quite happy to assert that a list of five was too difficult, while one of six was not, and to claim that seven was too many, but eight was okay. Whatever this tells us about the child's metamemory, it certainly tells us to beware of accepting a single verbal response as a measure of awareness.

Kreutzer et al. (1975) attempted to overcome this problem by requiring multiple responses to their test questionnaire, including adequate justification. The match between single yes/no answers indicating awareness and adequate justification increased dramatically with age. Would demanding adequate justification solve the problem? Kuhn (1974) has considered this problem in the context of Piagetian conservation studies. Apparently, there is more than one school of thought. Brainerd (1973) believes that justifications are inappropriate for evaluating the child's understanding of a problem, for operativity is supposed to precede the ability to express such knowledge linguistically. The risk of Type II errors is a problem as many children may well possess the requisite cognitive skills but fail to express them adequately. Brainerd (1973) advocates the use of yes/no, same/different responses, but as Kuhn points out, any dichotomous choice method is sensitive to response bias effects known to be developmentally sensitive (Brown & Campione, 1972). The dilemma is that demanding justification of responses entails the possibility of Type II errors, but relying on dichotomous responses risks the possibility of Type I errors. Kuhn's solution is the use of converging operations. As rich a variety of responses as possible should be elicited and the degree of awareness judged against the total picture revealed.

Since the responses that make up the majority of metamemory data are also dichotomous decisions or justifications, the same solution seems worthy of investigation in this area. Many different measures of awareness should be obtained, and at the very least, one should avoid accepting a single response as the only measure of the child's knowledge (Brown et al., 1977). There is also an obvious need to consider the problem of reliability of the measures obtained.

In the strategy-choice modeling task (Brown et al., work in progress), 23%, 44%, and 28% of normal 4-year-olds, MA 6 and MA 8 retardates respectively, were inconsistent in their choice of a preferred strategy when multiple measures were employed, thus demonstrating the necessity of obtaining reliability data. Note that Brown and Lawton (1977) found that children, sensitive to their own feelings of knowing in one situation, did not necessarily show the same sensitivity in a variant of that task. Albeit there were severe selection problems in those studies. If further cautionary tales are needed, note the "dishonesty" or "creative flexibility," depending on your viewpoint, of the children who deliberately failed a recall test so that they could play the popular feeling-of-knowing betting game. Of course, they had a reliable feeling of knowing concerning future recognition accuracy for items they could perfectly well have recalled. Thus, we agree with Belmont and Butterfield (1977) that measurement is a crucial problem in this area, and we would argue in favor of convergent operations (see Section V) in the quest for quantifying and qualifying the degree of awareness children have of their own mental operations.

F. Training and Transfer

Another powerful motivation for the current interest in metamemory, certainly the reason for our own interest in the area, stems from the controversy concerning the limited success of attempts to train specific mnemonic strategies in those who do not think this way. The argument is simple; if young children are totally unaware of the utility of mnemonic aids, why should they benefit from instruction? If trained to rehearse, they will rehearse, especially if the situation remains unchanged and they receive continual reminders. But, why should they then be expected to use their new skills insightfully if the reason for the activity was never made clear?

This leads us to the interesting question concerning which aspects of performance one should attempt to train — deliberate skills of remembering or the executive control of these skills. Butterfield and Belmont (1977) raised this issue by contrasting what they believed to be different positions taken by Brown (1974) and Butterfield, Wambold, and Belmont (1973). They characterized our position as one of opting for the training of individual strategies for the solution of specific tasks in the hope that the executive function would emerge as a result of mastery of a suitable subset of skills. In contrast, their preference was to focus on the executive function itself. Although this appears to be a difference of opinion, the importance of the distinction fades when one considers practical steps necessary to instigate a training program; for it is difficult to imagine how to train the executive control of strategies in the absence of a set of strategies to control. Thus, although it is feasible to attempt to inculcate planfulness by suggesting that the child "plan ahead," "be economic with cognitive effort," "use only the correct plan and then only as long as needed," etc., practically, it seems that one must proceed by initially training some memorization skills before attempting to induce the monitoring and control of these strategic behaviors.

Butterfield and Belmont (1977), in essence, agree with this position and, therefore, the difference of opinion is an artificial one, for they state: "since the control processes (skills, etc.) are the subject of the executive function, they would seem to be the most promising indices of its operation. A firm basis of measurement for the control processes would therefore precede measurement of their overseer [p. 9]." We believe their description of our position to be inadequate, for in the 1974 paper, it was states that "once a serviceable skill, or subset of skills had been inculcated, the next step would be to devise techniques to train retarded children to monitor their own strategy production and to evaluate realistically the interaction between the task demands, and their own capacity and repertoire of specific skills" (Brown, 1974, p. 102).

The apparent disagreement disappears under scrutiny; both positions advocate training preliminary skills as an essential prerequisite for the study of executive control. However, what looked like a difference in emphasis perhaps reflects a more fundamental difference in the direction that training attempts should take. In a subsequent paper, Belmont and Butterfield (1977) seem to have changed their empasis in that they call for detailed task analysis of both the training situation and all subsequent tests of transfer (e.g., train the specific skill). We will now change our emphasis and call for training, not of individual strategies, but of ways of approaching problems in general.

This argument needs elaboration. Belmont and Butterfield (1977) argue cogently for detailed task analyses of individual laboratory tasks and the strategies that subjects may use to perform them. The degree of detailed analyses that can be undertaken is well illustrated by their 10-year effort to refine the cumulative-rehearsal, fast-finish strategy deemed optimal in their paradigm. The effects of such detailed task analyses are clear. Given an intimate understanding of all aspects of the optimal strategy, it is possible to train children efficiently, to diagnose why training does not result in optimal performance, and to bring the level of performance at least to the standard set by untrained adults (Butterfield et al., 1973).

The main strength of the detailed task analysis approach to training mnemonic strategies is illustrated in this admirable set of studies, particularly those reported by Butterfield et al. (1973). If the aim of training is to see how close to mature performance one can render children's behavior, this approach is highly successful. Theoretically, such data are invaluable, for they demonstrate that one interpretation of a "structural limitation" (Brown, 1974) position is incorrect. If training fails, one should not implicate some fundamental capacity limitation of the child, but attempt to refine training (Belmont & Butterfield, 1977; Brown, 1974). The task analysis approach is also invaluable from a practical standpoint, if the desired end product is to improve performance on the training task itself. Gold's (1972) work with severely retarded individuals is an excellent case in point. Severely and profoundly retarded institutionalized people can be quickly trained to perform complex assembly jobs if the task is broken into easily manageable subunits, an intelligent task decomposition achieved through detailed task analysis (Wade & Gold, in press). The goal of the training procedure is to achieve quick, errorless performance on the training task, for, armed with this skill, the hitherto unemployable individual can earn a living wage (Gold, 1973).

The aim of those engaged in cognitive instruction is generally assumed to be somewhat different. Rather than regarding the goal as excellent performance on a specific task, the desired end product is to effect a general improvement in understanding, a much more demanding specification. This aim can again be defended both theoretically and practically. Theoretically, one could argue that without evidence of broad transfer, training may have resulted in the mastery of a rote rule, but may not have produced any real "structural change" (Kuhn, 1974) or general advancement in the child's knowledge of the world. Thus, there are at least two ways to consider the "anti-structuralist approach" (Belmont & Butterfield, 1977). Demonstrating adult-like performance on a single task is sufficient evidence for those who are interested in proving that intellectual immaturity is not necessarily an impediment to efficiency on any one task. The extreme position would be the claim that anything could be taught to anyone under the appropriate training conditions. Another version of a structural limitation position is one more akin to Piaget's, namely, that there are limitations to the young thinker's ability to reason; mere training on a particular task will not affect this ability until the appropriate level of maturity is reached. Intellectual maturation may be accelerated, but training can achieve only a small increment (Inhelder, Sinclair, & Bovet, 1974). Within the memory training field, advocates of this more conservative form of "structuralism" look for generalization as the index of successful training.

The problem is not one that Belmont and Butterfield ignore, but they appear to have a different end result in mind. Their aim is to "bring children up to adult levels of performance (on a specific task), in every measurable aspect," by providing a plan of sufficient detail that "anybody whose thoughts are put together according to that blueprint would recall very well." Given such a plan, young children should perform "exactly as if they had invented it themselves." "Instructional researchers and their young subjects are thus evidently engaged in the same enterprise and it is unimportant who makes the executive decision so long as they are made well." Finally, they assert that the most striking aspect of the instructional approach is to instruct the child "how or what to think."

This statement, how *or* what to think, encapsulates the difference between the two approaches, for there is an enormous gulf between training a child *how* to think and training a child *what* to think. The knowing how and knowing what controversy has played a prominent part in the history of educational philosophy and is still active today (Broudy, 1977). It is isomorphic with Greeno's (1976) distinction between cognitive and behavioral objects of instruction. Training a set rule or recipe (Holt, 1964) can effect significant improvement on a task, but we would argue that without a concurrent understanding of the reason why the skill must be used, it is unlikely that the result would be an improvement in the child's knowledge of how to think. We need not here add details of the long discussions of discovery learning vs. rote learning, and we refer the reader back to Section III.D.3 for examples of blind rule following.

Although there has been considerable interest in the need for transfer as a criterion of general cognitive improvement, the review of the literature illustrates the dearth of experimental endeavors in this area, an empirical gap generated not by lack of interest, but because of the formidable investment of time and effort needed to undertake such investigations. Belmont and Butterfield (1977) advocate an extension of their task analysis approach to a consideration of transfer: "the investigator who would demonstrate transfer must thoroughly understand both the task he uses during training and the task he uses to test transfer." Let us emphaisze that they mean "thorough," for they argued that both training and transfer tasks must be subjected to the type of in-depth analysis they have lavished on the cumulative rehearsal task. Failure to make an equally in-depth dissection of the transfer task would render the investigator incapable of inter-pretation transfer failures. A failure to perform adequately on transfer could be due to the trainee's inability to see the relation of the trained behavior to the new task, the usual interpretation, or to his inability to execute some other component of the transfer task which neither he nor the investigator fully appre-ciate.

The only answer then is to consider transfer from one well-analyzed task to another. We know of only one attempt that even approached this criterion and that was a failure. Retarded children who had been trained to cumulatively rehearse on a keeping-track task (Brown et al., 1973) and had maintained this activity over a 6-month retention interval (Brown et al., 1974) were given the Belmont and Butterfield probed-recall rehearsal task as a transfer test. Accuracy scores of naive and trained children were identical and poor. More importantly, there was no evidence of rehearsal activity (pause patterns, observed overt be-havior) in either group (Campione & Brown, 1977). True, it could be aruged that the transfer situation was less than ideal; the transfer test was taken some time after the maintenance task, and the keeping-track lists consisted of four items, whereas the probe-recall lists contained six. But, both tasks called for cumulative rehearsal in sets of three, the trained strategy, and there was no evidence of activity even on the first three items of the transfer task. We would not take this as the strongest evidence that such transfer could not be obtained; however, we were not encouraged by the results. Our interpretation of the Belmont and Butter-field position is that what would be needed before firm conclusions could be reached would be detailed task analysis of the first task, detailed task analysis of the second task, detailed task analysis followed by training on the noncommon elements of the two tasks, detailed analysis of the transfer setting, detailed analysis of. . . . Pragmatically, one has to face the problem of time and to assert a principle of cognitive economy on the part of both the trainer and trainee. If the aim of training is to effect generalization, the practical limitations of the task analysis approach must be taken into consideration (Brown & DeLoache, in press).

As we regard detailed task analyses of all possible transfer tasks as practically unfeasible, we must offer something in exchange, or at least a method of postponing or circumventing such time-consuming efforts. Our criterion for a suitable test of transfer (Brown et al., 1977) is that those persons who would spontaneously adopt the trained strategy on a pretest would also attempt to use it on the class of tasks used for transfer. One could obtain this information in several ways. For example, consider the use of cumulative rehearsal. One could ask successful and spontaneous rehearsers where and why they would think to use the strategy. Consideration of a series of such protocols should reveal prototypic rehearsal situations where almost anyone would rehearse; near cases, where there would be some disagreement concerning the suitability of rehearsal; and far cases, where no one who knew anything about rehearsal mechanisms would attempt it. The second method of obtaining the same information would be to devise a battery of tasks (prototypical instances, near and far cases) and observe when and where spontaneous producers use the strategy. Finally, within any study, a method of obtaining the desired information would be to consider the posttest generalization performance of those subjects who performed well on the pretest.

This third approach was adopted in the Brown, Campione, and Murphy (1977) study of span estimation (see Section III.E.2). Originally, realistic children performed well on all generalization tests, indicating their understanding of the task demands and their own ability. But trained realistic children did not perform well on the generalization tests, indicating the limitations of training (see Tables 16 and 17). Although it could be argued that the children efficient on the pretest differed from the other children on some underlying cognitive factor related to good performance on both the pretests and the generalization tasks, this is irrelevant. If the aim of training is to improve performance to match those who perform well, both in performance on the training task and in terms of general understanding, then the standards set by the originally efficient subjects are the obvious criteria of successful training.

From our point of view, the aim of training is not to get children to perform more like adults on a single task, but to get them to think more like adults on a single task, but to get them to think more like adults in a range of similar situations. If this is the desired goal, then why not train (1) generalization, or (2) skills that could conceivably be general enough to fit a variety of situations? We know of no studies where, far from attempting to train generalization, the experimenter has even hinted that this is the name of the game. The impression is that the child in an experiment of this kind is the enemy, rather than the ally, in the instructional approach. Granted that as mature learners generalize spontaneously, it is interesting to point out that immature trainees do not; however, the next step is to help the less efficient by hinting that they should or, better yet, attempt direct instruction in generalization.

Such training must go hand in hand with specific rule learning; otherwise, we would have come full circle in the Butterfield and Belmont (1977) and Brown (1974) controversy. Once we have trained mastery of a mnemonic skill in terms of the first two criteria, use and maintenance of the strategy, would it not be possible to intervene with some specific generalization training? For example, one could tell the child that the trained behavior could help him on a variety of similar tasks and that the trick is to know which ones. The child could then be exposed to a variety of prototypic tasks and the utility of the strategy in such situations demonstrated. At that point, far tasks could be considered, and the reason why the trained behavior would be inappropriate could be discussed and demonstrated. Finally, the child could be presented with a generalization test containing new prototypic and far tasks and his intelligent/unintelligent application of the strategy examined. We have no idea whether such an approach would work, but given the impressive evidence of the need for explicit training for slow-learning children, it certainly seems worth the attempt.

A final general point concerning transfer is that it might be judicious to rethink the type of skills we have attempted to train. How often does the mature memorizer rehearse? If children do not generalize a trained strategy because they fail to see its utility, this could be a realistic appraisal of the enterprise. After all, they all tell us that they write down telephone numbers.

An alternative strategy would be to train metacognition skills which could have broad generality across a variety of problem-solving situations. It was with this point in mind that we chose to organize the literature review with the headings of checking, planning, asking questions, self-testing, and monitoring. These skills are transsituational. Perhaps it would be possible to train the child to stop and think before attempting a problem, to ask questions of himself and others to determine if he recognizes the problem, to check his solutions against reality by asking not "is it right" but "it is reasonable," and to monitor his attempts to learn to see if they are working or are worth the effort. We appreciate that there are enormous problems associated with these suggestions. But, in the complete absence of data, we have no means of knowing whether such intervention would measurably improve memorial knowledge in the developmentally young. In view of the past dismal failures to induce generalization, however, we believe it would be worth the time and effort involved.

G. Training Limitations

A general point concerning training studies is that one must address the problem of limitations on the effects of training imposed by youth, lack of experience, or low intelligence. The problem of intelligence and how to define it is a difficult one, and some methodological and philosophical problems of comparative research will be considered in the next section. But, for the purposes of the following argument, the obvious needs to be stated; namely, that irrespective of the cause(s), individuals are not all equal in terms of their adaptation to the demands of schools and testing situations. In the case of educable retarded children, it is just this lack of adaptation which has singled them out for special notice in the schools and intensive training in laboratories. To clarify our position, it might help if I gave a working definition of intelligence that is used by my colleagues and myself, for we believe that the current controversy over developmentally imposed "capacity" or "structural" limitations is generated to a large extent by the lack of explicit definition of the terms used (Chi, 1976). Possibly the dominant reason why discussions of developmental changes in capacity are often irrational and confusing is because the key terms are used loosely, interchangeably, and often inappropriately. To understand such discussions, it is absolutely necessary to have a clear understanding of the underlying metaphor; not only is this rarely stated explicitly, but some authors appear to have no consistent metaphor. We cannot enter the capacity/no-capacity limitation argument here, but refer the reader to recent papers by Chi (1976) and Huttenlocher and Burke (1976).

To make explicit our position, the bias is toward a definition of intelligence based on executive functioning. To recapitulate, consider the range of responsibilities attributed to the executive in modern memory theories. The efficient executive is imbued with the capacity to undertake the complex coordination of routine selection, application, and control. Its duty is to monitor, check, and evaluate the chosen routine(s) against some criteria of effectiveness and to make inferences concerning the existing state of knowledge and the match between that knowledge and the desired goal. The executive must also estimate the probability that the goal can be reached by the methods available to the system. The characteristic features of the executive are just those that we have proposed as subjects for training: checking, planning, monitoring, etc. But this, in effect, means that we want to train efficient thinking. Thinking efficiently is a good definition of intelligence.

In this context, consider how intelligence is defined when the thinker is a machine. The similarity of the problems faced by those who wish to define intelligent operations either in the developmentally immature or in machines is quite striking. Moore and Newell (1974, pp. 203–204) define the essence of machine intelligence by two criteria. First, "S understands K if S uses K whenever appropriate." The distinction is between knowledge and the understanding of that knowledge. Immature thinkers fail to meet this criterion on our laboratory tasks, for this is the problem of maintenance and generalization.

The ability to use programs appropriately is the essence of machine intelligence; it is also a reasonable definition of human intelligence. It is the appropriate use of a skill that defines intelligent behavior, not adequate performance of that skill in a trained situation. The executive decision to employ the activity must be self-generated. If the routine is selected by an external agent (teacher, experimenter, etc.), he is the intelligent actor, not the child. Therefore, we believe that it does matter who acts as the executive. Although it may be "unimportant who makes the executive decision" (Belmont & Butterfield, 1977) if the object is to train improved performance on a specific task, it is vitally important who makes the decision if the aim is improved thinking; S must use K appropriately on his own volition.

Moore and Newell (1974, p. 204) gives as a further consideration for evaluating machine intelligence the extent of the ability to use knowledge appropriately; "Understanding can be partial, both in extent (the class of appropriate situations in which the knowledge is used) and in immediacy (the time it takes before understanding can be exhibited)." These criteria are similar to Resnick and Glaser's (1976) definition of human intelligence as the speed and efficiency of learning things important to one's environment. Thus, one might consider the efficiency of training in this light. How quickly and efficiently do children respond to training? And, how efficiently do they transfer the information, where efficiency is measured in terms of extent (broad generalization) and immediacy (without additionally prompting or training)? We would like to argue that if reasonable attempts to achieve generalization fail, even when the transfer tasks are appropriate (prototypic) and there have been explicit instructions concerning generalization, then a developmental limitation has been demonstrated, one which we would regard as a reasonable illustration of an intellectual limitation.

Resnick and Glaser (1976) also argue that intelligence is the ability to learn in the absence of direct or complete instruction. Therefore, if generalization could only be obtained by training it directly, we would not necessarily regard this success as a disaffirmation of an intellectual limitation position. For, if it can be achieved only with direct training, such generalization fails to meet the criterion of "in the absence of complete instruction." Furthermore, there is no reason to suppose that if transfer can be achieved in one domain only following detailed instruction, it would occur spontaneously in another.

We introduce these points because we have been cited as favoring an "antistructuralism" position (Belmont & Butterfield, 1977). That is, because of the emphasis in prior work on strategy training, it has been assumed that our position is that there are no "capacity" differences between the developmentally young and more mature thinkers; performance differences are attributed to inappropriate use (or no use at all) of mnemonic strategies and such strategy use can be trained. This argument rests on the definition of the term capacity. We would like to reaffirm the position that recourse to an unspecified "capacity limitation" when a particular training on a specific task fails is difficult to defend logically and is premature until alternative training methods have been examined (Brown, 1974). We also know of no compelling evidence that capacity differences in terms of the architecture of the system (e.g., STM), amount of space in the architectural units (e.g., the number of slots in STM), or in terms of durability of information in these systems differentiates the immature from the adult thinker (Belmont, 1972; Belmont & Butterfield, 1969; Brown, 1974; Chi, 1976; Wickelgren, 1975). This is not to say, however, that the developmentally young are not handicapped by limitations to their central processing resources, limitations that cannot be attributed to a simple notion of capacity. The effects of an impoverish knowledge base (LTM) alone can account for many of the reported developmental difficulties. Long-term memory is the repository of rules, strategies, and operations that can be used to make more efficient use of a limited-capacity system. In addition, the child's knowledge base is deficient in at least three ways: (1) the amount of information it contains; (2) the organization and internal coherence of that information; and (3) the number of available routes by which it can be reached. These differences impose several limitations on the child's information processing abilities, even in such simple situations as reading information in STM (Chi, 1975, 1976). Such basic cognitive processes as ease of retrievability and speed of encoding, naming, and recogniton are all influenced by restrictions imposed by an impoverished knowledge base.

The limitations to the knowledge base are clearly not susceptible to relatively brief training and intervention, no matter how ingenious. One cannot undertake to enrich the knowledge base in 3, or even 23, easy lessions. Of course, such "structural" limitations are not fixed, as age and experience will lead to reorganization and enrichment of the knowledge base, an enrichment and reorganization program that continues throughout the life span (Brown, 1975). Intervention could take the form of exposing impoverished children to a richer array of experiences, the rationale behind many Headstart programs, but it is difficult to imagine detailed training programs to effect this end. Training itself is limited by restrictions imposed by the current state of the knowledge base (Brown, 1975; Siegler, 1976; Klahr & Siegler, in press).

In addition, there are limitations placed on the effects of training due to low intelligence. We believe that both the extent of training needed to effect adequate performance and the efficiency of training in terms of extent and immediacy of transfer are indices of intelligence, although the cultural relativity of both the task and training must undergo careful scrutiny before such conclusions can be reached (see Section V).

A further characteristic of intelligence is that not only can old skills be used appropriately in new places, but they can be remodeled creatively to meet new task demands. Furthermore, new solutions can be invented on the basis of old knowledge alone. Resnick and Glaser (1976) have provided a recent discussion of the problem of intelligence and invention, and we do not want to reiterate it here. The point is included to demonstrate how weak a criterion of intelligent thinking is our demand for spontaneous generalization of a learned skill to prototypical transfer tasks.

The entire preceding section is in some ways trivial. First, it is obvious that there are functional differences between the developmentally young and mature problem solvers, for if there were not, intervention would not be required. Second, and more important, the position one assumes concerning the cause, type, or susceptibility to remediation of such developmental differences has little effect on the practical problem of training. The difference of opinion is theoretical not practical, descriptive not prescriptive. We believe as strongly as anyone that no attempt should be spared to provide intensive intervention to improve problem-solving abilities, particularly in slow learners. One major responsibility of an instructional psychologist is to devise increasingly ingenious training programs to induce enhanced performance. Furthermore, we have always been, and remain, optimistic concerning the success of well-designed training, and the real practical significance of such success in terms of worthwhile improvements in performance. We included this section because we believe there are limitations on the effectiveness of training and, therefore, would like to disassociate ourselves from an extreme anti-structuralism position.

V. MEMORY, INTELLIGENCE, AND INSTRUCTION

A major focus of our research efforts in the area of memory development has been an emphasis on the trainable, particularly with reference to slow-learning children. Although the research is "basic" in that it is conducted in laboratory settings to test hypotheses of theoretical interest, the underlying rationale has always been that information of practical significance would be forthcoming. Although we have neither the skill nor professional training to devise detailed curricula for instructive purposes, we hope that some of our training techniques could be implemented in instructional settings. In this section, we will first consider formal instruction, the schools, and their influence on metacognitive development. We will then examine the particular problems of the disadvantaged child in school settings. Finally, we will indicate the type of instruction that might prove practical and feasible.

A. The Effects of Formal Schooling: Intercultural Comparisons

It is interesting to note that the period of development when the major changes in memorization skills occur, from the first emergence of the child's awareness of himself as an active agent in knowing, to the establishment of the complex executive functions exhibited (sometimes) by high school and college students, coincides exactly with the period of formal education in most Western societies. Does this suggest that formal education is in some way implicated, that we have a case of educational rather than maturational development? The only meaning-ful way to consider such a question is by reference to cultures where the degree of formal schooling and chronological age are not hopelessly confounded as they are in Euro-America. A cursory review of the cross-cultural literature suggests some pertinent findings concerning the cultural relativity of many of the skills we have discussed in this chapter. Such a review also directs our attention to some basic philosophical and methodological problems associated with the type of experimentation employed by psychologists to gather comparative data and to the validity of the interpretations given to such data.

Consider first some cross-culture psychological evidence concerning the development of memorization efficiency. One of the consistent differences be-tween schooled and unschooled populations rests in the ability to deal with the kinds of mnemonic skills for deliberate memorizing that we have discussed in this chapter. Several years of formal schooling seem to be necessary before the emergence of spontaneous attempts to organize, rehearse, or categorize taxonom-ically for the purposes of rote remembering. In addition to a general lack of what we regard as routine memorization skills, unschooled populations differ in terms of their ability to transfer problems solutions readily across laboratory tasks. Scribner and Cole (1973) suggest that one cognitive characteristic of un-schooled populations is that they tend to treat the usual laboratory learning and memory tasks as independent, each as a new problem. In short, there appears to be a conspicuous absence of learning to learn. Schooled populations, however, show a marked tendency to treat such problems as instances of a general class. The application of common operations and rules to a universe of similar laboratory tasks appears to be an outcome of formal schooling.

Similar differences between schooled and unschooled populations have been found when the experimental task involves certain metalinguistic abilities. For example, children experience difficulty in dealing with decontextualized language. Osherson and Markman (1975) presented young children problems of the form: "either it is raining outside or it is not," or the "chip (hidden) in my hand is blue or it is not blue." The children indiscriminately sought empirical support for the truth value of the statements; they did not recognize the nonempirical nature of the simple contradictions, or at least were unwilling to evaluate these sentences in the absence of empirical evidence. A similar example of the need for empirical support to evaluate language comes from Scribner's (1977) studies of compre-hension of classical syllogims among schooled and unschooled Kpelle villagers. Given problems such as "All Kpelle men are rice farmers; Mr. Smith is not a rice farmer; Is he a Kpelle man?", unschooled villagers refused to consider the prob-lem if they had not met Mr. Smith. They did not appear to grasp the fact that the task involved logical implications determined solely by the structural relations between the stated propositions, independent of their factual status. Again, on the basis of the limited evidence, it would appear that certain forms of logical thinking in response to *traditional academic* problem-solving situations, far from being the natural outcome of maturation, are very much dependent on the intervention of formal schooling.

Piagetian experiments conducted cross culturally also support the idea that the degree of formal schooling is an important factor in determining progression to higher levels of abstract thought (Dasen, 1972). In keeping with the other psychological evidence, Lloyd (1972) suggests that the emergence of formal operations, as defined by the Piagetian system, depends heavily on Western-type schooling and that "this is hardly surprising since the structures of formal thought, the propositional calculus, and the mathematic four group are products of Western thinking. Their universality, as the goal of mature cognitive development, is an open question [p. 137]." In support of this position, Piaget (1972) himself has recently suggested that under some cultural conditions, formal propositional thinking may not emerge at all.

Finally, Olson (1976, 1977) and Bruner (1972) have suggested that the move from an oral to a literate culture imposes fundamental changes on people's ways of knowing. A strong case is made that the type of cognitive activities perfected by a culture are determined by the socioeconomic milieu (Luria, 1971) and that the invention of a phonetic writing system had profound historical consequences on the nature of human thought. We cannot give a full discussion here but would like to concentrate on three interconnected emphases of a literate tradition that are fostered by Western-type schooling — decontextualization and formalization of the language, an emphasis on the logical rather than the rhetorical function of language, and an emphasis on the general contex-free rule rather than the particular experience.

Briefly, an oral tradition depends heavily upon a particular form of thinking biased by the limitations of auditory memory. The system is well equipped to deal with proverbs, riddles, adages, etc., but:

Neither principles nor laws nor formulas are amenable to a syntax which is orally memorizable. But persons and events that act or happen are amenable. Orally memorized verse (including the epics) is couched in the contingent. It deals in a panorama of happenings not a program of principles [Havelock, 1971, p. 5].

Oral memory is biased in the direction of rhymes, riddles, proverbs, metaphors, and wise and witty sayings. Written messages, however, are uniquely adapted to an analysis of the implications and entailments of statements. When children learn to write, the dependence on context — on empirical support to validate statements — must be overcome. They must learn to write things which a reader, removed from them in time and space and unable to ask questions, can understand. They must learn to comprehend and produce a written language which is explicit and relatively context free.[2] Beyond mere literacy lies formal definition and scientific writing, which not only depend on context-free explicit language, but also demand formal definitions of terms and the analysis of the implications of propositions.

Olson (1976, 1977) has argued that the literate tradition has specialized the language to serve a logical function at the expense of the social, rhetorical function. The rhetorical function of language involves social, authoritative, and context-bound communication. The child in a literate society must come to single out the logical aspects of statements from the authority-maintaining, social functions.

Bruner and Olson (in press) believe that the emphasis on the formal, logical function of language in literate societies affect people's ways of knowing and biases the definition of intelligence in these societies, and the growing body of cross-cultural literature supports this *difference* hypothesis. Formal schooling in a literate tradition influences the course of cognitive growth; relatively un-schooled populations display different patterns of cognitive activities than do the products of formal schooling. Does this mean that one can accept a *defect hypothesis:* that unschooled populations are less intelligent than the schooled? After all, the tasks used to detect a difference are those associated with intelligence in our society.

Such an interpretation of the existing data is illegitimate. Since modes of thinking and ways of knowing are molded by cultural context, one cannot sensibly specify intelligence outside of the culture with which it is interacting. If we accept as one definition of intelligence, adaptation to real-life problems, quite different performances would be considered adaptive in different cultures. It is, therfore, an invalid inference to suggest that unschooled populations are less intelligent because they do not perform in a fashion comparable to Western children on a particular laboratory task or IQ test item; it is not reasonable to discuss intelligence (adaptation) without reference to the culture to which the developing child must adapt.

Cole and Scribner (1977) have provided a rich source of evidence to support a difference rather than a defect interpretation of cross-cultural findings, and they demonstrate that logical thinking, efficient communication, elaborate mnemonics, and generalization are features of thought in both traditional and schooled societies. It is the form that these aspects of cognition take, not their presence or absence, that distinguish schooled and unschooled populations. For example, Scribner (1977) gives many illustrations of "wrong" answers given by unschooled Kpelle to the totally unfamiliar logical syllogism problems. Neverthe-

---

[2]Strictly speaking, no message, even a written one, is truly context free in that the reader is free to disambiguate and instantiate utterances on the basis of world knowledge. The term decontextualization is used in Olson's sense of a written message's liberation from the immediate social context for interpretation.

less, the wrong answers contained elegant examples of chains of reasoning that followed logically from the evidence used by the subjects. Consider also this fine example of Kpelle cognition. Kpelle villagers, when asked to group together a set of items in the way that made Kpelle sense, grouped the items by their functional relationships. Next, when the villagers were asked how a stupid person might group them, they produced perfect taxonomic groupings. Interestingly, functional groupings appear to be universally accepted, but taxonomic categorization is influenced by degree of recency of exposure to formal schooling (Denney, 1974; Overcast, Murphy, Smiley, & Brown, 1975). Only taxonomic categorization is taken as a measure of higher intelligence within our society. It reflects our cultural bias that we call one activity more "intelligent" than the other. In a review of the cross-cultural studies on cognitive development, Lloyd (1972) concluded with the statement: "Men are fundamentally similar in their intellectual skills but these skills are differentially realized in culturally diverse settings . . . [and] no one setting should be acclaimed as superior [p. 153]."

Michael Cole and his associates have pointed out that anthropologists have, indeed, long advocated the similarity rather than the divergence of human intelligence in different cultural groups; it is psychologists who emphasize the difference. Anthropologists' tools, consisting mainly of ethnographic description of naturally occurring behaviors, are different from the tests and experiments imported by psychologists, and anthropologists object to the traditional laboratory task used by psychologists, not only on the obvious grounds that the experimental materials, tasks, and procedures developed in Western societies are ethnocentric and culturally biased, but because the experiment itself as a context for eliciting evidence of cognition has no ecological validity in the cultures to which it has been transported (Scribner, 1976).

Both Lloyd (1972) and Cole and Scribner (1975) believe that the traditional laboratory tasks can be used in cross-cultural research when due caution is paid to the interpretation of the outcome:

> Evidence of cultural differences in response to a particular task [should] become the starting point rather than the goal of cross-cultural research, and performance on a task should be scrutinized to determine whether it is a meaningful response or attempt to satisfy the arbitrary whim of an alien investigator [Lloyd, 1972, p. 153].

Cole and Scribner suggest a three-pronged research strategy for investigating cognitive development comparatively. First, one should investigate the subject's understanding of the experiment and his role as the subject. In light of the Kpelle example of clever vs. stupid answers, this is a vital point. Indeed, Campbell (1964) suggests that without compelling evidence to the contrary, we should regard any gross differences found in comparative research as failures of communication between the experimenter and his subject. The second research strategy is to "experiment with the experiment" (i.e., instead of using one fixed paradigm in many different cultures, the experimenter should work with many different variations of a single paradigm within one culture). An excellent example of this approach is the work of Cole and his colleagues (Cole & Scribner, 1977) concerning free recall in the Kpelle. The third strategy is to investigate the same process in a range of situations, including the naturally occurring contexts of the culture and also in experimental and quasi-experimental settings (Campbell & Stanley, 1966).

The basic theme is a call for an interweaving of experimental and ethnographic research to investigate a particular cognitive activity in a range of situations from the naturally occurring to the experimental. We argue later that such strategy is ideally suited for comparative research when the groups differ not in terms of national origin or degree of formal schooling but in terms of age or school success within a society. Similarly, we will argue that the same caution advised for the interpretations of group differences on traditional laboratory tasks or IQ test items be extended when interpretation is made concerning the developmentally immature and their "normal" counterparts.

B. The Sociohistorical Context: Intracultural Comparisons

The main emphasis of the cross-cultural, psychoethnographic approach espoused by Cole and Scribner (1975) is that it is difficult, if not impossible, to consider any psychological process separated from the context in and the content on which it must operate:

> The psychologist examining any mental mechanism is of necessity examining a mechanism normally operating with material given in society and culture and he cannot get away from such "living contents" even in the artificial isolation of an experiment. Similarly, if anthropologists are concerned with how "living contents" come into existence and change over history, they need to understand what operations (processes) individuals bring to the material that is culturally given [p. 126].

A similar emphasis on studying cognitive growth within a society in terms of sociohistorical context has been the underlying philosophy of Soviet investigation into memory development across the life span. In a recent review of Soviet investigations, Meacham (1977) points out that there are three major themes permeating the Soviet approach. We would like to focus on two of these themes. First, the individual's motives and activities interact with content to determine what will be remembered. Second, the particular cognitive activities shown by individuals are in large measure molded by cultural and historical conditions. We would like to point out the strong similarity in position between the Soviet-dialectic approach (Riegel, 1976) and the psychoethnographic position adopted by Cole, a similarity which is perhaps predictable given Cole's long interest in Soviet psychology.

The main thrust of the argument is to alert us to the fact that social-ecological factors must be considered as shapers of cognitive activities within our society, as well as between peoples of culturally diverse groups. We have argued elsewhere (Brown, 1975) that in order to understand memory efficiencies and weaknesses in young children, it is necessary to consider the ecological validity of traditional laboratory tasks in the light of naturally occurring situations of preschool life. The Soviets' definition of "leading activities" (Meacham, 1977) that dominate the organization of cognition at any one stage of development is particularly relevant to this point. Actions are organized around leading activities that change ontogenetically. The sequence of leading activities depends upon the specific social and historical conditions of the developing child. Thus, Soviet research in memory has as its main focus the development of cognitive activities in response to cultural forces, and there is a heavy concentration on memorization subordinated to a purpose, a leading activity of cultural relevance to the individual (e.g., practical settings rather than laboratory tasks, play activities for small children, and operating a telephone switchboard for adults). The focus is on the motivational and cultural historical context of remembering and relies predominantly on observational and descriptive techniques rather than experimental control. In contrast, Kvale (1975) has argued that nondialectic research in memory development has focused on meaningless materials and has ignored the fact that remembering always occurs within contexts and on contents. The contexts and contents powerfully influence memorization styles.

In summary, cognitive activities develop and change within a sociohistorical cultural context, and the nature of these acculturation processes influence the leading activities, motives, focus, and types of cognitive activity displayed by the individual. It is, therefore, profitable to view the memory abilities of the developing child in relation to the ecology of childhood. Furthermore, in order to assess the type of processes typical of an individual at any one stage of development, it is necessary to consider factors other than individual performance on artifically contrived laboratory tasks or IQ tests. The particular processes of interest should be considered in a variety of situations, including the naturally occurring leading activities of childhood (Istomina, 1975).

C. The School as a Cultural Context

Because formal schooling has such a powerful effect on the course of cognitive growth, it might prove instructive to think of schools as a miniculture within which certain specialized sets of skills are emphasized and refined. Techniques and qualities of memory are no less influenced by the school experience than are any other cognitive activities. It is in the context of formal schooling that many of the changes we have discussed take place, changes in the variety of available mnemonics and in the knowledge one has concerning one's own competence and fallibility as a memorizer of school materials. This should not be surprising, because schools represent the major cultural institution in technological societies where remembering as a distinct activity of specialized skill, in and for itself, in isolation from possible applications, is routinely undertaken. Outside the school setting and in unschooled populations, including that of the preschool child, such activities are rarely, if ever, encountered (Brown, 1975). Deliberate remembering as an end in itself rather than as a method of achieving a meaningful goal is very much a school inspired activity.

Therefore, one might expect formal schooling to result in the formulation and refinement of a specified set of skills specifically tailored to the needs of academic learning. The familiar memory strategies discussed here are the outcome of a specialized cultural force, schools, and not the inevitable results of human maturation. Adaption to a habitat forges the direction of cognitive development; schools are only one such habitat, and in historical perspective, a very recent development at that. Outside of school settings, other perfectly valid sets of cognitive activities may characterize the course of cognitive development.

Consider just one example of a "naturally occurring" strategy, the reliance placed on external aids to support mnemonic performance. Flavell (1976b) and his co-workers have shown many examples of the young child's preference for external means of memorizing real-world information; even remembering a telephone number elicits external (writing down) rather than internal (rehearsal) storage:

> In real, extralaboratory life situations, people make extensive use of external storage and retrieval resources, both human and nonhuman. In the outside world, people take notes on things and make notes of things: they exploit the capacious and leakproof memories of books, tape recorders, video-tapes, films, and computers; they get other people to help them store and retrieve information, both internally (i.e., in other people's heads) and externally. The real world's tasks generally have the properties of an open-book, take-home exam, even if the memory researcher's tasks do not [p. 233].

Preschool children rarely, if ever, encounter situations that call for deliberate internal memorization of decontextualized materials (Brown, 1975). Similiarly, members of traditional societies tend not to encounter such situations in everyday life, and adults in our society, when removed from the school setting, rarely, if ever, engage in such esoteric mental activities with the possible exception of rote memorization of a limited set of personal numbers (telephone, social security, etc.). Scribner (1976) has argued that the ubiquitous free-recall paradigm is particularly inappropriate for cross-cultural comparison as it does provide *external cues* for recall, but demands that internal cues be produced to structure performance. Scribner believes that such a heavy emphasis on internal retrieval cues is largely absent from naturally occurring, everyday-life memory rpoblems, and she quotes Margaret Mead's (1964) anecdotal observation of reliance on external cues in primitive peoples:

> The Aborigines of South Australia have cultivated a type of memory in which they have to walk through the terrain which is involved in a myth in order to be able to tell a long totemic myth correctly. The stimuli which call the correct incidents to mind are outside themselves in their territory [p. 103].

The similarity to the well-known "method of loci" (Yates, 1966) is striking. Recall that the method of loci was developed to meet the needs of Roman orators who required techniques for remembering the sequential order of the main points of their oration. That with minimum instruction, young children (Brown, 1973b) and adults (Bower, 1970) can all use such techniques effectively is a powerful testimony to the efficiency of externally cued recall.

The use of locations, settings, and physical reminders (notes, string, etc.) to mediate memory is a contextual form of cued recall, situated in real-life experience and, we would argue, a predominant form of human mnemonics. The use of decontextualized, internally cued mnemonics for remembering arbitrary contents, however, is a specialized form of cognitive activity not only typical of a Euro-American literate tradition, but possibly a product of formal schooling itself. Such skills are not necessarily representative of basic cognitive processes.

We would argue that there is a basic universality and continuity to human conceptual development based on forms of knowing which Nelson has referred to as scripted knowledge (for a full discussion, see Nelson, 1977), Nelson's description of a script for organizing the interaction of a number of different concepts around an action or a goal is very similar to Cole and Scribner's (1977) description of a natural type of memory concerned with personally experienced scenes or events that lend organization and predictability to the world around us. It is also similar to Havelock's (1971) characterization of the type of memory refined in oral traditions, knowledge centered around persons and events that act or happen in meaningful contexts.

Nelson points out that context-derived event structures and scripts involving actually experienced, meaningful, and repetitive sequences in space and time are the important organizing structures for young children (Nelson, 1977; Nelson & Brown, 1978). We believe that this may be the dominant form of knowing in both the mature in our society (Denney, 1974; Overcast et al., 1975) and unschooled young adults in other societies (Cole & Scribner, 1977). The further divorced one is from formal schooling, in terms of recency or extent of the experience, the more one's thinking is dominated by scripts based on real-life actions. Although based on context-constrained, actually experienced happenings, the scripts of everyday knowing are generative. General rules are "abstracted" from the particular repetitive experiences to allow interpretation of the novel, prediction of the familiar, and to provide an organizational structure for a *personal* universe.

Thus, we would argue that there is a fundamental universality to human conceptual development, and the basic way of knowing consists of the formation and refinement of increasingly richer event structures or scripts (Nelson, 1977), centered around action sequences which recur in personally experienced contexts. Later emerging, relatively context-free organization or rules are in addition to and not a replacement for the basic spatiotemporal scripts of knowing. Specifically, specialized elaborate skills for different kinds of remembering are developed in different contexts with differing leading activities (Meacham, 1977), for example, study skills for remembering texts in schools in our society vs. oral mnemonics for the transmission of epic poems (Colby & Cole, 1973) or for retaining totemic names for debating (Bateson, 1958) in traditional societies. There is considerable evidence that even in the absence of explicit instruction, the requirement of formal schooling determines the direction of mnemonic development in Western societies. The ability to comprehend and retain information couched in increasingly decontextualized and formalized language presented in texts is the leading activity in schools. Thus, the development of specialized cognitive activities to achieve this end must be seen in the sociohistorical context of schooling in advanced technological societies and not as a reflection of the natural end product of human cognitive growth.

D. Schools and the Disadvantaged Child

Each culture invents its own set of techniques for refining basic cognitive resources to meet a specialized need. Within our society, it is in the context of schools, particularly the later grades, that great emphasis is placed on decontextualized skills of knowing. As Bruner and Olson (in press) have pointed out, "whether for reasons of economy or effectiveness, schools have settled on teaching/learning out of the context of action and through media that are primarily symbolic and decontextualized [p. 1]." They continue in a latter part of the manuscript:

> Progressively aided by the decontextualized atmosphere of school, the literate child comes to manage statements as propositions with entailments, to recognize that a statement is true, not because it is empirically plausible or has been experienced, but simply because it is entailed by another proposition also in the text. *If not all achieve this skill* [italics mine], at least it is held up as an ideal [p. 21].

Although one might argue with the assumption that the modes of thinking of middle-class Western college students should be a goal for cognitive growth in all members of our society (Lloyd, 1972), it is certainly true that academic success in our schools, and to some extent, economic success in our society depend on achieving a reasonable degree of ease in this domain. Children are expected to make the transition from the context-bound, experientally based, play-centered culture of preschool life to the context-free, impersonal, learning-for-learnings-sake atmospheres of the schools. Some make the transition; others do not. Many that do not can be termed disadvantaged in terms of their preparation for school. Many that do not may become labeled as retarded if the transition is unduly troublesome.

Considered briefly what we know about disadvantaged children that might render the transition more difficult for them than for the middle-class child. Ignoring obvious problems such as facing a new language, either in terms of a different dialect or a second language, the disadvantaged child is hampered by a restricted language code (Bernstein, 1971) which favors the context-bound, social, rhetorical functions of language (Olson, 1976) rather than the context-free, explicit communicative mode demanded in school. Furthermore, we know that very early in their school career, disadvantaged children have difficulty dealing with problem solutions divorced from empirical support and difficulty generating aids, mnemonics, search strategies, etc. to enhance deliberate learning. They need explicit instruction in developing these skills and even then may fail to generalize the effects of training to similar classes of activity. Perhaps because of these problems, their metacognitive development is impaired. Simply stated, without considerable experience and success with this type of problem-solving activity, the child can hardly be expected to exert control (Brown & DeLoache, in press).

Perhaps there is a more basic problem. Early failure experiences can seriously erode children's self-concept. They may have no reason to believe in themselves as active agents in knowing what ther eis to know in school. If they have no expectations concerning their ability to control school performance, this would surely vitiate any attempts to achieve such control. Learned helplessness (Dweck, 1976) can be acquired early. The child's objective knoweldge of his own cognitive processes is obviously contaminated by his feelings of competence. Competence within a school setting may not be expected by many disadvantaged children and particulary not by those singled out for "special" education in response to their supposed incompetence.

Bruner (1972) has pointed out that schools as an institution are separated from both the early play activities thought suitable for childhood and even from most vocational activities demanded of adults. For example, in primitive societies, children learn by imitating adult models, initially in the context of play activity (mock hunting, weaving, cooking, ritualistic practices, etc.). The transition from play activities to the real adult occupation (i.e., play hunting to hunting) is gradual; there is no sharp division between the early exploratory play of childhood and the vocational pursuits of the adult. In our society, schools intercede between the two worlds, but they do not forge a necessary link. Not only is

entering into the school system an alienation process (play activities are discouraged, learning by listening and reading rather than acting is encouraged),
but the necessary link with the exit into adult society is also less than clear:

> School, separated from work which itself has grown difficult to under-
> stand, becomes its own world. As McLuhan (1964) insists, it becomes a
> medium and has its own message, regardless of what is taught. The message
> is its irrelevance to work, to adult life. For those who wish to pursue
> knowledge for its own sake, this is not upsetting. But for those who do
> not or cannot, school provides no guide — only knowledge, the relevance
> of which is clear neither to student nor to teachers. There are the condi-
> tions for alienation and confusion [Bruner, 1972, p. 703].

If schools do not relate to the real-life experiences of play or work activity
that the child encounters daily, it is not surprising that the enterprises valued in
the classroom do not "make sense" to many children. If lessons are not meant to
"make sense," why should the child check his performance against criteria of
the plausible or sensible? This problem of alienation was seen even in Holt's
(1964) middle-class, above-average children (see Section III.D.2), but it is much
more of a problem for the disadvantaged child for whom acculturation to a
school setting demands a more radical shift from preschool conditions. "Playing
the game of school" (Anderson, 1977), learning a script for how to behave in
school, may never be acquired by such children unless some form of intervention
is attempted.

Certain facts exist; all children do not make the transition to schooling with
equal ease, and some never make the transition and are marked for school failure.
Whether this is due to biological or socioeconomic reasons or any combination
of factors is irrelevant. The next question is, given the esoteric nature of many
school practices, should all children be expected to conform to the standards
set? Although the answer must surely be negative, the implications of accepting
that position in terms of selecting those that will enter higher-level academic
programs and those that will not are wide ranging, controversial, and cannot
concern us here. Rather, we assume the position that it is beneficial for as many
children as possible to acquire some facility with traditional school skills; therefore, intervention should be offered to all who need help. Schools come into
existence and are the way they are because they meet the needs of a technological
society. It is unlikely, therefore, that schools and the skills valued in schools
will change radically. Thus, we must prepare as many children as possible to
meet the demands of schools as they exist today. This means tailoring teaching
techniques for and expending resources on those who experience difficulty with
the transition.

It is for these reasons that we have been increasingly concerned with educable
retarded children and, more recently, children who risk being labeled retarded.
Many educable children suffer from school disease; they are only singled out

officially as retarded or slow in the school setting. Prior to school, they either experience no difficulty or their difficulties go undetected. After school, the majority are again absorbed within the community (Edgerton, 1967). Only during the school years are they segregated. If they can be helped to achieve minimal success with school tasks, the benefits would be enormous; they would avoid being branded in school as "special," together with the concomitant loss of their own feelings of competence.

An implicit defect theory often appears to guide our approach to those already singled out for special classes. Such children are characterized as those who do not learn quickly and are difficult to train. But these conclusions often derived from a consideration of data collected on isolated laboratory tasks and IQ test items, using procedures and materials unfamiliar to the child. We would like to argue that the same caution demanded by Cole and Scribner (1975) for cross-cultural comparisons of cognitive processes should also be extended to the interpretation of intracultural comparative data. That our subjects do not generalize a cumulative rehearsal strategy does not mean that they cannot generalize. They clearly can and do transfer knowledge flexibly in real-life situations. The need for multiple observations of a particular phenomenon, demanded in cross-cultural research, is no less apparent in any research program which seeks to make comparisons between groups that differ in terms of age, nationality, ethnicity, IQ score, etc. Therefore, we strongly endorse Cole and Scribner's (1975) three-point plan for comparative research: (1) investigate the subject's understanding of the experiment; (2) experiment with the experiment; and (3) investigate the same process in a range of situations, the naturally occurring, quasi-experimental, and the experimental. We know of no research program concerned with cognitive development in slow-learning children that meets these criteria.

The learning of isolated materials for a purpose neither understood nor appreciated is not an easy task for the skilled and far less so for the novice. If the slow-learning child comes to view this as the leading activity of school, he is doomed to failure. The aim should be to "recontextualize" (Anderson, 1977) early school activities in order to alleviate the transition difficulties of the disadvantaged child.

The distinction described earlier between oral and literate traditions may be helpful in suggesting new ways of approaching the school problems of the disadvantaged child. Rather than thinking of slow-learning children as lacking certain skills, it might prove profitable to reverse the emphasis and concentrate on the skills they do possess, those of an oral tradition. If we are searching for competencies to harness in the service of school settings, the competencies of the oral tradition could be a good place to start. Educable retarded children are adept at remembering places, people, and things experienced in their daily life. They have elaborate scripts for coping with their home and street environments. They show an amazing ability to recall lyrics from popular songs (retained over an equally amazing time period), baseball scores, the top twenty songs, and the times of television programs, etc. Thus, we would argue that the transition to formal schooling might be made easier for disadvantaged children if: (1) the emphasis is palced on their strengths in the skills of an oral tradition rather than their weakness in the not-yet acquired literate ones; (2) game-like learning by apprenticeship systems (watching and doing) are maintained for as long as possible; and (3) careful attention is paid to the content and context of any desired activity in terms of its interest and relevance to the child's knowledge of naturally occurring activities.

Such general exhortations are easy to make but hard to implement. But if they are to be taken seriously, practical step-by-step descriptions of how one might implement a single program are needed at the very least. From the perspective of an experimental psychologist, specifying the stages in a research program would provide the necessary instantiation, and we will try to do that here. However, we would like to emphasize that the program has as an underlying principle – the provision of basic information of practical value; that is, it could and maybe should be directly implemented in instructional settings.

Consider the progress to date of our attempts in training mnemonic and meta-mnemonic skills in educable children. We know that training specific traditional mnemonic routines is not a promising avenue to pursue as the benefits are restricted to a very small range of situations. Training such skills in meaningful contexts, together with explicit instruction concerning the *reasons why* such skills can be useful, looks more promising and is currently underway in our laboratory (see Section IV.F).

A more fundamental change in approach is that we believe that serious concern should be given to the skills that are the subject of training. The type of cognitive activity selected for intensive intervention should have certain properties: (1) it should have great transituational applicability; (2) it should be readily seen *by the child* to be a reasonable activity that works; (3) it should have some counterpart in real-life experiences; and (4) its component processes should be well understood so that effective training techniques can be devised. Our bias directs us to a subset of metacognitive activities that we feel admirably fit the prescription, checking, monitoring, and reality testing, etc. This is, of course, still too ambitious, and we would advocate the selection of a few basic skills for intensive study. The ones we have chosen can be subsumed under the general heading, self-interrogation.

The eventual aim is to train the child to think dialectically, in the sense of the Socratic teaching method. In the Socratic method, the teacher constantly questions the students' basic assumptions and premises, plays the devil's advocate, and probes weak areas, using such techniques as invious generalizations and counterexamples (Anderson, 1977; Collins, 1977). The desired end-product is that the student will come to perform the teacher's functions for himself via self-interrogation. Although the skills described by Collins are obviously not directly applicable to young slow-learning children, the basic principles underlying the approach are. We would start at the very simple level of teaching the child to self-interrogate when faced with a certain class of problems (instructions, math problems, a laboratory task, etc.). The type of self-interrogation that might work would be something like a routine set of n questions to ask oneself before proceeding. For example: (1) Stop and think! (2) Do I know what to do (i.e., understand the instructions, both explicit and implicit)? (3) Is there anything more I need to know before I can begin? and (4) Is there anything I already know that will help me (i.e., is this problem in any way like one I have done before)?

We are currently attempting to train educable children to follow both verbal and written instructions and to perform a variety of simple prose comprehension tasks, all in the context of a meaningful activity, like assembling a toy or following a recipe. In the course of these activities, they deliberately and overtly pass through a self-interrogation routine like the one described above. We believe that devising simple systems for eliciting self-awareness and conscious control over one's own activities is an important form of training because it is a desirable end-product in its own right; it should have transituational applicability, and it should improve both the child's cognitive and metacognitive skills and his feelings of personal competence.

VI. SUMMARY

The principal theme of this chapter has been the development of certain metacognitive skills that are indicative of efficient problem solving in a variety of situations, whether experimental, educational, or naturally occurring. We believe the distinction between knowledge and the understanding of that knowledge to be a valid and important distinction with great heuristic power for those interested in cognitive development. The emphasis in this chapter has been on the executive processes that underlie the cognitive products of the child; the executive processes of modern cognitive theory — predicting, planning, checking, and monitoring. We suggest that these are the basic characteristics of efficient thinking in a wide range of learning situations.

It is a reflection of the state of the art that the majority of developmental and training studies to date have been concerned with the conscious control of a few "simple" mnemonic skills for deliberate remembering. The cultural relativity of such skills was discussed both in terms of their ecological validity cross-culturally and with reference to the school problems of educable retarded children.

One main purpose of this chapter was to emphasize the paucity of experimental studies concerned with general metacognitive skills outside of the framework of traditional memory tasks. A particularly neglected research area has been the development of efficient training programs for the developmentally young, programs that concentrate on executive functioning rather than the perfection of a specific skill. Training techniques to induce simple checking skills in those who would not introduce them spontaneously, at least in the context of school learning or traditional laboratory tasks, have not been developed. Although the problems entailed in devising such training programs cannot be overestimated, both the practical and theoretical benefits that would accrue warrant the expenditure of effort and ingenuity.

ACKNOWLEDGMENTS

The majority of the empirical research reviewed here was undertaken at two research stations — at Peoria and Troy, Illinois. The author would like to extend her special appreciation to Mrs. Wilma Noynaert, Assistant Director of Special Education for the Peoria Publis Schools. She has continually provided support and encouragement and has made access to special education classes readily available. Thanks are also due to the following principals: Mr. William Jordan of Von Steuben School, Mr. Lee Nugent of Hines School, Mr. Dennis Bitner of Trewyn School, Mr. William Ricca of Roosevelt School, Mr. Robert Carruthers of Lincoln School, Mr. Robert Sorenson of Kingman School; and to all the teachers for their generous and willing cooperation. The author would especially like to thank Mrs. Carolyn Long for her patience and skill in testing the children and, of course, the children themselves for their willing and active participation and their sense of humor.

The author would also like to extend her special appreciation to William Orenic, Assistant Superintendent, Troy Community Consolidated School District, for allowing us to conduct studies in the Troy schools. Thanks are also due to Mr. Tom Staley and Mr. Bill Sparlin, principals of the Troy Craughwell School and the Troy Junior High School, for their generous and willing cooperation and to the children and teachers who gave so generously of their time and enthusiastic effort. Special thanks are due to Mr. James McCormick, Assistant Principal of Craughwell School, who acted as liaison officer, for his continued advice and support and to Mrs. Candy Mancuso for collecting data and supervising the smooth running of the studies.

The preparation of this manuscript was supported by Grant Nos. HD 06864 and HD 05951 and a Research Career Development Award No. HD 00111 from the National Institutes of Child Health and Human Development. The author would like to express her appreciation to Joseph C. Campione and Sandra S. Smiley for their collaboration and continual advice and support throughout the conduct of the research. The following colleagues have also contributed and collaborated at various stages of the research program: Craig Barclay, Norman Bray, Jeanne Day, Judy DeLoache, Lucia French, Roberta Jones, Susan Judd, Sallie Lawton, Barbara Lindauer, Martin Murphy, and Thomas Thieman, Many thanks also to Jane Thompson for her patient typing of this lengthy manuscript through at least three versions.

REFERENCES

Acredolo, L. P., Pick, H. L., & Olsen, M. G. Environmental differentiation and familiarity as determinants of children's memory for spatial location. *Developmental Psychology,* 1975, *11,* 495–501.

Anderson, R. C. The notion of schemata and the educational enterprise. In R. C. Anderson, R. J. Spiro, & W. E. Montaugue (Eds.), *Schooling and the acquisition of knowledge.* Hillsdale, N.J.: Lawrence Erlbaum Associates, 1977.

Anderson, R. C., & Biddle, W. B. On asking people questions about what they are reading. In G. H. Bower (Ed.), *The psychology of learning and motivation* (Vol. 9). New York: Academic Press, 1975.

Appel, L. F., Cooper, R. G., McCarrell, N., Sims-Knight, J., Yussen, S. R., & Flavell, J. H. The development of the distinction between perceiving and memorizing. *Child Development,* 1972, *43,* 1365–1381.

Bartlett, F. C. *Remembering: A study in experimental and social psychology.* Cambridge: Cambridge University Press, 1932.

Bateson, G. *Naven.* Stanford Calif.: Stanford University Press, 1958.

Becker, J. D. Reflections on the formal description of behavior. In D. G. Bobrow & A. Collins (Eds.), *Representation and understanding: Studies in cognitive science.* New York: Academic Press, 1975.

Belmont, J. M. Relation of age and intelligence to short-term color memory. *Child Development,* 1972, *43,* 19–29.

Belmont, J. M., & Butterfield, E. C. The relation of short-term memory to development and intelligence. In L. P. Lipsitt & H. W. Reese (Eds.), *Advances in child development and behavior* (Vol. 4). New York: Academic Press, 1969.

Belmont, J. M., & Butterfield, E. C. Learning strategies as determinants of memory deficiencies. *Cognitive Psychology,* 1971, *2,* 411–420.

Belmont, J. M., & Butterfield, E. C. The instructional approach to developmental cognitive research. In R. V. Kail, Jr., & J. W. Hagen (Eds.), *Perspectives on the development of memory and cognition.* Hillsdale, N.J.: Lawrence Erlbaum Associates, 1977.

Berch, D. B. Methodology in the study of memory development: A critique of the Perlmutter and Myers experiment. *Bulletin of the Psychonomic Society,* 1975, *6,* 285–286.

Berch, D. B., & Evans, R. C. Decision processes in children's recognition memory. *Journal of Experimental Child Psychology,* 1973, *16,* 148–164.

Bernstein, B. *Class codes and control* (Vol. 1). London: Routledge & Kegan Paul, 1971.

Binet, A. *Psychologie des grands calculateur et joueurs d'echess.* Paris: Hachette, 1894.

Blake, M. Prediction of recognition when recall fails: Exploring the feeling of knowing phenomena. *Journal of Verbal Learning and Verbal Behavior,* 1973, *12,* 311–319.

Bobrow, D. G. Dimensions of representation. In D. G. Bobrow & A. Collins (Eds.), *Representation and understanding: Studies in cognitive science.* New York: Academic Press, 1975.

Bobrow, D. G., & Norman, D. A. Some principles of memory schemata. In D. G. Bobrow & A. Collins (Eds.), *Representation and understanding: Studies in cognitive science.* New York: Academic Press, 1975.

Borkowski, J. G., & Wanschura, P. B. Mediational processes in the retarded. In N. R. Ellis (Ed.), *International review of research in mental retardation* (Vol. 7). New York: Academic Press, 1974.

Bower, G. H. Analysis of a mnemonic device. *American Scientist,* 1970, *58,* 496–510.

Brainerd, C. J. Order of acquisition of transitivity, conservation, and class inclusion of length and weight. *Developmental Psychology,* 1973, *8,* 105–116.

Bransford, J. D., Nitsch, K. W., & Franks, J. J. Schooling and the facilitation of knowing. In R. C. Anderson, R. J. Spiro, & W. E. Montague (Eds.), *Schooling and the acquisition of knowledge*. Hillsdale, N.J.: Lawrence Erlbaum Associates, 1977.

Broudy, H. S. Types of knowledge and the purposes of schooling. In R. C. Anderson, R. J. Spiro, & W. E. Montague (Eds.), *Schooling and the acquisition of knowledge*. Hillsdale, N.J.: Lawrence Erlbaum Associates, 1977.

Brown, A. L. Judgments of recency for long sequences of pictures: The absence of a developmental trend. *Journal of Experimetal Child Psychology*, 1973, *15*, 473–481. (a)

Brown, A. L. Mnemonic elaboration and recency judgments in children. *Cognitive Psychology*, 1973, *5*, 233–248. (b)

Brown, A. L. The role of strategic behavior in retardate memory. In N. R. Ellis (Ed.), *International review of research in mental retardation* (Vol. 1). New York: Academic Press, 1974.

Brown, A. L. The development of memory: Knowing, knowing about knowing, and knowing how to know. In H. W. Reese (Ed.), *Advances in child development* (Vol. 10). New York: Academic Press, 1975.

Brown, A. L. The construction of temporal succession by preoperational children. In A. D. Pick (Ed.), *Minnesota Symposia on Child Psychology* (Vol. 10). Minneapolis: University of Minnesota, 1976. (a)

Brown, A. L. Semantic integration of children's reconstruction of narrative sequences. *Cognitive Psychology*, 1976, *8*, 247–262. (b)

Brown, A. L. Development, schooling and the acquisition of knowledge about knowledge. In R. C. Anderson, R. J. Spiro, & W. E. Montague (Eds.), *Schooling and the acquisition of knowledge*. Hillsdale, N.J.: Lawrence Erlbaum Associates, 1977. (a)

Brown, A. L. Metacognitive development and reading. In R. J. Spiro, B. Bruce, & W. F. Brewer (Eds.), *Theoretical issues in reading comprehension*. Hillsdale, N.J.: Lawrence Erlbaum Associates, 1977. (b)

Brown, A. L., & Barclay, C. R. The effects of training specific mnemonics on the metamnemonic efficiency of retarded children. *Child Development*, 1976, *47*, 71–80.

Brown, A. L., & Campione, J. C. Recognition memory for perceptually similar pictures in preschool children. *Journal of Experimental Psychology*, 1972, *95*, 55–62.

Brown, A. L., & Campione, J. C. Training strategic study time apportionment in educable retarded children. *Intelligence*, 1977, *1*, 94–107.

Brown, A. L., & Campione, J. C. Memory strategies in learning: Training children to study strategically. In H. Pick, H. Leibowitz, J. Singer, A. Steinschneider, & H. Stevenson (Eds.), *Application of basic research in psychology*. New York: Plenum Press, in press.

Brown, A. L., Campione, J. C., Barclay, C. R., Lawton, S. C., & Jones, R. *Predicting the outcome of strategy intervention*. Work in progress, Center for the Study of Reading, University of Illinois at Urbana-Champaign.

Brown, A. L., Campione, J. C., Bray, N. W., & Wilcox, B. L. Keeping track of changing variables: Effects of rehearsal training and rehearsal prevention in normal and retarded adolescents. *Journal of Experimental Psychology*, 1973, *101*, 123–131.

Brown, A. L., Campione, J. C., & Murphy, M. D. Keeping track of changing variables: Long-term retention of a trained rehearsal strategy by retarded adolescents. *American Journal of Mental Deficiency*, 1974, *78*, 446–453.

Brown, A. L., Campione, J. C., & Murphy, M. D. Maintenance and generalization of trained metamnemonic awareness in educable retarded children. *Journal of Experimental Child Psychology*, 1977, *24*, 191–211.

Brown, A. L., & DeLoache, J. S. Skills, plans and self-regulation. In R. Siegler (Ed.), *Children's thinking: What develops?* Hillsdale, N.J.: Lawrence Erlbaum Associates, in press.

Brown, A. L., & Lawton, S. C. The feeling of knowing experience in educable retarded children. *Developmental Psychology*, 1977, *13*, 364–370.

Brown, A. L., & Scott, M. S. Recognition memory for pictures in preschool children. *Journal of Experimental Child Psychology*, 1971, *11*, 401–412.

Brown, A. L., & Smiley, S. S. *The development of strategies for studying prose passages* (Technical Report No. 66). Urbana-Champaign: University of Illinois, Center for the Study of Reading, October 1977. (a)

Brown, A. L., & Smiley, S. S. Rating the importance of structural units of prose passages: A problem of metacognitive development. *Child Development*, 1977, *48*, 1–8. (b)

Brown, R., & McNeill, D. The tip of the tongue phenomena. *Journal of Verbal Learning and Verbal Behavior*, 1966, *5*, 325–337.

Bruner, J. S. Nature and uses of immaturity. *American Psychologist*, 1972, *27*, 687–708.

Bruner, J. S., & Olson, D. R. Symbols and texts as tools of intellect. In G. Steiner (Ed.), *The psychology of the 20th century: Piaget's developmental and cognitive psychology within an extended context* (Vol. 7). Zurich: Kindler Publishing House, in press.

Butterfield, E. C., & Belmont, J. M. Assessing and improving the cognitive functions of mentally retarded people. In I. Bailer & M. Steinlicht (Eds.), *Psychological issues in mental retardation*. Chicago: Aldine Press, 1977.

Butterfield, E. C., Wambold, C., & Belmont, J. M. On the theory and practice of improving short-term memory. *American Journal of Mental Deficiency*, 1973, *77*, 654–669.

Campbell, D. T. Distinguishing differences of perception from failures of communication in cross-cultural studies. In F. S. C. Northrop & H. H. Livingstone (Eds.), *Cross-cultural understanding: Epistemology in anthropology*. New York: Harper & Row, 1964.

Campbell, D. T., & Stanley, J. C. *Experimental and quasi-experimental designs for research.* Chicago: Rand McNally, 1966.

Campione, J. C., & Brown, A. L. The effects of contextual changes and degree of component mastery on transfer of taining. In H. W. Reese (Ed.), *Advances in child development and behavior* (Vol. 9). New York: Academic Press, 1974.

Campione, J. C., & Brown, A. L. Memory and metamemory development in educable retarded children. In R. V. Kail, Jr., & J. W. Hagen (Eds.), *Perspectives on the development of memory and cognition.* Hillsdale, N.J.: Lawrence Erlbaum Associates, 1977.

Chi, M. T. H. *The development of short-term memory capacity.* Unpublished doctoral dissertation, Carnegie-Mellon University, 1975.

Chi, M. T. H. Short-term memory limitations in children: Capacity or processing deficits? *Memory & Cognition*, 1976, *4*, 559–572.

Chi, M. T. H. *Metamemory and chess skill.* Unpublished manuscript, University of Pittsburgh, 1977.

Christie, D. J., & Schumacher, G. M. Developmental trends in the abstraction and recall of relevant versus irrelevant thematic information from connected verbal materials. *Child Development*, 1975, *46*, 598–602.

Colby, B., & Cole, M. Culture, memory, and narrative. In R. Horton & R. Finnegan (Eds.), *Modes of thought: Essays on thinking in western and nonwestern societies.* London: Faber & Faber, 1973.

Cole, M., & Scribner, S. Theorizing about socialization of cognition. *Ethos*, 1975, *3*, 249–268.

Cole, M., & Scribner, S. Cross-cultural studies of memory and cognition. In R. V. Kail, Jr., & J. W. Hagen (Eds.), *Perspectives on the development of memory and cognition.* Hillsdale, N.J.: Lawrence Erlbaum Associates, 1977.

Collins, A. Processes in acquiring and using knowledge. In R. C. Anderson, R. J. Spiro, & W. E. Montague (Eds.), *Schooling and the acquisition of knowledge.* Hillsdale, N.J.: Lawrence Erlbaum Associates, 1977.

Collins, A., Warnock, E., Aiello, N., & Miller, M. Reasoning from incomplete knowledge. In D. G. Bobrow & A. Collins (Eds.), *Representation and understanding: Studies in cognitive science.* New York: Academic Press, 1975.

Danner, F. W. *Children's understanding of intersentence organization in the recall of short descriptive passages.* Unpublished doctoral dissertation, University of Minnesota, 1974.

Dasen, P. Cross-cultural Piagetian research: A summary. *Journal of Cross-Cultural Psychology,* 1972, *3*, 23–29.

Denney, N. W. Evidence for developmental changes in categorization criteria. *Human Development,* 1974, *17*, 41–53.

Denney, N. W., & Ziobrowski, M. Developmental changes in clustering criteria. *Journal of Experimental Child Psychology,* 1972, *13*, 275–283.

Drozdal, J. G., & Flavell, J. H. A developmental study of logical search behavior. *Child Development,* 1975, *46*, 389–393.

Dweck, C. S. Children's interpretation of evaluative feedback: The effect of social cues on learned helplessness. *Merrill-Palmer Quarterly,* 1976, *22*, 105–109.

Edgerton, R. *The cloak of competence.* Berkeley: University of California Press, 1967.

Flavell, J. H. Developmental studies of mediated memory. In H. W. Reese & L. P. Lipsitt (Eds.), *Advances in child development and behavior* (Vol. 5). New York: Academic Press, 1970.

Flavell, J. H. *The development of metacommunication.* Paper presented the Symposium on Language and Cognition, Twenty-first International Congress of Psychology, Paris, July 1976. (a)

Flavell, J. H. Metacognitive aspects of problem solving. In L. B. Resnick (Ed.), *The nature of intelligence.* Hillsdale, N.J.: Lawrence Erlbaum Associates, 1976. (b)

Flavell, J. H., Friedrichs, A. G., & Hoyt, J. D. Developmental changes in memorization processes. *Cognitive Psychology,* 1970, *1*, 324–340.

Flavell, J. H., & Wellman, H. M. Metamemory. In R. V. Kail, Jr., & J. W. Hagen (Eds.), *Perspectives on the development of memory and cognition.* Hillsdale, N.J.: Lawrence Erlbaum Associates, 1977.

Frase, L. T. Prose processing. In G. H. Bower (Ed.), *The psychology of learning and motivation* (Vol. 9). New York: Academic Press, 1975.

Gold, M. W. Stimulus factors in skill training of the retarded on a complex assembly task: Acquisition, transfer and retention. *American Journal of Mental Deficiency,* 1972, *76*, 517–526.

Gold, M. W. Factors affecting production by the retarded: Base rate. *Mental Retardation,* 1973, *11*, 41–45.

Greeno, J. G. Cognitive objectives of instruction: Theory of knowledge for solving problems and answering questions. In D. Klahr (Ed.), *Cognition and instruction.* Hillsdale, N.J.: Lawrence Erlbaum Associates, 1976.

Hart, J. T. Memory and memory monitoring processes. *Journal of Verbal Learning and Verbal Behavior,* 1967, *6*, 685–691.

Havelock, E. A. *Prologue to Greek literacy* (Lectures in memory of Louise Taft Semple). Cincinnati: University of Cincinnati, 1971.

Holt, J. H. *How children fail.* New York: Dell Publishing Co., 1964.

Huttenlocher, J. The origins of language comprehension. In R. L. Solso (Ed.), *Theories in cognitive psychology: The Loyola Symposium.* Washington, D.C.: Winston, 1976.

Huttenlocher, J., & Burke, D. Why does memory span increase with age. *Cognitive Psychology,* 1976, *8*, 1–31.

Inhelder, B., Sinclair, H., & Bovet, M. *Learning and the development of cognition.* Cambridge, Mass.: Harvard University Press, 1974.

Istomina, Z. M. The development of voluntary memory in preschool-age children. *Soviet Psychology,* 1975, *13*, 5–64.

James, W. *The principles of psychology* (Vol. 1). New York: Holt, 1890.

Jenkins, J. J. *Remember that old theory of memory? Well, forget it.* Paper presented at the meeting of the American Psychological Association, Montreal, August 1973.

Johnson, R. E. Recall of prose as a function of the structural importance of the linguistic unit. *Journal of Verbal Learning and Verbal Behavior,* 1970, *9,* 12–20.

Klahr, D. Understanding understanding systems. In L. W. Gregg (Ed.), *Knowledge and cognition.* Hillsdale, N.J.: Lawrence Erlbaum Associates, 1974.

Klahr, D., & Siegler, R. S. The representation of children's knowledge. In H. W. Reese (Ed.), *Advances in child development and behavior* (Vol. 12). New York: Academic Press, in press.

Kreutzer, M. A., Leonard, C., & Flavell, J. H. An interview study of children's knowledge about memory. *Monographs of the Society for Research in Child Development,* 1975, *40*(1, Serial Number 159).

Kuhn, D. Inducing development experimentally: Comments on a research paradigm. *Developmental Psychology,* 1974, *10,* 590–600.

Kvale, S. Memory and dialectics: Some reflections on Ebbinghaus and Mao Tse-Tung. *Human Development,* 1975, *18,* 205–222.

Lloyd, B. B. *Perception and cognition: A cross-cultural perspective.* Middlesex, England: Penguin Books, 1972.

Luchins, A. S. Mechanization in problem-solving. *Psychological Monographs,* 1942, *54,* 1–95.

Luria, A. R. Towards the problem of the historical nature of psychological processes. *International Journal of Psychology,* 1971, *6,* 259–272.

Markman, E. M. *Factors affecting the young child's ability to monitor his memory.* Unpublished doctoral dissertation, University of Pennsylvania, 1973.

Markman, E. M. Realizing that you don't understand: A preliminary investigation. *Child Development,* 1977, *48,* 986–992.

Masur, E. F., McIntyre, C. W., & Flavell, J. H. Developmental changes in apportionment of study time among items in a multitrial free recall task. *Journal of Experimental Child Psychology,* 1973, *15,* 237–246.

McLuhan, M. *Understanding media.* New York: McGraw-Hill, 1964.

Meacham, J. A. Society investigations of memory development. In R. V. Kail, Jr., & J. W. Hagen (Eds.), *Perspectives on the development of memory and cognition.* Hillsdale, N.J.: Lawrence Erlbaum Associates, 1977.

Mead, M. *Continuities in cultural evolution.* New Haven: Yale University Press, 1964.

Moore, J., & Newell, A. How can Merlin understand? In L. W. Gregg (Ed.), *Knowledge and cognition.* Hillsdale, N.J.: Lawrence Erlbaum Associates, 1974.

Moynahan, E. D. The development of knowledge concerning the effect of categorization upon free recall. *Child Development,* 1973, *44,* 238–246.

Moynahan, E. D. The development of ability to assess recall performance. *Journal of Experimental Child Psychology,* 1976, *21,* 94–97.

Neisser, U. *Cognitive psychology.* New York: Appleton-Century-Crofts, 1967.

Neisser, U. *Cognition and reality.* San Francisco: W. H. Freeman, 1976.

Nelson, K. Cognitive development and the acquisition of concepts. In R. C. Anderson, R. J. Spiro, & W. E. Montague (Eds.), *Schooling and the acquisition of knwoeldge.* Hillsdale, N.J.: Lawrence Erlbaum Associates, 1977.

Nelson, K., & Brown, A. L. The semantic-episodic distinction in memory development. In P. Ornstein (Ed.), *Memory development in children.* Hillsdale, N.J.: Lawrence Erlbaum Associates, 1978.

Norman, D. A. Memory, knowledge, and the answering of questions. In R. L. Solso (Ed.), *Contemporary issues in cognitive psychology: The Loyola Symposium.* Washington, D.C.: Winston, 1973.

Olson, D. Culture, technology and intellect. In L. B. Resnick (Ed.), *The nature of intelligence.* Hillsdale, N.J.: Lawrence Erlbaum Associates, 1976.

Olson, D. The language of instruction: On the literate bias of schooling. In R. C. Anderson, R. J. Spiro, & W. E. Montague (Eds.), *Schooling and the acquisition of knowledge.* Hillsdale, N.J.: Lawrence Erlbaum Associates, 1977.

Osherson, D. N., & Markman, E. Language and the ability to evaluate contradictions and tautologies. *Cognition,* 1975, *3,* 213–226.

Overcast, T. D., Murphy, M. D., Smiley, S. S., & Brown, A. L. The effects of instruction on recall and recognition of categorized lists in the elderly. *Bulletin of the Psychonomic Society,* 1975, *5,* 339–341.

Perlmutter, M., & Myers, N. A. Recognition memory development in two- to four-year-olds. *Developmental Psychology,* 1974, *10,* 447–450.

Piaget, J. Intellectual evolution from adolescence to adulthood. *Human Development,* 1972, *15,* 1–12.

Piaget, J., & Inhelder, B. *Memory and intelligence.* New York: Basic Books, 1973.

Reeves, J. W. *Thinking about thinking.* New York: George Braziller, 1965.

Reitman, W. What does it take to remember? In D. A. Norman (Ed.), *Models of human memory.* New York: Academic Press, 1970.

Resnick, L. B., & Glaser, R. Problem solving and intelligence. In L. B. Resnick (Ed.), *The nature of intelligence.* Hillsdale, N.J.: Lawrence Erlbaum Associates, 1976.

Riegel, K. F. From traits and equilibrium toward developmental dialectics. In W. J. Arnold & J. K. Cole (Eds.), *1974–75 Nebraska Symposium on Motivation.* Lincoln: University of Nebraska Press, 1976.

Robinson, F. P. *Effective study.* New York: Harper & Row, 1941.

Rogoff, B., Newcombe, N., & Kagan, J. Planfulness and recognition memory. *Child Development,* 1974, *45,* 972–977.

Rohwer, W. D., Jr. Elaboration and learning in childhood and adolescence. In H. W. Reese (Ed.), *Advances in child development and behavior* (Vol. 8). New York: Academic Press, 1973.

Rothkopf, E. Z. Structural text features and the control of processes in learning from written materials. In J. B. Carroll & R. O. Freedle (Eds.), *Language comprehension and the acquisition of knowledge.* Washington, D.C.: Winston, 1972.

Salatas, H., & Flavell, J. H. Behavioral and metamnemonic indicators of strategic behaviors under remember instructions in first grade. *Child Development,* 1976, *47,* 80–89.

Schaeffer, B., Eggleston, V. H., & Scott, J. L. Number development in young children. *Cognitive Psychology,* 1974, *6,* 357–379.

Scribner, S. Situating the experiment in cross-cultural research. In K. F. Riegel & J. A. Meacham (Eds.), *The developing individual in a changing world: Historical and cultural issues* (Vol. 1). The Hague: Mouton, 1976.

Scribner, S. Modes of thinking and ways of speaking: Culture and logic reconsidered. In R. O. Freedle (Ed.), *Discourse production and comprehension.* Norwood, N.J.: Ablex Publishing Corp., 1977.

Scribner, S., & Cole, M. The cognitive consequences of formal and informal education. *Science,* 1973, *182,* 553–559.

Shif, Z. I. Development of children in schools for the mentally retarded. In M. Cole & I. Maltzman (Eds.), *A handbook of contemporary Soviet psychology.* New York: Basic Books, 1969.

Sieber, J. *Secondary ignorance.* Paper presented at the UNESCO International Conference on Learning and the Education Process, Stockholm, August 1968.

Siegler, R. S. Three aspects of cognitive development. *Cognitive Psychology,* 1976, *8,* 481–520.

Smiley, S. S. Comment on mathemagenic activity, comprehension and development. *Proceedings of the Interdisciplinary Institute on Reading and Child Development.* Newark: University of Delaware, 1974.

Smiley, S. S., Oakley, D. D., Worthen, D., Campione, J. C., & Brown, A. L. Recall of thematically relevant material by adolescent good and poor readers as a function of written versus oral presentation. *Educational Psychology,* 1977, *69,* 381–387.

Spitz, H. H. Consolidating facts into the schematized learning and memory system of educable retardates. In N. R. Ellis (Ed.), *International review of research in mental retardation* (Vol. 6). New York: Academic Press, 1973.

Tenney, Y. J. The child's conception of organization and recall. *Journal of Experimental Child Psychology,* 1975, *19,* 100–114.

Thieman, T. J., & Brown, A. L. *The effects of semantic and formal similarity on recognition memory for sentences in children.* Unpublished manuscript, University of Illinois, 1976.

Tulving, E., & Pearlstone, Z. Availability versus accessibility of information in memory for words. *Journal of Verbal Learning and Verbal Behavior,* 1966, *5,* 381–391.

Wade, M. G., & Gold, M. W. Limitations of the retarded worker when maximizing the man –machine interface. *Human Factors,* in press.

Wellman, H. M. The development of memory monitoring: The feeling of knowing experience. *Child Development,* in press

Wellman, H. M., Ritter, R., & Flavell, J. H. Deliberate memory behavior in the delayed reactions of very young children. *Developmental Psychology,* 1975, *11,* 780–787.

Wickelgren, W. A. Age and storage dynamics in continuous recognition memory. *Developmental Psychology,* 1975, *11,* 165–169.

Yarmey, A. D. I recognize your face, but I can't remember your name: Further evidence of the tip-of-the-tongue phenomenon. *Memory & Cognition,* 1973, *1,* 287–290.

Yates, F. A. *The art of memory.* Chicago: University of Chicago Press, 1966.

Yendovitskaya, T. V. Development of memory. In A. V. Zaparozhets & D. B. Elkonin (Eds.), *The psychology of preschool children.* Cambridge, Mass.: M.I.T. Press, 1971.

Yussen, S. R. Determinants of visual attention and recall in observational learning by preschoolers and second graders. *Developmental Psychology,* 1974, *10,* 93–100.

Yussen, S. R., & Levy, V. M., Jr. Developmental changes in predicting one's own span of short-term memory. *Journal of Experimental Psychology,* 1975, *19,* 502–508.

3

Piaget and Beyond: Toward a Developmentally Based Theory and Technology of Instruction

Robbie Case
The Ontario Institute for Studies in Education

I. INTRODUCTION

As a number of authors have suggested, there is an important difference between a theory of learning and a theory of instruction (Ausubel, 1963; Bruner, 1966; Glaser, 1976). A theory of learning is intended to provide a model of the learning process. By contrast, a theory of instruction is intended to provide a model of how this process can be optimized to achieve particular goals. Depending on the class of goals that is of interest, a particular learning theory may or may not provide a valuable starting point for building a theory of instruction. No matter how appropriate a particular theory of learning may be, however, a theory of instruction must in some sense go beyond it, because it must provide a set of principles for making sound instructional decisions in specific educational settings.

A similar point can be made with regard to the difference between a theory of intellectual development and a developmental theory of instruction. The object of a theory of intellectual development is to provide a model of how the human intellect changes from birth to maturity. In contrast, the object of a developmental theory of instruction is to provide a model of how this process can be optimized to achieve particular goals. Depending on the class of goals that is of interest, a particular developmental theory may or may not provide a good starting point for building a developmental theory of instruction. No matter how relevant a particular theory of intellectual development may be, however, a developmental theory of instruction must in some sense go beyond it, because it must provide a set of principles for making sound instructional decisions for specific types of children at specific points in their development.

This chapter begins with a brief description of the dominant psychological theory in the area of intellectual development – the theory of Jean Piaget. This description is intended only to serve as a starting point, by indicating what instructional questions a developmental theory of instruction must ultimately be able to address. After these questions have been outlined, a theory is presented that goes beyond Piaget's in that it attempts to provide a more detailed model of the process by which the developmental competencies he described are acquired. Following a review of research related to the new theory, the instructional questions raised earlier are reconsidered, and an attempt is made to show how the new theory suggests answers to them. Finally, a number of instructional principles and techniques that are consistent with the new theory are proposed, and an illustration is provided of how they can be applied in a classroom setting.

II. PIAGET'S THEORY OF INTELLECTUAL DEVELOPMENT

The object of Piaget's theory is to describe and explain the development of human knowledge. Piaget is less concerned with the content of human knowledge than with its organization or structure. A central postulate of his theory is that human knowledge has the structure it does because the activities through which it is acquired are also highly structured. The central thrust of Piaget's research has been to investigate the structure of these knowledge-gathering activities.

Consider first the way in which knowledge is acquired during the first 2 years of life (Piaget, 1951, 1954). When an infant is born, he comes equipped with a number of basic action patterns (schemes) such as grasping, sucking, and visual tracking. It is by the exercise of these schemes that the child acquires his first knowledge of the world. At the same time as the child acquires this first knowledge, two important changes take place in the schemes themselves. The first is that they gradually become more differentiated; that is, they gradually become capable of being applied differentiatlly to a wider and wider variety of objects. The second is that they gradually become more coordinated. Although grasping starts out as a relatively isolated and reflexive scheme, for example, it gradually becomes coordinated with a large number of other schemes such as visual exploration, reaching, and manual rotation. As these sensorimotor schemes are applied and coordinated, the infant not only acquires a multifaceted and stable understanding of the objects in the immediate environment; the infant also acquires a flexible system of sensorimotor operations by means of which he can acquire further knowledge of new objects in new environments. A basic characteristic of the system of *sensorimotor operations* is that any effect produced by one scheme (e.g., grasping) can be reversed by another scheme (e.g., replacement).

A parallel trend occurs at a higher level during the next 6 years of life (Inhelder & Piaget, 1964; Piaget, 1952, 1960). Having mastered the basic sensorimotor operations of relevance to his immediate environment, the child begins to represent these operations symbolically and to manipulate objects mentally in addition to physically. The new schemes that the child develops during this period are similar to those developed during the first 2 years of life in that they can still be applied only in the presence of concrete objects. However, they are different in that they now involve actions that can be described as more internal in character: for example, procedures for combining and manipulating words, procedures for classifying objects, and procedures for quantifying. Initially, the symbolic schemes that emerge are again rather global and isolated. For example, the mental activity of finding the larger of two objects would be based on global appearances and would not yet be coordinated with the reciprocal activity of finding the smaller of two objects. With time, however, the schemes once again become more differentiated and coordinated so that by the age of 6 to 8, the child has begun to form a new system. Thus, during the years from 2 to 8, children not only acquire a knowledge of the basic categories and relations of relevance in their environments; they also acquire a system of *concrete operations* by means of which they can acquire further knowledge of this sort in new environments. As with the system of sensorimotor operations, a basic property of this system of concrete operations is that the effect of any one mental action (e.g., width increase) can be reversed or compensated for by some other mental action (e.g., width decrease, height increase).

From 8 to 12 years of age, the child's system of concrete operations becomes increasingly stable and generalized. At the same time, the groundwork is laid for the emergence of mental operations that are of a higher order still (Inhelder & Piaget, 1958). These are operations that take the products of the second stage (mental operations) as building blocks and operate on them directly rather than on the properties of concrete objects. At the concrete stage, for example, a child who witnessed an increase of weight on one arm of a balance could imagine a simple negation of this effect by the subtraction of the same amount of weight. He could also understand the reciprocal effect produced by an addition of weight to the other side. Children at the next stage of development, however, could take either the operation of negation or the operation of reciprocity as a starting point and generate the other mentally in the absence of any concrete example. They could further take the relation between these two relations as a given and imagine an inverse relation between relations in some other variable such as distance from the fulcrum. As children apply and compare operations, they become capable of generating many more combinations in their minds than are actually present before them. With time, they develop a system for generating *all* possible combinations in a given situation and, with this, a procedure for experimentally eliminating all combinations but one in order to isolate the effect of one particular variable. In addition to acquiring an understanding of the world that is more abstract and complex, the adolescent thus acquires a coordinated system of *formal operations* by means of which he can acquire similar abstract knowledge in new content areas.

What are the variables that affect a child's progress through these three developmental stages? According to Piaget, there are four basic factors: maturation, physical experience, social experience, and equilibration (Piaget, 1964). Of these, the fourth is seen as most important. Although the necessity of the first three factors is acknowledged, the exact mechanism by which they exert their effect is left largely undefined, and their importance is consistently downplayed (Piaget, 1964, 1970). Unfortunately, Piaget is also rather vague as to what the equilibration process entails (Piaget, 1964, 1970, 1971). At a global level of analysis, he is clear that the process involves a reflection on the adequacy of the current set of operations and an experimentation with new operations. He is also clear concerning the child's criterion for determining adequacy. It is consistency – consistency of predictions with events actually observed, consistency of judgments made in one situation with judgments made in another, or consistency of reasoning based on one system of operations with reasoning based on another (Piaget, 1971). Beyond this, however, he does not specify the exact mechanism by which equilibration occurs.

Although the equilibration process is not described in Piaget's theory in any great detail, the description that *is* given is sufficient to generate the conclusion that the process of development must necessarily be a rather slow one. Just as one would not expect a child to develop an adult identity in a few months if he were simply given hormone treatments to induce maturation or exposed to a massive variety of new physical and social experiences to induce learning, so one would not expect a child to develop an entire system of formal thought in a few months simply by the action of maturation or learning. Because the equilibration process is an internal one that involves reflection, coordination, and construction, and because the task of cognitive reorganization is such a massive and fundamental one, Piaget assumes that there is a limit to how much acceleration of development can be expected by any sort of environmental manipulation (Piaget, 1964, 1970).

To summarize, according to Piaget, children begin their life with a primitive repertoire of action schemes. Through the process of equilibration – and to some extent with the aid of maturation and externally induced learning – this initial repertoire gradually becomes more differentiated and coordinated. At a number of points in the child's life, the schemes that have been coordinated attain an interdependence that gives them the property of an organized system or operational structure. Intellectual development consists of a series of such structures, beginning with the structures of the sensorimotor period and terminating with the structures of formal thought.

III. QUESTIONS FOR A DEVELOPMENTAL THEORY OF INSTRUCTION

If Piaget's account of intellectual development is correct in its general outline (and I believe it is), at least two questions must be addressed by any theory that hopes to suggest how children's intellectual growth can be most appropriately fostered. The first question is how an educational environment should be structured so as to optimize the acquisition of the major systems of intellectual operations. This question is premised on two assumptions: (1) that the acquisition of these systems can be influenced by the sorts of environmental factors that are potentially under human control; and (2) that the sort of environment in which a child is currently being raised is not already optimal from a developmental point of view. Both of these assumptions would appear to be warranted. There is ample evidence that the rate of progress through the stages described by Piaget varies widely as a function of the human environment to which children are exposed (Dasen, 1972; Gaudia, 1972; Hollos, 1975). In addition, there is ample evidence that many (if not most) adults never reach the stage of formal operations under present environmental conditions (Karplus & Peterson, 1970; Kuhn, Langer, Kohlberg, & Haan, 1977; Piaget, 1972; Tomlinson-Keasey, 1972).

The second question that must be addressed is how the instruction of culturally valued facts and skills should be designed so that it is geared to the system of knowledge-gathering operations that the learner has available. This question is premised on the assumption that instruction that is not geared to a student's available system of operations will not be optimal. Once again, however, this assumption would appear to be warranted. When children are given explanations or demonstrations that utilize a more advanced level of thinking than they themselves employ, they do not appear to be capable of reproducing them even a few seconds later. Instead, they deform the material presented to their own developmental level (Blatt & Kohlberg, 1971; Turiel, 1972). The object of the present section is to explore the theoretical and technical problems that remain to be solved before either of the above questions can be answered.

A. Optimizing the Acquisition of Operational Structures

Consider first the question of how to structure an environment so as to optimize the development of operational structures. At a global level of analysis, a Piagetian method for accomplishing this objective may be suggested with little difficulty. The first step is to provide a detailed account of the way in which the major operational structures manifest themselves in the content areas that are of greatest importance to educators — mathematics, history, science, etc. The second step is to determine the stage at which the students to be taught are currently functioning. The third step is to structure the curriculum so that it includes exercises aimed at promoting a transition from this level of thought to a higher one. Although the general procedure for fostering operational development is clear, however, a great deal of further work remains to be done before any of the specific steps may actually be put into practice.

1. *Step 1: Structural Analysis.* As an illustration of the problems that are inherent in the structural analysis of conventional academic tasks, consider what

is perhaps Piaget's best-known analysis of an operational structure – that underlying the conservation of substance (Inhelder, Sinclair, & Bovet, 1974; Piaget, 1957; Piaget & Inhelder, 1941). The specific concept to be acquired in this case is that the amount of matter in a container remains invariant in spite of perceptible deformations. If two quantities of water are placed in identically shaped beakers and their initial identity is established, the child who has not yet acquired conservation will think that the two quantities of liquid are no longer equal when one is poured into a container that is taller and thinner. The child who has acquired the concept will realize that the two quantities of liquid must still be equal. His explanation will be that nothing has been added or taken away and that they were originally equal. Alternatively, the child may simply state that the liquid in the tall thin beaker could be returned to its original container, where it would once again be seen to be equal to the liquid in the standard beaker.

According to Piaget, children who grasp the conservation principle do so because they have acquired the following understanding: The increase in the salient dimension that occurs during the transformation is compensated for by a decrease in the less salient dimension. This knowledge may be symbolized as follows: $a_1 \times b_1 = a_2 \times b_2 = a_3 \times b_3 = \ldots$, where a and b represent the dimensions of height and cross-sectional area, and where the subscripts represent the different values these dimensions can assume. Piaget suggests that this knowledge can only be attained by a child who is capable of imagining an increase in one dimension and then reversing the result of this operation by imagining a decrease in the other. Because reversability is the hallmark of concrete operations, Piaget concludes that the knowledge underlying the concept of conservation cannot be acquired until the child has acquired the system of concrete operations.

Although this analysis may be adequate for Piaget's purposes, it also illustrates the problems inherent in any attempt to extend this sort of analysis to classroom tasks. First, it is by no means obvious what role a grouping of logical operations such as that described above might play in any academic area except perhaps mathematics or science. Second, it is not obvious what procedure was employed by Piaget in order to uncover the role of the above logical grouping in the first place. The actual performance that children exhibit on the conservation task gives no indication that they are making a mental compensation of the difference in height and the difference in cross sectional area. Thus, it seems clear that the procedure for determining the underlying operational structure was not simply to analyze children's responses to the task. Rather, the procedure must have been to analyze the knowledge that this performance was presumed to imply. Unfortunately, however, Piaget provides no general description of how such rational analyses were conducted. Thus, even in well-defined areas that clearly require logical reasoning such as science or math, it is not clear how the operational structures that underlie specific tasks should be identified.

2. *Step 2: Individual Assessment.*   Assuming that the problem of structural analysis could be solved, the next step in planning a developmental curriculum would be to determine the general operational level at which the children who were to be instructed were currently functioning. On the surface, this problem appears to be a trivial one. Because batteries of Piagetian tests have already been developed and standardized (Goldschmidt & Bentler, 1968; Tuddenham, 1970; Winkelmann, 1975), these tests could simply be administered, and students' operational levels determined using whatever scales are provided. In fact, matters are not quite so simple.

First of all, if one examines the correlations between items on Piagetian tests that supposedly tap very similar structures, one discovers that they are normally quite low and sometimes not even significant. Although it is not uncommon for two tests in the same mental battery to show a low intercorrelation, the implication from an instructional point of view is that the child's level of functioning must be assessed with regard to the specific structure that is required for a given task. Even then, to the extent that the low correlations across tests of related structures result from the action of uncontrolled task factors, it would not be possible to know whether a given child's performance resulted from the presence or absence of the particular operational structure of interest or from a response to one of the uncontrolled task factors.

If one looks at Piagetian tests of the *same* operational structure, one discovers a problem that is even more serious. Although the correlations between items are much higher, the absolute levels of success vary widely as a function of the particular test item that is employed. For example, while tests of conservation of number are passed by about the age of 6, tests of conservation of weight are not passed until about the age of 9 or 10, and tests of conservation of displaced volume are not passed until about the age of 11. From the point of view of developmental theory, the seriousness of this "decalage" among tasks in which the underlying structure is identical is a matter of some debate (Beilin, 1969; Pascual-Leone, 1972; Pinard, 1975). From the point of view of educational assessment, however, there can be no debate about the problems's seriousness. If a given structure is available by the age of kindergarten but may not be applied to certain tasks until the age of high school, then the utility of knowing whether or not a child has acquired this structure is greatly diminished. This knowledge can only be of use once it is also known whether or not the child can *apply* the structure to the sort of task that is of instructional relevance. Unfortunately, however, the factors that affect the application of intellectual structures to specific tasks are simply not specified by Piaget's theory.

3. *Step 3: Instructional Planning.*   Assuming that the problems of structural analysis and assessment could be solved, the final step in planning a developmental curriculum would be to design exercises to promote the transition from

the child's current level of functioning to the next highest level. As was mentioned in Section II, Piaget is rather vague as to what is involved in the stage-transition process. Consider his description of how children acquire the logical structure that is presumed to underly the acquisition of conservation. Piaget distinguishes several substages in this process (Piaget, 1957). In the first, children evaluate the relative quantity of two beakers primarily on the basis of height. In the second, they evaluate the relative quantity of two beakers primarily on the basis of cross-sectional area. In the third, their two schemes for evaluating quantity unidimensionally come into conflict. In the fourth, they resolve this conflict by constructing a higher-order operational structure in which the two lower-order schemes are coordinated. Finally, in the fifth, they consolidate and extend this structure.

As a model of the stages that children pass through in the acquisition of a sophisticated structure for evaluating quantity, this description seems to me to be quite compelling. It has also received some empirical support. In a recent study, Lefebvre and Pinard (1972) brought children through the above series of stages by presenting them with a carefully designed set of instructional activities. As a result, they succeeded in producing dramatic changes in the children's understanding of conservation. It should be noted, however, that although Piaget traces the substages children go through quite adequately, and although he makes clear that the general factor that motivates the progression is the child's search for consistency, he leaves the details of the transition from substage to substage unspecified. What is missing is an account of the internal process that the child goes through in the course of perceiving or resolving the conflict between height and cross-sectional area or any description of the specific maturational and experiential factors that can affect this process.

From the point of view of developmental theory, the importance of such an account might be questioned. It might be argued that it is sufficient, at least in the early phases of theory construction, simply to note the general set of factors that are at work (in this case maturation, experience, and autoregulative activity) and to describe their interaction. From the point of view of instruction, however, a theory that stops at this general level of analysis leaves almost all of the important questions unanswered. Although Lefebvre and Pinard's basic procedure was effective, for example, and although its success has been replicated with children of the same age (Case, 1977b; Lefebvre & Pinard, 1974), minor modifications in this procedure appear to render it a good deal less effective (Fortin-Theriault, 1977).

What are the critical features, then, that distinguish an effective instructional sequence from an ineffective one? What sort of internal process do children go through in response to conflict-inducing experience, and how can the benefits of this process be maximized? A similar set of questions may be raised with regard to the action of maturation. For example, Lefebvre and Pinard (1972) noted in their earliest attempts to induce stage transition that many young children seemed incapable of perceiving the conflict inherent in their two different schemes for assessing quantity. In line with this initial observation, subsequent attempts to replicate their results with very young children proved unsuccessful (Fortin-Theriault, 1977). Was this due to some limitation imposed by maturation? If so, how did maturation exert its effect, and how should children's maturational state be taken into account in planning instruction (Lefebvre & Pinard, 1974)?

Finally, a related set of questions can be raised with regard to the role of the child's equilibrative activity. Although Lefebvre and Pinard's procedure relies primarily on exercises that are designed to foster the child's own internal resolution of conflict, other approaches that have included more didactic measures appear to have produced results of similar magnitude (Bucher & Schneider, 1973; Gelman, 1969; Zimmerman & Rosenthal, 1974). To what extent, then, must the process that is induced by instruction replicate the process of spontaneous development? What is involved in each process, and how does experience, when it *is* helpful, affect each process? Although Piaget's theory describes the process of cognitive development quite adequately at a general level of description, the level of analysis that is necessary for instructional planning is much more molecular.

B. Adapting Instruction to Students' Current Operational Level

In principle, the adaptation of curriculum content to children's current operational level involves the same three steps as the stimulation of operational development. The only difference is that the objective of the third step is not to change children's current level of operative functioning, but simply to adapt the tasks and materials so that the children may work within their current level of functioning throughout each curriculum unit. In practice, however, the difficulties that are encountered at each step are even more severe.

1. Step 1: Structural Analysis. Consider first the problem of analyzing the structural underpinnings of different instructional tasks or materials. As will be remembered, although Piaget does not describe his method of structural analysis explicitly, his implicit approach is first to specify the underlying knowledge or competence that is required by a group of tasks and then to analyze this knowledge from an abstract logical point of view. When one's goal is to select a stage-appropriate method or task for teaching a particular concept, however, the knowledge to be imparted is normally determined ahead of time. What is of interest is the very sort of variation that Piaget's analyses do not take into account, namely variation in the ease with which this knowledge can be extracted from one task as opposed to another. The problem, then, is not just that Piaget's method of analysis is not easily specified or generalized. Rather, it is that his method of analysis is not appropriate for the goal that is of interest in the first place.

2. *Step 2: Individual Assessment.*   A similar difficulty is encountered when is comes to individual assessment. As will be remembered, the assessment of students' current level of operative functioning is rendered difficult by the failure of Piaget's theory to account for "performance" or "task" factors that may confound the results obtained. When the goal is to adapt curriculum material to children's current level of functioning, this lacuna in the theory is even more serious, because children's responsiveness to such task variations is the major focus of interest.

3. *Step 3: Instructional Planning.*   Finally, consider the problems that would be encountered in optimizing children's application of existing structures to new content areas. Since Piaget's theory concentrates only on the process of structional acquisition and ignores the process of structural application, there is little direct guidance to be obtained. To be sure, the task factors affecting structural application might turn out to be identical to those affecting structural acquisition. However, since these are not specified by Piaget's theory in any case, the net result is the same.

To summarize, if Piaget's theory is correct, two major questions must be addressed by any developmentally based theory of instruction. The first is how to promote the development of operational structures. The second is how to adopt the instruction of culturally valued skills and concepts to student's current operational level. The general procedure for accomplishing each of these objectives seems clear. The first step is to analyze the operational structure of the proposed instructional content. The second step is to determine the operational level at which students are currently functioning. The third step is to develop activities devoted either to fostering the further development of these structures (if that is the goal), or to fostering their application to the particular content areas that are of interest (if that is the goal). Although the general procedure for accomplishing each of these objectives is clear, major theoretical or technical difficulties present themselves at each step when an attempt is actually made to put this procedure into practice. When the goal is to foster operational development, the identification of operational structures is rendered difficult by the absence of a general model or procedure for task analysis. The assessment of students' current level of functioning is rendered difficult by the presence of potentially confounding task factors in Piagetian measures. Finally, the design of optimal instruction is rendered difficult by the absence of a model that specifies what maturational and experiential factors can affect the process of structural acquisition. When the goal is to select a developmentally appropriate method of instruction, the analysis of instructional methods, the assessment of student readiness for these methods, and the optimal sequencing of such methods are all rendered difficult by the same problem: Piaget's theory ignores the very sort of "performance" or "task" factors that are of primary interest.

IV. A NEO-PIAGETIAN THEORY OF COGNITIVE DEVELOPMENT

At first glance, it might appear that the theoretical and practical problems that were described in the previous section are so serious as to disqualify Piaget's theory completely as a basis for building a workable theory and technology of instruction. However, although the problems are indeed serious, it should be noted that they may all be traced to a common source: the fact that Piaget's theory is predominantly *structural* rather than *functional*. As Flavell and Wohlwill (1969) have pointed out, Piaget's primary concern has been to provide a logical description of the systems of intellectual operations that children possess at different points in their development, not to provide a psychological description of the processes by which these operations are acquired and utilized. If Piaget's account of intellectual development could be supplemented by a theory that provided a more detailed account of these latter processes, then the seriousness of the problems that were mentioned in the previous section would be greatly reduced.

Consider first the problem of fostering the development of operative structures. If a functional theory of development were available, the intellectual operations of relevance to various academic disciplines might more easily be identified. The reason for this would be that they could be induced more directly from children's actual performance, with a reduced dependence on abstract logical analysis. In addition, children's current level of functioning in any given content area might more easily be assessed. The reason for this would be that the factors that constrain performance would be better understood and that the type of assessment of interest would be one more closely related to observed performance. Finally, the conditions for fostering opeational development might also be specified more easily. The reason for this would be that the specification could be based on a more detailed understanding of how such operations are acquired in the first place.

Consider next the problem of adapting the materials or methods of instruction to the current operational level of the student. If a functional theory of development were available, it might be easier to provide an analysis of different presentation methods or materials in terms of their developmental appropriateness. The reason would be that the kind of task variation that was under the instructor's control would be an explicit focus of the theory. It might also be easier to assess the student characteristics that would determine their ability to profit from one method or another. The reason would be that the internal variables determining children's reactions to task factors would also be better understood. Finally, it might be easier to arrange a sequence of activities that would optimize the application of already existing structures to new conceptual domains. The reason would be that the theory would specify the performance factors that were of greatest relevance, not only to the process of structural acquisition, but also to the process of structural application (if in fact they are different).

In this section, a theory of intellectual development is described that takes Piaget's account of development as its starting point and attempts to supplement it with exactly the sort of functional theory that is necessary for addressing the instructional questions mentioned above. The theory was originally proposed by Pascual-Leone (1969) in a doctoral dissertation submitted to the University of Geneva. Because the theory had its roots in an attempt to provide a more detailed account of the functional factors that influence the acquisition and utilization of specific Piagetian structures, its basic concepts will be introduced by returning to the conservation task and presenting a more detailed and functional analysis of it.

A.   Conservation of Liquid Substance:
     A Neo-Piagetian Analysis

In the context of Pascual-Leone's theory, the stages that children pass through prior to the attainment of conservation are modelled as a series of intellectual strategies of increasing complexity and power (Case, 1977a; Pascual-Leone, 1972).

1. *Strategy 1: Unidimensional Scanning.*   When asked to justify their responses, children at Piaget's first stage refer primarily to the difference in height between the two liquid columns. Photographs of their eye movements also show that they scan the two beakers almost exclusively in the vertical dimension (O'Bryan & Boersma, 1971). The sequence of mental steps they go through in arriving at their response might therefore be modeled as follows:

1. Scan the vertical dimension of the water in Beaker A.
2. Scan the vertical dimension of the water in Beaker B (noting that the water in B continues past the point where the water in A ends).
3. Recognize that Beaker B contains a taller column of water.
4. Conclude that Beaker B contains more water than Beaker A.

At each of the above steps, it is assumed that some salient scheme will be activated directly by the perceptual field. In addition, it is assumed that the child must activate a number of schemes on his own: either operative schemes to effect the transformation involved, or figurative schemes that are no longer activated by the perceptual field but that must still be stored. All of these schemes are itemized in Table 3.1. As may be seen, the maximum number of

TABLE 3.1
Detailed Model of Unidimensional Scanning Strategy

Step or Operation	Specific Schemes	Symbol[a]	
1. Scan the vertical dimension of the water in Beaker A.	(1) Operative scheme scanning the vertical extent of an object and storing its highest point.	ψ	Vertical scan
	(2)[b] Figurative scheme representing visual input from the side of Beaker A, as the eye scans along it.	ϕ	A: side
2. Scan the vertical dimension of the water in Beaker B, noting that the water in Beaker B continues past the point where the water in Beaker A ends.	(1) Operative scheme scanning the vertical extent of an object, and noting whether it passes the (still visible) highest point of the previous object.	ψ	Vertical scan
	(2)[b] Figurative scheme representing the visual input from Beaker B. Note that if the difference in heights were not visually salient, an extra scheme would have to be stored at this step, representing the height of Beaker A.	ϕ	B: side
3. Conclude that the water in Beaker B is taller than the water in Beaker A.	(1) Operative scheme taking the perceived difference in vertical projection as input and generating a conclusion as to which is higher.	ψ	Height
	(2)[b] Figurative scheme representing the perceived difference in vertical projection that was noticed in Step 2.	ϕ	Visual difference in vertical extension
4. Conclude that there is more water in Beaker B than in Beaker A.	(1) Operative scheme representing the rule: taller things contain more.	ψ	Higher = more
	(2)[b] Figurative scheme representing the perception generated in Step 3; namely, that Beaker B is taller than Beaker A.	ϕ	B > A (height)

[a]The symbol ψ is used to represent an operative scheme. The symbol ϕ is used to represent a figurative scheme.
[b]In Pascual-Leone's system, it is assumed that visually activated schemes do not require activation by M. They are therefore not counted in estimating the M-demand.

schemes that have to be attended to (other than those directly triggered by the perceptual field) is only one — the operative scheme effecting the height comparison. If the difference in height were not salient, then the maximum number would be two, since the subject would have to construct this difference by first computing one height and then storing this value, while the second height was computed and compared to it.

2. Strategy 2: Bidimensional scanning. When asked to justify their responses, children at Piaget's second stage sometimes refer to the difference in height and sometimes to the difference in width, depending on which appears more salient. If neither difference is very salient, they sometimes take a long time in deciding which has more. Photographs of their eye movements reveal a more thorough scan of the two beakers, and one that is not restricted to the vertical dimension. The sequence of mental steps that they go through in arriving at their answer might therefore be described as follows:

1. Scan the vertical dimension of the water in Beaker A.
2. Scan the vertical dimension of the water in Beaker B (noting that the water in B continues past the point where the water in A ends).
3. Recognize that Beaker B contains a taller column of water.

4. If the difference is large, conclude that B contains more water than A, otherwise, proceed to step 5.
5. Scan the horizontal dimension of the water in Beaker B.
6. Scan the horizontal dimension of the water in Beaker A.
7. Note that Beaker A contains a wider column of liquid.
8. If the difference is large, conclude that Beaker A contains more water than B. Otherwise, recycle to step 1, setting the criterion for "large" at a lower value.

The schemes that would have to be activated at each step in the above process are summarized in Table 3.2. As can be seen, the maximum number of schemes that must be activated is only two — the additional one (in comparison with Table 3.1) stemming from the fact that there is no direct visual cue as to which of the two objects is wider. If a direct comparison were made between the difference in height and width, then the maximum number would be three since the product of the height comparison would have to be stored while the widths were evaluated and compared.

3. *Strategy 3: Reasoning in Terms of Initial State.*   As has already been mentioned, children who give a conserving response justify their answer most frequently by referring to the original equality of the liquids and the nature of

TABLE 3.2
Detailed Model of Bidimensional Scanning Strategy

Step or Operation[a]		Specific Schemes		Symbol[b]
5.	Scan the horizontal dimension of the water in Beaker B.	(1)	Operative scheme scanning the horizontal extension of an object and storing its magnitude (perhaps as an image, or as a record of scan time).	ψ Horizontal scan
		(2)[c]	Figurative scheme representing the visual input from the base of Beaker B, as the eye scans along it.	ϕ B: bottom
6.	Scan the horizontal dimension of the water in Beaker A, comparing it to that in Beaker B. (Note that, since there is no visual cue as to the relative extent as there is for height, the length of Beaker B must be stored briefly.)	(1)	Figurative scheme representing the width of Beaker B (generated in Step 1).	ϕ Horizontal magnitude B
		(2)	Operative scheme scanning the horizontal extension of the object and comparing its magnitude to a previously stored value.	ψ Horizontal scan
		(3)[c]	Figurative scheme representing the visual input from the base of Beaker B.	ϕ A: bottom
7.	Note that Beaker A is wider.	(1)	Operative scheme taking two horizontal distances as input and tagging the appropriate one as wider.	ψ Width
		(2)	Figurative scheme representing the horizontal magnitude of A (generated in Step 5).	ϕ Horizontal magnitude A
		(3)[c]	Figurative scheme representing the horizontal magnitude of B (generated in Step 6).	ϕ Horizontal magnitude B
8.	Conclude that there is more water in Beaker A (unless the difference was hard to detect in Step 7, in which case, recycle to Step 1, Table 3.1).	(1)	Operative scheme representing the rule: wider things contain more.	ψ Wider = more
		(2)	Figurative scheme representing the conclusion generated in the previous step that Beaker A is wider than Beaker B.	ϕ A > B (width)

[a]Operation for Steps 1-4, see Table 3.1.
[b] ψ = operative scheme; ϕ = figurative scheme.
[c] Activated by perceptual input.

TABLE 3.3
Detailed Model of Strategy for Reasoning in Terms of Initial State

Step or Operation		Specific Schemes	Symbol[a]	
1. Recall the original relative quantity of the two beakers.	(1)	Figurative scheme representing the fact that the quantity in Beaker A was judged equal to the quantity in Beaker B at the outset.	ϕ	A = B
2. Recall the nature of the transformation.	(1)	Figurative scheme representing the original equality (see Step 1).	ϕ	A = B
	(2)	Figurative scheme representing the fact that the water was poured from Beaker B to B' without addition or subtraction.	ϕ	B $\xrightarrow{Pour}$ B'
3. Draw conclusion about the present relative quantity.	(1)	Operative scheme representing the rule: if the original state was equal and nothing is added or subtracted, then the final state is equal.	ψ	Pour
	(2)	Figurative scheme generated in Step 2.	ϕ ϕ	B $\xrightarrow{Pour}$ B' A = B
	(3)	Figurative scheme generated in Step 1.		

[a] ψ = operative scheme; ϕ = figurative scheme

the transformation. Eye movement photography shows that their scan of the post-transformation array is often quite cursary (O'Bryan & Boersma, 1971). The series of mental steps that they go through in arriving at the answer might therefore be described as follows (Pascual-Leone, 1972):

1. Recall the original relative quantity of the two beakers. Store.
2. Recall the nature of the transformation.
3. If the transformation was simply pouring, state that the final relative quantity is the same as the original one.

The schemes that would have to be activated at each of the above steps are itemized in Table 3.3. As may be seen, the maximum number of schemes that would have to be activated at any one step is three — one to represent the initial equality, one to represent the fact of pouring, and one to represent the rule that pouring does not change quantity.

Consider now the problem of stage transition. Following Piaget (1957), two general mechanisms of stage transition could be postulated. The first is a relatively slow and probabilistic one in which the child gradually comes to perceive the dimension of the problem that was not taken into account in his first strategy and gradually evolves some new strategy for dealing with this dimension. Alternatively, the child might experience some cognitive conflict as a result of using his first strategy — either because he did not attain some external goal or because he encountered an internal contradiction — and the experience of this conflict might lead him to actively search for some new dimension and to work out a new strategy for taking it into account. From the point of view of instruction, the latter process is the more interesting because it corresponds more closely to the kind of sequence that might be able to be stimulated by direct intervention.

Consider, therefore, how such a transition might be modeled in the context of Pascual-Leone's theory. Although there are a number of ways in which a conflict might be experienced in using either the first or the second strategy, the simplest case to consider is probably that of the subject who is functioning at the second stage, and who gets one answer if he uses height as a basis for evaluation in certain situations and another answer if he uses width. This realization might be arrived at by the following sequence of mental steps (Case, 1977b, 1976):

1. Note that Beaker B has a taller column of liquid than Beaker A.
2. Conclude that Beaker B contains more water by this criterion. Store.
3. Note that Beaker B is narrower than Beaker A.
4. Conclude that Beaker B contains less water by this criterion. Store.
5. Note that the two stored conclusions are in conflict.

The schemes that would have to be activated at each of the above steps are itemized in Table 3.4. As may be seen, the maximum number of schemes that would have to be activated in any one step is three: two for drawing the conclusion about width, and one for storing the conclusion about height.

Once a child experienced some dissatisfaction with his current strategy, he would presumably initiate a search for a more adequate one. A possible series of steps by which he might discover the strategy of reasoning in terms of the initial state would be as follows (Pascual-Leone, 1972):

1. Remember that the two original beakers (A and B) started out with the same amount of water in them.
2. Remember that the water in Beaker B was transferred into the tall thin beaker (B') by pouring, without any water being added or subtracted.
3. Drawing on past knowledge of such pouring acts, conclude that the amount of water in B was unchanged in the course of its transfer to B'.
4. Putting together the fact that B' is still equal to B, and that A was equal to B to begin with, conclude that A is equal to B'.

The schemes that would have to be activated at each of the above steps are itemized in Table 3.5. As may be seen, the maximum number of schemes that would have to be activated is again equal to three.

Taken together, the above series of models may be viewed as an explanation not only of the sequence of stages through which a child might pass in acquiring conservation, but also of the type of process by which he might move from one stage to the next if he encountered an appropriate environmental event. The details of the models are speculative and as yet untested. However, from the

TABLE 3.4
Detailed Model of Conflict Discovery
While Applying Bidimensional Scanning Strategy

Step or Operation		Specific Schemes	Symbol[a]	
1. Note that Beaker B has a taller column of liquid than Beaker A.	(1)	Operative scheme taking the perceived difference in vertical projection between two objects as input and generating as output a conclusion as to which is higher.	ψ	Height
	(2)[b]	Figurative scheme representing the perceived difference in vertical displacement between the two columns. (For details of the scheme generation, see Table 1.)	ϕ	Vertical displacement
2. Conclude there is more water in Beaker B.	(1)	Operative scheme representing the rule: taller things contain more.	ψ	Higher = more
	(2)[b]	Figurative scheme representing the fact generated in Step 1, namely, that Beaker B is taller than Beaker A.	ϕ	B > A (height)
3. Note that Beaker B is narrower than Beaker A.	(1)[c]	Figurative scheme generated in Step 2, representing the conclusion that Beaker B contains more than Beaker A.	ϕ	B > A (height)
	(2)	Operative scheme taking a perceived horizontal projection difference as input and generating as output a conclusion as to which is wider. (See Table 2 for details.)	ψ	Width
	(3)	Figurative scheme representing the horizontal projections of Beaker B and of Beaker A. (For details of the scheme generation, see Table 2.)	ϕ	Horizontal displacement
4. Conclude that there is less water in Beaker B.	(1)[c]	Figurative scheme generated in Step 2 (B > A).	ϕ	B > A
	(2)	Operative scheme representing the rule: wider things contain more.	ψ	Quantity (width)
	(3)[b]	Figurative scheme representing the fact that Beaker B is narrower than Beaker A.	ϕ	B < A (width)
5. Note that the two stored conclusions are in conflict.	(1)[b]	Figurative scheme generated in Step 2 (B > A).	ϕ	B > A
	(2)	Figurative scheme generated in Step 4 (B < A).	ϕ	B < A

[a]ψ = operative scheme; ϕ = figurative scheme.
[b]Activated by perceptual input.
[c]Scheme being activated (stored) for subsequent use.

point of view of the present chapter, the important thing to notice is not the specific set of mental steps or schemes that are postulated in any case. Rather, the important thing to notice is the set of performance factors the relevance of which becomes apparent once this sort of approach to modeling children's development is adopted. If the approach is valid, even in its general outline, then the set of factors described below would be expected to affect the rate at which a child acquired the conservation concept.

The first factor would be the rate of growth of the child's capacity for attending to several schemes at once. Regardless of the specific set of schemes that is postulated, it is clear that fewer of these schemes must be activated simultaneously in order to execute the first intellectual strategy than to execute subsequent ones. There should, therefore, be a relationship between the maximum number of schemes that children can activate and their understanding of conservation (Pascual-Leone, 1969). Recent empirical work has provided support for this suggestion. It has been shown that children cannot normally activate three schemes at once until the age at which conservation is acquired

TABLE 3.5

Detailed Model of Conservation Acquisition

Step or Operation		Specific Schemes	Symbol[a]
1. Remember that the quantity in Beaker A = the quantity in Beaker B.	(1)[b]	Figurative scheme representing the fact noted at the outset of experiment, namely, that the quantity in Beaker A = the quantity in Beaker B. (For a description of the operation necessary to generate this conclusion to begin with, see Pascual-Leone (1972).	ϕ A = B
2. Remember that the quantity in Beaker B' was produced from Beaker B by pouring.	(1)[b]	Figurative scheme representing the fact that the quantity in Beaker A = the quantity in Beaker B (see above).	ϕ A = B
	(2)[b]	Figurative scheme representing the transformation which was observed, namely, that B was transferred into B' by pouring, with no addition or subtraction of liquid.	ϕ B $\xrightarrow{Pour}$ B'
3. Deduce that the quantity in Beaker B = the quantity in Beaker B'.	(1)[b]	Figurative scheme representing the fact that the quantity in Beaker A = the quantity in Beaker B. (See Step 2.)	ϕ A = B
	(2)	Operative scheme applying on various transformations and generating the conclusion that they have or have not changed quantity. This scheme is equilivant to the rule: if nothing is added or subtracted, then the quantity remains identical.	ψ Pour = identical
	(3)	Figurative scheme representing manner in which liquid was transformed. (See Step 2, Scheme 2.)	ϕ B $\xrightarrow{Pour}$ B'
4. Conclude that, since the quantity in Beaker A = the quantity in Beaker B and the quantity in Beaker B = the quantity in Beaker B', the quantity in Beaker A = the quantity in Beaker B'.	(1)[c]	Operative scheme representing transitivity rule: if A = B and B = C, then A = C.	ψ Transformation
	(2)	Figurative scheme representing the conclusion generated in the previous step, namely, that the quantity of Beaker B was unchanged, i.e., that the quantity in Beaker B = the quantity in Beaker B'.	ϕ B = B'
	(3)	Figurative scheme representing memory of original state A = B.	ϕ A = B

Note. Adapted from "A Theory of Constructive Operators, a Neo-Piagetian Model of Conservation, and the Problem of Horizontal Decalages" by J. Pascual-Leone, unpublished manuscript, York University, 1972.

[a] ψ = operative scheme; ϕ = figurative scheme.
[b] Scheme being activated (stored) for use in subsequent step.
[c] An alternative is that no operative scheme is necessary. The answer is chosen because A = B' represents a simpler and more consistent conceptual field when combined with B = B' and A = B than does A $\neq$ B'. (For an explication of this possibility see Pascual-Leone (1972, 1974b).)

(Case, 1972b; Pascual-Leone, 1970). It has also been shown that tests of this capacity correlate significantly with tests of conservation, even after age is partialled out (Case, 1977b; Parkinson, 1976).

The second factor that might affect a child's success or failure would be his attraction or resistance to the influence of perceptual sets. The first two strategies for approaching the conservation problem both involve an evaluation of the most salient perceptual aspects of the problem. In contrast, the final strategy requires children to move their attention away from their current visual field and work out their answers on the basis of prior knowledge. There should, therefore, be a correlation between the cognitive style of field dependence (Witkin, Dyk, Faterson, Goodenough, & Karp, 1962; Witkin, Lewis, Hertzman, Machover, Meissner, & Wapner, 1954) and performance on the conservation task. In his doctoral work, Pascual-Leone verified this hypothesis (Pascual-Leone, 1969). He also showed that the relationship between field dependence and conservation performance is remarkably strong: Intelligent *adults* who are extremely field-dependent still frequently fail the conservation task.

A third factor that might affect a child's success or failure would be his previous experience with liquids, beakers, and judgments of relative quantity.

For example, if children encounter a large number of quantity comparison situations in which height and width factors act in opposite directions, they should be much more likely to go through the series of mental steps itemized in Table 3.4 than if they encounter no such situations. Similarly, if children encounter a situation in which the difficulties inherent in the bidimensional strategy are pointed out to them and the more sophisticated strategy is modeled, they should be even more likely to go through the series of steps itemized in Table 3.4 and to adopt the strategy outlined in Table 3.5. The first type of experience should provide the child the *opportunity* for development; the second type of experience should provide him with actual *guidance* in development. Recent empirical work has demonstrated that both these kinds of experience can be beneficial. If children are simply provided with a large number of exposures to situations where bidimensional evaluation leads to unpredictable results, they spontaneously develop an understanding of conservation – provided, that is, that they can attend to at least three schemes at once (Case, 1977a). If, in addition, the inadequacy of the bidimensional strategy is actively pointed out to them and they are guided to a realization of the correct strategy, the acquisition of conservation comes even more easily and at a lower level of M-power (Case, 1977a).

Finally, a fourth factor that might affect a child's success or failure would be his affective disposition. If children are intimidated by the testing situation, they should be unlikely to provide a true indication of their understanding when the conservation question is posed. More importantly, however, if there is anything about the quantity judgment situation itself that elicits anxiety, they should be unlikely to explore the situation very thoroughly to begin with or to go through the series of mental steps itemized in the tables. Although this latter possibility might seem remote, it must be remembered that the motivation for going through the series of steps itemized in Table 3.5 is the cognitive uncertainty experienced in the course of going through the steps itemized in Table 3.4, and that the situation of uncertainty is inherently an affective one (Kagan, 1971) to which different children exhibit different reactions.

When detailed analyses of the sort described above are conducted for other Piagetian problems (e.g., class inclusion), the same four factors frequently emerge as underlying successful or unsuccessful acquisition. On the basis of such analyses, then, Pascual-Leone was led to construct a general theory of the process by which children acquire and apply the cognitive structures described by Piaget. Although the main tenets of this theory are implicit in the analysis of the conservation problem that has been presented, it is worthwhile to make them explicit before proceeding any further.

A number of extensions and modifications of the theory have recently been suggested (Case, 1978b; Pascual-Leone, 1976a). However, for present purposes, only those aspects of the theory which are most firmly established and which are of greatest direct relevance to education will be summarized. In addtion, the language in which the theory is presented will be a close as possible to that used in the rest of this volume. For a more complete presentation of the theory, see Pascual-Leone (1970, 1972, 1976b) or Ammon (1977). For a description of the proposed extensions and modifications, see Case (1978a).

B.   The Basic Units of Knowledge

As was illustrated in the analysis of conservation, all human knowledge, whether it is factual or procedural, is assumed to be stored in the psychological system by means of entities called *schemes*. Like the units of knowledge postulated by computer simulators (Newell & Simon, 1972), schemes are presumed to consist of two components: an initial set of conditions under which they apply (their releasing component), and a subsequent set of conditions that they generate (their effecting component). Consider, for example, the capability most 4-year-olds exhibit at the beginning of the conservation task: comparing the two beakers and concluding that they contain an equal amount of water. In the context of the theory, this capability is assumed to exist because the children already possess a scheme for equality in their cognitive repertoire. The effecting component of this scheme is the particular meaning that children attach to equality at their particular stage of development. The releasing component is the set of possible conditions under which this meaning may be legitimately assigned. In the language of the theory, one can say either that children's conclusions regarding initial equality are "released" by the stimulus situation, or that their understanding of equality is "applied" to the stimulus situation and satisfied by it.

As was also illustrated in the conservation analysis, schemes can serve a variety of functions. Schemes that serve a representative function – that is, schemes that represent facts, states, or meanings – are referred to as *figurative*. Schemes that serve a transformational function – that is, schemes that operate on one set of figurative schemes and that generate as products a new figurative scheme or set of schemes – are referred to as *operative*. Finally, schemes that serve a control function – that is, schemes that represent the series of operations a subject intends to execute in order to get from one figurative state to another – are labeled *executive*.

The differences among these three types of schemes are not presumed to have a structural basis. At different points in time, and depending on the problem in question, the same structural unit might serve any one of the three functions. For analytic purposes, however, it is convenient to have a terminology for specifying the function of a scheme. The above terms have the advantage of being congruent with the sort of processing distinctions used in contemporary cognitive psychology, while at the same time being consistent with the Piagetian terms from which they were derived (Pascual-Leone, 1976b; Piaget, 1969).

C. The Content of Intellectual Development

In the context of Pascual-Leone's theory, the sequence of structures described by Piaget may be viewed as a series of executive schemes of increasing power and complexity. As was suggested by the previous analysis, the executive schemes of relevance to conservation have to do with the evaluation of quantity.

To begin with, subjects evaluate quantity on a unidimensional basis, normally relying on height alone. Then, when they perceive that this does not always work, they search for a basis for improving their evaluations (Klahr & Wallace, 1973; Piaget, 1957). At first they use width and height alternately, then width and height jointly. Although the bidimensional executive is more powerful, it, too, is inadequate for certain situations, in particular, for the sort of compensation comparisons where the height and width vectors are close in magnitude but act in opposite directions. When subjects perceive the contradictions or difficulties this latter comparison entails (perhaps by going through a process such as that illustrated in Table 3.4), they again search for a better basis for quantification. Finally, either in the course of their everyday experience, or in the context of the conservation test itself, they go through the mental steps indicated in Table 3.5 and discover that relative quantity can be determined by using equal size containers as standards for measurement. Although the particular executive schemes in question are very different, a similar sequence of events can be seen to account for the observed changes on a variety of other Piagetian problems (Noelting, 1975; Siegler, 1976). Once the content of intellectual development is characterized as a sequence of executive schemes of increasing power and complexity, it becomes possible to take the sort of model described in Tables 3.1 to 3.5 as a prototype and to provide a general characterization of the equilibration process.

D. The Process of Equilibration

In the context of the new theory, the following general postulates may be assumed to characterize the sort of spontaneous conflict resolution that Piaget refers to as equilibration:

1. At any time when, in the course of some goal-directed activity, two pragmatically incompatible schemes are coactivated (e.g., scheme 1 — *A has more*; scheme 2 — *B' has more*), the organism experiences cognitive conflict.

2. When the organism experiences such conflict, it temporarily abandons its current executive scheme and initiates a search for any other information that might help it resolve the conflict. In the language of computer simulation, one could say that it activates a heuristic executive scheme (HES) that directs a search of the problem situation, the problem given, and any stored information

of relevance. (The development of the first heuristic executive probably occurs during the sensorimotor stage. By the age of 1½, a child who is frustrated in one strategy will be seen to actively search for another.)

3. The search for relevant information occurs in discrete "mental steps," each of which takes a specifiable amount of real time. [The minimum unit of such time corresponds to what has been termed a "psychological moment" (Stroud, 1955).]

4. In each mental step, either (a) a figurative scheme or set of schemes is retrieved, or (b) an operative scheme applies on some already active figurative scheme and generates a new scheme.

5. Unless it is maintained directly by some salient aspect of the immediate perceptual input, the activation or rehearsal of any scheme requires the application of "mental energy." Because the amount of mental energy that can be applied at any one moment is limited, the number of schemes that can be activated in any one mental step is also limited. This number is referred to as the organism's M-power. [Although this construct is very similar to short-term memory (STM), several important differences should be noted. From a theoretical point of view, STM is defined in terms of external responses, not internal schemes; thus, schemes triggered by sensory (e.g., acoustic) effects would be counted in STM estimates, whereas they would not be counted in estimates of M-power. From an empirical point of view, tests of STM would require only that subjects perceive and reproduce a number of units. Tests of M-power would also require that the units be transformed in some fashion. The distinction is thus akin to the one between short-term memory and operating memory (Posner, 1970).]

6. If the conflict is not eliminated, the organism will, other things being equal, favor the response that is congruent with the greatest number of currently activated schemes.

7. After a very few trials in which the organism arrives at the resolution to its experienced conflict, the sequence of steps by which it did so becomes consolidated as a strategy, and the subject is able to generate the new solution on subsequent trials without the aid of any heuristic executive. In short, the organism forms a new executive routine (ES2) for which the original problem situation is a releaser (e.g., $A > B$ on height, $B > A$ on width) and for which the final solution constitutes the effector (e.g., check pretransformation state, check type of transformation; if equal to begin with and no addition or subtraction, conclude still equal). [For a formal specification of the conditions under which such learning occurs, see Pascual-Leone, Parkinson, and Pulos (1974).]

E.   Factors Affecting the Rate of Intellectual Development

Given this general characterization of equilibration, it may be seen that four distinct factors can affect the rate of a subject's spontaneous intellectual development. These are the size of his *M*-power, his degree of field independence, his content-related experience, and affective factors.

1. *Size of M-Power.* The first factor is the rate of growth of the subject's *M*-power. In the conservation task, it will be remembered that the minimum *M*-power required for perceiving the conflict and for discovering the solution was 3. On other Piagetian tasks, the minimum *M*-power is sometimes as high as 5 or more, and sometimes as low as 2. On the basis of a large number of such analyses, together with an examination of the ages at which the tasks in question are normally passed, Pascual-Leone postulated that *M*-power increases linearly with age according to the scale indicated in Table 3.6. He also postulated that the growth of *M*-power is dependent primarily on factors such as maturation or general experience, that is, that it is independent of the effects of specific experience (Pascual-Leone, 1970).

2. *Field Independence.* The second general factor that can affect a subject's rate of intellectual development is his degree of field independence. In the conservation task, it will be remembered that the two beakers do not look as though they contain the same amount of liquid. Perhaps because the menisci are so salient and the surface area of the liquid is not, even adults tend to overestimate the importance of the difference in height relative to the difference in surface area. Thus, if they have not witnessed the original equality and the transformation, they will also tend to judge that the beaker with the taller column of liquid contains more to drink (Case, 1976). It follows that subjects who are highly influenced by the structure of the perceptual field will be slower to notice the inherent difficulty with either of the perceptually based executives for

TABLE 3.6
Hypothesized Modal *M*-Power Values at Different Ages

Age (years)	Piagetian Substage	Value of M^a
3-4	Early preoperations (Intuitive thought)	$e + 1^b$
5-6	Late preoperations	$e + 2$
7-8	Early concrete operations	$e + 3$
9-10	Middle concrete operations	$e + 4$
11-12	Late concrete operations Early formal operations	$e + 5$

[a]Pascual-Leone (1970) has proposed that M may continue to grow to $e + 7$ at 15 or 16. However, the growth in this age range has been less adequately documented.
[b]The symbol e represents the space taken up by the executive, which is presumed to be constant.

determining quantity and will, therefore, take longer to search for a way to construct a more adequate executive. This same formal property is shared by a good many other Piagetian tasks and, in fact, constitutes a frequent criterion for testing operational development. Knowing that the field suggests an incorrect response is, in Piaget's system, one sure way to know that correct responses do not result from some automatic response to an impinging stimulus (Piaget & Inhelder, 1941).

Given that some (but not all) of Piaget's tasks present subjects with misleading field effects, it may be hypothesized that subjects who are extremely sensitive to the influence of such effects should be slower than normal to develop sophisticated executive schemes in content areas that present such effects, but that they should not be slower than normal to develop such schemes in other content areas (Pascual-Leone, 1969).

3. *Content-Related Experience.* The third factor that can affect a subject's rate of intellectual development is the quantity and quality of the experience that he encounteres in any given content area. In the conservation task, it will be remembered that two kinds of experience were of relevance, experience that would provide the child with an *opportunity* to abandon the perceptual strategy for the more conceptual one, and experience that would provide the child with direct *guidance* in this process. The same is true for most other Piagetian tasks: Performance may be facilitated either by experience that provides children with the opportunity for constructing a more adequate strategy or by experience that provides them with guidance in doing so.

The proposal that experience can play an important role in influencing a child's cognitive development is of course not a new one. Piaget and his followers have for some time emphasized the importance of experience that provides children with the opportunity for learning. They have assumed that this experience has its effect primarily by providing the child with a chance to exercise individual schemes, thus exploring their limitations, or by provoking disequilibrium between two apparently contradictory schemes (Inhelder et al., 1974; Piaget, 1964, 1971; Strauss & Langer, 1970). Similarly, investigators in the neobehaviorist tradition have for some time emphasized the importance of experience that provides direct guidance in the learning process. They have assumed that such experience has its effect by drawing the child's attention to the cues on which a more adequate response must be based (Gelman, 1969) or by providing a clear model of how these cues must be dealt with (Beilin, 1965; Zimmerman & Rosenthal, 1974).

What is distinctive about the new position is that it emphasizes the potential importance of both kinds of experience. The first kind of experience is seen as being of significance in reducing the importance of the subject's set to use his current executive strategy. The second is seen as being of significance in facilitating the process of discovering the problem with this executive and in constructing a more adequate one. As a consequence, the first kind of experience is seen as being the mainspring of spontaneous intellectual development — that is, development where the child's learning is under the control of his own heuristic repertoire and subject to all the vagaries that this implies. In contrast, the second kind of experience is seen as being the mainspring of instructionally induced development — that is, development in which the child's mental steps are directed, simplified, and monitored by someone who already knows what the more adequate strategy is.

From the viewpoint of the new theory, then, the debate between the two traditional schools of thought has actually been a controversy at cross purposes. Developmentalists have investigated the mechanisms of spontaneous development and obtained data that show only moderate effects of experience (Inhelder et al., 1974). In contrast, learning theorists have investigated the mechanisms of instructionally induced development and have obtained data that show a strong effect of experience (Bucher & Schneider, 1973; Gelman, 1969).

4. *Affect.* The fourth and final factor that can influence a subject's rate of intellectual development is affect. Certain situations in which detection is of particular importance to the survival or well-being of the species are privileged in that they elicit the immediate and strong activation of whatever executive scheme the organism has available for dealing with them. An affectively triggered scheme can completely preempt whatever other executive scheme is currently controlling behavior (Simon, 1967), or it can interact with it in complex ways.[1]

At first glance, it might appear that affective factors play a relatively unimportant role in the process of intellectual development. As was suggested in the analysis of the conservation task, however, this is not necessarily the case. It is quite possible, for example, that a child might have an affective reaction to some particular content area which sets that area apart from other areas in his mind. The child might find it particularly exciting, particularly boring, or particularly anxiety-producing. In such cases, his rate and terminal level of development in that area would either be accelerated or retarded accordingly.

Much more importantly, however, a child might experience an affective reaction to the executive acquisition situation itself. As Piaget has frequently pointed out, and as is also highlighted by the neo-Piagetian account of the equilibration process, one situation that can serve as an impetus for spontaneous intellectual development is that of cognitive uncertainty or conflict. In cases where children acquire a new executive strategy without conflict, in cases where they have sufficient M-power to assemble an executive that overcomes conflict, and in cases where their search for the components of a conflict-reducing executive is not a long one, the conflict and uncertainty that they experience

---

[1] For a description of such complex interactions in lower animals, see Hess (1962).

may be fleeting and insignificant. In situations where children are exposed to conflict, however, and where (1) they have insufficient M-power to assemble a more powerful executive, or (2) their search for the appropriate components is a difficult one, the conflict and uncertainty that they experience may be prolonged and of considerable magnitude. Because both uncertainty and conflict constitute situations to which human beings exhibit affective reactions virtually from birth (Kagan, 1971), the child's rate and terminal level of general intellectual development may be significantly influenced by the nature of his affective response to uncertainty. As a function of cultural, familial, or idiosyncratic factors, the child may learn to avoid such uncertainty and conflict at all costs. He may become timid in his search for conflict resolution and simply wait for a resolution to be suggested by an adult. On the other hand, as a result of the very same sorts of factors, the child may learn to actively seek out uncertainty and conflict. He may become confident in his ability to resolve such conflicts on his own and may develop strategies for doing so both independently and boldly. In the former case, his rate of development would be relatively slow and in the latter relatively rapid.

F. Relationship Between Piagetian and Neo-Piagetian Theory

At a global level of analysis, the characterization of the process of intellectual development is exactly the same within the neo-Piagetian system as it is within the classic Piagetian system. As the reader will no doubt have noticed, however, there are a number of important differences in the manner and in the degree of precision with which the central constructs are defined.

1. *Operational Structures.* Operational structures are conceptualized in both theories as sets of schemes that reflect previous knowledge and that govern the acquisition of new knowledge by their control of the equilibration process. However, in Piaget's theory these structures are modeled as logical competencies whose mathematical properties can best be specified with the aid of symbolic logic. In contrast, in the new theory, these structures are modeled as sets of executive schemes whose releasing cues and sequences of effecting acts can be inferred directly from children's performance and specified in standard English.

The notion of a set of executive schemes is perfectly compatible with the notion of a logical structure (Cellerier, 1972). However, because the content of an executive scheme can be specified more easily and concretely than that of a logical structure, the shift in conceptualization permits a modeling of children's thought that is more detailed, more precise, and more closely tied to potentially observable behavior. Because the notion of an executive scheme has its origins in work on computer stimulation (Newell, Shaw, & Simon, 1958), as does the notion that operational structures may be equated with such schemes (Simon, 1962), the modeling of Piagetian stages as sequences of executive schemes also permits a conceptual bridge to be built between work in developmental psychology and work in human information processing (Case, 1970; Klahr & Wallace, 1973; Siegler, 1976).

2. *Equilibration.* In Piaget's theory, equilibration is conceptualized as a process of structural reorganization in response to cognitive conflict. In the new theory, equilibration is modeled as a particular type of problem solving. The problem solving process is unique in that it is initiated by an inconsistency or contradiction that is generated by the organism's current executive repertoire and in that it results in a change in that repertoire. Nevertheless, in its underlying process, it obeys the same set of general rules as does all problem solving. Again, although perfectly consistent with Piaget's notion, the new characterization of equilibration permits a much finer grain of analysis – one that employs a much briefer time frame and one that can be tied much more closely to children's behavior in specific contexts. Again, too, this characterization provides a link between classic developmental theory and current information processing theory.

3. *Maturation and General Experience.* In the context of traditional Piagetian theory, the process by which maturation and/or general experience affect intellectual development is not specified. In contrast, in the new theory, these factors are hypothesized to exert their effect by producing a change in the size of the organism's field of centration or M-power. Here again, the new definition permits a more precise and operational specification of the construct in question than is possible within the traditional Piagetian system. The result is that the consequences of maturational limitations can be predicted in particular contexts. In addition, the nature of the proposed construct is again such that a conceptual bridge can be built between traditional developmental theory and current theory in human information processing (Broadbent, 1973; Kahneman, 1973; Miller, 1956; Pascual-Leone, 1970).

Unlike the equation of operational structures with executive schemes, however, or the modeling of the equilibration process as a sequence of mental steps directed at problem solving, the equation of maturational limitations with limitations in M-power introduces two fundamental alterations in the basic struc-structure of Piagetian theory. First, the hypothesis reverses the direction of the proposed relationship between what Piaget refers to as the size of the field of centration and the complexity of operational structures. For Piaget, the child's increasing field of centration is a result, not a cause, of the increasing complexity in his operational structures (Piaget, 1920, 1928). Second, the emphasis on M-power changes the factors that are assumed to limit the speed with which new structures can be acquired. For Piaget, the limiting factors are the inherent slowness of equilibration, together with the magnitude of the task of operational reorganization (Piaget, 1970). For Pascual-Leone, the only limiting factor is the limit in the size of the field of centration (*M*-power). As will become apparent in the next two sections, the result of this shift in emphasis is a drastically changed evaluation of the role that instruction can play in influencing the course of intellectual growth.

4. *Perceptual Effects.* Perceptual effects are mentioned in Piaget's theory as a possible source of variance on cognitive tasks. However, the mechanism by which they exert an effect is not clearly specified. In contrast, perceptual effects are conceptualized in the new theory as deriving from the same sensory and organizational properties of stimulus fields as have been studied by Gestalt psychologists. It is assumed that these factors exert their effect by influencing the selection of executive schemes, and that, under certain circumstances, they can affect the *M*-demand of a task as a result. It is further assumed that individual differences in sensitivity to these factors are stable and equivalent to the cognitive styles that have been studied by Witkin and his collaborators. Once again, these extensions of Piagetian theory permit predictions to be made about performance on specific tasks that are not possible within the context of traditional Piagetian theory (Case & Globerson, 1974; Pascual-Leone, 1969; Scardamalia, 1977c).

5. *Externally Induced Vs. Spontaneous Learning.* The distinction between learning that is externally induced via social experience and learning that occurs spontaneously in the normal course of development is preserved in the context of the new theory. Again, however, the similarities and differences between the two types of learning are specified more clearly and operationally with the result that a particular experience may be classified as preserving the developmental demands of everyday experience (i.e., maintaining the same demand for use of an heuristic executive and requiring the same *M*-power) or as introducing an externally induced reduction in these developmental demands (i.e., by facilitating the heuristic search and reducing the *M*-demand).

6. *Affect.* Affect is mentioned as a factor of potential importance in both theories. Again, however, the manner in which the construct is presumed to have its effect in the new theory is such that affective influences in specific contexts can, potentially at least, be identified more easily. As a consequence, connections with work in other areas of psychology (e.g., Abelson, 1973; Hess, 1962; Steiner, 1974) may be easier to make.

To summarize, the theory originated by Pascual-Leone introduces a number of refinements in traditional Piagetian theory, with the result that it becomes possible to identify the operational structures underlying performance on Piagetian tasks more easily and precisely and to specify the maturational, perceptual, experiential, and affective factors that affect the acquisition of these structures in greater detail. In most of its refinements, the new theory preserves the essential structure of traditional Piagetian theory. However, in its equation of maturational limitations with limitations in M-power, the new theory introduces one important deviation.

V. RESEARCH RELATED TO THE NEW THEORY

Although the new theory has not yet generated a large body of research, the research that has been done has provided a substantial degree of support for its fundamental hypotheses. In this section, I discuss this research and, in Sections VI and VII, the implications that the neo-Piagetian theory has for instruction.

A. Growth of M-Power with Age

Because M-power is defined as the maximum number of independent schemes that can be attended to at any moment in the absence of direct support from the perceptual field, any test of M-power must meet the following five requirements:

1. It must demand some transformation of the input in order to reduce the possibility that the schemes might be activated perceptually.
2. It must provide thorough pretraining on the transformations in question in order to insure that the requisite executive and operative schemes are available to all subjects and require a minimum amount of M-energy for activation.
3. It must utilize units to be transformed that are thoroughly learned, yet that are not part of higher-order chunks that are relevant to the test. This is necessary in order to insure that the relevant figurative schemes require one and only one unit of M-energy for activation.
4. It must not admit of solution by any power-saving or mnemonic strategy that might make the number of units counted by the experimenter greater than the number of schemes the subject is actually activating.
5. It must engage the subject affectively so that he will apply his full M-power to the task.

One example of a task that meets these requirements is the Digit Placement Test (Case, 1972c). On this test, the transformation children are required to execute is to place a given digit (e.g., 4) in its correct position with respect to an ordinal series of other digits that are in fixed positions and that ascend in magnitude from left to right (e.g., 2, 9, 11). Pretraining in executing this operation is provided and is continued until the child can quickly and successfully execute the task five times in a row. After the criterion has been reached, children are seated in front of the apparatus shown in Fig. 3.1. This apparatus

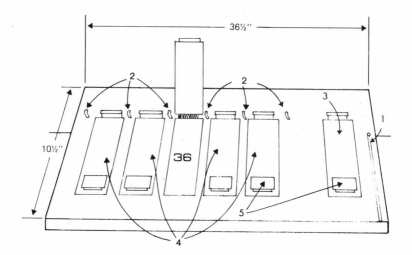

FIG. 3.1.   Experimental apparatus used for testing. 1 — token; 2 — hooks
on which it may be placed; 3 — door concealing final numeral; 4 — doors
concealing ascending series; 5 — door handles. (Adapted from "Validation
of a Neo-Piagetian Mental Capacity Construct" by R. Case, *Journal of Experimental Child Psychology,* 1972, *14,* 287–302. Copyright 1972 by
Academic Press, Inc. Reprinted by permission.)

presents the numbers in the fixed series one at a time. Then it presents the digit
to be placed. In order to insure that subjects are familiar with the basic units
that the test employs, the numbers are restricted in range to those under 20. In
addition, children who cannot label these numbers quickly and accurately are
screened out in the pretraining. In order to eliminate the possibility of chunking,
the number series are chosen with a view to avoiding any common and recognizable patterns (e.g., 5, 7, 9). In order to discourage mnemonic strategies such as
grouping and rehearsal, children are required to label each number as it appears
and are presented with a new number as soon as they have labeled the one that
is currently in view. Finally, in order to sustain the high degree of motivation
initially elicited by the apparatus, the feedback is tailored to the child's performance and mood.

When this task is administered to children aged 6, 8, and 10, the norms that
are obtained are those that would be predicted on the basis of the theory. Six-
year-olds perform virtually perfectly until the number of digits presented is
three. Eight-year-olds perform virtually perfectly until the number of digits
presented is four. Finally, 10-year-olds perform virtually perfectly until the
number of digits presented is five. After these critical points, the distribution of
scores at each age group becomes indistinguishable from what would be
expected simply by chance (Case, 1972c).

The Digit Placement Test is not the only task that meets the basic require-ments for a measure of M-power. So far, a total of eight different measures have been designed, using a variety of different formats and materials and involving both auditory and visual modalities. Although none of the tests are suitable for the entire age range, they have all shown the norms hypothesized for the age range to which they have been administered (Burtis, 1974; Diaz, 1974; Parkin-son, 1976; Pascual-Leone, 1970; Toussaint, 1974).

B. Relationship of M-Power to Performance on Piagetian Tasks

Because a child's M-power is supposed to be a major factor that affects the sophistication of the executive strategies he can construct and apply, it follows that there should be a significant relationship between M-power and performance on Piagetian tasks. The nature of this relationship has been investi-gated in several different ways.

First, tests of M-power have been administered together with tests of Piagetian operations, and the results of the two types of measures have been correlated. When this has been done, the correlations that have emerged have been moderate (e.g., .4 to .6) at both the concrete and formal operational levels (Case, 1977b; Dale, 1976; DeRibeaupierre, 1975; Parkinson, 1976; Toussaint, 1974). When regression analyses have been conducted to remove the effects of age, the correlations have dropped (as would be expected) but remained statistically significant (Case, 1977a, 1977b; Dale, 1976).

Second, Piagetian tasks have been modified so as to increase or decrease their M-demand and administered to groups of children with different M-powers. A particularly well-designed study of this sort has recently been reported by Scardamalia (1977b). Scardamalia was interested in children's ability to generate all possible combinations of objects from a given set. She presented children with arrays of cards such as those illustrated in Fig. 3.2 and asked them to make as many different sets of 3 cards as they could with the constraint that each set always contain one card from each column. The majority of successful children appeared to employ a strategy that she likened to the working of an odometer. They treated each column of cards as though it were a series of digits on an odometer. Beginning at the right hand side of the display they first cycled their way through all the cards in the first column, exchanging them one by one in order. Once that column had been exchanged completely, they moved to the next column to the left, exchanged the first card there, and then once again worked their way through the cycle in the right hand column. By proceeding in this fashion, it was possible to generate all the possible combinations of cards from the columns in exactly the same manner as an odometer generates all the possible combinations of numbers on its dials. They did not always proceed in

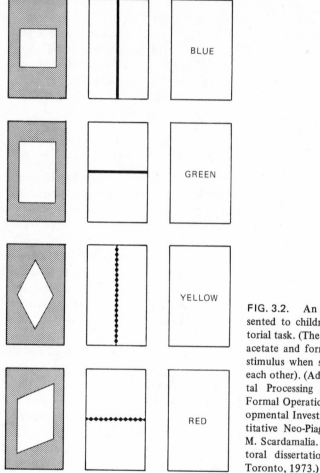

FIG. 3.2.   An array of cards presented to children in a combinatorial task. (The cards are made of acetate and form one compound stimulus when stacked on top of each other). (Adapted from "Mental Processing Aspects of Two Formal Operational Tasks: Developmental Investigation of a Quantitative Neo-Piagetian Model" by M. Scardamalia. Unpublished doctoral dissertation, University of Toronto, 1973.)

the same direction across columns; that is, on some columns, they went from top to bottom and on others from bottom to top. However, within any column, they always proceeded systematically from one end to the other. This being the case, Scardamalia reasoned that they would need to keep track of where they were going in any given column by activating an independent scheme, but that they would *not* need to activate an independent scheme for each individual card in each column. Accordingly, she concluded that the M-demand should equal the number of columns of cards and should be independent of the number of cards per column.

On the basis of this analysis, Scardamalia investigated the performance of three different M-groups on a set of tasks that varied in the number of columns and the number of cards per column. The subjects were selected so as to have M-powers of 4, 5, and 7. After practice on problems with very few columns, the number of columns was systematically increased for each group until it exceeded the subject's measured M-power. As shown in Table 3.7, the great majority of subjects passed the task with ease until the number of columns exceeded their available M-power. Similar results have been reported for modified versions of the Control of Variables Test (Scardamalia, 1977c), the Water Level Test (Pascual-Leone, 1969), and several tests of classification (Pascual-Leone & Smith, 1969).

A final strategy that has been employed for investigating the hypothesized relationship between M-power and performance on Piagetian tasks involves the use of instruction. A strategy for approaching a standard Piagetian task is taught to children from several different age groups, and the youngest age at which the strategy will be mastered is predicted on the basis of the M-demand required to understand and apply it. A good illustration of this approach is provided by a recent study on teaching children to control variables (Case, 1974b). The strategy for controlling variables is a relatively simple one, at least in situations where the variables of interest are known ahead of time and are relatively salient perceptually. All the subject must do is to identify an object with an extreme positive value on the dimension to be tested (e.g., a long stick), then identify an object with an extreme negative value (e.g., a short stick), and then check to see if there is any *other* difference between these two objects that might affect the result of interest (e.g., bending). An analysis of the strategy is presented in Table 3.8, from which it can be seen that the M-demand of the task is only 3.

In order to teach children this strategy, an instructional sequence was devised that presented children with both sorts of guidance mentioned earlier: (1) guid-

TABLE 3.7

Percentage of Subjects Possessing Combinatorial Strategy
Who Could Apply It at Different Levels of Complexity[a]

M-power of Group	Number of Columns in Display						
	2	3	4	5	6	7	8
$(N^4 = 15)$	100%[b]	100%	87%	15%	0%	c	c
$(N^5 = 15)$	c	100%[b]	80%	73%	18%	0%	c
$(N^7 = 3)$	c	100%[b]	100%	100%	100%	100%	0%

[a]Reanalysis of data presented in Scardamalia, 1977.
[b]At the lowest complexity level, the percentage is 100 by definition. Subjects not evidencing the strategy after practice at this level are presumed not to possess it.
[c]Not tested.

TABLE 3.8

Detailed Model for Control of Variables[a]

Step or Operation	Specific Schemes	Symbol[b]
1. Identify the object with extreme positive value on the dimension to be tested (e.g., long).	(1) Operative scheme corresponding to the working definition of the positive pole of the dimension to be tested (e.g., for length, if the object sticks out the most, call it the longest).	ψ Dimension to tested (+)
	(2)[c] Figurative scheme representing the array of the objects in the visual field.	ϕ Array
2. Identify the object with value at the other extreme of dimension to be tested.	(1) Operative scheme corresponding to the working definition of the other pole of dimension to be tested (e.g., for length, if the object is recessed the most, call it the shortest).	ψ Dimension to be tested (−)
	(2)[c] Figurative scheme representing the array of the objects in the visual field.	ϕ Array
3. Check to see if there is any difference between the two objects, other than the one to be tested.	(1) Figurative scheme representing the dimension to be tested.	ϕ Dimension to be tested.
	(2) Operative scheme representing the routine for scanning back and forth between the two objects and isolating any salient difference between them.	ψ Find difference
	(3) Figurative scheme representing object A.	ϕ Object A
	(4)[c] Figurative scheme representing object B.	ϕ Object B
4. If a difference is found recycle to Step 2.		
5. If no difference is found, conduct the test for property (i.e., see if object A > B on property of interest, e.g., bending).		

Note: Adapted from "Structures and Strictures: Some Functional Limitations on the Course of Cognitive Growth" by R. Case, Cognitive Psychology, 1974, 6, 544-573. Copyright 1974 by Academic Press. Reprinted by permission.

[a]Problem Question: Given a set of multidimensional objects with property X (e.g., bending), does dimension Y effect magnitude of X?

[b]ψ = operative scheme; ϕ= figurative scheme.

[c]Scheme activated by perceptual field. No M-power necessary.

ance in realizing the inadequacy of their current strategy; and (2) guidance in how to construct a new one. Because a task analysis had revealed that the M-demand for responding to the guidance was also equal to 3 (Case, 1974b), it was predicted that 7- and 8-year-olds would be able to acquire the control of variables strategy and would apply it to genuinely novel problems such as those designed by Piaget. It was also predicted that 5- and 6-year-olds would not. As is shown in Table 3.9, both predictions were confirmed quite strongly. Since then,

TABLE 3.9

Percentage of Subjects Passing Two
Novel Tasks Requiring Control of Variables

Age (years)	Instructed		Uninstructed	
	Task 1	Task 2	Task 1	Task 2
7-8	80	80	20	40
5-6	0	0	0	0

the results have been replicated with a population of 6- and 7-year-olds who were divided into two groups of approximately equal age but unequal M-power (Case, 1977a). Similar results have also been obtained for tests of conservation (Case, 1977b) and classification (Case, 1972a), as well as for several tests that are not, strictly speaking, Piagetian (Case, 1974a, 1975).

C. Relationship Between Field Independence
and Performance on Piagetian Tasks

Because field dependence is hypothesized to affect the rate of a subject's intellectual development only in content areas that contain field effects, it follows that there should be a significant relationship between tests of field independence and Piagetian tasks that contain field factors. It also follows that there should be a weaker or insignificant relationship between tests of field independence and Piagetian tasks that do not contain such factors.

As it is defined by Witkin, the cognitive style of field independence refers to a subject's ability or tendency to overcome the influence of the perceptual field with which he is confronted or to separate an item from its context. The standard measure for assessing a subject's degree of field independence is the Rod and Frame Test. In this test, subjects are led into a dark room that contains an illuminated stick surrounded by an illuminated frame. The subject's task is to align the stick to the true vertical, in spite of the fact that the frame surrounding it is tilted at an angle of 28° and that no other visual cues to verticality are present. Individual differences on such tests have been shown to be highly reliable and to remain remarkably stable over time (Witkin, Goodenough, & Karp, 1967).

In his doctoral dissertation, Pascual-Leone (1969) administered the Rod and Frame Test, together with several other tests of field independence and a battery of concrete operational measures to a group of 9-year-olds and a group of adults. He found substantial within-group correlations between the measures of field independence and the Piagetian measures that he had previously judged to contain field effects and much lower or insignificant correlations between the tests of field independence and the Piagetian measures that he had judged not to contain such effects. A related study has recently been conducted by Dale (1976). Dale administered a standardized group test of field independence, a test of M-power, and several Piagetian tests of formal operations to a group of 10-year-olds and a group of 13-year-olds. He found substantial within-group correlations between the measure of field independence and the Piagetian measures, even after the variance due to M-power and age had been removed. Although less comprehensive in their design, similar studies have also been conducted by other investigators with similar results (Case, 1973a, 1974b; Saarni, 1973).

D.   Relationship Between Experience and
     Performance on Piagetian Tasks

As was mentioned in the previous section, the relationship between experience and performance on Piagetian tests has already been subjected to a great deal of experimental scrutiny. By and large, developmental psychologists in Geneva have been interested in the mechanisms of spontaneous development and have obtained data that show only moderate effects of experience (Inhelder et al., 1974). In contrast, developmental psychologists in North America have been interested in the mechanisms of programmed development and − in recent studies, at least − have obtained data that show strong effects of experience (Gelman, 1969; Lefebvre & Pinard, 1972). The neo-Piagetian position is that both types of experience can produce genuine cognitive change and that the fundamental mechanisms underlying change in each case are very similar. The hypothesis is that the two types of experience differ only in that they place different demands on subjects' heuristic repertoire and M-power.

Early experimental work designed to test this hypothesis was devoted primarily to showing that the effects of programmed development could be extremely large, but that a subject's M-power would still place a ceiling on the complexity of the strategy he could construct. The most well-controlled example of this sort of study was the experiment on the control of variables which was cited earlier (Case, 1974b). However, a number of other studies were conducted, all of which showed a strong training effect and an equally strong interaction between the size of this effect and the subject's M-power (Case, 1972a, 1974a, 1974b, 1977a, 1977b).

More recently, an attempt has been made to show that the theory can predict the effects of experience not only in highly programmed but also in more spontaneous learning situations. Although much of this work is still in progress, three recent studies involving the conservation paradigm have been completed. In the first, subjects were exposed to the sort of highly programmed experience employed by Lefebvre and Pinard, and it was shown that the M-demand of the task was reduced by this training to 2. Of the subjects who had M-powers of 2 or greater, 50% showed improvement. Of the subjects who had M-powers of 1, none showed any improvement (Case, 1977b). In the second study, children were provided with experience that was similar in the general types of materials that were employed but that differed in one fundamental respect. Although children were provided with the opportunity to make quantity comparisons and received feedback on the adequacy of their judgments, they were never led through the series of mental steps described in Tables 3.4 and 3.5, with the result that the M-demand for constructing the conservation strategy remained at 3. The results were extremely strong. Subjects who had M-powers of 3 were able to go through this sequence on their own and to construct the conservation principle without any help from the experimenter. In contrast, subjects with

TABLE 3.10
Percentage of Subjects Passing Two Conservation Tasks

	Type of Instruction	
M-power	Direct	Indirect
3	100	50
2	57	13
1	0	0

Note. Adapted from "The Process of Stage Transition in Cognitive Development" by R. Case. (Final Report, ROIH DO 9148-01, NIMHCD, 1977). Berkeley, Calif. University of California, 1977.

M-powers of 2 showed no grasp of the conservation principle whatever. In both the first and second studies, the effects of M-power and age were confounded. However, as shown in Table 3.10, the same basic pattern of results was obtained in a third study, in which age was experimentally controlled.

E. Relationship Between Field Independence and M-Power

In the context of the theory, performance on tests of field independence may be analyzed in exactly the same fashion as performance on Piagetian tasks, by tracing the series of mental steps necessary to construct the correct solution. According to Pascual-Leone, such analyses reveal that the correct solution not only requires subjects to apply an executive scheme that is cued by the instructions rather than the perceptual field, but also to coordinate a greater number of schemes than they would need to if they applied an executive scheme that was directly triggered by the perceptual field (Pascual-Leone, 1969). This being the case, Pascual-Leone ascribes the developmental increase that Witkin and his colleagues have found in field independence to the known developmental increase in M-power. In contrast to Witkin, he ascribes the within-age variance in field independence to variance in field sensitivity itself, together with variance in the tendency to mobilize whatever M-power is available.

The relationship between field independence and M-power has been investigated in two recent studies. In the first, a battery of M-measures was administered, together with a battery of field independence measures to a group of children in second grade (Case & Globerson, 1974). In accordance with the theory, the two batteries of tests loaded on distinct but moderately correlated factors. In a second study, an attempt was made to determine whether the relationship between these two factors was due to differences in M-mobilization or to differences in M-power itself (Globerson, 1976). A similar battery of tests was administered to a group of children in the same grade and in the same school.

This time, however, the measures were modified to permit concurrent assessment of children's pupillary dilation, which has been shown to increase reliably and predictably as mental effort increases (Hess, 1972; Kahneman, 1973). The relationship between field independence and M-power did indeed disappear after the effect of pupillary dilation was removed via anlaysis of covariance. However, it was also noted that: (1) the relationship between field dependence and M-power was curvilinear, not linear; and (2) covariance of test scores and pupillary dilation appeared almost exclusively on the M-measures. On the field dependence measures themselves, where the effect should have been greatest if field-dependent subjects really did achieve low scores due to low M-mobilization, there was no tendency for subjects who did poorly to have smaller pupillary dilations. For the time being, then, the most conservative conclusion is that the nature of the within-age relationship between M-power and field independence still needs to be clarified.

To summarize, although the number of studies that have been conducted to date is not large, the fundamental hypotheses of the theory have already received a good deal of empirical support. It has been shown that M-power grows linearly with age, according to the scale that was originally hypothesized. In addition, it has been shown that M-power, field independence, and experience all make independent contributions to the rate of children's intellectual development. What has not yet been determined is the nature of the underlying relationship between field independence and M-power.

VI.   TOWARD A NEO-PIAGETIAN THEORY OF INSTRUCTION

In Section III of this chapter, it was suggested that, if Piaget's theory is correct, two questions must be addressed by any developmentally based theory of instruction. The first question is how to optimize the development of children's operational structures. The second question is how to adapt the content of instruction to the structures that children already have available. At a general level of analysis, it was suggested that the answer to each of these questions is clear. The first step is to analyze the structural underpinnings of the academic discipline that is to form the content of instruction. The second step is to assess children's current level of functioning in that discipline. The third step is to tailor the instructional activities that are presented to the level of functioning that is assessed, either with a view to promoting a transition from this level of functioning to a higher one (if that is the goal), or with a view to adopting the material presented to the current level of functioning (if that is the goal).

Because the neo-Piagetian theory that has been described preserves the essential conceptual framework of Piaget's theory, the general instructional procedure that it suggests is identical to that which is suggested by Piaget's theory. On the other hand, since the new theory is a functional rather than a structural one, it eliminates many of the difficulties that are encountered when an attempt is made to translate the general procedure into practice. In the present section, each of the three steps mentioned above will be reconsidered, with a view to showing how the practical difficulties that are encountered are either reduced or eliminated when the task is approached from a neo-Piagetian perspective.

A. Fostering the Development of Operational Structures

1. *Step 1: Structural Analysis.* In the context of traditional Piagetian theory, it is difficult to conduct a structural analysis of conventional academic tasks for two reasons. The first is that the type of structure to be analyzed is a logical one, and the operation or relevance of logical structures is not obvious in most conventional academic areas. The second is that the type of analysis that must be provided is not a performance analysis but a competence analysis. Because students' performance is an uncertain guide to their competence, and because no general method has been suggested by Piaget for going from one type of analysis to the other, it is hard to know where to begin or how to proceed.

In the context of neo-Piagetian theory, both of the above problems are eliminated. First, the type of structure to be analyzed is an executive one, and the importance of such structures is obvious in most academic domains. Second, since the function of an executive structure is precisely to control subjects' performance in a given task domain, the nature of the structure that is required to execute a given task may be inferred directly from the performance of skilled subjects on that task. Although there is no necessary sequence of steps that must be followed in generating an executive analysis of a task, the following set of steps are extremely useful and normally sufficient:

1.1. The first step is to identify the goal of the task to be performed. This may be accomplished quite simply by examining the question children are asked. For example, in the conservation task, children are asked, "What has more?" Thus, the goal toward which their underlying executive scheme must be oriented is the determination of relative quantity.

1.2. The second step is to map out a series of steps by which a successful subject might reach this goal. One technique that is useful in doing this is to execute the criterion task oneself and to list the sequence of operations one went through in order to reach the goal. When using this sort of introspective approach, it is helpful to map out one's general sequence of steps first and then, on subsequent trials, to list the sequence of suboperations one executed within each of these general steps. If one were attempting to describe one's strategy for bidimensional quantification, for example, the first thing to note would be simply that one glanced at both the height and the width. One could then re-execute the task and monitor the substeps by which each of these dimensions was actually compared.

In some tasks, an introspective technique may be difficult to apply, because the answer to the problem question may appear to leap into one's mind without any mental steps at all. This is the case, for example, with the conservation task itself. One simply "knows" that the two quantities must still be the same, without necessarily being aware of how one knows. A technique that is useful under these conditions is to explore the problem from a purely rational point of view and to set out a series of steps that would logically be necessary in order to prove the answer that appears to be so obvious. It was this sort of procedure that led Pascual-Leone to the analysis of the conservation executive that was described in Table 3.5.

1.3. Having mapped out a hypothetical series of steps that should lead to the correct answer, the next step is to compare this hypothesized series of steps to the performance subjects actually exhibit. One technique that is useful for doing this is to note the sequence of motor and eye movements that experienced subjects exhibit as they execute the task. As has been described, this sort of approach has been used with great precision for conservation tasks by actually photographing subjects' eye movements while they are engaged in the task (O'Bryan & Boersma, 1971). For most problems of instructional relevance, however, an informal analysis of this sort is sufficient.

Another useful technique is to interview a skilled performer and ask him how he did the task or ask him to describe the content of his thoughts as he actually proceeds throgh the task (Newell & Simon, 1972). This sort of protocol analysis is particularly useful for subjects who are old enough to be aware of their own thinking processes and for tasks that take an appreciable amount of real time to execute.

1.4. Having checked out the hypothesized series of steps against the subject's actual performance, one may wish to modify the series of steps one has hypothesized and to recycle through steps 1.1 to 1.3. If any ambiguity still remains, one may wish to invent a new problem in which the parameters are altered such that subjects would be expected to give one response if they were using the first possible strategy and a different one if they were using the second possible strategy. For example, if there was some question as to whether conserving children really were paying attention to the nature of the liquid transformation or simply responding on the basis of the original state of the two liquids, one could change the type of transformation executed and see if their response changed accordingly (Lefebvre & Pinard, 1972; Watson, 1968).

1.5 Finally, having satisfied oneself that the series of mental steps hypothesized really does correspond to that used by skilled performers (or at least some subclass of skilled performers), one may occasionally wish to test the description for completeness. A useful technique for doing this is analogous to that used in computer simulation: read the sequence of steps as described to a naive subject and instruct him to do only what he is told. If a point is reached where the instructions must be supplemented or modified in order to insure that the subject behaves as expected, then a corresponding modification or addition must be introduced in the original description of the strategy.

2. *Step 2: Assessment of Students' Current Level of Functioning.* In the context of traditional Piagetian theory, assessment of children's current level of functioning is rendered difficult by the presence of uncontrolled performance factors. The existence of these factors is made apparent by the presence of low intercorrelations among tasks that supposedly tap closely related underlying structures and by the presence of unexplained décalages between tasks that supposedly tap the same underlying structure. Given the existence of these two phenomena, it becomes impossible to be certain whether a given test result stems from the presence or absence of an underlying logical structure or from the individual's success or failure in coping with one of the unidentified performance factors that the task entails.

As was mentioned in the previous section, the neo-Piagetian theory that has been summarized specifies the performance factors inherent in most Piagetian tasks with sufficient accuracy that the presence or absence of high inter-task correlations and the presence or absence of décalages can be predicted (Pascual-Leone, 1969; Scardamalia, 1977b; Toussaint, 1974). Given that this is the case, it becomes possible to attribute a given subject's failure to utilize a given executive structure as being due to any of the following factors: (1) the absence of adequate *M*-space (indicated by an abnormally low score on a measure of this construct); (2) an unusual sensitivity to the perceptual cues involved (indicated by an abnormally high score on tests of field dependence); or (3) the absence of specific experience in the domain in question (indexed by average scores on both the above measures but an inability to perform the task nonetheless).

From the viewpoint of special education, the ability to localize the source of a particular child's difficulty holds considerable promise (Bachor, 1976; DeAvila & Havassy, 1974). When a particular child's problems are severe and are observed across a variety of content areas, it may be useful to know their etiology. This may help in setting realistic goals and in prescribing a program of effective remediation. From the viewpoint of most regular education, however, the power of the new theory comes not from its ability to diagnose a particular child's reason for not being able to use a particular executive structure, but from its redefinition of the nature of the structure that is of relevance in the first place. As will be shown in subsequent sections, the reason a child uses an inadequate executive structure in a particular context is often relatively unimportant. The important thing is what executive structure he actually *does* use. It is this that must be assessed, and it is this that must be known in order to plan effective instruction.

Because the most important entity to assess is the child's current executive strategy in the domain or task in question, the method of assessment is the same as that mentioned in the previous section. The only difference is that the strategy that one must attempt to analyze is one that leads to an incorrect, rather than to a correct answer.

In practice, it is often a good deal more difficult to assess the strategy of a student who fails a task than it is to assess the strategy of a student who succeeds. There may be a number of reasons for this. Because one uses the correct strategy oneself, it may be harder to imagine oneself in the child's position and to mentally generate a strategy that would lead to his answer. Because children who fail at problems are often much less articulate than those who pass, data on their introspections or justifications may also be more difficult to come by. Finally, because one's goal is always the teaching of the "correct" approach, it may be difficult to decenter and to view the child's answer as anything but "wrong" (or at best, deficient in some particular component). Because the analysis of an incorrect strategy is more difficult than the analysis of a correct strategy, it is often helpful to be able to convert the former problem ino the latter one. There are at least two techniques by which this may be accomplished:

2.1. One useful technique is to determine a question for which the child's response would have been correct and then to cycle through steps 1.2 to 1.5 as though this were really the goal of the task. In the case of conservation, for example, the child's response would be correct if the question were, "Which of these two beakers *looks* as though it has more?" If adults are asked this question, they adopt a strategy that is very similar to that employed by children and that may be analyzed in the same fashion.

2.2. An alternate technique that is equivalent to the first one is to assume that the subject does not have access to some crucial piece of information that he appears to have ignored. By presenting the task to mature learners without this piece of information, one may again hypothesize a rational procedure for reaching the goal and compare this hypothesized procedure to that which is actually used. In the case of conservation, for example, children clearly act as though they had no knowledge of the original state or of the transformation. If one simply presents two unequal diameter beakers to adults and asks them which has more (or even if one imagines how one would solve such a problem oneself), it becomes much easier to understand the rationale for the child's strategy and to specify the mental steps that the strategy entails.

3. *Step 3: Instructional design.* In the context of traditional Piagetian theory, stage transition is described as a five phase process. In the first phase, children rely exclusively on some pragmatically useful but isolated scheme. In the second phase, they acquire a new scheme that is a potential source of conflict. In the third phase, they experience a conflict between the two schemes. In the fourth phase, they construct a higher-order structure by means of which the conflict is resolved. Finally, in the fifth phase, they consolidate and extend their new structure. While this general description is compelling, the diffi-

culty with it is that it provides insufficient guidance to those who are interested in optimizing the acquisition of operative structures, since it does not specify any of the maturational or experiential variables that might affect the stage transition process.

In the context of neo-Piagetian theory, this difficulty is greatly reduced. One maturational variable is specified, namely M-power. In addition, three classes of experiential variables are specified, each of which is potentially manipulable. These are: (1) the familiarity of the situation in which the child is placed; (2) the salience of the cues to which he must attend; and (3) the number of items of information that he must coordinate. From a neo-Piagetian point of view, then, the most effective way to enable a child to acquire a particular executive strategy is to lead him through each of the five phases isolated by Piaget, while at the same time taking care to maximize the familiarity of the situation, to render the relevant cues as salient as possible, and to minimize the M-power required to effect the relevant scheme coordinations. Although the size of the child's M-power will still set a limit on the complexity of the strategy he can acquire, use of this general approach will guarantee that for any given level of M, the complexity of the strategy that can be acquired will be much greater than it would be under normal circumstances. In short, it will guarantee that a low M-power will interfere with learning as little as is possible.

The following set of procedures are useful for accomplishing this objective:

3.1. The first step is to set up a paradigm where the subject may assess the effectiveness of the strategy that he currently employs. It is at this step that the greatest care must be devoted to maximizing situational familiarity and cue salience and to minimizing cognitive complexity. Suppose, for example, that one's objective were to teach children a sophisticated strategy for controlling variables. In the sort of paradigm that is normally used for assessing children's skill in this domain, at least three sources of difficulty are introduced other than the basic requirement for manipulating one variable while another is held constant (Scardamalia, 1977c). The first difficulty is that the dependent and independent variables are often unfamiliar to the subject. The second difficulty is that the independent variables are not particularly distinct from each other and that variation along any one of them is often hard to detect. The third difficulty is that the total number of variables that must be dealt with is quite large. If one's objective is instruction rather than assessment, then, the first step is to remove each one of these difficulties from the task and to incorporate some procedure whereby the subject can test the effectiveness of the strategy he employs. A paradigm that meets these requirements is illustrated in Fig. 3.3 (Kenzie, 1970). The instructions for the task are as follows. "This is a balance, do you know how it works? Good, can you use it to tell me which weighs more, grey rods or silver rods?"

Note how this paradigm removes all the above mentioned difficulties. The dependent and independent variables are both familiar ones: the only novelty is

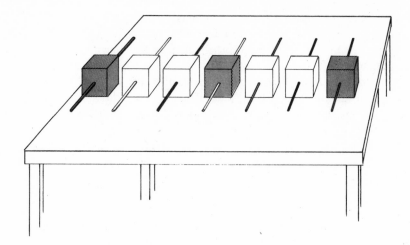

FIG. 3.3.   Array of rods and blocks used for training chldren to control variables. (Adapted from "Structure and Structures: Some Functional Limitations on the Course of Cognitive Growth" by R. Case, *Cognitive Psychology*, 1974, *6*, 544–573. Copyright 1974 by Academic Press, Inc. Reprinted by permission.)

in the particular values they assume (i.e., the particular types of materials that are used and their particular weights). The two independent variables, rods and blocks, are also highly distinctive, and variation in each one is easily detected (being marked by different colors). Finally, the number of independent variables is reduced to a bare minimum, namely two.

Note, too, that the paradigm introduces one additional feature in order to set the stage for cognitive conflict. The efficiency of the subject's spontaneously employed strategy may be evaluated by means of a simple and direct procedure. Once the child has conducted a test and drawn a conclusion, he is allowed to remove the rods from the blocks, and to weigh them directly.

3.2. Having designed a paradigm where the child can evaluate the effectiveness of his current strategy, the next step is to demonstrate its insufficiency. If the child's initial strategy has been correctly diagnosed in the assessment phase, this can normally be accomplished simply by selecting an appropriate problem. To continue with the control of variables example, young children's spontaneous strategy is normally to select the first two rods of different colors on which their glance falls and to weigh them without bothering to check the type of block in which they are embedded. The inefficiency of this strategy can be demonstrated simply by setting up the blocks such that the nearest pair to the subject are made of different material, with the heavier block containing (and obscuring the effect of) the lighter rod. When this is done, children invariably conclude that aluminum is heavier than brass and are surprised when they remove the blocks and discover that this is not so.

3.3. Having demonstrated to the subject that his initial strategy does not work, the next step is to help him discover the reason why this is so.[2] Once again, the constraints of scheme familiarity, cue salience, and cognitive complexity must be taken into consideration. Thus, if the child does not see the reason for his failure himself, the instructor should point out the critical feature by gesture or word and then explain its action repeatedly, using simple concrete sentences and active verbs. A possible explanation for the block problem might be the following: "How do you think you got fooled? You don't know? Feel these blocks. You got fooled because this block was so heavy that it pulled the balance down and made the silver rod *look* heavier, even though it really isn't."

3.4. Having pointed out to the student the reason why his current strategy did not work, the next step is to facilitate his construction of a more adequate strategy. Once a child understands the reason for his initial failure, he may construct this strategy spontaneously. Again, however, this may be too difficult a step for him to do alone, since the act of strategy reconstruction is potentially a complex one.

3.5. Having taught the child a new strategy that overcomes the difficulties inherent in his original strategy, the final step is to provide for consolidation and extension of this strategy. The basic technique for achieving this is to provide practice, punctuated by periodic modifications in the nature of the task. As the child's new strategy becomes automatized, less and less attention (M-power) has to be devoted to executing it. As a consequence, more and more attention becomes available for other matters. Thus, the complications that were stripped from the task during the first step (1) may now be gradually reintroduced. Each time a new component is introduced, it may be helpful to "back down" to the simplest form of the problem. Thus, if the components to be added are symbolized by the letters a through d, it may be helpful to sequence the transfer activities as follows: $a, a + b, a + c, a + b + c, a + d, a + b + d, a + b + c + d$. When this was done for the control of variables task, the results that were obtained were quite dramatic (Case, 1974b). Although none of the subjects exhibited the sophisticated control-of-variables strategy at the outset, by the end of the program the majority of the 8-year-olds were performing better than the average uninstructed 15-year-old.

B. Adapting the Content of Instruction to the Operational Level of the Learner

In the context of traditional Piagetian theory, the phrase "adapting the content of instruction to the operational level of the learner" can have two meanings. It can mean modifying the tasks children are presented so that they do not

---

[2]This step does not appear as one of Piaget's five phases of stage transition. However, it fits well with the extended model of stage transition presented in Section IV and would appear to make good sense from an instructional point of view in any case.

require a higher level of operative functioning than that which they have already developed. Alternatively, it can mean presenting children with tasks that would normally require a higher level of operative functioning but teaching them some special procedure or trick for approaching the tasks that obviates this necessity. Certain formal tasks, for example, can actually be solved using concrete operations, providing that a simplified procedure of this sort is devised and taught (Case, 1974b).

In the context of neo-Piagetian theory, the situation is somewhat more complicated. Because a child's operative level may be defined either in terms of the strategies that he currently employs, or in terms of the M-level he has reached,[3] the same phrase can actually have three meanings. It can mean adapting tasks to fit the strategy that the learner has available (the first meaning above), it can mean teaching simplified strategies for solving complex tasks (the second meaning above), or it can mean teaching complex strategies for solving complex tasks, but doing so in a way that the subjective complexity of the learning sequence never exceeds the subject's available M-power. In this latter sense, the set of procedures that were described in the previous section already constitutes a technology for adopting the content of instruction to the operational level of the learner. Even if one of the first two senses of the phrases is employed, however, the set of procedures described in the previous section still constitutes the *core* of the basic technology that is appropriate.

In order to see why this is so, consider first the objective of modifying an instructional task so that it does not demand the application of a strategy that is more sophisticated than that which the learner already has available. In order to do this, the first step would be to redesign the task so that it was in its simplest and most familiar form (cf. 3.1). The second step would be to administer the task to children of several different age levels and to determine the age at which the correct strategy was first employed (cf. 1.1—1.5). The third step would be to design a series of exercises for bringing children of this age level from success on the simple and familiar version of the task, to success on the task that was originally of interest (cf. 3.5). When stated in this manner, it may be seen that the set of procedures that would have to be employed are identical to those that would have to be employed for inducing operative development, with the exception that their order of application is rearranged and that the procedures for the analysis of incorrect strategies (cf. 2.1) and for strategy modification (cf. (cf. 3.2—3.4) are deleted.

Consider next the objective of discovering and teaching a simpler strategy than that which is normally used by skilled performers for solving a complex task. In this case, the first step would be to analyze the strategy that is used by

---

[3]The disagreement between Lefebvre (1976) and Pascual-Leone (1976a), as to whether or not Lefebvre's learning procedures induced "true" operative development, can be traced to a difference between which of these two definitions is preferred.

skilled performers (cf. 1.1–1.5). The next step would be to analyze the strategy that is used by the age group of primary interest (cf. 2.1). The next step would be to experiment with modifications of, or alternatives to, the strategy used by skilled performers. The object here would be to see whether a strategy could be discovered that was as adequate as that used by successful performers, yet that was no more complex than that used by naive performers. Having discovered or constructed such a strategy, the final step would be to teach it (cf. 3.1–3.5). Once again, it may be seen that the procedures that would have to be employed would be very similar to those that were described in the previous section. The only difference would be that one additional step would have to be added. An example of how this extra step might be added will be presented in the next section.

To summarize, the instructional suggestions that may be derived from neo-Piagetian theory are identical in general form to those that may be derived from traditional Piagetian theory. However, since the new theory presents a detailed model of the processes of structural acquisition and application, the difficulties that are encountered in actually trying to apply this general procedure are considerably reduced. When the goal is fostering operational development, structural analysis is rendered easier by virtue of the fact that the structure to be analyzed is one that may be directly inferred from subjects' performance. Individual assessment is rendered easier since the entity to be assessed is simply the strategy that a particular subject employs on the task that is of primary interest. Finally, instructional planning is rendered easier because the performance factors to be controlled in bringing a child from one strategy to the next are explicitly sepcified. When the goal is adapting the content of instruction to the developmental level of the learner, the procedures and benefits at each stage are very similar. The only difference is that one may wish to delete the steps of analyzing and modifying incorrect strategies or add the step of inventing a novel and simplified strategy.

VII. FROM THEORY TO PRACTICE: A NEO-PIAGETIAN ANALYSIS OF A CLASSROOM TASK

As was mentioned in the previous section, most of the procedures that have been suggested for fostering the acquisition of complex executive schemes have already been applied — either explicitly or implicitly — in the successful training studies that have been reported in the recent developmental literature. As yet, however, their applicability to training situations of a more conventional nature has not been demonstrated. Given the broad gap that often separates the psychological laboratory from the classroom, this seems an important task to accomplish.

The classroom task that will be used as an illustration is called the missing addend problem. The task requires children to look at the equation, $4 + \Box = 7$, and to fill in the missing number. Although the task appears quite simple on the surface, and although it forms a part of most standard grade one curricula, it is, in fact, extremely difficult. Most first-grade teachers either admit that they do not succeed in teaching it or else say that they no longer try (O'Hara, 1975). In addition, the task appears to elicit responses from children that, although they are incorrect, are highly consistent and systematic. As a test of the power of the neo-Piagetian approach, then, the task would appear to be a good one. What follows is a description of how the principles and techniques described in the previous section were applied to the task of designing an improved sequence of instruction.

A. Step 1: Structural Analysis

The first step in determining the nature of the difficulty in the missing addend problem is to conduct an analysis of the strategy that is used by skilled adults in solving the task. Assuming that the numbers that are used in the equation are relatively large, adults appear to go through a sequence of steps such as the following:

1. Read the symbols from left to right.
2. Notice that the quantity to be found is one of the two addends.
3. Decide that the addend that is known must therefore be subtracted from the total (which is also known).
4. Note the value of the given addend. Store.
5. Note the value of the total. Store.
6. Subtract the addend from the total.

Within the context of traditional Piagetian theory, the most difficult step in the above sequence would be presumed to be step 3, because in order to execute this step the subject would have to utilize one operation (subtraction) to mentally reverse the effect of another (addition). As will be remembered, the ability to execute this sort of reversal is the hallmark of concrete operations.

Within the context of neo-Piagetian theory, the same step would be presumed to be the most difficult one, at least in the learning phase. The presumption would be that in order to carry out this step, the subject would have had to have some prior exposure to a situation where he could realize the reversibility of addition and subtraction. It would also be presumed that he would need an M-power of from 3 to 5, depending on the simplicity of the demonstration that was provided.

Finally, within the context of either theory, it would be expected that if one were to teach children a strategy that did *not* require an appreciation of reversibility, they should be able to solve the task at a younger age. One strategy that meets this requirement is a "counting-up" procedure analogous to that used by clerks in stores for making change:

1. Read the problem from left to right, looking for the operation sign (+).
2. Look at the symbols on either side of the addition sign.
3. Note that one of the numbers to be added is given, but the other is not (indicated by the presence of a box).
4. Find the equal sign and note the number on the other side of it. Store this number (7).
5. Begin with the number after the given addend and count in increments of one (5, 6, etc.). For each number counted, advance a token (e.g., a finger).
6. When the stored total is reached (7), stop.
7. Count the number of tokens advanced and enter this number in the box (3).
8. (Optional.) Reread the symbols from left to right, checking the verbal statement against one's knowledge of number facts to be sure that it is correct (e.g., Does 4 plus 3 equal 7?).
9. If the statement does agree, stop. If it does not, re-enter the task at step 4.

Although the above strategy was generated by a purely rational analysis (cf. 1.2), there is empirical evidence that children who learn to succeed at the problem, in contrast to adults, tend to use a strategy of this sort (Groen & Poll, 1973).

B. Step 2: Assessment of Current Functioning

When children do not succeed at the above problem, the vast majority of them tend to make one of two errors. Those who have had very little training in addition or who are slow learners tend to give either 4 or 7 as the answer. Those who have had adequate training in addition and who are normal learners tend to write in the number 11. Once either of these errors is known, it becomes easy to diagnose the strategy that is being used (cf. 2.5). The first answer would be correct if the instructions were simply to copy one of the numbers in the space provided. The second answer would be correct if the problem were $4 + 7 = $ _____ . Accordingly, the first strategy may be described as follows:

1. Look at the symbols, read one of them.
2. Copy this symbol in the box.

The second strategy may be described as follows:

1. Look at the first symbol. Store.
2. Count out that many tokens (e.g., fingers).
3. Look at the second symbol. Store.
4. Count out that many tokens.
5. Count the total number of tokens advanced. Store.
6. Write this number in the box.

7. (Optional.) Check to see if the two smallest numbers add up to the biggest number. (Does 7 + 4 = 11?).

8. If it does, stop. If it does not, re-enter the problem at step 1.

From even a casual inspection, it may be seen that the complexity of the second incorrect strategy and the complexity of the second correct strategy are very similar.

C.   Step 3: Instructional Design

Depending on one's goal, one could design a sequence of instruction to bring children from either of the incorrect strategies to either of the correct ones. For the purpose of the present illustration, I consider only the example of the child whose current strategy has already been diagnosed as the second one (i.e., addition), and for whom the goal is to teach the simpler of the two correct strategies — that is, to work within his current strategically defined developmental level. Readers interested in a sequence for improving the developmental level of functioning (i.e., teaching the more complex "reversal strategy") are referred to Lam (1977).

3.1. The first step in the process of instructional design is to create a paradigm where the child has some simple way for evaluating the adequacy of his current strategy. Any number of paradigms would be equally valid for this step. One with which I have actually experimented, however, is the following:

Do these faces look the same? This (=) says that they are the same.

Here are two more faces. Can you make this one the same as this one? Pick up some of these shapes and make this side just the same as this side.

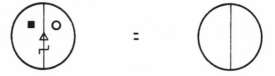

This (+) says put these together. Can you see that when we put these together we get a face that is the same as this one?

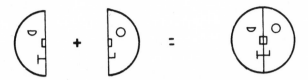

Remember, this says put these together. Now can you make this side the same as this side?

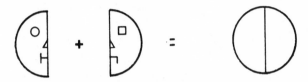

Note that this paradigm meets all of the criteria specified in the previous section. It is familiar. The relevant cues are salient, and it is stripped of all demands that are extraneous to the goal of matching each side of the equations, demands such as counting and reading numbers. Note, too, that the form of feedback is such that the child can tell at a glance, and by himself, whether or not he has attained his objective.

3.2. The second step is to provide the child with problems where the inadequacy of his preferred strategy can be demonstrated. The sorts of tasks for which this strategy might be exhibited are the following:

Remember, this (=) says make both these the same. Pick up some of these shapes and make this side just the same as this side.

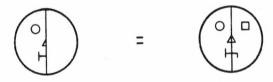

Remember, this says put these together. Now can you make this side the same as this one?

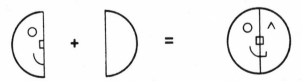

3.3. The third step is to provide the child with an explanation for why his preferred strategy is incorrect. Thus, when a child exhibits the incorrect strategy, he can be presented with an explanation such as the following. "Remember, this

(+) says put these two together so they will be the same as that one. When you put these two together do you get the same as that?"

Note how this meets the criteria that were specified in the previous section. It draws children's attention to the relevant cue that they have ignored (+), and it provides an explanation for why their response is incorrect in terms that are simple, brief, and concrete.

3.4. The fourth step is to provide a model of the correct strategy. Since the face paradigm deals with very concrete materials, this is unlikely to be necessary at this stage. In principle, however, one could draw the child's attention to the way the complete facial pattern can be broken down into parts, and each part can be checked to make sure that it is the same as one on the other side of the equal sign.

3.5. The final phase is one of consolidation and transfer. The first thing to do during this phase is to re-introduce the complications which were originally stripped from the task. Note that this should be done one at a time, in order to minimize the M-demand. In the present situation, this would mean giving children problems of the following sort:

Numbers

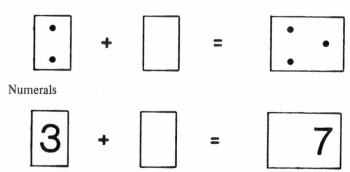

Numerals

As each complication is re-introduced, one can drop back and retrace one's way through the original series of steps, reminding the child first of the meaning of the equal sign and then of the meaning of the plus sign. One can also provide coaching, especially in the details of the counting strategy by which the missing addend can first be obtained. Finally, one can provide a number of practice items to consolidate the child's strategy at each stage. These practice items can involve a variety of different numbers and formats (e.g., box on the right, box on the left).

Although this analysis has been presented simply as an illustration, a curriculum that was based on this analysis has actually been designed by Allan Gold and myself. When the curriculum was administered to normal kindergarten children, the results were quite similar to those previously reported for Piagetian tasks. Eighty percent of the kindergarten children receiving the neo-Piagetian training attained criterion on the posttest. In contrast, only 10% of the children receiving a control treatment based on the standard California arithmetic workbook (*Modern School Mathematics: Structure and Use*) reached criterion in the same length of time (Case, 1978a; Gold, 1974). Similar results were obtained subsequently using retarded children whose mental age was equivalent to that of the normal kindergarten children. Although no attempt has yet been made to isolate the precise locus of the effect, it seems clear that the instructional approach, considered as a totality, can be just as powerful in a classroom setting as in a developmental laboratory.

D. Limitations, Costs, and Benefits of the Neo-Piagetian Approach

Although the missing addend problem is a good illustration of a classroom developmental task, it is by no means the only one. A similar pattern of over-simplified and misleading strategies is displayed by young or slow learners in areas as diverse as calculating perimeter, telling time, adding fractions, sounding out words, and solving ratio problems. In each of the areas where such strategies are observed, preliminary data suggests that a neo-Piagetian approach can be highly successful in designing more effective instruction (Frazer, 1977; Hunt, 1977; Steinbach, 1977; Stevens, 1977). It should be noted, however, that although the above mentioned set of tasks are quite diverse, they all share two distinctive features: (1) they all require the acquisition of a complex cognitive skill, not just a concept or set of facts; and (2) they are all sufficiently well defined that the nature of the skill they require can be fairly clearly specified from the outset. For areas or tasks in which this is not the case, application of a neo-Piagetian approach at the present moment is not feasible.[4].

Even limiting the discussion to task domains where the neo-Piagetian approach to instructional design is feasible, however, the question of which of the various possible instructional goals should be adopted still arises. As will be remembered, it is possible: (1) to attempt to bring children to the operational level of skilled performers via the set of procedures described in the previous section; (2) to attempt to teach children a simpler operative routine that will nevertheless be effective for solving the task in question, as was demonstrated

---

[4]It is worthwhile to note in passing, however, that the number of domains for which strategic skills are being identified is rapidly expanding. Collis and Biggs (1976), for example, drawing an earlier work by Hallam (1967) and Rhys (1972), are charting some of the executive strategies that are of use in geography and history. Bereiter (1977) and Scardamalia (1977a) are conducting similar analyses in the area of English composition. In my own work, I have attempted such analyses for the areas of social science and critical thinking (Case, 1972b). As tasks in these areas become more clearly defined, and as the nature of the effective solution strategies are better understood, the possibility of applying the neo-Piagetian method should become much more feasible.

with the missing addend problem; or (3) simply to select the type of tasks that children are given so that they will not need to apply more sophisticated operative routines than they already have available in their repertoires.

For many tasks, the third of the above three goals may be the most realistic and economical. A criticism that has been voiced of attempts to accelerate the acquisition of developmental competencies is that the cost is not worth the benefit, since the competencies to be taught are by definition ones that students would acquire spontaneously in a few years anyway (Case, 1973b). The same sort of criticism could be applied to the various principles and techniques that were itemized in the previous section. It might reasonably be suggested that, although the techniques may be useful in accelerating the acquisition of skills such as solving the missing addend problem, the same effect could be achieved without any change in current methods simply by placing the task several years later in the curriculum. In a sense, the techniques that were listed may be thought of as analogous to a technology for rebuilding a ship that has been erected in a bottle: There is no limit to the elegance and complexity of the new structure one can erect, providing one can find a way around the limits imposed by the narrow neck of the bottle, and providing one can take account of the structure that is already present. However, under what conditions is it worthwhile going to the trouble of adopting all of the procedures itemized and attempting to work within these sorts of constraints? Certainly not when the neck of the bottle is going to be bigger in another 2 years anyway, or when the pre-existing structure will become closer to the one that one wants to build on its own during that time. If anything, it would appear that one should *postpone* the instruction of such tasks until all the children in a class have more than sufficient capacity to process them. If this were done, minor lapses of attention or fatigue would not play such an important role, the pace of instruction would be quicker, and children would experience a greater sense of mastery and self-confidence (Rohwer, 1973).

There are at least four instances, however, where this reasoning does not apply, and where the technology that has been suggested could probably be employed to great advantage. The first case is when the pupils to be instructed are mentally retarded. By definition, a retardate is one whose development lags behind that of his peers and reaches a lower terminal level. In fact, as Wechsler (1958) has pointed out, one of the most salient characteristics of retarded individuals is precisely that their performance on tests of information processing capacity is so poor. If an individual has a capacity of only two or three in his teens, it is clear that the strategy of simply waiting for him to acquire a larger capacity will not pay off. Furthermore, it is clear that there are many valuable skills to which he will be denied access if a technology for circumventing his processing limitations is not discovered.

A second case where the techniques that have been described might be valuable is for material that is not mastered easily, even if its teaching is delayed until adulthood. Adults' *M*-power is not nearly as low as young children's. Nevertheless, it is still the case that they can be misled into thinking a simple and previously successful strategy is appropriate where it is not, and it is still the case that their information processing capacity can be seriously overloaded with the demands of learning a new concept or skill (Case, 1975; Kahneman & Tversky, 1973; Smedslund, 1967; Wason, 1971). In any situation where this is the case, then, adults are in essentially the same position as retardates: their capacity is never going to be larger than it is at present, so the alternative of simply delaying instruction is not a viable one. When the complexity of materials is beyond the normal adult span, then, and incorrect strategies of the sort described are elicited, the techniques that have been suggested might again be extremely valuable.

The third instance where the techniques might be appropriate is for children from atypical or minority backgrounds whose performance lags behind that of their peers. Regardless of the cause of the lag, the results in social terms are probably quite similar: the individual feels inferior and disturbed by his inability to grasp the material that his peers appear to acquire with such ease. Remedial approaches based on learning hierarchies are presumably already of considerable benefit in such cases (Gagné, 1970; Hackett, 1971; Resnick, 1967). However, the present approach might well provide some added benefit.

A fourth instance where the techniques that have been suggested might be useful is for tasks that present the developmental properties described, yet where for one reason or another, the alternative of delaying instruction several years is not acceptable. It might be that the task would have to be delayed until a stage of development where students' interests would no longer dispose them to learn the material (e.g., adolescence). It might be that the task in question is a prerequisite for some other culturally valued skill and that to delay its introduction would mean increasing the number of years of formal schooling. It might simply be that early acquisition of the skill in question is so valued by the culture in its own right that delay would not be tolerated. In any of these instances, it seems possible that a neo-Piagetian approach would be extremely valuable in diagnosing the reasons for current learning difficulties and in suggesting instructional procedures for overcoming them.

VIII. CONCLUSION

It seems worthwhile to conclude by reviewing the basic line of argument that has been advanced and setting it in a broader perspective. The object of a developmental theory of instruction is to provide a workable basis for optimizing young children's acquisition of culturally valued skills and concepts. Piaget's theory provides a good starting point for building such a theory since it focuses attention on the importance of intellectual operations in the process of learning, on the fact that these operations are highly structured, on the fact that they go through a fixed sequence of reorganization in the course of develop-ment, and on the fact that the perception of inconsistency can play a major role in motivating these reorganizations. On the other hand, Piaget's theory is insuffi-cient for building a developmental theory of instruction since it leaves three important questions unanswered: how to identify the operational structures of relevance to the sorts of skills normally taught in school, how to assess child-ren's current level of operational functioning, and how either to bring children from their current level of functioning to that which is desired, or to adapt the method of instruction such that the material in question can be mastered without a change in the current level of functioning. In order to answer these questions, it is necessary to have a theory that provides a more detailed model of the process by which intellectual operations are acquired and utilized and that specifies the environmental and maturational factors that can affect this process.

Recently, a theory has been advanced that meets these specifications. In the context of this new theory, operational structures are characterized in a fashion originally suggested by Simon — as sets of executive strategies. The development of operational structures is characterized as the process by which these strategies are reorganized, either in response to a gradually increasing awareness of the complexity of a given problem domain or in response to perceived failures to reach specific goals. The model of the reorganization process that is provided draws attention to the role of four different factors: the size of the subject's M-power, his cognitive style, the complexity and perceptual organization of the experience he encounters, and his affective disposition. Research on the first three of these factors has shown that they make independent contributions to the acquisition of operational structures and that their interaction in specific situations is both lawful and predictable.

Given that the new theory has demonstrated some empirical validity, it seems reasonable to use it to suggest answers to the problems that Piaget's theory leaves unanswered. The answers that were proposed in the present chapter were as follows: First, the executive strategies that are of relevance in a given discipline may be determined by specifying the goals of the tasks children must learn to perform and the step-by-step process by which skilled performers normally arrive at these goals. Second, children's current level of executive func-tioning may be assessed by giving them the same tasks and analyzing the actual set of steps that they go through in attempting to reach the goal. Third, the gap between children's current executive strategy and the desired strategy may be bridged either: (1) by presenting them with a task in which the inadequacy of their current strategy may be demonstrated and a model of the correct strategy may be provided; (2) by finding a qualitatively simpler executive strategy than the one normally used by adults and teaching this strategy; or (3) by finding qualitatively simpler tasks so that they are solvable by means of the strategy children currently have available. Whichever of the three approaches is adopted, care must be taken to maximize the salience of the information or cues to which children must attend and to minimize the complexity of the mental coordination that is required.

There are a number of ways in which the neo-Piagetian approach to instruction is similar to other contemporary approaches. The suggestion that the structure of a task should be analyzed prior to instruction is one which has been advocated for some time by Gagné (1968). The suggestion that children's readiness for instruction should be assessed with reference to such analyses has also been suggested by Gagné and forms an integral part of most other analytic approaches to instruction as well. Finally, the suggestion that the analysis of task performance should take the form of a step-by-step description through time is also not completely new. It has been advocated or practiced by several other learning theorists who have been influenced by the contemporary revolution in cognitive psychology (Anderson & Faust, 1973). Where the neo-Piagetian approach most clearly differs from other contemporary approaches, and where it most clearly reflects its developmental origins, is in the suggestions that: (1) children's current level of functioning cannot simply be assessed in terms of components of skilled performance that are already available but must be seen as having a distinct organizational structure of its own; and (2) the optimal procedure for dealing with a child's current organizational structure is one which combines elements of Piaget's model of equilibration with Pascual-Leone's model of the performance parameters which affect the equilibration process.

ACKNOWLEDGMENTS

Preparation of this chapter was facilitated by the resources of the Institutes of Human Learning and Human Development at the University of California, Berkeley, as well as by grants from the Spencer Foundation and the National Institute of Child Health and Human Development. The author is indebted to Paul Ammon for his encouragement and criticism during all phases of the preparation, and to Micki Chi, Veroncia Fabian, Robert Glaser, Monique Lefebvre, Wendy Portnuff, Bill Rohwer, Marlene Scardamalia, and Irene Subelman for their comments on an earlier draft of the manuscript. Finally, he is indebted to Ruth Brazier, Joan King, and Mary Macri for their patience and assistance in typing this manuscript.

REFERENCES

Abelson, R. P. The structure of belief systems. In K. Colby & R. Schank (Eds.), *Computer simulation of thought and language.* San Francisco: Freeman, 1973.

Ammon, P. R. Cognitive development and early childhood education: Piagetian and neo-Piagetian theories. In H. L. Hom & P. A. Robinson (Eds.), *Psychological processes in early education.* New York: Academic Press, 1977.

Anderson, R. C., & Faust, G. W. *Educational psychology: The science of instruction and learning.* New York: Dodd, Mead & Co., 1973.

Ausubel, D. P. *The psychology of meaningful verbal learning.* New York: Grune & Stratton, 1963.

Bachor, D. G. *Information processing capacity and teachability of low achieving students.* Unpublished doctoral dissertation, University of Toronto, 1976.

Beilin, H. Learning and operational convergence in logical thought development. *Journal of Experimental Child Psychology,* 1965, *2,* 317–339.

Beilin, H. Stimulus and cognitive transformation in young children. In D. Elkind & J. H. Flavell (Eds.), *Studies in cognitive development.* New York: Oxford University Press, 1969.

Bereiter, C. *Integration of skill systems in the development of textual writing competence.* Unpublished manuscript, The Ontario Institute for Studies in Education, 1977.

Blatt, N., & Kohlberg, L. Effects of classroom discussion on moral thought. In L. Kohlberg & E. Turiel (Eds.), *Moralization reasearch: The cognitive-development approach.* New York: Holt, Rinehart & Winston, 1971.

Broadbent, D. E. The magic number seven after fifteen years. In A. Kennedy & A. Wilkes (Eds.), *Studies in long term memory.* New York: Wiley, 1973.

Bruner, J. S. *Toward a theory of instruction.* Cambridge, Mass.: Harvard University Press, 1966.

Bucher, B., & Schneider, R. E. Acquisition and generalization of conservation by preschoolers, using operant training. *Journal of Experimental Child Psychology,* 1973, *16,* 187–204.

Burtis, P. J. *Two applications of measurement theory in developmental psychology.* Unpublished manuscript, York University, 1974.

Case, R. *Information processing, social class, and instruction: A developmental investigation.* Unpublished doctoral dissertation, University of Toronto, 1970.

Case, R. Learning and development: A neo-Piagetian interpretation. *Human Development,* 1972, *15,* 339–358. (a)

Case, R. *Thinking critically, Book 2: Evaluating controversial arguments.* Toronto: The Book Society of Canada, 1972. (b)

Case, R. Validation of a neo-Piagetian capacity construct. *Journal of Experimental Child Psychology,* 1972, *14,* 287–302. (c)

Case, R. *Field independence and formal operations.* Unpublished manuscript, University of California, 1973. (a)

Case, R. Piaget's theory of child development and its implications. *Phi Delta Kappan,* 1973, *45,* 20–25. (b)

Case, R. Mental strategies, mental capacity, and instruction: A neo-Piagetian investigation. *Journal of Experimental Child Psychology,* 1974, *18,* 382–397. (a)

Case, R. Structures and scrictures: Some functional limitations on the course of cognitive growth. *Cognitive Psychology,* 1974, *6,* 544–573. (b)

Case, R. Gearing the demands of instruction to the development capacities of the learner. *Review of Educational Research,* 1975, *45,* 59–87.

Case, R. *Maturation, experience, and intellectual development.* Final report, The Spencer Foundation, 1976.

Case, R. *The process of stage transition in cognitive development* (Final report, Project #ROIHD09148-01, NIMHCD). Berkeley: University of California, 1977. (a)

Case, R. Responsiveness to conservation training as a function of induced subjective uncertainty, *M*-space, and cognitive style. *Canadian Journal of Behavioral Science,* 1977, *9,* 12–26. (b)

Case, R. Implications of developmental psychology for the design of effective instruction. In A. M. Lesgold, J. W. Pellegrino, S. D. Fokkema, & R. Glaser (Eds.), *Cognitive psychology and instruction*. New York: Plenum, 1978. (a)

Case, R. Intellectual development from birth to adolescence: A neo-Piagetian interpretation. In R. Siegler (Ed.), *Children's thinking: What develops?* Hillsdale, N.J.: Lawrence Erlbaum Associates, 1978. (b)

Case, R., & Globerson, T. Field independence and central computing space. *Child Development*, 1974, *45*, 772–778.

Cellerier, G. Information processing tendencies in recent experiments in cognitive learning: Theoretical implications. In S. Farnham-Diggory (Ed.), *Information processing in children*. New York: Academic Press, 1972.

Collis, K. F., & Biggs, J. B. *Classroom examples of cognitive development phenomena*. Unpublished manuscript, University of Newcastle, Australia, 1976.

Dale, L. *A neo-Piagetian investigation of some factors affecting performance on Piaget's flexibility of rods problem*. Unpublished doctoral dissertation, La Trobe University, Australia, 1976.

Dasen, P. R. Cross-cultural Piagetian research: A summary. *Journal of Cross-Cultural Psychology*, 1972, *3*, 23–39.

DeAvila, E., & Havassy, B. *Intelligence of Mexican American children*. Austin, Tex.: Dissemination Center for Bilingual and Bicultural Education, 1974.

DeRibeaupierre, A. *Mental space and formal operations*. Unpublished doctoral dissertation, University of Toronto, 1975.

Diaz, S. *Cucui scale: Technical manual. Multilingual assessment program*. Stockton, Calif.: Stockton Unified School District, 1974.

Flavell, J. H., & Wohlwill, J. F. Formal and functional aspects of cognitive development. In D. Elkind & J. H. Flavell (Eds.), *Studies in cognitive development*. New York: Oxford University Press, 1969.

Fortin-Theriault, A. *Comparaison de deux methodes d'apprentissage par conflit cognitif*. Unpublished doctoral dissertation, University of Montreal, 1977.

Frazer, A. *Teaching Michael to sound out words*. Unpublished course assignment, The Ontario Institute for Studies in Education, 1977.

Gagné, R. M. Contributions of learning to human development. *Psychological Review*, 1968, *75*, 177–191.

Gagné, R. M. *The conditions of learning* (2nd ed.). New York: Holt, Rinehart & Winston, 1970.

Gaudia, G. Race, social class, and age of achievement of conservation on Piaget's tasks. *Developmental Psychology*, 1972, *6*, 158–165.

Gelman, R. Conservation acquisition: A problem of learning to attend to relevant attributes. *Journal of Experimental Child Psychology*, 1969, *7*, 167–187.

Glaser, R. Components of a psychology of instruction: Toward a science of design. *Review of Educational Research*, 1976, *46*, 1–24.

Globerson, T. *Field independence, information processing capacity, and mental effort*. Unpublished doctoral dissertation, University of California, Berkeley, 1976.

Gold, A. *The effects of four teaching methods on learning the missing addend problem* (Divisional Review Paper). Berkeley: University of California, Division of Educational Psychology, 1974.

Goldschmidt, M. L., & Bentler, P. M. *Concept assessment kit – conservation*. San Diego: Educational and Industrial Testing Service, 1968.

Groen, G. J., & Poll, M. Subtraction and the solution of open sentence problems. *Journal of Experimental Child Psychology*, 1973, *16*, 292–302.

Hackett, M. G. *Success in the classroom: An approach to instruction.* San Francisco: Holt, Rinehart & Winston, 1971.

Hallam, R. N. Logical thinking in history. *Educational Review,* 1967, *19,* 183–202.

Hess, E. H. Ethology: An approach toward the complete analysis of behavior. In T. Newcomb (Ed.), *New directions in psychology.* New York: Holt, Rinehart & Winston, 1962.

Hess, E. H. Pupillometrics. In N. S. Greenfield & R. A. Sternbach (Eds.), *Handbook of psychophysiology.* New York: Holt, Rinehart & Winston, 1972.

Hollos, M. Logical operations and role taking abilities in two cultures: Norway and Hungary. *Child Development,* 1975, *46,* 638–649.

Hunt, J. *Teaching perimeter.* Unpublished course assignment, The Ontario Institute for Studies in Education, 1977.

Inhelder, B., & Piaget, J. *The growth of logical thinking from childhood to adolescence.* New York: Basic Books, 1958.

Inhelder, B., & Piaget, J. *The early growth of logic in the child: Classification and seriation.* New York: Routledge & Kegan Paul, 1964.

Inhelder, B., Sinclair, H., & Bovet, M. *Learning and the development of cognition.* Cambridge, Mass.: Harvard University Press, 1974.

Kagan, J. *Change and continuity in infancy.* New York: Wiley, 1971.

Kahneman, D. *Attention and effort.* Englewood Cliffs, N.J.: Prentice-Hall, 1973.

Kahneman, D., & Tversky, A. On the psychology of prediction. *Psychological Review,* 1973, *80,* 237–251.

Karplus, R., & Peterson, R. W. Intellectual development beyond elementary school. II. Ratio, a survey. *School Science and Mathematics,* 1970, *0,* 813–820.

Kenzie, R. Personal communication, July 1970.

Klahr, D., & Wallace, J. G. The role of quantification operators in the development of conservation of quantity. *Cognitive Psychology,* 1973, *4,* 301–323.

Kuhn, D., Langer, J., Kohlberg, L., & Haan, N. S. Operational thought structures in adolescence and adulthood. *Journal of Genetic Psychology Monographs,* 1977, *95,* 97–188.

Lam, J. *Finding the sum or addend in subtraction.* Unpublished course assignment, The Ontario Institute for Studies in Education, 1977.

Lefebvre, M. Les experiences de Geneve sur l'apprentissage: un dossier peu convaineant (meme pour un Piagetian). *Canadian Psychological Review,* 1976, *17,* 103–109.

Lefebvre, M., & Pinard, A. Apprentisage de la conservation des quantites par une methode de conflit cognitif. *Canadian Journal of the Behavioral Sciences,* 1972, *4,* 1–12.

Lefebvre, M., & Pinard, A. Influence du niveau initial de sensibilite au conflit sur l'apprentissage de la conservation des quantities par une methode de conflit cognitif. *Canadian Journal of Behavioral Science,* 1974, *6,* 398–413.

Miller, G. A. The magical number seven, plus or minus two: Some limits on our capacity for processing information. *Psychological Review,* 1956, *63,* 81–97.

Newell, A., Shaw, J. C., & Simon, H. A. Elements of a theory of human problem solving. *Psychological Review,* 1958, *65,* 151–166.

Newell, A., & Simon, H. A. *Human problem solving.* Englewood Cliffs, N.J.: Prentice-Hall, 1972.

Noelting, C. *Stages and mechanisms in the development of the concept of proportion in the child and adolescent.* Paper presented at the 5th Interdisciplinary Seminar on Piagetian Theory and Its Implications for the Helping Professions, Los Angeles, University of Southern California, February, 1975.

O'Bryan, K. G., & Boersma, F. J. Eye movements, perceptual activity, and conservation development. *Journal of Experimental Child Psychology,* 1971, *12,* 157–169.

O'Hara, E. Piaget, the six-year-old child, and modern math. *Today's Education,* 1975, *64,* 33–36.

Parkinson, G. M. *The limits of learning.* Unpublished doctoral dissertation, York University, 1976

Pascual-Leone, J. *Cognitive development and cognitive style.* Unpublished doctoral dissertation, University of Geneva, 1969.

Pascual-Leone, J. A mathematical model for the transition rule in Piaget's developmental stages. *Acta Psychologica,* 1970, *63,* 301–345.

Pascual-Leone, J. *A theory of constructive operators, a neo-Piagetian model of conservation, and the problem of horizontal décalages.* Unpublished manuscript, York University, 1972.

Pascual-Leone, J. On learning and development, Piagetian style: A reply to Lefebvre–Pinard. *Canadian Psychological Review,* 1976, *17,* 270–289. (a)

Pascual-Leone, J. A view of cognition from a formalist's perspective. In K. F. Riegel & J. Meacham (Eds.), *The developing individual in a changing world.* Hague: Mouton, 1976. (b)

Pascual-Leone, J., Parkinson, G. M., & Pulos, S. *Constructive abstractions (structural learning) and concept development.* Paper presented at the meeting of the Canadian Psychological Association, Windsor, June 1974.

Pascual-Leone, J., & Smith, J. The encoding and decoding of symbols by children: A new experimental paradigm and a neo-Piagetian model. *Journal of Experimental Child Psychology,* 1969, *8,* 328–355.

Piaget, J. Une forme verbale de la comparaison chez l'enfant. *Archives de Psychologie,* 1920, *18,* 141–172.

Piaget, J. *Judgement and reasoning in the child.* New York: Harcourt-Brace, 1928.

Piaget, J. *Play, dreams, and imitation in childhood.* New York: Norton, 1951.

Piaget, J. *The language and thought of the child.* London: Routledge & Kegan Paul, 1952.

Piaget, J. *The construction of reality in the child.* New York: Basic Books, 1954.

Piaget, J. Logique et equilibre dans les comportements du sujet. In L. Apostel, B. Mandelbrot, & J. Piaget (Eds.), *Etudes d'epistemologie genetique, II.* Paris, Presses Universitaires de France, 1957.

Piaget, J. *The psychology of intelligence.* Totowa, N.J.: Littlefield, Adams, 1960.

Piaget, J. Development and learning. In R. E. Ripple & V. N. Rockcastle (Eds.), *Piaget rediscovered.* Ithaca, N.Y.: Cornell School of Education Press, 1964.

Piaget, J. *The mechanisms of perception.* New York: Basic Books, 1969.

Piaget, J. Piaget's theory. In P. Mussen (Ed.), *Carmichael's manual of child psychology* (Vol. 1). New York: Wiley, 1970.

Piaget, J. Problems of equilibration. In C. F. Nadine, J. M. Galalgher, & R. D. Humphreys (Eds.), *Piaget and Inhelder on equilibrium.* Philadelphia, Pa.: The Jean Piaget Society, 1971.

Piaget, J. Intellectual evolution from adolescence to adulthood. *Human Development,* 1972, *15,* 1–12.

Piaget, J., & Inhelder, B. *Le developpement des quantites chez l'enfant.* Neuchatel & Paris: Delachaus & Niestle, 1941. (English translation by Routledge & Kegan Paul, 1974.)

Pinard, A. Note sur la compatibilité des notions de stade et de décalage dans la theorie de Piaget. *Canadian Psychological Review,* 1975, *16,* 255–260.

Posner, M. I. Short term memory systems in human information processing. In A. F. Sanders (Ed.), *Attention and performance I.* Amsterdam: North Holland, 1970.

Resnick, L. B. *Design of an early learning curriculum.* Pittsburgh: University of Pittsburgh, Learning Research and Development Center, 1967.

Rohwer, W. D. Children and adolescents: Should we teach them or let them learn. In M. C. Wittrock (Ed.), *Changing schools: Alternatives from educational research.* Englewood Cliffs, N.J.: Prentice-Hall, 1973.

Rhys, W. The development of logical thinking. In N. Groves (Ed.), *New movements in the study and teaching of geography.* London: Temple Smith, 1972.

Saarni, C. I. Piagetian operations and field independence as factors in children's problem solving performance. *Child Development,* 1973, *44,* 338–345.

Scardamalia, M. *Mental processing aspects of two formal operational tasks: Developmental investigation of a quantitative neo-Piagetian model.* Unpublished doctoral dissertation, University of Toronto, 1973.

Scardamalia, M. *How children cope with the cognitive demands of writing.* Unpublished manuscript, The Ontario Institute for Studies in Education, 1977. (a)

Scardamalia, M. Information processing capacity and the problem of horizontal décalage: A demonstration using combinatorial reasoning tasks. *Child Development,* 1977, *48,* 28–37. (b)

Scardamalia, M. *The interaction of perceptual and quantitative load factors in the control of variables.* Unpublished manuscript, York University, 1977. (c)

Siegler, R. S. Three aspects of cognitive development. *Cognitive Psychology,* 1976, *8,* 481–520.

Simon, H. A. An information processing theory of intellectual development. *Monographs of the Society for Research in Child Development,* 1962, *27*(2, Serial No. 83).

Simon, H. A. Motivational and emotional controls of cognition. *Psychological Review,* 1967, *74,* 29–39.

Smedslund, J. The concept of correlation in adults. In C. P. Duncan (Ed.), *Thinking: Current experimental studies.* Toronto: Lippincott, 1967.

Steinbach, R. *Teaching Eric how to tell time.* Unpublished course assignment, The Ontario Institute for Studies in Education, 1977.

Steiner, C. *Scripts people live.* New York: Grove Press, 1974.

Stevens, R. *Teaching the addition of fractions.* Unpublished course assignment, The Ontario Institute for Studies in Education, 1977.

Strauss, S., & Langer, J. Operational thought inducement. *Child Development,* 1970, *41,* 163–175.

Stroud, J. M. The fine structure of psychological time. In H. Quastler (Ed.), *Information theory in psychology.* Glencoe, Ill.: Free Press, 1955.

Tomlinson-Keasey, C. Formal operations in females from eleven to fifty-four years of age. *Developmental Psychology,* 1972, *6,* 364.

Touissaint, N. A. Analysis of synchrony between concrete-operational tasks in terms of structural and performance demands. *Child Development,* 1974, *45,* 992–1001.

Tuddenham, R. A "Piagetian" test of cognitive development. In B. Docherell (Ed.), *On intelligence.* Toronto: The Ontario Institute for Studies in Education, 1970.

Turiel, E. Stage transition in moral development. In R. M. Travers (Ed.), *Second handbook of research on teaching.* Chicago: Rand McNally, 1972.

Wason, P. C. Problem solving and reasoning. *British Medical Bulletin,* 1971, *27,* 206–210.

Watson, J. S. Conservation: An S–R analysis. In I. E. Siegel & F. H. Hooper (Eds.), *Logical thinking in young children.* New York: Holt, Rinehart & Winston, 1968.

Wechsler, D. *The measurement and appraisal of adult intelligence* (4th ed.). Baltimore: Williams & Wilkins, 1958.

Winkelmann, W. *Test batterie zur erfassung kognitiver operationen* (TEKO). Brainschweig: Westermann, 1975.

Witkin, H. A., Dyk, R. B., Faterson, H. F., Goodenough, D. R., & Karp, S. A. *Psychological differentiation.* New York: Wiley, 1962.

Witkin, H. A., Goodenough, D. R., & Karp, S. A. Stability of cognitive style from childhood to young adulthood. *Journal of Personality and Social Psychology,* 1967, *7,* 291–300.

Witkin, H. A., Lewis, H. B., Hertzman, M., Machover, K., Meissner, P. B., & Wapner, S. *Personality through perception.* New York: Harper, 1954.

Zimmerman, B. J., & Rosenthal, T. L. Observational learning of rule governed behavior by children. *Psychological Bulletin,* 1974, *8,* 29–42.

4
The Role of Global
Psychological Models in
Instructional Technology

Patrick Suppes
Elizabeth Macken
Mario Zanotti
*Institute for Mathematical Studies
  in the Social Sciences*
Stanford University

1. INTRODUCTION

There is a long history of detailed work in educational psychology relevant to the learning of various skills and subject matters taught in schools, colleges, and universities throughout the world. Much of this tradition of psychological investigation that is related to education has concentrated on a microscopic analysis of the individual learning process. Some of the earliest examples were Thorndike's studies of reading and elementary arithmetic. Thorndike devoted the second volume of his monumental treatise *Educational Psychology* (1913–1914) to the psychology of learning. His scientific objective was to show how the learning of elementary courses such as arithmetic could be accounted for in terms of three fundamental laws, which he named *readiness, exercise,* and *effect.* Although the language of Thorndike's formulation sounds somewhat strange today, the central point of the Law of Readiness is the importance of the connection between stimulus and response being satisfying to the organism. The Law of Exercise actually has two parts. One is the Law of Use, which asserts that when a connection is made between a stimulus and a response, the strength of the connection is increased, other things being equal. The Law of Disuse states that when such a connection between a stimulus and a response is not employed for a period of time, then that strength of connection is decreased. We might today formulate the Law of Exercise in terms of the strength of a response being increased by repeated trials and to formulate the Law of Disuse as a law of extinction, but the central idea is well stated by Thorndike. The most famous of the three laws, the Law of Effect, states that if a connection is made between a stimulus and a response, and it is accompanied by a satisfying state of affairs or, as we might put it now, a positive reinforcement, then the connection is strengthened; similarly, if the connection is accompanied by a negative reinforcement it is weakened.

In a later work, *The Psychology of Arithmetic* (1922), Thorndike attempted to apply in a detailed way his principles of learning to the psychology of drill and practice in arithmetic. He conceived the psychological purpose of drill as being to strengthen the bonds between stimuli and responses. There is a strong tendency to think of Thorndike as emphasizing mindless rote exercise as the heart of arithmetic, but in fact he emphasized throughout his writing the importance of the student's having an understanding of the deductive theories of arithmetic, even though he did not provide a sharp intellectual basis for the concept of understanding such a deductive theory.

In any case, the point of the historical excursus here is not to enter into the details of Thorndike's treatment but to emphasize that he began a historical pattern that has been followed for most of this century in research on the psychology of basic skills, ranging across arithmetic, language, and reading. A fairly extensive summary of the many good empirical studies done of arithmetic in the first third of this century is to be found in Suppes, Jerman, and Brian (1968), but the great volume of literature about any of these skills, especially reading, is far too extensive to review here. A good recent reference on reading is Carroll and Chall (1975).

The central point of this chapter is to argue strongly by example for the value of moving away from the kind of detailed analysis of the learning of particular items characteristic of Thorndike and his successors to more global models of student progress and curriculum organization. It is desirable that the global models be based upon psychological principles, but the essential change is that the details of each response are now ignored and the focus is on two aspects of learning and performance uncharacteristic of this earlier literature. The first focus is on mean or average performance, without attention to the structure of individual items, and the second is on progress over substantial periods of time rather than over the short period required for a few exercises or a limited test.

This emphasis on global models is illustrated with two applications in the context of instructional technology. It is no accident that the use of global models is coupled with instructional technology because it is especially in technological settings that we can exercise the control necessary for quantitative analyses thereby making the use of such models meaningful and interesting from both a conceptual and an empirical standpoint. It is not our point to argue that the models cannot be applied in ordinary classroom settings. We are not interested in trying to develop such a negative thesis but, rather, in establishing positively what can be done when instruction is taking place in an environment that uses one of the three major technologies of radio, television, or computers.

Before we enter into the details of some examples, there are one or two more general remarks we want to make about global models. In the tradition of educational psychology mentioned earlier and in the tradition of experimental psychology, it is hard for many researchers to deal with global models that ignore the many interesting details of each response. We want to emphasize our own continuing interest in these details. In fact, the analyses of individual learning and performance studied in the context of computer-assisted instruction and published in Suppes, Jerman, and Brian (1968) and Suppes and Morningstar (1972) are substantial. But the development of a global theory based on these extensive analyses is quite difficult. In this chapter, we have formulated global models in terms of general psychological principles.

To readers who have not investigated these matters in some detail, it may be surprising to find how little discussion there is in the educational or psychological literature of what global principles are considered appropriate in organizing curriculum. Let us just mention two examples. The first is what principles are back of decisions regarding the proportion of time in a school day that should be devoted to a given subject and the proportion of time that should be devoted to particular concepts or skills within that subject — for example, how much time should be devoted in the teaching of arithmetic at, let us say, the fifth-grade level, to problem solving, and how much to the manipulation of fractions. These matters concerning relative allocations of time have had little if any rational discussion. Second, and perhaps even of more importance, is the absence of discussion of how we should think about students moving through a curriculum — for example, what is the right way to think about the progress of the student in reading in the second grade, in language arts in the fourth grade, or in elementary mathematics in the seventh grade. It is not that the topic is controversial — it is really that detailed technical discussions of such matters are almost nonexistent. We are not claiming that there is no literature on these topics but that, relative to their importance in the organization of curriculum and teaching, they are noticeably absent as major topics of discussion.

The examples we have just introduced are large and complex. They expand into even larger and more complex issues, and we do not pretend to have answers of a general sort as to how to deal with them. Our aim in the present chapter is considerably more modest. We would like to give in some detail two examples of the application of global models and to sketch how these models can be of use in more systematic thinking about curriculum and teaching.

The first example is drawn from some of our work in computer-assisted instruction (CAI) and develops further the work begun in Suppes, Fletcher, and Zanotti (1976) on student trajectories. The second example is drawn from recent work on the use of radio as an instructional technology in developing countries. Here we draw on our experience in the Nicaragua Radio Mathematics Project, described in Searle, Friend, and Suppes (1976), and in this case, we are concerned with optimizing the organization of instruction for group learning rather than for individual learning. The second example emphasizes questions of optimization more directly than the first, but we also make some remarks following the first example to show how a theory of student trajectories can itself be used to consider questions of optimization.

Both of the examples considered deal with basic skills in the elementary school, but it is important to note that this restriction to elementary-school curriculum and teaching is in no way essential. In fact, the trajectory model developed in the first example has been applied to a CAI course at the university level — namely, the teaching of introduction to logic, and this application is reported in Larsen, Markosian, and Suppes (1978). It is also obvious that the kind of optimization that is the main focus of the second example could be applied to other subjects than those characteristic of the elementary-school curriculum.

II. STUDENT TRAJECTORIES IN THREE CAI CURRICULUMS

A. Model and Theory

In this section, we extend a new approach to evaluating curriculum begun in Suppes et al. (1976). The essential idea of our new approach is to develop a theory of prediction for individual student progress through a curriculum, to use this theory as a means of control by regulating the amount of time spent on the curriculum by a given student, and thereby to achieve agreed-upon objectives for the grade-placement gains of each student. We thus avoid the wait-and-see attitude required when classical evaluation of a new curriculum in terms of pretests and posttests is used.

This predictive evaluation calls for individualization, for it is unrealistic to expect all students to make the same gains even when variation in time is permitted. The intuitive idea is to study the trajectory of a student through a curriculum — a method similar to the study of the paths or trajectories of objects in physics. An important feature of the prediction of student progress is to separate the global features of the curriculum from the global individual parameters characteristic of a particular student. The details of this separation become clear in the sequel.

We tested directly the robustness of the theory of the earlier work (Suppes et al., 1976) regarding a power-function model using CAI grade placement as the dependent variable and time on the system as the independent variable. As already remarked, the theory is aimed at the student's global progress and does not consider his performance on individual exercises. By using such a global approach, it is possible to state general axioms about information processing from which we may derive a basic stochastic differential equation that seems to be characteristic of several different curriculums. The equation we obtain is

$$y(t) = bt^k + c,$$

where the parameters b, c, and k can be estimated separately for each individual student, although it is often convenient and interesting to estimate the parameter k for the entire population. For purposes of subsequent reference here, for each student and each curriculum we write the basic equation as:

$$GP_{ij} = bt_{ij}^{k} + c,$$

where

GP_{ij} = grade placement of student i at the jth observation,
t_{ij} = time on system of student i at the jth observation, and
b, c, k = parameters to be estimated for each student.

In the axioms, which we review here briefly, we speak of new *pieces* of information. This nontechnical use of piece is to avoid a technical commitment to the concept of bit of information. Actually, the axioms were formulated in such a way that little about information is assumed. This is more or less characteristic of global theories and is not meant to be exhibited as a virtue. A more detailed theory would aim to say more about the structure of the information transmitted to students in a given curriculum.

The first axiom deals with a student's rate of processing or sampling information in a course. The second axiom postulates what happens to the student's mean rate of processing information when a new piece of information is introduced. The third axiom deals with the basic assumption about the rate of introducing new information. The fourth axiom postulates that the student's current position in a course is closely related to the sum of information introduced up to this point, and the fifth axiom states a similar assumption about his rate of progress in the course. Readers not interested in the technical statement of the axioms and the derivation of the basic stochastic differential equation should skip to the next section.

For statement of the axioms and later use, we define the following quantities: $y(t)$ = position of student in the course, and at $t = 0$ we set $y = 0$ for the present purposes, but later consider a translation; $dy(t)/dt$ = rate of progress through the course; $A(t)$ = cumulative amount of information introduced in the course up to time t; $dA(t)/dt$ = rate of introduction of information in the course; and $s(t)$ = student's rate of processing or sampling information.

Axiom 1. A student's mean rate, $s(t)$, of processing or sampling information is directly proportional to the rate of introduction of information in a course and inversely proportional to the total amount of information introduced up to time t; that is, $s(t)$ is proportional to $[dA(t)/dt]/A(t)$.

Axiom 2. Upon introduction of a new piece of information, a student's new mean rate of processing information is decreased by an amount equal to the product of his current rate and the difference of his current rate and his asymptotic rate; that is, for a small interval of time h,

$$s(t + h) = s(t) - [s(t) - s(\infty)] s(t).$$

Axiom 3. The probability of a new piece of information being introduced for a given student at time t is independent of t and the previous introduction of information.

Axiom 4. The position of a student in a course is directly proportional to the total information introduced thus far in the course; that is, $y(t)$ is proportional to $A(t)$.

Axiom 5. The rate of progress of a student in a course is directly proportional to the rate of introduction of information in the course; that is $dy(t)/dt$ is proportional to $dA(t)/dt$.

We turn now to the derivation of the basic stochastic differential equation. By Axiom 3, the introduction of new information is a Poisson process, let us say with parameter λ. Thus, by Axiom 2, with probability λh in a small time interval h,

$$s(t + h) = s(t) - [s(t) - s(\infty)] s(t); \tag{1}$$

with probability $o(h)$, more than one piece of information is introduced, and with probability $1 - \lambda h - o(h)$,

$$s(t + h) = s(t), \tag{2}$$

whence from Eqs. (1) and (2), and setting $s(\infty) = 0$, which seems intuitively sound,

$$\frac{s(t + h) - s(t)}{h} = -\lambda s(t)^2 + \frac{o(h)}{h}.$$

Hence, as $h \to 0$, we obtain the differential equation,

$$ds(t)/dt = -\lambda s^2(t),$$

whose solution is

$$s(t) = \frac{1}{\lambda t + c_1}.$$

By Axiom 1,

$$s(t) = \frac{k_1 dA(t)/dt}{A(t)}, \qquad k_1 > 0,$$

but by Axiom 4,

$$\frac{dy(t)}{dt} = k_2 \frac{dA(t)}{dt}, \qquad k_2 > 0,$$

and by Axiom 5,

$$\frac{dy(t)}{dt} = k_3 \frac{dA(t)}{dt}, \qquad k_3 > 0;$$

whence, combining results,

$$\frac{dy(t)/dt}{y(t)} = \frac{k_4}{\lambda t + c_1}, \qquad k_4 > 0.$$

Integrating this last equation, we obtain

$$\ln y(t) = \frac{k}{\lambda} \ln(\lambda t + c_1) + \ln |b_1|,$$

and so

$$y(t) = b_1 (\lambda t + c_1)^{k_4/\lambda}.$$

Here, if $t = 0$, $y(t) = 0$, and so $c_1 = 0$. Assuming the student has some knowledge, c, of the course at $t = 0$, we obtain as our final equation,

$$y(t) = bt^k + c.$$

B. Student Data and Curriculum Descriptions

To test the model, we used learning data for deaf and hearing-impaired students in several schools for the deaf throughout the United States and for Indian children at the Bureau of Indian Affairs public school at the Isleta Pueblo in New Mexico. Six geographical regions are represented in the data from the deaf schools: Florida, Dallas (which includes 105 students from Fort Worth), Oklahoma, Houston, San Antonio, and Austin. The research project from which the data were drawn was aimed at providing support services, especially in the form of data evaluation and teacher and proctor training, for CAI in the schools. It was conceived as a follow-on project to a large three-year project, running from July 1, 1970 to June 30, 1973, in which CAI was introduced into the schools by the Institute for Mathematical Studies in the Social Sciences (IMSSS) at Stanford University, under the sponsorship of the Bureau of the Handicapped (U. S. Office of Education) and the National Science Foundation. As the delivery of CAI from the central computer at the Institute reached a natural completion point with the end of the three-year project, the Isleta school and 10 of the 13 schools for the deaf active in the project contracted with Computer Curriculum

Corporation (CCC) in Palo Alto, California for hardware and curriculum. The new hardware consisted of minicomputers installed in each school; the students used teletype terminals to interact with the computer.

The main body of data collected consists of pre- and posttest achievement scores and grade-placement scores in three curriculum areas — language arts, mathematics, and reading — with observations on grade placement in each curriculum being made essentially every 2 weeks. Exactly how the courses are structured to provide this grade placement is described in the following section on curriculum. Because there was considerable variability in the extent to which students used CAI instruction in the various schools, we show in Table 4.1, Column P, the number of students participating in each location and, in Column I, the number of students who had, in a given curriculum, a change (up or down) in grade placement of at least three-tenths of a year, that is, had moved at least three tenths of a year during the course of a year. For a variety of reasons, in almost every location there were a number of students who were on the system for short periods only, and we have excluded them from the analysis. The total number of students remaining is still substantial and provides more than an adequate basis for the statistical analysis of our model.

One of the complicated aspects of data analysis in the present project arose from the wide variety of achievement tests used by the various schools. Table 4.2 gives the code number and the associated name of the test that was administered. These code numbers are used later and refer to the specific tests listed in this table.

The students in our sample used one or more of the following courses from CCC: Mathematics Strands, Grades 1–6; Reading, Grades 3–6; and Language Arts, Grades 3–6. We shall describe each curriculum briefly, beginning with an explanation of the strands instructional strategy. Further details can be found in the *Teacher's Handbook* for each course (Adkins & Hamilton, 1975; Fletcher, Adkins, & Hamilton, 1972; Suppes, Searle, Kanz, & Clinton, 1975).

TABLE 4.1
Number of Students Who Participated (*P*) and Number of Students
Included (*I*) in Analysis by Region and Curriculums

Curriculum	Florida		Dallas		Isleta		Oklahoma		Texas		Houston		Total	
	P	I	P	I	P	I	P	I	P	I	P	I	P	I
Math	251	175	388	163	184	128	197	146	650	341	198	90	1,868	1,043
Reading			388	97	184	70	197	49	650	55	198	17	1,617	288
Language			388	204	184	78	197	102	650	297	198	45	1,617	726

TABLE 4.2
Code Numbers for Achievement Tests

Code	Meaning
1	Stanford Achievement Test, Primary Level 1, Form A[a]
2	Stanford Achievement Test, Level 2, Form A[a]
3	Stanford Achievement Test, Advanced Battery, Form A[a]
4	Stanford Achievement Test, Primary 1 Battery, Form W, 1964[b]
5	Stanford Achievement Test, Primary 2 Battery, Form W, 1964[b]
6	Stanford Achievement Test, Intermediate 2 Battery, Form Y, 1965[b]
7	Stanford Achievement Test, Advanced Battery, Form W, 1964[b]
8	Stanford Achievement Test, Intermediate 1 Battery, Form W, 1964[b]
9	Stanford Achievement Test, Intermediate 2 Battery, Form W, 1964[b]
10	Science Research Associates, Achievement Series, Primary 2, Form E, 1972[c]
11	Science Research Associates, Achievement Series, Primary 2, Form F, 1972[c]
12	Science Research Associates, Achievement Series, Multi-Level Form E & F, 1972[c]

[a] For use only with hearing-impaired students as part of the special achievement testing procedures devised by the Annual Survey of Hearing Impaired Children and Youth, Office of Demographic Studies, Gallaudet College, Washington, D.C., 1972; Richard Madden, Eric F. Gardner, Herbert C. Rudman, Bjorn Karlsen, Jack C. Merwin; Harcourt Brace Jovanovich, Inc., New York.

[b] Truman L. Kelley, Richard Madden, Eric F. Gardner, and Herbert C. Rudman; Harcourt Brace Jovanovich, Inc., New York.

[c] Robert A. Naslund, Louis P. Thorpe, D. Welty Lefer; Science Research Associates, Inc., Chicago.

1. *Strands Strategy.* A strand represents one content area within a curriculum. For example, a division strand, a decimal strand, and an equation strand are included in the Mathematics Strands curriculum. Each strand is a string of related items whose difficulty progresses from easy to hard. A computer program keeps records of the student's position and performance separately for every strand. By comparing a student's record of performance on the material in one strand with a preset performance criterion, the program determines if the student needs more practice at the same level of difficulty within the strand, should move back to an easier level for remedial work, or has mastered the current concept and can move ahead to a more difficult level. Then the program automatically adjusts the student's position to the correct level within the strand. The process of evaluation and adjustment applies to all strands and is continuous throughout each student's interaction with a curriculum.

Evenly spaced gradations in the difficulty level of the material allow positions within a strand to be matched to school grade placements by tenths of a year. Grade placement in a specific subject area can then be determined by examining a student's position in the strand representing that area. Since performance in each strand is recorded and evaluated separately, the student may have a different grade placement in every strand of a curriculum. Teachers' reports, available as part of each curriculum, record progress by showing the student's grade placement in each strand at the time of the report.

In a curriculum based on the strands instructional strategy, a normal lesson consists of a mixture of exercises from different strands. Each time an item from a particular curriculum is to be presented, a computer program randomly selects the strand from which it will draw the exercise. Random selection of strands ensures that the student will receive a mixture of different types of items instead of a series of similar items.

Each curriculum also provides for rapid gross adjustment of position in all the strands as the student is first beginning work in the course. Students who perform very well at their entering grade levels are moved up in half-year steps until they reach a more challenging level. Students who perform poorly are moved down in half-year steps. This adjustment of overall grade level ensures that students are correctly placed in the curriculum and is in effect only during a student's first 10 sessions.

2. *Mathematics.* The Mathematics, Grades 1–6, curriculum contains 14 strands, or content areas. Table 4.3 lists the strands in the mathematics curriculum. The curriculum begins at the first-grade level and extends through grade

TABLE 4.3
Mathematics Strands, Grades 1–6

Strand	Content	Abbreviation
1	Number Concepts	NC
2	Horizontal Addition	HA
3	Horizontal Subtraction	HS
4	Vertical Addition	VA
5	Vertical Subtraction	VS
6	Equations	EQ
7	Measurement	MS
8	Horizontal Multiplication	HM
9	Laws of Arithmetic	LW
10	Vertical Multiplication	VM
11	Division	DV
12	Fractions	FR
13	Decimals	DC
14	Negative Numbers	NG

level 7.9. The seventh-grade material does not constitute a complete curriculum for that grade year but is intended as enrichment for students who complete the sixth-grade material.

Each strand is organized into equivalence classes, or sets of exercises of similar number properties and structure. During each CAI session in mathematics, students receive exercises from all the strands that contain equivalence classes appropriate to their grade levels. For example, a student at grade level 2.0 will receive exercises from the first seven strands listed in Table 4.3. Students do not receive an equal number of exercises from all strands. The program adjusts the proportion of exercises from each strand to match the proportion of exercises covering that concept in an average textbook.

The curriculum material in Mathematics Strands, Grades 1–6, is not stored in the computer's memory but takes the form of algorithms that use random-number techniques to generate exercises. When a particular equivalence class is selected, a program generates the numerical values used in the exercise, produces the required format information for the presentation of the exercise, and calculates the correct response for comparison with student input. As a result, the arrangement of the lesson and the actual exercises presented differ between students at the same level and between lessons for a student who remains at a constant grade placement for several lessons.

3. *Reading.* The Reading, Grades 3–6, curriculum consists of reading practice items designed to improve the student's skills in five areas: word analysis, vocabulary extension, comprehension of sentence structure, interpretation of written material, and development of study skills (see Table 4.4). It contains material for 4 years of work at grade levels 3, 4, 5, and 6 as well as supplementary remedial material that extends downward to grade level 2.5.

The program is divided into two parts: Basic Sentences and Strands. The Basic Sentences section begins at grade level 2.5 and ends at grade level 3.5. The items in this section are short and easy. They represent the simplest type of reading-practice exercise that can be presented in a contemporary computer-assisted instructional system.

TABLE 4.4
Strands in Reading, Grades 3–6

Strand	Content
A	Word Attack—analyzing words as units
B	Vocabulary—building a reading vocabulary
C	Literal Comprehension—understanding the literal meaning of sentences and short paragraphs
D	Interpretive Comprehension—reading sentences for interpretation
E	Work-Study Skills—learning to use resources effectively

The Strands section starts at grade level 3.5 and continues through grade level 6.9. When working in the Strands section, the student receives items from all five strands during every session.

4. *Language Arts.* The Language Arts, Grades 3–6, curriculum covers Grades 3 through 6 with enough material for a year's work at each grade level. It also offers a supplement of lessons for students with special language problems. These include hearing-impaired students and students for whom English is a second language.

The Language Arts curriculum stresses usage instead of grammar and presents very few grammatical terms. It is divided into two courses, Language Arts Strands and Language Arts Topics. Both courses cover the same general subject areas, but their structures are very different. Language Arts Strands uses a strands structure to provide highly individualized mixed drills. In Language Arts Topics, the entire class receives lessons on a topic assigned by the teacher. The schools included in this survey used only the Language Arts Strands course. See Table 4.5 for the content of the Language Arts Strands.

C. Results

As we stated earlier (Section II.A), the global model we tested is

$$GP_{ij} = bt_{ij}^k + c,$$

where

$\quad GP_{ij}$ = grade placement of student i at the jth observation,
$\quad t_{ij}$ = time on system of student i at the jth observation, and
$\quad b, c, k$ = parameters to be estimated for each student.

The parameters b and c were estimated for each student for 50 values of k ranging from .001 to 4.00. (The exact values are shown in the first column of Table 4.6.) The triple (b, c, k), which minimized the standard error, and the standard error itself were recorded for each student.

TABLE 4.5
Language Arts Strands, Grades 3–6

Strand	Content
A	Principal Parts of Verbs
B	Verb Usage
C	Subject-Verb Agreement
D	Pronoun Usage
E	Contractions, Possessives, and Negatives
F	Modifiers
G	Sentence Structure
H	Mechanics

TABLE 4.6
Number of Students for Whom the k Values
Gave the Minimum Average Squared Deviation

k	DL	DM	DR	FM	HL	HM	HR	OL	OM	OR	TL	TM	TR	IL	IM	IR
.001	0	3	13	4	0	1	0	0	1	4	1	6	6	0	1	6
.002	56	8	16	8	6	7	0	22	1	3	3	20	1	20	3	7
.003	2	13	8	9	0	8	1	0	5	0	1	21	2	0	13	1
.004	1	8	2	16	0	7	0	0	7	0	0	23	1	0	8	1
.005	0	0	1	11	0	4	0	0	7	2	0	16	4	0	9	1
.006	0	1	0	12	0	2	0	0	6	0	0	12	1	0	4	1
.007	1	0	0	10	0	0	0	0	7	2	0	7	1	0	9	1
.010	0	2	0	2	0	0	0	0	8	0	0	10	0	1	4	2
.020	1	4	0	1	0	0	1	0	2	1	0	3	1	0	2	2
.030	2	3	0	2	0	0	0	0	0	0	0	0	1	0	0	0
.040	1	0	0	0	0	1	0	0	1	0	0	0	1	0	0	1
.050	0	1	0	0	0	0	0	1	2	0	0	0	0	0	0	0
.060	0	0	0	0	0	0	0	0	1	2	0	1	1	0	0	1
.070	0	0	0	1	0	2	0	0	0	0	0	1	0	0	0	0
.080	1	0	0	0	0	1	0	0	0	0	0	1	0	1	0	0
.090	0	2	1	1	0	0	0	0	1	0	1	1	0	0	0	2
.100	6	5	3	1	0	1	0	0	2	2	0	4	0	2	2	0
.150	2	1	2	2	0	0	0	0	2	2	0	7	0	2	0	3
.200	3	9	0	3	1	1	1	0	1	1	1	5	1	1	1	0
.250	12	6	3	3	2	0	0	1	1	1	0	8	0	1	4	1
.300	9	7	0	3	0	3	0	1	2	1	0	3	0	1	3	2
.350	10	7	1	1	2	3	0	1	3	1	0	6	1	3	2	0
.400	7	8	1	2	1	2	0	2	1	1	0	5	2	3	3	1
.450	7	8	0	2	2	1	0	1	1	0	1	3	0	2	0	0
.500	7	6	2	3	0	1	0	0	2	1	1	3	3	0	2	0
.550	5	8	1	7	3	3	0	2	4	0	1	9	1	2	1	0
.600	6	5	0	2	1	2	2	3	2	1	0	2	1	4	2	2
.650	4	4	1	1	1	0	0	0	1	0	0	10	0	4	1	0
.700	5	5	1	1	0	1	1	2	1	1	1	5	0	2	1	1
.750	2	4	1	1	1	1	0	6	0	3	0	10	0	0	1	1
.800	3	4	1	4	0	1	0	3	3	2	0	10	0	4	1	0
.850	2	3	1	1	0	0	2	2	1	0	0	8	0	2	3	0
.900	4	4	2	1	2	2	1	4	0	0	0	4	0	5	3	1
.950	4	2	3	3	0	1	1	3	1	0	1	5	4	1	1	0
1.00	1	0	3	3	0	2	1	0	1	0	1	5	0	2	0	0
1.05	5	1	3	0	0	5	0	3	2	1	1	3	0	2	3	0
1.10	1	1	0	4	2	1	1	4	3	1	0	8	1	0	1	1
1.15	1	5	1	0	0	3	1	2	1	0	0	9	0	3	1	1
1.20	1	2	0	0	0	2	0	1	3	0	0	2	2	1	3	1
1.25	0	3	1	5	2	2	0	1	3	0	1	3	0	1	4	2
1.30	4	1	3	4	0	2	0	3	5	0	9	12	0	1	0	2
1.40	1	0	1	2	2	0	2	5	4	3	8	6	2	0	4	2
1.50	6	3	3	2	2	3	1	0	3	1	6	2	0	0	2	3
1.60	1	0	2	5	0	0	0	1	2	1	4	9	0	0	1	0
1.70	1	0	3	3	1	1	0	2	3	0	9	6	0	1	2	2
1.80	2	0	1	2	1	1	0	0	3	1	9	2	0	1	4	0
1.90	0	0	1	3	2	1	0	3	3	1	5	3	1	1	1	1
2.00	5	2	3	12	1	7	0	5	7	2	114	14	3	0	3	3
3.00	8	2	3	6	5	2	0	8	11	0	102	16	1	1	3	5
4.00	4	2	5	6	5	2	1	10	15	7	16	12	12	3	12	9
Sum	204	163	97	175	45	90	17	102	146	49	297	341	55	78	128	70

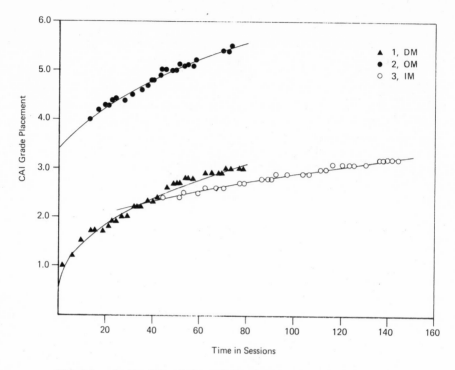

FIG. 4.1.   Scatterplot and theoretical trajectory for gain in grade placement over time for three students in the mathematics curriculum.

Figures 4.1 through 4.3 show how closely the model fits a variety of student
trajectories; CAI grade placement is plotted on the ordinate and a measure of
time on the system is plotted on the abscissa. Figure 4.1 shows data for three
students in the mathematics curriculum.[1] All students progressed steadily, but
Student 3 progressed at a much slower rate than Students 1 or 2. All three curves
fit the observed data points very closely. The data for Student 1 are fit by the
curve $y = .295t^{.50} + .509$ with a standard error[2] of .072; this student gained 2

---

[1]In these figures and subsequent figures and tables, the following notation is used: The
first initial indicates the region as follows: D stands for Dallas, F for Florida, H for Houston,
I for Iseleta Pueblo, O for Oklahoma, and T for Texas, which includes data from Austin and
San Antonio. The second initial is the letter M, R, or L to indicate the mathematics, reading,
or language arts curriculum.

[2]Standard error is defined by the equation

$$SE_j = \left[\frac{1}{n_j} \sum_{i=1}^{n_j} (o_{ij} - t_{ij})^2 \right]^{\frac{1}{2}}$$

where o_{ij} is observation i for student j, t_{ij} is the corresponding theoretical prediction, and n_j
is the number of predictions for student j. Then, the mean standard error for the sample
population of students is just the mean of their standard errors.

years in eighty 10-minute sessions. For Student 2 the equation of the theoretical curve is given by $y = 3.142t^{.20} - 2.313$ with a standard error of .252 and for Student 3 by $y = .118t^{.55} + 1.419$ with a standard error of .030.

Figure 4.2 shows data for two students in the reading curriculum. Notice that the unit of time on the abscissa is minutes: Student 1 gained about one-third of a year in fifty 10-minute sessions and Student 2 gained about half a year in one hundred 10-minute sessions. Approximately 150 days are available for working in a school year, and students are scheduled for one CAI reading session per day. On that basis, Student 1, a deaf student, gained one-third of a year in one-third of a year's time and Student 2, an American Indian, gained about one-half a year in two-thirds of a year's time. The curve for Student 1 is given by $y = .00017t^{1.25} + 2.935$, and the curve for Student 2 is given by $y = .009t^{.6} + 5.748$; the standard errors are .025 and .026, respectively.

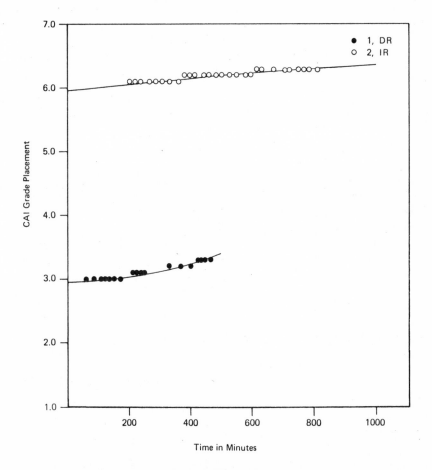

FIG. 4.2.   Scatterplot and theoretical trajectory for gain in grade placement over time for two students in the reading curriculum.

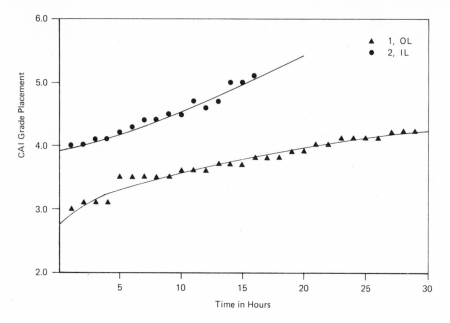

FIG. 4.3.   Scatterplot and theoretical trajectory for gain in grade placement over time for two students in the language arts curriculum.

Figure 4.3 shows data for two students in the language arts curriculum. Both
students gained over a year in 20 hours; Student 2, who worked 30 hours, gained
1.4 years. The curve for Student 1 is given by $y = .035t^{1.25} + 3.938$, and the
curve for Student 2 is given by $y = .224t^{.55} + 2.774$; the standard errors are
.059 and .062, respectively. Again, the curves give quite good fits to the data.

It is useful to see the distribution of best values of k as evidence of wide student variability in rate of progress. Table 4.6 shows for each k value the number
of times it gave the minimum standard error in each group; the region and curriculum are denoted by initials as explained earlier.

Figure 4.4 is a histogram showing the distribution of the best individually
estimated k for all students in the study. Each value of k gave the minimum
standard error for at least five students, and most values gave the minimum for
at least 25 students.

In the previous work by Suppes et al. (1976), the distribution of the mean
standard error over fixed values of k for the entire population was relatively flat.
The data for the deaf schools and Isleta supported this; we found that if a fixed
k is used for the entire population, there is no necessity to have a highly exact
estimate of it. For most populations using the reading and mathematics curriculum, any value in the range from .07 to .90 gives about as good an estimate as
any other, with appropriate adjustments of the two individual parameters b and
c. At Isleta, for example, the mean standard errors in the mathematics curricu-

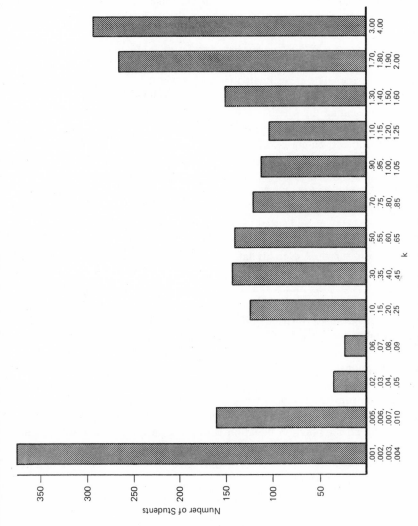

FIG. 4.4. Histogram of the exponent *k* individually estimated for 2057 students over all curriculums.

245

lum for these values of k range from about .05 to .06. For the language arts curriculum, the lower bound for values of k is smaller. In fact, for three of the four regions that used the language arts curriculum, the minimum mean standard error was given by $k = .002$. However, the standard errors for values of k within the range from .07 to .90 are not large; for Oklahoma, for example, the mean standard errors for these values of k range from about .2 to .3.

D. Joint Distribution of the Parameters

When several parameters are estimated for each student, it is natural to ask what can be said about the joint distribution of the parameters. The results fall into two cases depending on whether k is fixed for a population or whether k is selected for each individual. Consider first a population k that is determined for each region and curriculum by averaging the best individual k's and the correlation of the pairs (b_1, c_1) obtained for each student by fitting the equation $y = b_i t^k + c_i$. We found these correlations for 16 groups; for all but three of the groups, the correlation between b and c is close to zero. The three exceptions are (Dallas, Language Arts) where $r(b, c/k = .628) = -.6$, (Oklahoma, Reading) where $r(b, c/k = 1.081) = -.9$, and (Isleta, Language Arts) where $r(b, c/k = 9.06) = -.8$.

On the other hand, if we find for each student the triple (k_i, b_i, c_i) that best fits the curve $y = b_i t^{k_i} + c_i$ to his data, then the correlation between any two of the three values given the third is high. To be explicit, $|r(b_i, c_i)| \simeq 1$, $|r(k_i, c_i)| \simeq 1$, and $|r(k_i, b_i)| \simeq 1$. This means that to fit the individual curves, only two of the three variables are necessary. In terms of k, the results indicate that if k is fixed, b and c are independent; we need both variables to fit the data. But if k is allowed to vary by individual, then b and c are dependent.

There are several different remarks to be made abou these results. First, under weak assumptions, the results on conditional independence and correlations of absolute value one between any two parameters satisfy the hypotheses of a probabilistic lemma proved in Suppes and Zanotti (1976). Namely, if $r(b_i, c_i|k) = 0$ and $|r(b_i, c_i)| = 1$, then $|r(b_i, k_i)| = |r(c_i, k_i)| = 1$. Second, a power series representation of the power function equation shows the source of some of the constraints. For $t > 0$, we can represent t^k by:

$$t^k = e^{k \ln t} = \sum_{n=0}^{\infty} \frac{k^n (\ln t)^n}{n!}.$$

Thus the model can be written in the following equivalent form for $t > 0$:

$$y = \sum_{n=0}^{\infty} a_n (\ln t)^n.$$

It follows that

$$a_0 = b + c$$

$$a_n = \frac{bk^n}{n!}$$

In particular, $b = a_1/k$, which is approximately linear for a small range of k. A deeper analysis of the model is not pursued here.

1. *Predicting Posttest Scores.* We examined the possibility of using the parameters b, c, and k that had been estimated for each individual along with final grade placement (FGP) and pretest score (PRE) to predict posttest (POST) score. The model is defined by the following equation:

$$POST_i = a_0 + a_1(b_i) + a_2(c_i) + a_3(k_i) + a_4(FGP_i) + a_5(PRE_i).$$

We were able to test the model with 20 groups; we needed groups with $N > 6$ and with pre- and posttest data available. There were eight groups with $6 < N \leqslant 10$ and 12 groups with $N > 10$; of these 12, five had $N > 30$. In the discussion that follows, groups are labeled by the ordered quadruple (region, curriculum, pretest, posttest); pre- and posttest codes were given in Table 4.2.

Among the eight groups with between six and 10 students, the multiple correlations are, with two exceptions, all greater than .8. (We attach little significance to the large multiple correlations for the groups with small N's.) The two exceptions to the .8 generalization are (Oklahoma, Reading, 4, 8) and (Texas, Language Arts, 6, 1), which gave the worst fit of all 20 groups. For (Texas, Language Arts, 6, 1), there were only 4 degrees of freedom left in the residual after the regression took in all independent variables, yet the multiple correlation was .562. For five of the eight groups, the variable b entered the regression on the first or second iteration; no other trends were apparent with respect to the entering of the independent variables in this grouping.

Among the 12 groups with more than 10 students, there are seven regressions with multiple correlations greater than .85: (Oklahoma, Mathematics, 4, 9) had a multiple correlation of .967 with 5 degrees of freedom; (Oklahoma, Mathematics 4, 5) had a multiple correlation of .941 with 8 degrees of freedom; (Oklahoma, Mathematics, 5, 9) had a multiple correlation of .914 with 13 degrees of freedom; (Texas, Mathematics, 4, 4) had a multiple correlation of .862 with 20 degrees of freedom; and (Isleta, Mathematics, 10, 11), the largest group, had a multiple correlation of .864 with 64 degrees of freedom. In these 12 larger groups, b entered last or next to last eight times out of 12, in marked contrast to the results for the groups with 10 or fewer observations. FGP and PRE were the important independent variables for these groups. FGP was the first variable to enter the regression seven times out of 12; PRE entered first or second eight times out of 12. A less important independent variable in these regressions tended to be k; it never entered on the first iteration and entered on the second iteration only once.

Although the pretest was often an important independent variable, there were many students for whom pretest data were not available and who therefore could not be used in the preceding model. In addition, a model without the pretest as an independent variable would allow those students with the same geographical region, lesson, and posttest to be grouped. Thus, the following model was considered in order to increase the degrees of freedom.

$$POST_i = a_0 + a_1(b_i) + a_2(c_i) + a_3(k_i) + a_4(FGP_i) \tag{3}$$

We were able to test this model with 29 groups of data with $N > 5$. In the following discussion, groups are labeled with the ordered triple (group, lesson, posttest).

There were several instances in this set of regressions where it was clear that a linear function of the independent variables could not adequately explain the observations. An extreme example is (Texas, Mathematics, 1), for which a multiple correlation of .190 with 48 degrees of freedom was computed. However, of the 24 groups of 11 or more students, eight regressions had multiple correlations above .8, and of the 16 groups of 25 or more students, eight regressions had multiple correlations above .7. FGP entered first in the stepwise regression calculations 17 times out of 29.

To increase group size further, we tested the model given by Eq. (3) with students across regions grouped according to curriculum and posttest. There are nine regressions that are new to this group (i.e., regressions where grouping increased the sample size). Of these, seven have more than 10 students, and six have more than 30. For this set of regressions, groups are labeled by the ordered pair (lesson, posttest).

Several groups in this set had high multiple correlation coefficients. (Language Arts, 5) had a multiple correlation of .816 with 21 degrees of freedom. FGP entered first, followed by c and k; b did not enter because of the high negative correlation between b and c, $r(b, c) = -.999$. (Language Arts, 8) had a multiple correlation of .812 with 29 degrees of freedom. Again, the order in which variables entered was FGP, c, and k, with b not used because $r(b, c) = -.995$. (Mathematics, 5) had a multiple correlation of .853 with 36 degrees of freedom; (Mathematics, 4) had a multiple correlation of .897 with 35 degrees of freedom, and (Reading, 5) had a multiple correlation of .753 with 3 degrees of freedom. FGP entered the regression first for all except one of the 11 groups.

E.   Some Conclusions and Applications to Questions of Optimization

Use of the power function model as a global trajectory model fit individual data of student progress extremely well in a large number of cases. The close fit to the data supports the extensive analysis of the fit of this model already reported (Suppes, Fletcher, & Zanotti, 1975, 1976). Achievement in the CAI curriculums of language arts, mathematics, and reading was found to be closely related to scores on achievement tests given at the end of the school year. The highest correlations were obtained in the mathematics curriculum, which is to be anticipated in view of the greater difficulty for hearing-impaired students in mastering either reading or language arts skills.

The success of the trajectory models in fitting extremely well the individual data suggests some possible applications that optimize the use of technology in instruction. We shall sketch here some of the questions that we are presently analyzing in considerable detail and will publish subsequently. The first thing to note is that a trajectory model makes possible a global prediction of student grade placement based upon the amount of time spent on systematic drill, practice, and review. Given that a cost must be assigned to the use of computers in the schools, the question naturally arises then of how time should be allocated to various students. Such a question of allocation leads in turn to a question of what function are we trying to optimize. We mention here a few of the alternatives.

A first possibility would be to maximize the expected grade-placement increase as measured by curriculum grade placement or by external pre- and post-tests. If we take this expectation as the unrestricted goal for the given population for which computer-assisted instruction will be available, then the conclusion is that any unused or marginal unit of time should be assigned to the student with the fastest rate of increase in grade placement per unit of time. (We use *marginal* here in the sense of economics.) In general, this will mean assignment of time to the brighter and better students, contrary to what is ordinarily intended in programs for the disadvantaged. Second, we may take the opposite tack — namely, that the goal we want to maximize is not increase in expected grade placement for the population under consideration but rather decrease in the variance in grade placement across the population. In this case, our optimization function would be that of minimizing the variance in final grade placement or in grade-placement gain. In either case, the qualitative outcome would be to assign most of the time to the poorest performers and to assign essentially no time to the ablest students in the population. (We describe all these various optimal solutions in qualitative and somewhat vague terms. It is easy to see how they can be converted into precise quantitative formulas.) We believe that neither of these extremes is really suitable for actual allocation of technological resources.

A third form of allocation of time would be to optimize the expected gain but with the constraint that the variance in the grade-level achievement of the population not be increased. A fourth possibility would be to maximize the number of students who make at least a one-year gain in grade placement. In many ways, this last goal corresponds to much of the intuitive thinking of many school people.

It is important to recognize that each of the goals we have stated would lead to a particular algorithm of allocation that runs contrary to a general philosophy of equality of opportunity. We may want to adopt an egalitarian attitude toward opportunity and insist that time should be allocated equally to all students in the given population. We suspect that there are aspects of the equality-of-opportunity philosophy that have to be brought to bear in allocating time under any global model. This leads to a formulation of optimization that is probably close in working spirit to the intuitive thinking of many people. This model is to apply first equality of opportunity and to give a routine time on a daily basis, for example, to each student on the assumption that there will be unused technological resources after this allocation is made; the remainder of the resources are then allocated to optimize one of the functions we have mentioned above. Many people might choose to allocate by decreasing the variance. It is important to recognize that the use of a global model to decrease variance after an allocation according to a principle of equality of opportunity is a very different matter from using the goal of decreasing variance as the sole goal with respect to which allocation is made.

The range of possibilities permitted by the kind of global model we have developed in this section is by no means exhausted by the alternatives just sketched. There is a different and in many ways still more attractive way of thinking about optimization. Rather than imposing some external function to be optimized, the predictive aspects of the trajectory model can be used to work with the individual student toward achieving a goal that is set in consultation with his teacher. For example, a student might work with his teacher to make a grade-placement gain of 1.1 years. The trajectory model could be used to give a continual updated prediction to the teacher and to the student of how well he is progressing toward his goal, and time could be allocated to individuals as necessary according to the prediction. It is easy for us to underestimate the ability of even relatively young children to absorb information about their own progress and to act accordingly. In some preliminary work we have recently done, we have found that students can be very motivated to achieve a curriculum-related goal and will find, in terms of their own schedules, ways and means of taking advantage of the extra technological resources available in the school. It may well be that time allocation based on individual goals and individual initiatives and using a global model effectively to provide prediction and guidance will provide a better way to move in the future. We may turn away from an allocation of resources that does not take into account the student's own ability to be self-motivated.

III. OPTIMIZING REVIEW EXERCISES IN
THE RADIO MATHEMATICS PROJECT

The use of radio for instructional purposes has a long history, yet the number of studies directed toward the development and improvement of instructional techniques appropriate for radio is relatively small. Among the various technologies of instruction now being used around the world, ranging from programmed instruction booklets to color television and computers, a good case can be made that radio is the most economical for mass distribution of instruction.

Responding to the growing use of instructional radio in developing countries and the need for research, the Technical Assistance Bureau, within the division of Education and Human Resources of the United States Agency for International Development (AID), has provided funds for research on improving the effectiveness of teaching by radio in the primary grades. Under the aegis of AID, the Institute for Mathematical Studies in the Social Sciences has initiated a project to teach mathematics by radio in the lower primary grades and is presently working in Nicaragua.

The Radio Mathematics Project assumes responsibility for all of the mathematics instruction children receive. A daily lesson consists of a 25-minute radio presentation followed by approximately 20 minutes of teacher-directed activities; instructions for the teacher are provided in a project-developed teachers' guide. No textbooks are used, but teachers are asked to supply simple materials, such as bottle caps and sticks. The focus of our research is how best to use these limited resources to teach mathematics effectively.

In discussing the current project, we have found some skepticism that mathematics can be effectively taught by means of radio, and it is a primary purpose of the project to test this hypothesis. The success of this experiment would be of some importance because of the low cost of radio technology. If good achievement results can be obtained, then at least in the case of teaching primary school mathematics, the cost–benefit ratios for radio may be the best of any of the feasible technologies, including even traditional instruction with adequately trained teachers.

A. Location of the Project

The project is located in the Department of Masaya, an area close to Managua, the capital city of Nicaragua. The Department has one large and several small municipalities. The total primary-school population is close to 18,000 with approximately two-thirds of the children in urban schools and the remainder in rural schools. Class size ranges from 15 to 60; rural schools frequently have more than than one grade in the same classroom. Roughly 30% of the urban and 50% of the rural school population is in first grade.

Children attend school for 3 to 4 hours a day during a school year that extends from mid-February to mid-November. Student performance is evaluated at the end of each school year by final tests constructed by the teacher or school. Students who fail one or two subjects may be reexamined before the start of the next school year; those who fail more than two subjects are held back. Most teachers in the Department are school graduates (with 5 years of post-primary education), and they are, on the average, better qualified than teachers in areas more remote from the capital. As of the time of writing this chapter, several thousand students have received the radio lessons, and the number is continuing to expand.

B. Overview of a Mathematics Lesson

Each mathematics lesson consists of two parts, the broadcast portion and the teacher-directed portion, with the broadcast designed to be presented first. During a typical lesson, two main characters join one or two subordinate characters to sing, play, and talk mathematics, and they often invite the listening children to participate. The children are asked to respond in a variety of ways to about 50 exercises during each 25-minute lesson. Sometimes children are asked to handle concrete materials; for example, they may count or group bottle caps. Sometimes children are asked to respond orally to new mathematical material, and sometimes they respond individually by writing exercises and answers in their notebooks. After the radio transmission, the teacher continues the lesson, following directions given in the teachers' guide.

C. Structure of the Curriculum

Broadly speaking, the mathematics curriculum is that specified by the Nicaraguan Ministry of Education, although some changes in emphasis and some reorganization have been necessary in structuring the radio lessons. The process of constructing lessons from the rather general curriculum guide of the Ministry of Education involved several steps. First, the mathematical content was divided into topics or strands, similar to the CAI curriculum described in the first section of this chapter. For first grade, there are six strands, namely, basic concepts, number concepts, addition, subtraction, applications, and measurement. Then, for each strand, a set of goals or objectives was formulated, which defined the behavior expected of a student who had successfully completed one year of the instructional program. The goals were then broken down into subgoals, called classes, that are appropriate units for instruction.[3] Consider, for example, a goal that states: *The student will count the number of objects in a set of* N *objects, where* N *is less than or equal to 25.* The first subgoal might restrict the number of objects to five or fewer, a second might use from six to 10 objects, and so on. The classes may be sampled at any time to provide test items to measure student progress in attaining curriculum goals.

The first consideration in determining the instructional sequence was that all classes that are prerequisites to a given class come before it in the sequence; this must be true within and across strands. Second, each class must appear several

---

[3]In Tables 4.7 and 4.8, these classes or subgoals are referred to in abbreviated form. These abbreviations, listed here in alphabetical order, have the following interpretations: HA = horizontal addition, HM = horizontal multiplication, HS = horizontal subtraction, NC = number concepts, OA = oral addition, OC = oral combinations of addition and subtraction, OM = oral multiplication, OS = oral subtraction, SN = selecting numerals, SP = subtraction word problems (oral), VA = vertical addition, VS = vertical subtraction, and WN = writing numerals. The numbers following the abbreviations in the tables are the class numbers.

times throughout the year — the first appearance for introducing and explaining the material and the remaining appearances for providing practice and review.

D. Optimal Allocation of Time to the Various Curriculum Objectives

It is accepted by a great many people that curriculum designers and writers should make explicit the curriculum goals that are being served by the materials. In broad terms, we have tried to do this in the Radio Mathematics Project. More importantly, the curriculum structure outlined above lends itself naturally to a quantitative approach. The model that is presented provides specific quantitative results that should serve as a sophisticated guide to those constructing the curriculum.

As mentioned already, there are approximately 50 exercises per 25-minute radio lesson. On the basis of approximately 150 lessons per school year, this means that there are about 7500 exercises to allocate to the various goals. The optimization problem then is to group the total number of exercises into blocks of N exercises and then to divide the number of exercises in each block among the goals in such a way as to optimize performance at the end of the block.

It is desirable that a problem of this complexity have additional constraints placed upon it insofar as this is possible. Our optimization problem has the following components. First, there is the number s of objectives. Second, there is the weight r_i assigned to each goal i with the obvious constraints that $r_i > 0$ and $\Sigma r_i = 1$. Third, there is the initial probability of a correct response to an exercise in a given block of exercises. This initial probability of a correct response we denote by p_i or occasionally, when an indication of sequence position j is needed, $p_{i,j}$. Correspondingly, we use the standard notation for the probability of an error, q_i and $q_{i,j}$, with $q_i = 1 - p_i$. Fourth, there is the mean learning rate a_i. Note that we could simplify matters by not introducing a different learning rate for items associated with different goals, but we do not make that simplifying assumption here. Fifth, there is the mean forgetting rate b_i. Sixth, there is the number N of exercises in a given block or segment, with m_i to be allocated to the ith goal. For example, at the beginning of the year, N could be 7500 exercises. Our formal problem is to allocate the m_i exercises to each goal in such a way that performance at the end of the block is optimized. The measure of optimization is the expected mean error rate, and thus, we want to minimize the expectation of the mean probability of an error.

There are, of course, a very large number of ways of ordering presentation of exercises related to different goals, but we shall restrict ourselves to a periodic pattern as a first approximation. Thus, an exercise relevant to goal i is offered on a given trial followed by k_i trials dealing with other goals. This pattern of $k_i + 1$ trials is repeated periodically throughout the block. Note that, as we show later, a relation exists between k_i, m_i, and N, so that the value of k_i is fixed by the value of m_i and N. Thus, in finding the optimum allocation of the m_i exercises to each goal, we are also determining k_i, the optimum number of trials before the next presentation of an exercise related to goal i. Obviously, in actually writing curriculum materials, one would sometimes deviate from the exact $k_i + 1$ periodicity, but the effects of minor deviations will not be significant, and by making this periodic assumption, we are able to make explicit computations that otherwise are considerably more difficult.

We assume mean learning and forgetting rates across students. Within these mean or averaging assumptions, a variety of individual models can be fitted, as is well known from the literature of mathematical learning theory. In particular, the models of individual learning that can be accommodated to the mean learning assumptions may range from the all-or-none model, on the one hand, to the linear incremental model, on the other. The two mean equations are the following:

Learning: $\quad q_{i,n+1} = a_i q_{i,n}$ (4)

Forgetting: $\quad p_{i,n+1} = b_i p_{i,n}$ (5)

We can write the recursion for forgetting in terms of the probability of an error:

$$q_{i,n+1} = b_i q_{i,n} + (1 - b_i)$$ (6)

After one learning trial and k_i forgetting trials, which constitutes a cycle of $k_i + 1$ trials, we can easily show the following:

$$q_{i,k_i+2} = b_i^{k_i} a_i q_{i,1} + (1 - b_i^{k_i})$$ (7)

The derivation of this result and others that closely follow are to be found in Suppes (1964).

After m_i cycles of $k_i + 1$ trials, we can show that we have the following:

$$E(q_{i,m_i k_i + m_i + 1}) = b_i^{m_i k_i} a_i^{m_i} q_{i,1} + (1 - b_i^{m_i k_i} a_i^{m_i}) \frac{1 - b_i^{k_i}}{1 - a_i b_i^{k_i}}$$ (8)

As noted previously, N is the total number of trials in a block. Because, under the assumptions made here, forgetting occurs on all trials that are not learning trials, the following simple relation holds between N, m_i, and k_i:

$$N = m_i k_i + m_i$$ (9)

It should be noted that this equation holds for every goal i with, of course, the following constraint:

$$N = \Sigma m_i$$ (10)

Finally, to obtain the weighted expectation of q, the probability of an error, at the end of a block, we obtain the following equation from Eqs. (8), (9), and (10):

$$E(q) = \Sigma\, r_i E(q_{i,m_i k_i + m_i + 1}) \tag{11}$$

The expected probability of error for objective i, $E(q_{i,m_i k_i + m_i + 1})$, is a convex combination (weighted average) of $q_{i,1}$ and $f(k_i) = (1 - b_i^{k_i})/(1 - a_i b_i^{k_i})$. The following inequality must be statisfied if learning is to occur:

$$\frac{1 - b_i^{k_i}}{1 - a_i b_i^{k_i}} < q_{i,1}. \tag{12}$$

When this is the case, $f(k_i)$ being an increasing function of k_i, we have:

$$\frac{1 - b_i}{1 - a_i b_i} \leqslant \frac{1 - b_i^{k_i}}{1 - a_i b_i^{k_i}} \leqslant E(q_{i,m_i k_i + m_i + 1}) \leqslant q_{i,1}. \tag{13}$$

Furthermore, a lower bound for $E(q)$ is obtained:

$$\Sigma\, r_i \frac{1 - b_i}{1 - a_i b_i} \leqslant E(q). \tag{14}$$

As it stands, Eq. (11) is rather difficult to work with in terms of finding an optimal solution — that is, the allocation of the learning trials m_i so as to minimize the expected error. Detailed analytical results will be published elsewhere.

On the other hand, by making the overly strong simplifying assumption that there is no forgetting, that is, that $b_i = 1$, we can get an explicit solution of the allocation problem, which will give us a first approximation that in many cases will also be a useful one. Thus, we want to minimize

$$E(q) = \Sigma\, r_i q_{i,1} a_i^{m_i}, \tag{15}$$

subject to the constraint that $\Sigma\, m_i = N$. We use Lagrange multipliers to find a solution (where z replaces the standard lambda). Our basic function is

$$f(m_1, ..., m_s) = \Sigma\, r_i q_{i,1} a_i^{m_i} + z(\Sigma\, m_i - N).$$

Thus taking derivatives, we have for $i = 1, ..., s$,

$$r_i q_{i,1} a_i^{m_i} \ln a_i + z = 0, \tag{16}$$

with

$$\Sigma\, m_i - N = 0,$$

$$m_i > 0.$$

Summing the s equations in z, we then obtain

$$r_i q_{i,1} a_i^{m_i} \ln a_i = \frac{1}{s} \Sigma\, r_i q_{i,1} a_i^{m_i} \ln a_i, \tag{17}$$

but the right-hand side of Eq. (17) is independent of i, and so we conclude that the condition for optimal allocation is the simple qualitative condition of equality that for every i and j

$$r_i q_{i,1} a^{m_i} \ln a_i = r_j q_{j,1} a^{m_j} \ln a_j. \tag{18}$$

The results represented in Eq. (18) can be used to make allocations for the entire remaining year. The algorithm is simply that of finding those exercises for which practice will increase their expected score at the end of the year by the greatest amount. Extensive work on this algorithm and actual implementation have been made. The results are too complicated to enter into here in complete detail, and there are still certain central conceptual problems that need to be solved before a completely successful implementation can be made.

To give a sense of one of the more pressing conceptual problems, we shall focus on a single but highly important aspect. As Eq. (18) indicates, to determine where to make the next optimal allocation of exercise time, we need to know the current probability q_i of an error on an exercise of a given type — that is, as represented in terms of a given goal or subgoal. Because our analysis is in terms of the finer breakdown represented by subgoals, we shall confine ourselves to these and ignore the goals in terms of which subgoals are clustered.

The problem is how to estimate the q_i's. If unlimited test data were possible, a direct solution would be feasible. Unfortunately, the number of subgoals in each year of the curriculum is approximately 200, so that it is not practical on a weekly basis to get current estimates of the q_i's. Our approach to this problem was the following quasi-Bayesian method. First, we assigned a prior probability distribution with a mean based upon extensive past experience in primary-school mathematics. Second, we asked the curriculum designer and coordinator in Nicaragua to give her estimates of the preteaching and postteaching performance levels to be expected of the students. These estimates took the form of simple probability estimates of the proportion of correct responses. We asked her to make an estimate for each of the subgoals. We then tested a restricted number of the subgoals on which we had test data.

The results for 10 second-grade subgoals tested prior to teaching are shown in Table 4.7. As is clear from the table, the estimates were strikingly and systematically low for all subgoals. In Table 4.8, we show the comparison of the estimates with test data on 16 second-grade subgoals for which test data were collected after teaching had taken place. In this case, there is no systematic trend in the data when the test data and the estimates are compared, as shown in the final column of the table, but the discrepancies are large in a number of cases, in fact, more than .10 for over half of the subgoals.

TABLE 4.7
Comparison of Estimates with Test Data
on 10 Subgoals Prior to Teaching

Subgoal[a]	Teaching Week	Testing Week	Estimated P	Test P Range	Mean	Difference Estimate − Test
VS4	7	6	.30	.46 − .80	.66	.36
OM1	7	6	.10	.24 − .76	.53	.43
SP2	7	6	.20	.83 −1.00	.94	.74
SN3	8	7	.30	.73 − .83	.76	.46
OS3	9	8	.20	.69 − .71	.70	.50
HS4	9	8	.15	.45 − .78	.59	.44
HM	9	7	.10	.35 − .95	.70	.60
HS3	10	7	.25	.53 − .63	.59	.34
OA8	10	9	.35	.53 − .75	.63	.28
VA9	10-11	9	.10	.24 − .46	.35	.25
		Mean	.205		.645	.440
		S.D.	.093		.154	.148

[a]The symbols are explained in footnote 3, p. 252.

These discrepancies present formidable conceptual and statistical problems of inference to determine the values of the q_i's that should be used in making an optimal allocation. It is worth noting that the literature on Bayesian inference does not provide much in the way of help when the problem is that of absorbing nonfrequency estimates of the kind given by the curriculum designer and as shown in Tables 4.7 and 4.8. The move from a Bayesian prior to a posterior is ordinarily made on the basis of frequency data. It is almost a paradox of the Bayesian emphasis on subjective probability that such poor tools are available for absorbing probability estimates that are not based on frequency into the formation of a new posterior.

In the case of Table 4.7, it is at least apparent that a systematic correction can be estimated and used for modifying the estimated q_i's required to apply Eq. (18). This has been done by straightforward regression methods, but the details are not given here. The situation is much less hopeful with respect to the data shown in Table 4.8. There is a slight tendency for the estimated p_i's to be higher than the observed p_i's, but the trend is not a strong one, and there seems no reasonably useful systematic generalization possible of the relation between the test data and the estimated p_i's.

It must be emphasized that the efficacy of the global allocation model developed in this section depends on having reasonably accurate estimates of the q_i's (or p_i's, with always $q_i = 1 - p_i$) and also on similar sorts of estimates for the rates of learning. The design of an innovative curriculum effort and the pro-

TABLE 4.8
Comparison of Estimates with Test Data
on 16 Subgoals After Teaching

Subgoal[a]	Teaching Week	Testing Week	Estimated P	Test P Range	Mean	Difference Estimate−Test
NC7	3	5	.70	.81 −1.00	.90	.20
OA2	3	5	.80	.64 − .95	.80	.00
VA2	3-4	5	.90	.89 −1.00	.96	.06
WN3	3-4	6	.70	.07 − .69	.48	−.22
NC8	4	5	.70	.90 −1.00	.95	.25
NC10	4	5	.80	.56 − .75	.64	−.16
HA3	4	5	.65	.88 −1.00	.91	.26
VA4	5	6	.85	.80 − .80	.84	−.01
OC1	5	6	.75	.14 − .69	.36	−.39
HS2	5	7	.75	.48 − .55	.51	−.24
WN4	6	7	.70	.55 − .70	.63	−.07
VA3	6	7	.90	.88 − .95	.93	.03
VS3	6	7	.85	.70 − .75	.73	−.12
VS4	7	8	.85	.71 − .78	.76	−.09
OM1	7	8	.75	.46 − .87	.72	−.03
SP2	7	8	.80	.42 − .66	.57	−.23
		Mean	.778		.730	−.048
		S.D.	.077		.185	.183

[a]The symbols are explained in footnote 3, p. 252.

vision of resources adequate to this task of data collection and analysis is not impossible, but it is difficult to put in place.

Thus, the example we have dealt with in this section is in one sense incomplete. On the one hand, the conceptual framework is clear and the intended application is well defined. On the other hand, successful application is as yet impeded by difficult problems of data collection and analysis. In our view, systematic thinking about curriculum, especially the global organization of curriculum, has usually proceeded without concern for any serious systematic appraisal of empirical data. Part of our reason for considering the example of the Radio Mathematics Project is to illustrate that this nonempirical attitude need not prevail and that, with sufficient perseverance and determination, the application of global psychological models to the detailed design and organization of curriculum is possible. We hope to be able to report in the future our own results in carrying this kind of analysis through to a conclusion. We believe that the problems of statistical inference we have outlined can be solved in a constructive way.

ACKNOWLEDGMENTS

The research reported in this chapter was supported in part by the Bureau of Education for the Handicapped, U.S. Department of Health, Education, and Welfare, under Office of Education Contract No. OEC-0-74-1006; in part by National Science Foundation Grant No. NSF-EC-443; and in part by Agency for International Development Contract No. AID/cm/ta-C-73-40. The extensive computations in Section II have been made with the assistance of Robert Poling during the period that he was a research assistant at the Institute for Mathematical Studies in the Social Sciences. The work reported in Section III has been conducted in collaboration with Jamesine Friend and Barbara Searle, both of whom are research associates at the Institute. Jamesine Friend serves as coordinator in Nicaragua of the Radio Mathematics Project, and Barbara Searle is project coordinator at Stanford.

REFERENCES

Adkins, K., & Hamilton, M. *Teacher's handbook for language arts 3–6* (3rd ed., rev.). Palo Alto, Calif.: Computer Curriculum Corp., 1975.

Carroll, J. B., & Chall, J. S. (Eds.). *Toward a literate society: A report from the National Academy of Education.* New York: McGraw-Hill, 1975.

Fletcher, J. D., Adkins, K., & Hamilton, M. *Teacher's handbook for reading, grades 3–6.* Palo Alto, Calif.: Computer Curriculum Corp., 1972.

Larsen, I., Markosian, L. Z., & Suppes, P. Performance models of undergraduate students on computer-assisted instruction in elementary logic. *Instructional Science*, 1978, *7*, 15–35.

Searle, B., Friend, J., & Suppes, P. *The radio mathematics project: Nicaragua 1974–1975.* Stanford, Calif.: Institute for Mathematical Studies in the Social Sciences, Stanford University, 1976.

Suppes, P. Problems of optimization in learning a list of simple items. In M. W. Shelly, II, & G. W. Bryan (Eds.), *Human judgments and optimality.* New York: Wiley, 1964.

Suppes, P., Fletcher, J. D., & Zanotti, M. Performance models of American Indian students on computer-assisted instruction in elementary mathematics. *Instructional Science*, 1975, *4*, 303–313.

Suppes, P., Fletcher, J. D., & Zanotti, M. Models of individual trajectories in computer-assisted instruction for deaf students. *Journal of Educational Psychology*, 1976, *68*, 117–127.

Suppes, P., Jerman, M., & Brian, D. *Computer-assisted instruction: Stanford's 1965–66 arithmetic program.* New York: Academic Press, 1968.

Suppes, P., & Morningstar, M. *Computer-assisted instruction at Stanford, 1966–68: Data, models, and evaluation of the arithmetic programs.* New York: Academic Press, 1972.

Suppes, P., Searle, B. W., Kanz, G., & Clinton, J. P. M. *Teacher's handbook for mathematics strands, grades 1–6* (rev. ed.). Palo Alto, Calif.: Computer Curriculum Corp., 1975.

Suppes, P., & Zanotti, M. On the determinism of hidden variable theories with strict correlation and conditional statistical independence of observables. In P. Suppes (Ed.), *Logic and probability in quantum mechanics.* Dordrecht: Reidel, 1976.

Thorndike, E. L. *Educational psychology.* New York: Columbia University, Teachers College, 1913–1914.

Thorndike, E. L. *The psychology of arithmetic.* New York: Macmillan, 1922.

5 Assessment of Learning Outcomes

Robert M. Gagné
Jacob G. Beard
Florida State University

I. INTRODUCTION

Several educational trends have contributed to the strong current interest in examining the logical foundations and the technology of assessing the outcomes of learning. The widespread employment of carefully defined objectives in instructional programs, the increasing use of various forms of individualized instruction, and the application of the concept of accountability to educational efforts have all helped to generate requirements for assessing student learning in ways that have a sound rational basis. Of particular note in this connection has been the discussion of the concept of criterion-referenced testing, introduced by Glaser (1963) and elaborated by Glaser and Klaus (1963). The technical literature in this field, summarized and reviewed by such authors as Donlon (1974), Hambleton (1974), Messick (1975), Millman (1974), and Popham (1975), begins to have a form and substance that makes possible the transmission of an assessment rationale to practitioners as well as to researchers. Although writings on criterion-referenced measurement are plagued by novel and sometimes arbitrary terminology, they nevertheless contribute a core of meaning that continues to be influential in the formulation of a systematic technology of learning assessment. The basic point made by writings in this field is that assessment must give primary consideration to *what is learned* and only secondary consideration to the detection of *individual differences* in what is learned.

Criterion-referenced measurement has itself received a number of different definitions, and several alternative phrases have been proposed to take its place. Among others are *objective-based* (cited in Millman, 1974), *standard-referenced, behavior-referenced* (Donlon, 1974), and *domain-referenced* (Hively, Maxwell,

Rabehl, Sension, & Lundin, 1973) measurements. Some of these distinctions may be of value, although they do not appear by themselves to offer the best route to clarity of understanding. The most frequently cited definition is that of Glaser and Nitko (1971):

> *A criterion-referenced test is one that is deliberately constructed to yield measurements that are directly interpretable in terms of specified perform-ance standards.* Performance standards are generally specified by defining a class or domain of tasks that should be performed by the individual. Meas-urements are taken on representative samples of tasks drawn from this domain, and such measurements are referenced directly to this domain for each individual measured [p. 653].

This definition appears to be carefully drawn. It is both broad enough and pre-cise enough to include the special meanings that are given to such phrases as "objective-referenced," "domain-referenced," and "standard-referenced." Its major contribution to the clarification of what is meant by assessing "what is learned," however, lies in its pointing out that such measurements must be directly interpretable by being directly referenced to a defined task domain (Messick, 1975).

Besides the efforts at definition, several sources of the idea of measuring what is learned have had important influences on current thought. Glaser and Klaus (1963) proposed the development of a rationale for *proficiency measurement*, which they defined as follows: "the assessment of criterion behavior — the determination of the characteristics of present performances or output in terms of specified standards [p. 240]." These authors were concerned particularly with describing a form of measurement that focused on a current state of individual performance as opposed to an inferred trait or basic ability. That is, they envisaged assessment techniques that had the purpose of measuring *proficiency* of criterion performance itself, in contrast to *aptitude measurement*, which is designed to predict criterion performance.

A second concept relevant to the assessment of learning outcomes is the notion of *classifying learning objectives*, described by Bloom and his associates (1956), Krathwohl, Bloom, and Masia (1964), and more recently by Bloom, Hastings, and Madaus (1971). Categories of learning outcomes were proposed and exem-plified, conceived of as finer divisions of the more comprehensive general outcome categories called *cognitive, affective,* and *psychomotor.* These important works make the fundamental point that measures of learning outcomes must be designed and interpreted in terms of different classes of learned capabilities, not simply in terms of score distributions representing different degrees of achievement.

The idea of a defined domain of tasks for the specification of "performance standards" (as reflected in the Glaser and Nitko definition) has been developed in some detail by Hively et al. (1973). These investigators undertook to describe exactingly precise methods of specifying domains from which assessment items could be drawn. Task domains were identified as *item forms*, with defined stimulus and response characteristics, and specified *replacement sets* of items to be constructed according to designated rules. Thus, a rational basis was provided for determining the representativeness and appropriateness of individual items selected for assessment of a given learning objective. Although these methods are viewed by some investigators as impractically cumbersome (e.g., Popham, 1975), their importance lies in their demonstration of what is meant by *specifying task domains.*

With an awareness of the urgency of these fundamental contributions, we wish to review current formulations of measurement rationale and technology directed toward the aim of assessing what is learned, or the *assessment of learning outcomes.* We have in mind the entire range of capabilities and dispositions that may be engendered by learning in the school, in programs of training, and in other organized educational ventures. We intend to incorporate into this review many of the ideas contributed by the sources previously cited, as well as others, insofar as they contribute to this central purpose. Some of the questions to be considered are the following:

1. What kinds of learning outcomes are there?
2. What is the significance of measures of learning outcomes that assess quality vs. those that assess quantity?
3. What are the differences among measures in respect to the "directness" of performance assessment?
4. What are "directly interpretable" measures?
5. How are items sampled from a domain of tasks?
6. What meaning can be given to the "adequacy" of assessment measures?
7. What are the ways in which the results of testing can be expressed?

II. SPECIFYING THE TASK DOMAIN

We assume that the process of designing measures to assess learning outcomes begins with carefully defined objectives. The methods for unambiguous definition of learning objectives have been described by a number of authors, including Mager (1975), Popham (1975), and Gagné and Briggs (1974), among others. There is general agreement that definitions of objectives in forms suitable for the derivation of test items include at least the following components: (1) a description of the stimulus situation; (2) an action verb indicating the intended capability (the "major" verb, or "main intent"); (3) the object or objects acted upon; (4) a verb or verb phrase describing how the action is to be done (as, "by writing"); and (5) the tools and environmental constraints to be present.

Beginning with a suitably defined learning objective, the designer of learning assessment procedures undertakes first the step of *specifying the task domain*. This step looks backward at the definition of the objective to determine the accuracy with which the specifications reflect this definition. Thus, a determination is made of the validity of the task domain. At the same time, the specification looks forward to the derivation of items for assessment of the learning outcome of interest. In pursuit of this aim, the specification must achieve as precise a description as possible of the class or classes of items that are appropriate for the desired measurement.

Specifications for the task domain require greater detail of description than is contained within the learning objective itself. The method proposed by Hively et al. (1973) using *item-forms* has already been mentioned. Popham (1975) suggests specification in the form of an *amplified objective*, which includes stimulus elements, response alternatives, a criterion of correctness, and format specifications. In the following sections, we undertake to describe a basis for task domain specification in as comprehensive a manner as possible. A major suggestion to be made is that some decisions about the task domain are best made early and others later. We shall attempt to describe the composing of task domain specifications by consideration of: (1) types of learning outcomes; (2) intentions for quality and quantity measurement; (3) directness of measurement; and (4) criteria of performance. Our implicit suggestion is that these determinations, in at least this approximate order, lead most clearly to the desired precision in task domain specification.

A. Types of Learning Outcomes

Specifying the domain from which assessment items are to be drawn begins by recognizing that what is learned falls into a number of distinct categories. These classes of learned entities are not determined by curricular content (such as science, mathematics, history). Rather, they are best conceived of as different classes of organization of the contents of human memory. The learner acquires and stores a number of different kinds of memorial organizations, and it is these organizations for which we try to find indicators or "probes" when we devise tests to sample human performance. Assessment must be designed with specific consideration of the type of memory organization one wishes to probe. If the learning outcome to be measured is skill at shooting baskets, for example, one chooses a test that adequately represents the stimuli and responses of this kind of task and avoids a test that asks verbal questions about the dimensions of the basket. The determination of the type of learning outcome reflects the major intent (Mager, 1975) of what is to be learned as defined by the objective.

Five major categories of learning outcomes have been described by Gagné (1972, 1974, 1976) as: (1) intellectual skills; (2) verbal information; (3) cognitive strategies; (4) motor skills; and (5) attitudes. These five are conceived to represent different classes of memorial organization. They require different conditions of learning for their optimal establishment as acquired capabilities. Furthermore, as might be expected, they exhibit themselves in human performances that require different kinds of probes for their assessment.

Our discussion of types of learning outcomes employs these five categories. They appear to be most consistent with the assumptions of modern learning theories of the cognitive variety (e.g., Atkinson & Shiffrin, 1968; Bower, 1975; Kintsch, 1974; Rumelhart, Lindsay, & Norman, 1972) in the distinctions they make concerning memory organizations. We note, however, that other categorizations might serve as well to establish the necessity of distinguishing among varieties of learning outcomes. The approximate correspondence of these categories with those proposed by Bloom et al. (1971) as the cognitive domain, the affective domain, and the psychomotor domain will be apparent. Obviously, the common intent is to describe the purpose of learning assessment as one of obtaining indicators of certain classes of learned capabilities (or dispositions), conceived of as memory organizations that are inferred from systematic observations of the learner's performance.

As defined by Gagné (1972, 1974), the five major varieties of learning outcome are as follows:

Intellectual skills — concepts and rules that are exhibited as rule-governed performances in which the learner manipulates symbols representing his world, exemplified particularly by rules of language and mathematics. Example: Correct the sentence: "The leaves stirred gentle in the wind."

Verbal information — information about the world that is stored in such a way that it can be retrieved as verbally stated propositions. Example: What does the First Amendment prohibit with respect to freedom of speech?

Motor skills — sequences of activity that exhibit themselves as motor performances characterized by smoothness and precision of timing. Example: Printing the letter R.

Cognitive strategies — executive control processes through which the learner modifies his own internal processes of attending, learning, remembering, and thinking. Example: Inventing a humorous visual image that can be readily retrieved when recollecting a person's name.

Attitudes — acquired internal states, usually conceived as having both cognitive and affective components, which modulate the individual's choices of action toward classes of objects, persons, or events. Example: Choosing to listen to classical music.

The emphasis on measuring what is learned that pervades writings on criterion-referenced testing would lead one to expect adequate consideration and coverage of these five kinds of learning outcomes. Such is the case with one of the seminal articles in this field — namely, Glaser and Klaus (1963). The variety of performances used as examples by these authors is obviously great enough to encompass all classes of learning outcomes. They base their analyses of testing requirements on such varied tasks as radar operation, equipment maintenance, solving geometry problems, prescribing medication, leadership behavior, and resourcefulness in problem solving, among others.

There is, however, a marked contrast between this broadly conceived basis for learning assessment and the examples to be found in current literature on criterion-referenced testing. Virtually all of the examples (e.g., Hively et al., 1973) are from the field of mathematics, although a few pertain to language usage. The principles of criterion-referenced test construction have been derived almost solely in the area of *intellectual skills*, and little attention has been paid to test characteristics required for the measurement of other types of learning outcomes (Popham, 1975).

Controversies about the distinctive meaning of "criterion-referenced" sometimes hinge upon the particular selection of examples used to illustrate learning outcomes. For instance, the assessment of intellectual skills is described by Hively et al. (1973) in terms of an example such as "completing a multiplication equation by writing the product of two factors." In contrast, some writers (Donlon, 1974; Ebel, 1970; Traub, 1972) employ examples of the assessment of verbal information such as percentage grades on teacher-made tests requiring students to "answer ten questions on the U.S. Constitution." The two outcomes reflect different kinds of learned capabilities (memory organizations). The basic requirement is to determine how tests can best be designed to assess what has been learned for both kinds of outcomes. There is no *a priori* reason to suppose that the two kinds of assessment require measures having the same formal characteristics regardless of whether or not they should both be called "criterion referenced."

Learning Outcomes and Domain Specification. It would seem a desirable requirement that task domain specifications be developed for all types of learning outcomes. The ideas and concepts of learning assessment will have an unduly limited value if they can be applied only to assessing performance in such subjects as mathematics and grammar. Although intellectual skills such as these are undoubtedly essential components of school curricula, the range and variety of school learning make it equally important to have sound methods of measuring other kinds of learning outcomes.

The formulation of specifications for learning assessment in areas other than intellectual skill poses a number of challenges. In the case of *verbal information*, there must be a resolution of the question as to whether the objective of learning is broader knowledge, "deeper" knowledge, or both. When a learner studies a history text about the Great Depression, is he expected to acquire more extensive knowledge or a deeper understanding? In describing the task domain, this question cannot be resolved by making the assumption that higher scores mean both broader and deeper knowledge, as is now often done. Problems of definition and conceptualization must also be faced in other areas of learning outcome. How is the increased precision and smoothness of a *motor skill* to be assessed? Various alternatives are described by Singer (1975). It would appear possible to relate these scoring procedures to defined dimensions of domains. Turning to *attitude* measurement, it is an intriguing question as to how these learned dispositions can be conceived in a framework of learning assessment. Can an attitude domain be described from which items can be selected to yield directly interpretable scores? This possibility has not been definitively demonstrated, although the works of Triandis (1964) and of Guttman (1969) appear to offer promising leads. A first step would appear to be to formulate an operational definition of "attitudes" in terms reflecting the means employed for their measurement. There are similar difficulties in regard to the rational derivation of measures of the *cognitive strategies* involved in problem solving and original thinking. For example, how can an objectively defined domain be specified which reflects "originality" as a learning outcome (cf. Johnson & Kidder, 1972)? On the whole, it would appear that there is much new technology to be developed if the assessment of what is learned is to be demonstrated as a distinctive and useful conception.

B. Quality and Quantity Dimensions

A conception basic to the definition of domains of learning outcomes is the distinction between *quality* of performance and *quantity* (or amount) of performance. In traditional achievement testing, these two aspects of human performance are often equated by assumption. Thus, answering eight out of ten questions about the Boston Massacre is often assumed to yield the same kind of assessment as answering eight out of 10 whole number multiplication problems. Actually, two different dimensions of the task domain are involved. A score of 80% on items pertaining to the Boston Massacre reveals something about *how much* is known — that is, how many relevant propositions have been stored in the learner's memory. The same percentage score applied to multiplication problems is intended to tell us *how well* the intellectual skill of multiplying whole numbers has been learned. To interpret the latter as "how much" would be to assume that the product of each combination of whole numbers has been separately memorized by the student — an assumption that cannot seriously be entertained.

In assessing learning outcomes, a quantity score is sometimes desired; that is, a score which is directly interpretable as "how much." In other instances, a quality score ("how well") is what is sought. Since we have previously introduced the five major varieties of learning outcome with which learning assessment must deal, we can now proceed to describe some differences among these varieties with respect to requirements for quality and quantity measures as characteristics of the task domain.

1. *Intellectual Skills.* When the concern of assessment is with an intellectual skill (the application of a rule or concept), interest centers upon the question of "how well." One wishes to measure how well the student has mastered the capability of multiplying two-place numbers, or subtracting mixed fractions, or finding the roots of simultaneous equations. Unambiguous specification of the task domain can be accomplished in the manner described by Hively et al. (1973). This method involves the definition of item forms, replacement schemes, and replacement sets in terms that specify the range and dimensions of the domain from which assessment items are to be drawn.

It is of some importance to note the evidence that indicates that the learning of a *unitary* intellectual skill is all-or-none. That is to say, when the domain of a single intellectual skill has been appropriately defined, items drawn from that domain yield scores that are either all correct or at the chance level — the answer to the question "how well" is mastery or nonmastery. For example, Graham (1974) found distinctly binary distributions on tests of mathematical skills when the domain from which items were drawn could be precisely defined in a unitary fashion (e.g., computing a rate of interest or a sales tax). Scores distributed over several values, however, were found when the items employed represented task variation in two or more dimensions (e.g., computing travel time having both integer and fractional solutions). Comparable results were obtained by Horwitz (1975) with tasks requiring the addition of positive and negative numbers. Again, the findings showed all-or-none learning for tasks that could be defined by a unitary item-form domain (such as $-4 + 9$, $-3 + 7$), and a dispersion of scores for domains that contained variations in replacement sets (such as the addition of $-7 + 3$, and $3 - 7$).

Sometimes, the desired assessment of intellectual skills is not one of quality but of quantity. If a student has studied the subject of fractions, for example, it may be desirable to test a whole group of skills composing this topic — adding fractions, subtracting fractions, multiplying fractions, reducing fractions, and so on. A test on fractions can readily be constructed that samples from this larger domain — a domain that would itself be composed of several item forms, each with its own replacement sets. The score on such a test would answer the question of "how much" the student is able to accomplish with fractions.

2. *Verbal Information.* The typical task domain for the learning of verbal information (or "knowledge") would seem to be one that has the purpose of assessing *quantity*. How much does the student know about the Boston Massacre, or about the Federalist Papers, or about the provisions of the U.S. Constitution? How much does he know about the occurrence of the chemical

elements in nature or about the manufacture of illuminating gas? The answers to quantity questions of this sort are usually sought by devising items (questions) selected from a domain that is more or less well defined. It may be as well defined as the designation of a specific paragraph in a particular textbook or a specific longer passage of textual material. Or it may be more loosely defined as the information a student is expected to learn from lectures, text, and references available to him on a particular subject. In any case, however, it is a domain specifying quantity and can only in the loosest (and incorrect) sense be considered to define measures of "how well" the student knows a subject.

Suggestions made by several investigators (Anderson, 1972; Bormuth, 1970) imply the possibility that *quality* of knowledge can be assessed as a learning outcome. One proposal, for example, is that this might be accomplished by the use of syntactic or semantic transformations (paraphrases) of the specific propositions that represent the items of knowledge for which learning is to be assessed. A similar interpretation may be made of Bloom's (1956) categorization of the cognitive domain as knowledge, comprehension, application, analysis, synthesis, and evaluation. The basic idea is that something like the "depth" of knowledge can be measured by specifying domains that make increasing demands on information processing. This is an appealing notion, the rationale for which does not yet appear to have been fully developed. What kind of memorial organization can be conceived that corresponds to "deeper understanding" of verbal information (cf. Kintsch, 1974)? Considerable additional research and theoretical development will probably be required before specifications for direct measures of this aspect of learning can be devised with confidence.

3. *Motor Skills.* For motor skills, the task domain most clearly appropriate is one designed to make possible measures of *quality*. We wish to know how well the student is able to perform a particular motor act — how well can he bat a baseball or how well can he print the letter N. The domain of a motor skill can usually be defined with reasonable precision, and replacement sets can be used to indicate the limits of variation in tools and environment to be permitted. As is well known, most motor skills can be assessed in terms of either accuracy or speed, and an item form requires the specification of these factors. Once these dimensions of the domain are determined, there would seem to be little difficulty in obtaining a measure of the quality of the learning outcome.

Quantity measures of motor skills may be desirable in instances such as those associated with a particular sport or a particular occupation. Thus, one might wish to know *how many* of the skills of playing tennis (serve, backhand, net shot, etc.) have been acquired, or *how much* of the job of automobile body repair has been mastered. The domain to be described would accordingly contain item forms for multiple measures. As Glaser and Klaus (1963) point out, a checklist is often employed to obtain quantity measures of this sort.

4. *Cognitive Strategies.*   This interesting and highly important kind of learning would appear to require considerable systematic thought, so far as the requirements of learning assessment are concerned. Certain specific types of cognitive strategies, such as rehearsal and the use of mnemonics, have been identified for relatively simple learning tasks (cf. Brown, 1975; Flavell & Wellman, 1976; Mandler & Stephens, 1967). Much has yet to be discovered, however, about strategies involved in thinking and problem solving. Evidently, what is desired in the specification of a domain for a capability like original problem solving is a measure of the "degree of originality" — obviously a quality measure. One major difficulty, however, is that it is not clear whether such a capability is unitary or is instead several different capabilities working together as an integrated set to affect human performance and its product. Such a suggestion, for example, was made by Olton and his colleagues (Olton, Wardrop, Covington, Goodwin, Crutchfield, Klausmeier, & Ronda, 1967) in their study of productive thinking in fifth-grade children.

Various attempts have been made to identify, isolate, and measure a number of different cognitive strategies. It is possible to view most, if not all, of Guilford's (1967) intelligence dimensions as aiming to specify particular kinds of cognitive strategies. For example, a test like Thurstone's Flags, which Guilford classified as Cognition of Figural Systems (CFS), may be seen as assessing a strategy of rotating a visual image of a printed figure. Despite the operational descriptions of categories which Guilford presents, however, the domains from which the items of many tests are selected are not unambiguously interpretable. In many instances, the items of tests of intellectual abilities require the application of rules (intellectual skills) and the recall of information, in addition to the use of cognitive strategies, which might be their most cogently intended measurement. Thus, the measures they provide are not *distinctive* (Gagné, 1970), in that it is not clear which learning outcomes they assess. Similar considerations apply to Bloom's (1956) suggested items for the assessment of problem-solving capabilities classified as "analysis," "synthesis," and "evaluation." In these instances, also, the strategies that may be involved are not separated from the intellectual skills required for successful item completion. Consequently, it cannot be said that distinctively defined domains of cognitive strategies have been achieved.

The use of a quantity measure to assess a cognitive strategy does not seem appropriate. Except by making inadmissible assumptions, one would not be inclined to interpret a score of "how many problems solved" as an indication of the quantity of a strategy. However, the use of a multi-item test with a time limit may make possible the assessment of quality in the sense of efficiency of the strategy being measured. In fact, this may be the common implicit assumption to be made by tests of aptitude, insofar as they may be conceived as yielding measures of cognitive strategies.

5. *Attitudes.*   The problems of attitude measurement are many and have been the subject of several critical reviews (Kiesler, Collins, & Miller, 1969;

McGuire, 1968; Scott, 1968). An attitude is most clearly conceived as a learned memorial state that affects behavior. In this view, attitudes are measured as consistency in *choices of personal action* toward some class of objects, persons, or events (Gagné, 1976). The domain that defines these choices may be carefully specified along several dimensions (Triandis, 1964). For example, in assessing the choices of personal action, "social contact with Negroes," Triandis and Triandis (1960) chose items from a domain that was structured in terms of: (1) forms of social contact; and (2) sociopersonal characteristics of Negroes (occupation, age, etc.). This method, or a variant of it, can presumably be employed to define domains that make possible the direct interpretation of attitude scores.

Measures of a single attitude (such as an attitude toward disposal of personal trash or an attitude toward reading modern novels) need to reflect the "strength" of the attitude. Some people have a strong attitude toward attending church services and some a weak one, as indicated by frequency of church attendance. Attitude strength is conceived as varying in both positive and negative directions. These considerations imply that attitude strength should be viewed as an assessment of *quality*, although quality may itself be inferred from such measures as frequency or consistency of action choices.

Most existing attitude scales and instruments are quantity measures, since they depend upon cumulative scores obtained from a number of different, though logically related, item domains (see, for example, the variety of attitude-measuring instruments described by Shaw and Wright, 1967). Thus, it is not uncommon for an instrument employed in assessing attitude toward school to be composed of statements that actually pertain to "attitude toward the teacher," "attitude toward classmates," "attitude toward studying," "attitude toward recess," and many other specific item domains. Cumulative scores are then used as aggregate indicators of "attitude toward school." Obviously, the measures obtained from such instruments indicate *quantity,* in the sense of "how many aspects of the object class are responded to in a positive fashion?" Since the scores obtained usually cannot be separately related to defined domains of action choices, they are at best crude measures of learning outcomes.

6. *Implications for Task Domain Specification.* The identification of a type of learning outcome and the appropriateness of quality or quantity measurement to this outcome enable the designer of assessment procedures to determine the general nature of the *content* of the task domain. The choice of a type of learning outcome will usually be apparent from the classification of the learning objective (Gagné & Briggs, 1974) or, in other words, from its major intent (Mager, 1975; Popham, 1975). The quality or quantity measurement possibilities afforded by the type of outcome must then be considered and decided upon. This decision affects the interpretability of scores to be obtained from the items drawn from the domain. For example, the learning outcome "intellectual skill" requires a measure of the quality of that skill as a learned

entity, and this cannot be inferred from a quantity measure. In contrast, the usual measure of the learning outcome "verbal information" is one of quantity, and the inference of quality of performance from such measures cannot currently be made with confidence.

There are, of course, additional reasons for choosing between task domains yielding quality or quantity measures, which will be discussed in a later section. These pertain to the intended uses of scores obtained from learning assessments. Thus, the use of a test for summative evaluation of a course of study may require a quantity measure, summed over several related task domains, each of which by itself most appropriately yields a measure of quality.

A summary of design decisions for the determination of the content of the task domain is given in Table 5.1. As the table indicates, the nature of the content specifying the task domain is expected to differ according to whether quality or quantity measures are sought. The appropriateness of the type of

TABLE 5.1
Content of the Task Domain for Types of Learning Outcome,
as Dependent on Choice of Quality or Quantity Measures

Type of Learning Outcome	Type of Measure	Content of Task Domain
1. Intellectual Skills	Quality	Item forms and replacement sets explicitly defined.
	Quantity	Item forms and replacement sets for several different skills, separately identified.
2. Verbal Information	Quality	Insufficient rational basis for item form definition.
	Quantity	Item forms and replacement sets defined as general or specific propositions to be recalled ("main ideas," "specific details," etc.).
3. Motor Skills	Quality	Item forms explicitly defined in terms of dimensions of performance, including accuracy and/or speed.
	Quantity	Sets of separately defined item forms for specific skills related to particular human activities.
4. Cognitive Strategies	Quality	Item forms defining measures of performance such as "efficiency," "originality," etc.
	Quantity	Inappropriate.
5. Attitudes	Quality	Item forms and replacement sets of personal action choices toward classes of objects, persons, or events; explicitly defined in terms of attributes of the class.
	Quantity	Collections of related attitudes, each defined as a quality measure; sets of separately defined item form for each related attitude.

measure is in turn influenced by the kind of learning outcome identified as the intended capability or disposition to be assessed.

C. Directness of Measurement

Another aspect of the task domain requiring specification is usually conceived as a matter of directness of measurement. Such specification involves a determination of the appropriate *stimulus situation* and *respone provisions* of the task to be defined (Hively et al., 1973; Popham, 1975). These components of the specification are derivable from corresponding parts of the instructional objective, as indicated in the following examples:

1. Given a printed equation of the form 3 $\square$ 6 = 18 and oral instructions to supply the proper operation sign (stimulus situation), applies rules of arithmetic operation to complete the equation by printing the appropriate sign (response).

2. Given printed sentences in which adjectives have been used for adverbs and printed instructions to correct the sentences (stimulus situation), applies rules of adverbial construction and usage by writing adverbs in the place of wrongly used adjectives (response).

3. Given a 1" x 6" board with a marked line across its face (stimulus situation), executes a cut through the board by sawing a straight edge with a tolerance of one-half a degree, using a handsaw (response).

1. Variations in Directness of Measurement. A number of reasons may make necessary a departure of the stimulus and response characteristics of the instructional objective (and consequently of the specified task domain) from the "real" or "ultimate" goal of instruction. The distinction between proximate and ultimate objectives of educational programs has been discussed by Glaser and Nitko (1971) and earlier by Lindquist (1951). As these authors point out, the proximate objectives of a course of study are those that can reasonably and feasibly be measured at the end of some period of instruction. They are related to ultimate goals by some process of rational analysis or, more rarely, on the basis of empirical evidence. Thus, the ultimate educational goal of a vocational education course may be to produce highly competent television repairmen. The proximate objectives, however, can do no more than define the various competencies of television repair and maintenance that are possible to assess with the use of equipment and materials available in the instructional situation.

Even the proximate objectives and the task domains derived from them may have to be constrained by feasibility factors of expense, of time limitations, or of risks to the examinee's life and limb. The specification of the task domain may require variations in the directness of measurement on account of these considerations. For example, students of elementary mechanics may learn to find the amount of force needed to be employed in lifting weights attached to various pulley systems. The proximate objective in this case could conceivably contain several different "situation" descriptions. It might state "Given a system of pulleys . . ."; or "Given a diagram showing a system of pulleys . . ."; or "Given a printed description of a system of pulleys . . .". Obviously, these different situations would imply different degrees of convenience or feasibility in assessment were they to be reflected in task domain descriptions.

Four categories of degrees of directness of measurement are described by Lindquist (1951) as: (1) identical elements; (2) related behavior; (3) verbalized behavior; and (4) student's knowledge. Glaser and Klaus (1963) identify three categories of directness as: (1) "on the job"; (2) simulations; and (3) correlated behaviors. These categories are similar to Lindquist's, although the additional distinction of simulated performance measures is of some importance and is further explicated by Fitzpatrick and Morrison (1971). The latter authors provide a number of examples of simulation measures exhibiting varying degrees of directness and describe their assessment characteristics.

2. *Validity in Relation to Directness of Measurement.* It seems clear that the choice of the degree of directness of measurement, as represented by various categories discussed in the articles cited, may be of considerable value in design-ing practical measures. Conceptually, though, the matter of directness of measurement is related to the content validity of the tests that are being designed. It would seem that the rational justification for content validity of the task domain itself must ultimately be made in terms of the components of the definition of the task, as given in the objective. The task components generally recognized by designers of assessment procedures include not only the *stimulus situation* and the *responses*, but also the *process* (Bloom et al., 1971; Cronbach, 1971; Popham, 1975). Presumably, content validity of task domains is achieved by specifying the *least possible degree* of departure from the desired objective description in all three of these factors.

As implied by previous sections, our treatment of domain specification views "process" as being indicated by the "major verb" (Gagné & Briggs, 1974) or the "main intent" (Mager, 1975) of the objective. It may be as some writers have suggested (e.g., Cronbach, 1971; Messick, 1975), that the determination of process is a matter of *construct validity*, the constructs referred to being derived from theory. Such a view is at least consistent with the idea that task domains describe different forms of memorial organization, as implied by various contemporary cognitive learning theories now under active development (Bower, 1975).

Departures of the task domain from the processes implied by objectives are likely to result in lowered validity. For example, specifying the domain in ways that allow the usage of multiple-choice items, as opposed to completion items, may sometimes be seen as involving a process change. In many instances (not all), responses to multiple-choice items require the process of recognition, rather than the entire set of processes involved in recall. Although the hypothesis that recognition and recall require the same processes cannot be said to be disproved, the mounting evidence of the involvement of different processes is worthy of serious note (Anderson & Bower, 1974; Klatzky, 1975).

Directness of representation of the stimulus situation described in the learning objective has particular cogency to the question of content validity of the task domain. Stimuli serve as cues to the retrieval and recall of whatever memorial entity is called for in assessment. Thus, variations in stimulus aspects of the task may have significant direct effects upon the learner's performance in the assessment situation. Variations in the cues for performance may include not only those inherent to the task itself, as when a verbal description of the task of measuring fluid ounces is substituted for an actual graduated container of fluid. Also, cues of the surrounding "test situation," such as those of the location, the people present, the extraneous noise, the mental set of the learner, usually differ considerably from those of the "real situation" (Gagné, 1975). Thus, some degree of simulation is likely to be inevitable in assessment, particularly with respect to the stimulus situation.

The responses required for assessment may also differ from those of the real situation. It is not as clear, however, that response variation per se has as distinct an effect upon validity of the assessment procedure. As a simple example, writing a sentence in answer to a verbal information question does not appear to yield a different measure from speaking a sentence in answer to the same question. The discrepancy between attitude scores and direct measures of behavior may best be viewed, according to some authors (cf. Kiesler et al., 1969), as resulting from the considerable difference in the stimulus situation to which the individual responds, rather than to a difference in the responses themselves. Even motor skills, in which response-generated stimuli are prominent, generally exhibit high degrees of learning transfer over wide ranges of variation in response speed and accuracy (Singer, 1975). The concern for maintaining high fidelity in specified responses often turns out to be more appropriately seen as a matter of accurately identifying the *process* involved in the activity.

D.   Performance Criterion

Most writings on the assessment of learning outcomes include the idea of direct reference of the scores to a "criterion." Glaser and Nitko use the phrase "performance standard." Popham (1975) states that the domain description should include "a section that indicates in clear language just what constitutes acceptable answers [p. 145]." The item form used by Hively et al. (1973) provides "scoring specifications." Mager's (1962) influential book incorporates a component of "performance criterion" into the definition of an instructional objective. And as the phrase itself indicates, criterion-referenced testing is conceived as a measurement technique yielding scores that can be directly referred to a performance "criterion."

The word "criterion" has a number of meanings. As Glaser and Nitko (1971) point out, two different meanings are common in the literature on educational and psychological testing. One of these is a continuum of measures with which a given test score correlates, as vocabulary test scores correlate with the "criterion" of success in school. The second meaning is an acceptable score level as an index of attainment, such as the designation of 80% of items correct. The distinction between these two meanings is discussed by Donlon (1974), who sees the neglect of this distinction as a source of much confusion.

For purposes of item domain specification, *both* these meanings of "criterion" must be rejected, as Glaser and Nitko recommend (1971). Instead, the criterion is the specified domain of tasks from which items are drawn for assessment purposes. It may be noted that such a domain defines a class of tasks, but these tasks are not themselves arranged on a continuum; accordingly, they are not necessarily expected to yield a continuum of scores with which some other measure can be compared by correlation. Neither does the domain necessarily specify a "passing score" in the sense of how many items out of a given number will be considered acceptable. The domain is a "criterion" in the sense that it permits the identification of a class of items that clearly and unambiguously assess what is learned, as defined by the learning objective.

The idea of "directly interpretable" scores of learning outcome would have little value as a measurement concept if it meant only that such scores were referable to a level of attainment of some collection of items from some ill-defined domain. As a number of writers have pointed out (Donlon, 1974; Ebel, 1970; Traub, 1972), a "criterion of mastery" such as "80%," or "70 words per minute" does not in itself make the scores of criterion-referenced tests any more directly interpretable than those that refer to norms such as an IQ scale.

A *criterion of correctness*, however, can be given a precise meaning with reference to the task domain. It may be used to designate the criterion as a standard against which the performance of *each item* is to be judged or scored, as opposed to the number of items in a collection or test. For example, the motor skill of threading a needle may need to include the specification of a needle slot of 0.5 mm as a criterion of correctness. One of Mager's (1962) examples is the adjustment of a radar range marker to the form of a standard template within 1/8 inch. Thus, the correctness criterion refers to an *inherent* characteristic of the class of tasks defined by the domain, not to the arbitrary assignment of a "level of mastery." The mastery level for threading a needle with a 0.5 mm slot, for example, might be set as eight out of 10 successful threadings. The latter kind of standard may be of usefulness in the administration of programs of instruction (Bloom et al., 1971; Hambleton, 1974). But it is not the inherent standard that may be required in specifying the domain from which each item of a test is drawn. The "correctness criterion" provides such a standard for each item described by a task domain.

III.   CONSTRUCTING THE TEST

The process for constructing tests to directly assess specific learning outcomes differs in several ways from the classical process used in constructing instruments for measuring broader traits or attributes of persons. The most fundamental differences between these two types of measurement is usually rendered interpretable by referencing the performance of individuals to a defined "norm" group. Because there is the implicit requirement for variance of persons in norm-referenced testing, statistical procedures have been developed that assume that such variance will be present. For norm-referenced measurement, test construction procedures are followed which optimize these statistical indices.

There are, however, many learning outcomes that are not best measured with the classical norm-referenced model. The last two decades have seen a marked increase in interest in alternative models that assess learning outcomes more directly and that do not require reference groups for interpretation. Test builders have often been frustrated by the lack of theoretical guidelines for constructing and evaluating criterion-referenced tests. We do not propose here to provide a comprehensive treatment of this problem area. Three issues in test construction, however, seem especially important and will be discussed in this section. These issues are: selecting items for the test, assessing quality and quantity, and test length.

A.   Selecting Items for the Test

There are two fundamental criteria to be considered in selecting items for a criterion-referenced test. First, the sample of tasks included in the test must be representative of those in the larger domain of interest. Second, the number of items included must be large enough to permit a dependable inference about the performance of the individual. The first of these criteria has to do with the content validity of the test and the second with the reliability of the resulting scores.

The score from the test should be interpretable in terms of the expected performance on the larger domain of tasks. A probability sample of test tasks facilitates deriving such a score. Osburn (1968) pointed out that in such a testing model the basis of generalization lies in the operational definition of procedures for sampling items from the domain. Therefore, the interest of the test builder and the test user should be on the description of the domain and on the procedures for sampling items from it rather than on the characteristics of any one test.

There is general agreement that the appropriate model for sampling items from the domain is a random or stratified-random one. The desirability of the random-item sampling model in assuring meaningfulness of test scores has been pointed out by Osburn (1968), Millman (1974), Hively et al. (1973), and

Kriewall (1972). When the item sampling is truly random, the absolute value of the score may be interpreted as a ratio measure. That is, neglecting error, it becomes possible to say that a score of 80% indicates that twice the number of tasks in the domain can be accomplished as for a score of 40%. Kriewall (1972) points out that such ratio properties can be assumed only if the item sampling is in fact random. The common practice of treating a purposive sample of items as *random* yields scores of unknown validity. Furthermore, selection of items having large discrimination indices and preferred distributions of difficulty values may lead to similar validity problems.

When a domain has been explicitly defined and procedures have been designed for selecting items from it, parallel forms of the test can be readily created. This model of test construction is highly consistent with the needs of instructional systems for which successive parallel test forms may be needed for pretesting and retesting purposes (Kriewall, 1972).

B. Assessing Quality and Quantity

Some writings on criterion-referenced testing discuss problems and procedures that are unique to a particular type of learning outcome, without making clear the limits of the generalizations that can legitimately be drawn. This over-generalization from specific problem settings to all criterion-referenced testing may be a source of confusion because it neglects differentiation among the different types of testing problems and their solution strategies. Our position is that methods of assessing learning outcomes are to a large degree dictated by the type of learning outcome and the associated task characteristic of *quality* or *quantity*.

As discussed in Section II, quantity measures are intended to answer the question, *how much*, and the test result should provide an estimate of the proportion of tasks in the domain that can be correctly done. For example, the results of a spelling test might indicate the proportion of words on a given list or of a given type that could be correctly spelled. Achievement on such a test is expected to vary over a number of score points. The strategies used for selecting items and for interpreting results of criterion-referenced quantity tests are distinctly different from those of norm-referenced tests, and although the statistical characteristics of most criterion-referenced quantity scores will be similar to those obtained from norm-referenced instruments, the indices of item and test adequacy are not the same. (However, it should be kept in mind that the norm-referenced model may be appropriate for some quantity assessments.)

In contrast, measures of quality tell us *how well* a task can be performed, and it is with quality measures that dichotomization into mastery and nonmastery scores is most meaningful. Quality measures of unidimensional intellectual skills have been found to yield distinctly bimodal distributions (Graham, 1974; Horwitz, 1975). The data of these studies show that the shape of the distribution of scores is dependent upon the complexity (or dimensionality) of the objective. For example, Graham (1974) developed a criterion-referenced test to measure proficiency on the following objective:

"Given the distance between two points and a rate of travel, the student will determine the required travel time."

Items were developed according to the following item format: A car travels ___d___ miles at an average speed of ___r___ miles per hour. How many hours does the trip take?

Answer: _____

A 10-item test (Form A) of this objective was prepared in which five of the items yielded integer solutions, and five items yielded fractional solutions of 1/2 hour (e.g., 1-1/2, 3-1/2 hours, etc.). The test was administered to 558 middle-school students. A frequency polygon of the resulting scores is shown as the dashed line in Fig. 5.1.

The distribution is distinctly trimodal. The test apparently differentiated among three major groups of students: (1) those who could perform the task with integer and fractional solutions (the mode at a score of 10); (2) those who

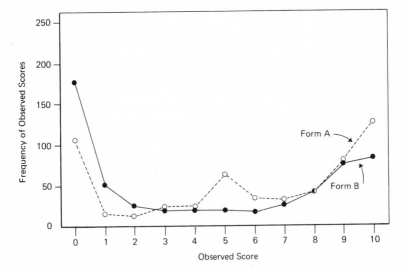

FIG. 5.1.   Distribution of scores on a criterion-referenced test on computing travel time. (Items of Form A had both integer and fractional solutions; items of Form B had only fractional solutions.) (Adapted from "An Empirical Investigation of the Application of Criterion-Referenced Measurement to Survey Achievement Testing" by D. L. Graham. Unpublished doctoral dissertation, Florida State University, 1974. Copyright 1974 by D. L. Graham. Reprinted by permission.)

could perform the task with integer solutions only (the center mode at a score of 5); and (3) those who could do neither (the left mode at a score of 0). In order to test this hypothesis, Graham constructed a second test (Form B) containing all fractional solutions and administered it to the same group of students. The frequency polygon for the "all fractional solution" test is shown as the solid line in Fig. 5.1. The center mode at five is absent in this distribution, leaving a bimodal distribution of scores. The frequencies at the lower-extreme mode increased, presumably including many of the students who were at the center mode in the Form A distribution. The second set of items is more nearly uni-dimensional, and the distribution of scores bimodal. The data show that the skill was either mastered or not mastered for most students, with relatively few showing partial mastery. A dichotomous representation of scores from such distributions is obviously more appropriate than from a rectangular or normal distribution. These data, as well as others presented by Graham (1974) and by Horwitz (1975), indicate clearly that the dimensionality of an objective deter-mines the shape of the distribution of scores and consequently the interpreta-bility of dichotomous scores. It can also be shown theoretically that any set of extremely homogeneous items, having intercorrelations near unity, yields a bimodal or two-point distribution of total scores.

The terms "quantity" and "quality" seem to communicate effectively the major distinctions between two test types. Tests of quality are designed to be directly interpretable in terms of precisely defined knowledge of skills. The items of such tests should be homogeneous or unidimensional. Furthermore, there is evidence that subjective judgments of the dimensionality of items are frequently unreliable (Graham, 1974), and it would appear desirable that the homogeneity of such items be empirically demonstrated. Extremely homogen-eous tests may be quite short and still provide reliable results.

Tests of quantity also aim to be directly interpretable in terms of proficiency on a defined task domain. The items for quantity measures may not demonstrate the high degree of homogeneity required for quality measurement. The shape of score distributions from such tests will depend upon the dimensionality of the domain; that is, upon the homogeneity of test items selected to represent the domain.

C.   Test Length

The question of length for criterion-referenced tests has proven to be one of the most difficult to answer. Major testing programs have used as few as one item per objective while some research studies have used as many as 30 items. Some work has been done in developing a technology for criterion-referenced measure-ment that might answer such questions, but the effort has accomplished so little that Popham (1974) referred to the area as a "technical wasteland."

The lengths of norm-referenced measuring instruments are typically determined through compromises between time required for administration and internal consistency reliability. Since reliability is a function of the number of items, the test is made long enough to provide reliable scores but not long enough to require more than a school period to complete. The result of the compromise usually yields tests having from 20 to 50 items. The square root of the reliability coefficient obtained from such a set of items is interpreted as the correlation between obtained and true scores.

When criterion-referenced tests are developed, scores are sometimes obtained that have little or no variance. In such cases, traditionally used indices of reliability and validity may be indeterminate or meaningless. Several alternate procedures for assessing the adequacy of criterion-referenced tests have been proposed, but none has currently achieved full acceptance as an adequate determiner of test length. The formulation of general principles for arriving at criterion-referenced test lengths may have been impeded by the existence of such a great variety of kinds of criterion-referenced tests and test applications. One can find under this descriptive title a variety of tests ranging from one-item diagnostic tests to final examinations for an entire course. This diversity of applications makes difficult the formation of a single set of guidelines for the determination of test length.

One application that has been extensively researched is the kind of testing that governs a student's progress through individually prescribed instruction (IPI). Millman (1973) has studied the length problem for such tests. He treats the percentage correct score on the test as an estimate of the students' percentage correct in the domain of items. Binomial probability tables are then employed to estimate the percentage of students at each of several true performance levels who would be incorrectly passed when they should have failed and failed when they should have passed. Millman's tables provide considerable insight into the nature of errors from such tests, including the relationships among test length, cutting score, and percentage of errors arising from each type of misclassification. However, his work does not appear to provide the simple decision procedure for determining test length that test developers have been seeking.

Novick and Lewis (1974) point out that Millman's tables provide probabilities of a student's attainment of a particular test score given his true level of functioning. This approach has limited utility because an individual student's true level of functioning is not known. They proposed a framework for specifying test length which begins with the student's test score, which is known, and provides estimates of the probability that his true level of functioning exceeds a specified criterion level. Bayes' theorem is applied to combine knowledge about the student's expected performance, based on prior knowledge about the performance of students having similar training, with the student's test score to improve the probability of correct classification. They also address the problem of difference in relative losses arising from false-positive and false-negative errors. For example, it might be determined that advancing a student who should have failed is twice as costly as retaining a student who should have passed. Procedures for handling differing loss ratios are described in their paper. Novick and Lewis present some specific test length recommendations for selected criterion-of-mastery levels, prior distributions of students' functioning levels, and relative losses associated with false advancement and false retention. These recommendations have been carefully worked out and should be of genuine benefit to anyone faced with the test length problem.

We believe that the practical problem of determining test length can be somewhat simplified by distinguishing between the major categories of learning, especially between verbal information and intellectual skills and between the quality and quantity dimensions. For example, measures of the quality type for unidimensional intellectual skills may be quite short, even as short as one item. The length of quantity measures will depend upon the homogeneity of the task domain and may need to be quite long. For either type of measurement, the length required for adequate assessment will depend upon the considerations stated by Millman (1974) and Novick and Lewis (1974) and upon the intended use of the measure. In addition, decisions about length should take into account whether guessing is a factor in the test and whether individual or group decisions are to be based upon the score.

It is emphasized that the focus of our discussion is on the assessment of learning outcomes in terms of the performance of the learner. The use of such measures in controlling progress through an individualized instructional program, or a mastery learning program, usually rests on the premise that the content is hierarchically arranged, so that knowledge of proficiency on the objectives of a unit of instruction provides the most useful information for advancing the student to the next task. Alternative assumptions about the structure of content might lead one to approach the controlling function from other perspectives. Such alternative perspectives might materially affect the design of test instruments.

IV.   ADEQUACY OF ASSESSMENT MEASURES

Test scores are usually based on a sample of tasks from a larger domain and provide probabilistic estimates of proficiency in that domain. The closeness with which these estimates approach the true values for the domain is of primary interest to the test user. A major part of measurement theory deals with this difference between obtained and true values — called *measurement error.*

Criteria of adequacy for different scaling models are established through theoretical investigations and through empirical studies. These studies yield criteria or standards of acceptability for test results. The criteria are then routinely applied to the results of test applications to determine and document the adequacy of the scores. Until the advent of criterion-referenced testing, there were agreed-upon procedures for evaluating test adequacy, under the broad categories of validity and reliability. Validity was subdivided into the finer procedural subcategories of content, construct, concurrent, and predictive validity. Except for content validity, the correlation coefficient was the common index of validity. The reliability of a test was indicated by correlations between scores from re-administration of the same or alternate forms of the test or by a coefficient of internal consistency. Tests were considered adequate only if their validity and reliability met acceptable standards.

The traditional indices of validity and reliability, based upon product moment correlations, are indeterminable when the variance of measures approaches zero. Popham and Husek (1969) have pointed out, however, that when criterion-referenced tests are used in the instructional setting, distributions of scores having no variance may in fact be desired. For example, it is expected that all students will successfully complete the posttest following a well-designed unit of programmed instruction. If that were to happen, the scores would all have the same value, the variance would be zero, alpha or KR-20 indices of internal consistency would be indeterminate, and correlations with other variables would be zero. When such distributions of scores arise, the traditional indices of test adequacy are invalid.

A number of indices of adequacy for criterion-referenced tests have been proposed. These have been reviewed by Brennan (1974) and summarized by Millman (1974). Many of these techniques are designed to assess the adequacy of items and tests for making certain instructional decisions, such as controlling progress through an instructional program, and are not our major concern in this chapter. Instead, we focus on appropriate indicators of adequacy for measures of learning outcomes in a more general and unrestricted sense.

A. Validity

For both quality and quantity measures, the most appropriate type of validity is content validity. Content validity is assured by the process of test domain specification and by appropriate item sampling. The primary aim is that the items in the test be representative of the task domain. The use of item forms (or expanded objectives) and random sampling procedures provide a basis for content validity. The documentation of such validity is to be accomplished by the clear statement of domain specification and sampling procedures.

There may be occasion to consider construct validity as well as content validity. We have expressed the view that domain specification and test construction should be based on the type of learning outcome implied by the objective and the related specification of quantity or quality. The search for empirical evidence to support the contention that different memorial organizations are involved in completing the test tasks would constitute construct validation (Cronbach, 1971; Messick, 1975).

B. Statistical Model

The theoretical model for assessing learning outcomes proposed here is essentially an item-sampling model. This model has been discussed at length by Lord and Novick (1968) and reiterated in the context of criterion-referenced testing by Kriewall (1972). The basic idea underlying this model is quite simple. There exists a hypothetical domain of items. A given individual can respond correctly to a certain percentage of the items in the domain. This percentage correct for the domain is the student's true score. The test consists of a sample of items from the domain, and the percentage correct for the test is an estimate of the percentage correct for the entire domain.

The major statistical properties of such a model are: (1) the observed test score is an unbiased estimator and a sufficient statistic for estimating the true score; and (2) the error variance for the "number correct" score for an individual is:

$$\sigma^2 \text{ meas}(a) = \frac{1}{n-1} x_a (n - x_a),$$

where

> x_a = the obtained score of person a, and
> n = the number of items in the text.

Except for the use of $n - 1$ in the denominator to correct for bias of the sample, this is the familiar expression for the variance of a binomial distribution (npq), where n is the number of observations in the sample, p is the probability of a given event, and q is $1 - p$. Therefore, measurement error is determined by the number of items in the test and the proficiency level of the examinee. Measurement error is less when tests have more items and when proficiency is extremely high or extremely low.

It appears that the appropriate measure of proficiency is the probability of a correct response measured on a scale from zero to one. The standard error of such proficiency measures (for a person) is given by:

$$\sigma_{\text{meas}(a)} = \sqrt{\frac{pq}{n}}$$

where

> p = the proportion of domain items known, usually estimated by the proportion correct on the test.

This coefficient is an adequate index of the amount of error associated with the measure. Indices of reliability, such as alpha, test–retest, or parallel forms, are directly related to the variance of the group of persons tested. Such indices give the expected stability of relative position among the group upon retesting and are meaningless in criterion-referenced testing where reference to other persons is not needed. We believe that the standard error of measurement described above is sufficient.

V. DECISIONS REQUIRED IN TEST DESIGN

Inherent in the conceptual framework described in this chapter is a set of critical questions to be answered in the process of test selection or design. The careful consideration of these questions in the early stages of design should enhance the appropriateness of the resulting test instrument. The set of questions and some alternative answers are shown in Table 5.2. Questions in the table are ordered in the sequence in which they would usually be dealt with. The ordering is convenient but not fixed, and in some cases, two or more questions may require simultaneous consideration. Also, the answers to some questions may restrict the choices available for a later question. The test descriptions that result from application of these concepts to different assessment problems may differ widely.

It is proposed that the initial decision in designing a test is one which depends on classification of the learning objective into one of the five classes of learning outcomes previously described. The next decision will determine whether quality or quantity is to be measured. For example, is a single intellectual skill (such as using the prefix *anti-*) to be assessed in quality, or is a test of quantity covering "use of prefixes and suffixes" to be given? The directness of measurement now becomes a matter for decision. Does one wish to measure in a direct fashion, or is there an advantage to using a simulation of the task? These determinations should lead naturally to the next step (D, in Table 5.2) in test design which involves a description of the item domain in terms of its dimensions and its replacement sets.

Having described the domain, it is possible next to consider the question of item sampling. If a quality measure is being designed, sampling is done for each objective or subobjective in the domain, from item forms having defined replacement sets, with primary attention to content validity. Alternatively, if a quantity measure has been chosen, particular attention must be paid to sampling for representativeness of content employing stratified random sampling. The question of number of items requires consideration of what constitutes an acceptable standard error of measurement, and this, in turn, may involve the matter of intended usage of scores. Once the results of testing are at hand, one can proceed to choose an expression of scores that best fits the usage expected. For example, the use of scores for diagnostic purposes normally requires something like percentage scores indicating quality of performance for specific domains or subdomains. In contrast, scores obtained on a quantity measure covering a particular curriculum topic might be expressed either as percentages or as percentiles or other measures related to group norms.

A.   Examples of Test Design

Two examples are described to illustrate the planning of a test through consideration of the set of questions given in Table 5.2. These examples illustrate the process of test conceptualization by considering the questions, in turn, and suggesting possible implications of the answers for test design.

1.   *Example 1.*   The first objective has been taken from the "Essential Mathematical Skills" part of the Florida State-Wide Eighth-Grade Testing Program:

> "Given the price of an article and denomination of currency to be used in paying for it, the student will compute the amount of change to be returned."

From Table 5.2, the series of questions and their possible answers would be as follows:

(a) *What is the type of learning outcome?*   The learning outcome is an intellectual skill and can be clearly differentiated from the other four types of learning. Some verbal information is required to complete the task (the names of units of currency) but can be assumed as known. The behavior of interest is the repeated application of rules for computing change to problems having different values for price and for currency denomination.

(b) *Is quantity or quality being assessed?*   The basic inference to be made from the test result concerns the quality of performance, not its quantity. That is, the objective is to find out how well the examinee can compute change. It would be of little interest to know that one examinee could correctly compute change for 40% of a set of problem tasks and another examinee 60%, since the inference in both cases would be that neither could adequately perform the task.

(c) *How direct should the measurement be?*   It is the ultimate performance of the student in actual consumer situations which is of interest; however, the efficiency of the "verbal description" test format is appealing. The question must ultimately be decided on the basis of the relationship between the response to the "verbal description" and to the "actual" spending situations. In this case, "verbal description" is chosen because it is assumed that the skill can be easily transferred to the real situation when learned through verbal descriptions, and the mistakes made because of the change in stimulus properties would not be critically important ones. If the assessment situation were an integral part of the instructional situation, then "simulation" might well have been chosen.

TABLE 5.2
Decisions in Design of Assessment Tests

Question for Decision	Choices
A. What is the type of learning outcome?	1. Motor skills
	2. Verbal information
	3. Intellectual skills
	4. Cognitive strategies
	5. Attitudes
B. Is quantity or quality being assessed?	1. Quantity — how much?
	2. Quality — how well?
C. How direct can the measurement be?	1. Actual situation
	2. Simulated situation
	3. Verbal description
	4. Knowledge
D. How can the domain be described?	1. Item forms, including task dimensions and replacement sets
E. How will the items be sampled?	1. For content validity
	2. For representativeness
	3. Number of items
F. How should the test results be expressed?	1. Criterion-referenced a. Mastery b. Percentage
	2. Norm-referenced a. Percentile b. Standard score c. Grade equivalent

(d) *How can the domain be described?* The "item form" approach would be appropriate for this objective. The test-task domain would be specified by establishing an item form with replacement sets for variable elements. The example is a somewhat simplified version of the procedure described by Hively et al. (1973):

Item Form:
   If you bought something which cost __ X __ and gave the clerk a __ Y __ dollar bill, how much change would you receive?
Replacement Sets:
   X equals any amount from amount from $.01 to $99.99.
   Y equals 1, 5, 10, 20, 50, or 100 $(Y > X)$.

(e) *How will items be sampled?* An item for the test would be constructed by randomly selecting a value from replacement set X and from set Y, and substituting these values for the appropriate blanks in the item form. A number of items could be generated by repeating this process. The set of items generated would constitute a random sample of items from the task or item domain. These procedures would insure that all items so constructed are valid measures of the objective. The number of items selected should be large enough to include a representative set of cost and money combinations, so as to make possible a dependable inference about the student's proficiency in making change.

(f) *How should the test results be expressed?* The test results must be expressed in a way that will serve the basic purpose of the assessment. As indicated by answers to questions (a) and (b), this purpose is to determine whether or not the examinee can compute change. The best form of score report would be one which directly conveys this information to the user. A dichotomous score showing mastery or nonmastery of the objective would serve this purpose well.

2. *Example 2.* A second example is based on a "vocabulary" objective proposed for a state-wide assessment program. The student must demonstrate a knowledge of the meaning of words typically encountered in eighth-grade instructional materials by associating words with their literal definitions. The series of questions from Table 5.2 would be answered in the following way:

(a) *What is the type of learning outcome?* The type of learning outcome is verbal information. Acquisition of a reading vocabulary is a matter of learning the meaning of words, stored in such a way that they can be retrieved as verbal propositions. It may be noted that other objectives might require that words be defined through application of intellectual skills, for example, by applying rules about suffixes or by determining the meanings of words from context; however, these approaches are not suggested by this objective.

(b) *Is quantity or quality being measured?* In this example, what is being measured is quantity or how much is known. Interest lies in a summary score giving the number, or proportion, of words defined correctly by each person. In contrast, if the assessment were an integral part of an instructional program, knowledge of the correctness of each definition by each student might be useful for diagnostic purposes.

(c) *How direct should the measurement be?* The measurement of verbal information is called for in this case. Because the objective implies that the acquisition of this knowledge is for reading purposes, the use of printed words as stimuli is appropriate. A paper-and-pencil test format should provide a suitable medium for presenting the stimulus situation and for recording responses.

(d) *How can the domain be described?* The task is to associate words with their literal definitions. An appropriate item form would be one in which a word is given along with one correct and three incorrect definitions. The student is required to select the correct definitions from the list. An example of such an item form is: The most correct definition for __X__ is: (1) __Y_1__ ; (2) __Y_2__ ;

(3) Y_3 ; and (4) Y_4 ; where the five lettered blank spaces are variable parts to be filled by selecting elements from defined replacement sets. The replacement set for X would be all words encountered in eighth-grade instructional materials. The replacement sets for the Y variables include a correct definition for the selected X word, randomly assigned to be one of the Y variables, and definitions for three other words selected as the same part of speech in the same way as X, but not being correct definitions of the selected X word.

(e) *How will the domain be sampled?* A sample of items from the task domain could be generated by randomly selecting words from currently adopted eighth-grade textbooks to replace the variable parts of the item form. Such a procedure would yield a sample of items that could be used to derive a proficiency score, that is, an estimate of the probability of defining correctly a randomly selected word from the domain. However, the strictly random selection of a sample from all words in the texts might include relatively few of the new or complex words in which greatest interest centers. The characteristics of the sample of words could accordingly be altered by imposing various kinds of restrictions on the sampling procedure. For example, one might include only nouns, verbs, adjectives, and adverbs; or one might exclude one-syllable words from the sample. Any departure from a random sampling procedure would make questionable the interpretation of the scores as proficiency measures unless the objective and domain description were rephrased to correspond to the sampling procedure used.

(f) *How should the test results be expressed?* The basic inference to be made from the test score is one of quantity of words and definitions known. However, it is unlikely that a percentage score on the test would be optimally meaningful without knowing how particular groups of other students performed on the test. Therefore, one might choose to report both percentage and norm-referenced scores until sufficient information was gathered to interpret percentage scores directly.

VI. SOME GENERAL CONCLUSIONS

In reviewing the work which has been done to date on the assessment of learning outcomes, it appears to us that the ideas of criterion-referenced, or domain-referenced, testing have exerted considerable influence on current thought. Perhaps the most general effect of this line of thinking has been the identification of priorities in the decisions involved in the design of tests for assessing outcomes of learning. The criterion-referenced view would require that decisions be made first concerning what is to be measured in the precisely defined manner of the domain or "item form" corresponding to a specific learning objective. In the second step, decisions are made about how to construct the test — whether one can appropriately employ measures of quantity or quality, how direct the measurement can be, and how items should be selected from the defined domain. In making this second set of choices, however, the "looking back" to reconsider and perhaps revise the learning objective has a strictly limited purpose of insuring that the item domain and objective are consistent. Revision is not undertaken to meet certain other desiderata of measurement. The domain that defines what is to be measured (the "criterion") remains uncompromised. Third, a decision is made as to how to express test results. Here, there is recognition that reference to a norm may be useful for some purposes, while reference to a defined standard is often useful for others.

The necessity for precise specification of task domains makes it essential that test design be concerned with the differentiation of types of learning outcomes. An adequate technology of achievement testing must address itself to the variety of *classes of memory organization* identified by modern cognitive theories of learning and memory, including verbal knowledge, attitudes, and cognitive strategies, as well as the intellectual skills that have frequently served as examples for criterion-referenced test design. Attending to the categories of memory states in designing measures of learning outcome will help to assure comprehensive coverage of the varieties of human performance. In addition, the incorporation of the constructs of modern cognitive learning theory would appear to be a promising direction of thought for the development of a rational theory of human performance assessment.

The insistence on the primacy of the defined performance criterion carries a number of implications for test design. In the first place, it requires that there be rigorous methods for defining the domain from which items are selected and equally rigorous procedures for generating and selecting items from that domain. Validity estimates are to be made in terms of matches of test performance with performance in the criterion situation. Descriptions of such situations are exemplified by statements of instructional objectives as, for example, "given an incomplete printed sentence with a missing verb and a set of four printed verbs, identifies the appropriate verb to complete sentence meaning." In contrast, content validity of the criterion-referenced variety cannot be judged on the basis of the names of content topics such as "verb meaning or "sentence completion."

The primacy of the criterion implies certain problems in the development of test-construction techniques, not all of which have been adequately solved as yet. The definition of the item domain can be undertaken with a fair degree of confidence when intellectual skills are being measured using methods such as those described by Hively et al. (1973) and by Popham (1975). However, similarly useful methods have not been developed for the specification of domains of verbal information ("knowledge"), motor skills, cognitive strategies, or attitudes. For example, how is one to specify item forms and replacement sets for the knowledge attained in reading Lincoln's Gettysburg Address, or a paragraph describing the nesting habits of robins? Or how can the attitudinal domain "rejection of harmful drugs" be described so that it provides a criterion? It may be, of course, that these difficulties of measurement will ultimately be used to demonstrate the inutility of the criterion-referenced conception. We prefer instead to adopt the working hypothesis that such problems can be solved. Obviously, they need much attention.

When the defined criterion to be measured remains inviolate, still other kinds of measurement problems appear. For example, when an intellectual skill is assessed by means of items drawn from a defined domain, the selection of items must be done in a manner that assures their representativeness. This means that items cannot be selected for their difficulty or "discriminative power." As a result, the variance of test scores often approaches zero, and traditional correlational methods of determining the dependability of scores become inapplicable. The problems of differentiating "true score" from "error," and of specifying confidence limits for such scores, continue to be areas for current and future investigation. Comparisons of actual test results with statistical models will be required. On the whole, one may expect that an extended period of time will be needed to develop, refine, and disseminate statistical theory and methodology for criterion-referenced testing as thoroughly as has been done for norm-referenced testing.

When one views objectively the question of how testing results should be expressed, it becomes apparent that the overriding factor in this decision must be that of how the test scores are to be used. If precise attainment of performance is to be reported, or if diagnosis is to be made of skills needed by a learner, expression of test scores as patterns of achievement or as percentages may be desirable. Such scores typically denote achievement in relation to a defined criterion. However, if a quantitative measure of amount of achievement over a specified set of objectives or topics is desired, as is often true in school situations, meaning may be added to test scores when they are related to a well-defined norm. In other words, as many authors have been at pains to point out, scores which are "criterion-referenced" may readily become "norm-referenced" when the results of testing a group are known.

The conception of criterion-referenced testing, then, has contributed the idea of the *priority of the criterion* in test construction. What this means is that the criterion, a domain of items derived from a precisely defined human performance, must remain inviolate to the exigencies of measurement methods. Whatever characteristics tests must have to insure their adequacy, these must be achieved by techniques that avoid compromising the criterion. Many of these techniques remain to be developed and tested for their appropriateness and efficiency.

REFERENCES

Anderson, J. R., & Bower, G. H. A propositional theory of recognition memory. *Memory & Cognition*, 1974, *2*, 406–412.

Anderson, R. C. How to construct achievement tests to assess comprehension. *Review of Educational Research*, 1972, *42*, 145–170.

Atkinson, R. C., & Shiffrin, R. M. Human memory: A proposed system and its control processes. In K. W. Spence & J. T. Spence (Eds.), *The psychology of learning and motivation* (Vol. 2). New York: Academic Press, 1968.

Bloom, B. S. (Ed.). *Taxonomy of educational objectives: Handbook 1: Cognitive domain.* New York: McKay, 1956.

Bloom, B. S., Hastings, J. T., & Madaus, G. F. *Handbook on formative and summative evaluation of student learning.* New York: McGraw-Hill, 1971.

Bormuth, J. R. *On the theory of achievement test items.* Chicago: University of Chicago Press, 1970.

Bower, G. H. Cognitive psychology: An introduction. In W. K. Estes (Ed.), *Handbook of learning and cognitive processes* (Vol. 1). Hillsdale, N.J.: Lawrence Erlbaum Associates, 1975.

Brennan, R. L. *The evaluation of mastery test items* (Project No. 213118). Washington, D.C.: U.S. Office of Education, 1974.

Brown, A. L. The development of memory: Knowing, knowing about knowing, and knowing how to know. In H. Reese (Ed.), *Advances in child development and behavior* (Vol. 10). New York: Academic Press, 1975.

Cronbach, L. J. Test validation. In R. L. Thorndike (Ed.), *Educational measurement* (2nd ed.). Washington, D.C.: American Council on Education, 1971.

Donlon, T. F. *Some needs for clearer terminology in criterion-referenced testing.* Paper presented at the annual meeting of the National Council on Measurement in Education, Chicago, 1974.

Ebel, R. L. *Some limitations of criterion-referenced measurement.* Paper presented at the annual meeting of the American Educational Research Association, Minneapolis, March 1970.

Fitzpatrick, R., & Morrison, E. J. Performance and product evaluation. In R. L. Thorndike (Ed.), *Educational measurement* (2nd ed.). Washington, D.C.: American Council on Education, 1971.

Flavell, J. H., & Wellman, H. M. Metamemory. In R. V. Kail & J. W. Hagen (Ed.), *Memory in cognitive development.* Hillsdale, N.J.: Lawrence Erlbaum Associates, 1976.

Gagné, R. M. Instructional variables and learning outcomes. In M. C. Wittrock & D. E. Wiley (Eds.), *The evaluation of instruction: Issues and problems.* New York: Holt, Rinehart & Winston, 1970.

Gagné, R. M. Domains of learning. *Interchange,* 1972, *3,* 1–8.

Gagné, R. M. Task analysis – Its relation to content analysis. *Educational Psychologist,* 1974, *11,* 11–18.

Gagné, R. M. Observing the effects of learning. *Educational Psychologist,* 1975, *11,* 144–157.

Gagné, R. M. The learning basis of teaching methods. In N. L. Gage (Ed.), *The psychology of teaching methods: Seventy-fifth yearbook of the National Society for the Study of Education* (Part I). Chicago: NSSE, 1976.

Gagné, R. M., & Briggs, L. J. *Principles of instructional design.* New York: Holt, Rinehart & Winston, 1974.

Glaser, R. Instructional technology and the measurement of learning outcomes: Some questions. *American Psychologist,* 1963, *18,* 519–521.

Glaser, R., & Klaus, D. J. Proficiency measurement: Assessing human performance. In R. M. Gagné (Ed.), *Psychological principles in system development.* New York: Holt, Rinehart & Winston, 1963.

Glaser, R., & Nitko, A. J. Measurement in learning and instruction. In R. L. Thorndike (Ed.), *Educational measurement* (2nd ed.). Washington: D.C.: American Council on Education, 1971.

Graham, D. L. *An empirical investigation of the application of criterion-referenced measurement to survey achievement testing.* Unpublished doctoral dissertation, Florida State University, 1974.

Guilford, J. P. *The nature of human intelligence.* New York: McGraw-Hill, 1967.

Guttman, L. Integration of test design and analysis. In *Proceedings of the 1969 Invitational Conference on Testing Problems.* Princeton, N.J.: Educational Testing Service, 1969.

Hambleton, R. K. Testing and decision-making procedures for selected individualized instructional programs. *Review of Educational Research,* 1974, *44,* 371–400.

Hively, W., Maxwell, G., Rabehl, G., Sension, D., & Lundin, S. *Domain-referenced curriculum evaluation: A technical handbook and a case study from the Minnemast Project.* Los Angeles: University of California, Center for the Study of Evaluation, 1973.

Horwitz, S. P. *Effects of some review processes on retention of mathematical rules.* Unpublished doctoral dissertation, Florida State University, 1975.

Johnson, D. M., & Kidder, R. C. Productive thinking in psychology classes. *American Psychologist,* 1972, *27,* 672–674.

Kiesler, C. A., Collins, B. E., & Miller, N. *Attitude change.* New York: Wiley, 1969.

Kintsch, W. *The representation of meaning in memory.* Hillsdale, N.J.: Lawrence Erlbaum Associates, 1974.

Klatzky, R. L. *Human memory: Structures and process.* San Francisco, Calif.: Freeman, 1975.

Krathwohl, D. R., Bloom, B. S., & Masia, B. B. *Taxonomy of educational objectives: The classification of educational objectives: Handbook 2: Affective domain.* New York: McKay, 1964.

Kriewall, T. E. *Aspects and applications of criterion-referenced tests.* Downers Grove, Ill.: Institute for Educational Research, 1972.

Lindquist, E. T. Preliminary considerations in objective test construction. In E. F. Lindquist (Ed.), *Educational measurement.* Washington, D.C.: American Council on Education, 1951.

Lord, F. M., & Novick, M. R. *Statistical theories of mental test scores.* Reading, Mass.: Addison-Wesley, 1968.

Mager, R. F. *Preparing instructional objectives.* Belmont, Calif.: Fearon, 1962.

Mager, R. F. *Preparing instructional objectives* (2nd ed.). Belmont, Calif.: Fearon, 1975.

Mandler, G., & Stephens, D. The development of free and constrained conceptualization and subsequent verbal memory. *Journal of Experimental Child Psychology,* 1967, *5,* 86–93.

McGuire, W. J. Nature of attitudes and attitude change. In G. Lindzey & E. Aronson (Eds.), *Handbook of social psychology.* Reading, Mass.: Addison-Wesley, 1968.

Messick, S. The standard problem. Meaning and values in measurement and evaluation. *American Psychologist,* 1975, *30,* 955–966.

Millman, J. Passing scores and test lengths for domain-referenced measures. *Review of Educational Research,* 1973, *43,* 205–216.

Millman, J. Criterion-referenced measurement. In W. J. Popham (Ed.), *Evaluation in education: Current applications.* Berkeley, Calif.: McCutchan, 1974.

Novick, M. R., & Lewis, C. Prescribing test length for criterion-referenced measurements. *Problems in criterion-referenced measurement* (Monograph Series in Evaluation, No. 3). Los Angeles: University of California, Center for the Study of Evaluation, 1974.

Olton, R. M., Wardrop, J. L., Covington, M. V., Goodwin, W. L., Crutchfield, R. S., Klausmeier, H. J., & Ronda, T. *The development of productive thinking skills in fifth-grade children.* Madison: University of Wisconsin, Research and Development Center for Cognitive Learning, 1967.

Osburn, H. G. Item sampling for achievement testing. *Educational and Psychological Measurement,* 1968, *28,* 95–104.

Popham, W. J. *Technical travails of developing criterion-referenced tests.* Paper presented at the annual meeting of the National Council on Measurement in Education, Chicago, 1974.

Popham, W. J. *Educational evaluation.* Englewood Cliffs, N.J.: Prentice-Hall, 1975.

Popham, W. J., & Husek, T. R. Implications of criterion-referenced measurement. *Journal of Educational Measurement,* 1969, *6,* 1–9.

Rumelhart, D. E., Lindsay, P. H., & Norman, D. A. A process model for long-term memory. In E. Tulving & W. Donaldson (Eds.), *Organization of memory.* New York: Academic Press, 1972.

Scott, W. A. Attitude measurement. In G. Lindzey & E. Aronson (Eds.), *Handbook of social psychology.* Reading, Mass.: Addison-Wesley, 1968.

Shaw, M. E., & Wright, J. M. *Scales for the measurement of attitudes.* New York: McGraw-Hill, 1967.

Singer, R. N. *Motor learning and human performance* (2nd ed.). New York: Macmillan, 1975.

Traub, R. E. *Criterion-referenced measurement: Something old and something new.* Address delivered at the University of Victoria, 1972.

Triandis, H. C. Exploratory factor analyses of the behavioral component of social attitudes. *Journal of Abnormal and Social Psychology,* 1964, *68,* 420–430.

Triandis, H. C., & Triandis, L. M. Race, social class, religion and nationality as determinants of social distance. *Journal of Abnormal and Social Psychology,* 1960, *61,* 110–118.

Author Index

Subject Index

Date Due